Macroeconomics

Paul Middleditch

Macroeconomics

Paul Middleditch

McGraw Hill

Macroeconomics
Paul Middleditch
ISBN-13 9781526850737
ISBN-10 1526850737

Published by McGraw-Hill Education (UK) Limited
Unit 4, Foundation Park,
Roxborough Way,
Maidenhead SL6 3UD
T: +44 (0) 1628 502500
Website: www.mheducation.co.uk

British Library Cataloguing in Publication Data
A catalogue record for this book is available from the British Library

Library of Congress Cataloguing in Publication Data
The Library of Congress data for this book has been applied for from the Library of Congress

Portfolio Manager: Felicity Baines
Content Developer: Jo O'Neill
Content Product Manager: Ali Davis
Marketing Manager: Ros Letellier

Text design by Kamae Design
Cover design by Adam Renvoize
Printed and bound by CPI Group (UK) Ltd, Croydon, CR0 4YY

ISBN-13 9781526850737
ISBN-10 1526850737
eISBN-13 9781526850744

G10966 CPI 2026

Dedication

To my wonderful children Lucienne, Charles and Louis. Thank you for your endless support, patience and love. You have been my inspiration through every chapter. To my incredible partner Kernprit, whose unwavering encouragement and belief has been my guiding light through the challenges I have faced bringing this book to publication.

To my reviewers, Eric, Juergen, Matheus and Sambit, your insightful feedback has been invaluable. I am truly grateful for your time and expertise. To the fantastic publishing team at McGraw Hill, Jo and Felicity – thank you for your professionalism and dedication. Finally, to my colleagues at the University of Manchester, especially Horst and Kyriakos, whose thoughtful comments have shaped this work over the years.

With heartfelt thanks, Paul

Brief Table of Contents

Detailed Table of Contents

CHAPTER 12
The Open Economy IS/LM/BP Model 155

CHAPTER 13
The AS/AD Model 171

CHAPTER 14
The Flexible Price Model 187

CHAPTER 15
Modelling Economic Growth 199

Preface

This textbook has evolved from many years of teaching the subject of macroeconomics as an undergraduate instructor. Along the way it has been shaped by the insights, questions and enthusiasm of my wonderful students. Their curiosity and engagement have motivated me to refine my own teaching as this book has developed – it is as much a product of those classroom conversations as it is of my own scholarship.

My aim in writing this book has been to integrate the latest ideas, pathologies and alternative perspectives into the taught subject of macroeconomics. Events such as the global financial crisis and the COVID-19 pandemic have highlighted the importance of making the subject of macroeconomics relevant to the real world. The book adopts a 'markets and models' structure, where we begin by exploring the three central macroeconomic markets before introducing key models one by one. This approach has proven effective in my teaching, helping students to first build a more fundamental understanding of the wider subject before progressing to more analytical material and economic policy analysis.

A distinctive feature of this textbook is the expanded treatment of the financial system that facilitates economic activity. By including the sector of financial instruments, I have sought to broaden the discussion surrounding the money market to include topics in finance that play a vital role in the economy and add relevance to students trying to understand the world around them. In addition, the text includes extensive discussions on the nature of economic modelling and the role of empirical investigation. My intention here is to equip students with the ability to think critically, learning how economists construct models and how they are tested against reality.

Since the inception of this book my main objectives have to been to write a relevant, complete and, above all, accessible text for students in undergraduate macroeconomics. I hope that the instructors and students who use this textbook get as much value from reading it as I have had writing it.

About the Author

Dr Paul Middleditch is an associate professor of macroeconomics at the University of Manchester, founding director of the UK Centre for Innovation in Pedagogy, and academic author in the field of economics. He has taught the subject of macroeconomics at the University of Manchester since 2009, across all years at the undergraduate level, and before that at the University of Surrey, where he taught both macroeconomics and econometrics at the undergraduate and postgraduate level.

He received his BA in economics at Kingston University and his MSc in economics at Birkbeck College, University of London before going on to the University of Surrey to complete his PhD, also in economics. His research interests include macroeconomic time series, economic volatility, monetary policy and economic growth. His research in pedagogy involves the design of educational frameworks for higher education more generally.

Paul has published his research in the *Journal of Government and Economics*, the *Review of Development Economics*, the *Cambridge Journal of Economics*, the *Scottish Journal of Political Economy*, *The Manchester School*, *Cogent Economics and Finance*, the *International Review of Economics Education* and the *Journal of Perspectives in Applied Academic Practice*. He has received the Economics Network 'Outstanding Teaching Award' in 2013 and a University of Manchester Distinguished Achievement Medal 'Teacher of the Year' in 2014.

Development Reviewers and Digital Contributors

Eric Golson is an Associate Professor of Economics and the former Deputy Head of Economics and Undergraduate Programme Director at the University of Surrey. As an economist with expertise in economic warfare, trade, finance and international political economy, Eric has travelled the world exploring complex economic warfare issues for governments and businesses.

We would like to thank him for his invaluable feedback during the development of the text, and his work on authoring the Smartbook for Connect, together with Paul Middleditch.

Sambit Bhattacharyya is a Professor of Economics and Head of Department of Economics at University of Sussex. His research interests are in the areas of development economics, macroeconomics, and economic history. He is an Associate Editor of the Review of Development Economics.

Juergen Amann is an Economist at the OECD Centre for Entrepreneurship, SMEs, Regions and Cities (CFE). His main research interests lie in applied econometrics, environmental economics, industrial development, Input-Output analysis, price setting and structural change. Juergen has a PhD from the University of Nottingham and studied at Duke University on a Fulbright scholarship. He holds graduate degrees in economics and econometrics.

We would like to thank him for his invaluable feedback on the text during its development.

Matheus Trotta Vianna is a Lecturer at University of Manchester. His research interests include economic policies to promote growth, stability, and development and he designs computer simulation models to analyse policy implementation and performance. Matheus holds a Ph.D. and an M.Sc. in Economics at the Federal University of Rio de Janeiro, Brazil.

Drew Woodhouse is a Senior Lecturer in Economics at Sheffield Hallam University. Drew specialises in the areas of Macroeconomics, Political Economy and Institutional Economics. His research involves interdisciplinary approaches to the study of economic agency & behaviours, deriving policy-led conclusions and interventions using a range of cutting-edge quantitative modelling.

We would like to thank him for developing the Instructor Manuals accompanying the text, aimed at supporting lecturers in their teaching.

Acknowledgments

Our thanks go to the following reviewers for their comments at proposal stage:

Luca Andriani, Birkbeck, University of London

Sambit Bhattacharyya, University of Sussex

Mikael Randrup Bryialsen, Aalborg University

Carlos Cortinas, University of Exeter

Paul Cowell, University of Stirling

Dr Ceri Davies, University of Birmingham

Thomas Eidfeld, Copenhagen Business School

Gabriel A. Giménez Roche, NEOMA Business School

Faith Kansoy, University of Warwick

Kaushik Mitra, University of Birmingham

William Tayler, Lancaster University

Tom Verbeke, KU Leuven

Yuan Wang, Sheffield Hallam University

Drew Woodhouse, Sheffield Hallam University

Francesco Zanetti, University of Oxford

Endorsements

"Paul Middleditch's Macroeconomics is an excellent new resource for students and professionals alike. Aimed at those without a background in macroeconomics, it presents complex economic theories with clarity and depth, making even advanced concepts accessible. It gradually builds understanding through real-world explanations which help to explain and cement key theoretical ideas, helping bridge the gap between abstract ideas and practical application. Case studies and data-driven insights together with Smartbook features like AI explanations further enrich the learning experience. Whether you're new to macroeconomics or looking to deepen your knowledge, this textbook provides a strong foundation and valuable context for understanding today's complex and ever-changing global economy."

– ***Dr. Eric Golson,*** *University of Surrey*

"Compared to other textbooks I've used in the past, this book stands out as it is unique and innovative."

–***Dr. Sambit Bhattacharyya,*** *Professor of Economics and Head of Department of Economics, University of Sussex*

"The book's structure is robustly set up for continuing the evolution of economics education. I truly think it is the way forward for Macroeconomics teaching."

– ***Dr. Drew Woodhouse,*** *Senior Lecturer in Economics, Sheffield Hallam University*

"Macroeconomics has been written with clear, easy language making it much better than the majority of economics textbooks that have gone before it."

– ***Yuan Wang,*** *Senior Lecturer in Economics, Sheffield Hallam University*

Guided Tour

At a Glance: At the start of each chapter, this section provides a snapshot of the chapter and what can be expected in terms of the economic questions addressed by the individual chapters.

At a Glance **Introduction**

The issue

How we define the subject area of macroeconomics? How can we use data to help us understand the workings of the economy? What does a macroeconomist do?

The understanding

This chapter helps develop a definition and understanding of the subject area of macroeconomics. We will look at an example of macroeconomic time series data and discuss the role of the macroeconomist. Finally, we look at how the profession presents ideas and policy advice to peers and policymakers.

The usefulness

Understanding the workings of the wider economy is central to developing useful economic policy; it is also useful to understand the macroeconomic climate when drawing up plans that require some estimate of the economic climate in the future, not only for policymakers, but also for firms and businesses.

Learning Outcomes

By the end of this chapter you should be able to:

- Define the subject area of macroeconomics as a subfield of economics.
- Describe the typical role of a macroeconomist interested in the higher workings of the financial interactions across a society.
- Interpret basic macroeconomic time series.
- Explain the purpose of a typical macroeconomic two-dimensional analysis.

Learning Outcomes: Every chapter begins with a set of learning outcomes, or objectives, summarizing what you will take away from each chapter.

Key Definitions: Highlighted throughout the text to reinforce key terms and aid understanding.

The preliminary data analysis

From our plot of macroeconomic data we can make a visual inspection and a basic **preliminary data analysis**. Firstly, we can see that across the whole sample, UK unemployment ranges from around 4 per cent to 8 per cent and from this observation we might propose that a normal unemployment rate be in the region of 6 per cent. Further, we can see that there are prolonged periods where unemployment is either increasing or declining; these periods correspond to episodes in the general condition of the macroeconomy, such as economic activity or other economic and political factors. When output is declining during a recession, we would expect unemployment to be rising.

Preliminary Data Analysis: An analysis, or visual inspection, that comes from the observation of a basic presentation of economic data. This may be in the form of summary statistics, or from the profiles and directions of the time series data itself.

ASSESSMENT ADVICE

It is important that you make clear your understanding of the importance of the price level in the economy as the adjusting mechanism between the short-run equilibrium in our models and the long-run equilibrium. The AS/AD model, and also the IS/LM model, described in Chapter 8, allow us to capture this change.

A change in economic policy will have a short-run real effect on output (policy will affect output) but it is generally agreed that the effect of policy is limited in duration. In the long run, policy is said to be neutral because prices adjust fully (policy will not affect output). We discuss this in more detail at the end of this chapter.

Assessment Advice: These offer tips and context behind the types of exams and assessments you will come across in your degree and in practice.

Exercises: These exercises challenge you to apply the information covered in the chapter to facilitate practice and reinforce learning, as you progress through the material.

EXERCISE 1.1

An important characteristic of a macroeconomic series is the frequency in which it is presented. What key difference would you expect to see in the variance of a series presented in a quarterly frequency to that of an annual frequency?

Examples: Split into three types, these boxes explore how theory is applied in practice. **Real World Examples** provide lively and engaging examples from the real world to demonstrate economic principles in a relevant context, **Worked Examples** take students through some of the more complicated calculations step by step, and **Hypothetical Examples** use a fictional situation to demonstrate the application of a theory in practice. Pathologies cover historical events, but in such a way that they could be applied to future economic events.

EXAMPLE 1.1

Real world example: Relating the components of a model to the game of chess

Another way to see how a model works is to relate it to something we are familiar with in real life. Consider the components of an economic model and how they relate to a game of chess.

The landscape

The axes in an economic model are like the board in a game of chess; they are the economic space which frames the analysis and the space in which the game is played.

The operators

The agents in an economic model are similar to the players in a game of chess. The buyers and sellers in the model and the players in the game both interact.

Modus operandi

The schedules in the model map the behaviour of the agents in the same way that the players in a game choose moves.

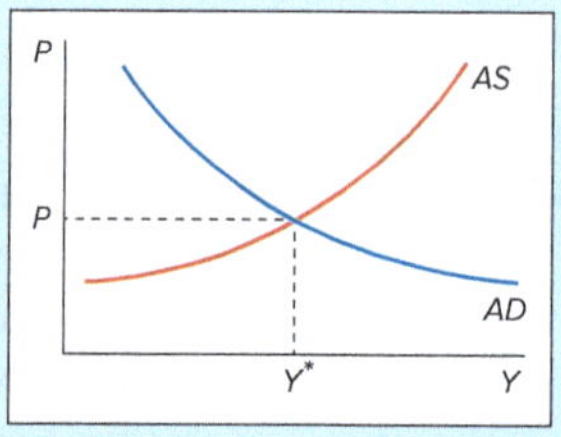

Figure 4.8 **Equilibrium in the AS/AD model with upward-sloping AS curve**

Table 4.2 **Fiscal and monetary policy models**

Policy Type	Detail	Modelled By
Fiscal policy	Changes to government expenditure and taxation: Variables *G* and *T*	Via aggregate demand $\Uparrow G \Rightarrow \Uparrow AD$ $\Uparrow T \Rightarrow \Downarrow AD$
Monetary policy	Changes to the money supply: Variable *M*	Via aggregate demand $\Uparrow M \Rightarrow \Uparrow AD$

Figures and Tables: Each chapter provides a number of figures, graphs and tables to help you visualize key economic theories and concepts, to aid visual learners specifically.

1.4 Chapter summary: Putting it all together

What have we learnt from this chapter? We have defined macroeconomics as the science of the economy – a branch of economics that interests itself with the measurement of the macroeconomic variables including output, growth, inflation, unemployment and international trade. The values of these aggregated variables are of concern to economists and policymakers who seek to understand and explain the linkages between them, and in doing so recommend economic policy that can produce positive or better macroeconomic outcomes.

To understand the higher workings of the economy we can make use of the profiles of macroeconomic variables in the form of time series plots. A visual inspection of these time series can give our economic research direction and motivation; if we can see that unemployment and output are negatively correlated then our theory should take this into account. A preliminary inspection of macroeconomic data should always precede good economic research.

A macroeconomist will communicate macroeconomic theory with an economic model. To familiarize ourselves with the models that will appear in later chapters, we have presented a bare bones economic model to understand the concepts of economic agents, *ceteris paribus* and equilibrium. Forward from here, this knowledge will be assumed, though we will highlight exceptions where schedules (curves) instead refer to sectors or dynamic differences.

Chapter Summary: Pulling it all together: Every chapter ends with a summary that highlights the key theories, topics and concepts within the chapter. They serve as a revision aid and to reinforce the content from the chapter.

Assessment Question

Economic activity can be measured using three different methods; the production method, the income method and the expenditure method. In theory, these three methods should produce exactly the same calculation. Explain:

a. Why this might not actually be the case in reality because of measurement error and time lags.
b. Why having three different ways of measuring the same variable might be a benefit when it has to be estimated.

Assessment Question: This question is designed to be challenging and more aligned with the questions and tasks you might face under assessment, perhaps in a mid-term assignment or final exam.

Cases: These case studies help to reinforce your learning across the whole chapter and subject topic. In some cases they will go further than the scope of the material covered in the book to encourage you to engage with your own enquiry.

Cases

Economic growth in the UK

Introduction

Economic growth refers to the increase in a country's output over time, typically measured by the rise in its gross domestic product (GDP). The UK, as one of the world's largest economies, has experienced varying rates of economic growth over recent decades. This case study examines the key drivers of economic growth in the UK, the challenges faced and the policy responses implemented by the government and the Bank of England.

Background

Over the past 30 years, the UK has seen periods of significant economic growth, particularly following the global financial crisis of 2007–2008. From 2010 to 2016, the UK experienced a recovery in GDP growth rates, often outperforming other European countries. However, this growth has been uneven, with some years of stagnation or contraction, especially during periods of economic uncertainty, such as the Brexit referendum in 2016 and the COVID-19 pandemic in 2020.

Key drivers of economic growth in the UK

1. **Investment in infrastructure and technology:** The UK government has consistently invested in infrastructure projects and technological advancements. From the HS2 rail project to the focus on digital infrastructure, these investments have helped drive productivity and long-term growth.
2. **Labour force and education:** The UK's strong labour force, supported by high levels of education and skills development, has contributed to its economic growth. The service sector, particularly in finance, technology, and professional services, remains a major contributor to GDP growth.
3. **Monetary and fiscal policies:** The Bank of England's monetary policy, including interest rate management and quantitative easing, has been central in stabilizing the economy. Fiscal policies such as government spending on public services and social welfare have also played a role in supporting demand during times of recession.
4. **Trade and global integration:** The UK's trade relations, particularly with the European Union, the United States, and emerging economies, have been vital to its growth. While Brexit has led to uncertainty regarding future trade agreements, the UK's historical trade networks have been an important growth factor.

Challenges to economic growth

1. **Brexit:** The decision to leave the European Union has created significant uncertainty around trade, investment and labour supply. The UK faces new barriers to trade with the EU, reduced access to the single market and challenges in attracting foreign investment.

Problems

EASY

1. How would you define macroeconomics?
2. Which of the following macroeconomic variables would be studied in relation to economic growth?
   a) The price level and inflation
   b) Output and its change over time
   c) Consumer spending and sentiment
   d) Exchange rate movements
   e) Government borrowing and debt

MEDIUM

3. What does a macroeconomist typically use to explain economic linkages and predict reactions to economic shocks?
4. What is a 'macroeconomic time series'?
5. Which would be an example of a negative correlation often observed in macroeconomic data?
6. Why are economic models said to be 'simplified' representations of the economy?

HARD

7. Explain the importance of time series data in macroeconomics. How can visual inspection of macroeconomic time series help economists develop new theories? Discuss the potential limitations of relying solely on visual inspections for economic analysis.

Problems: These questions test your understanding of the learning objectives so that you can confidently progress to the next chapter to discover which topics you may need to revisit before moving on. They are split by difficulty to provide a wide range of questions across different depths of understanding.

Connect® for Economics

We have a wide selection of interactive excercises and activites on hand to help students gain valuable practice applying key concepts to real-world scenarios. Featured below are our Application-Based Activities and Graphing Tools.

Application-Based Activities

The Connect Application-Based Activities (ABAs) provide students valuable practice using problem solving skills to apply their knowledge to realistic scenarios. Students' progress from understanding basic concepts to using their knowledge to analyse complex scenarios and solve problems.

Available ABA's include:

1. Basics of Money
2. Demand and Supply
3. Econ Production and Cost
4. Externalities
5. Fiscal Policy and Multipliers
6. Government Intervention
7. International Trade
8. Labour Market Indicators and Unemployment
9. Oligopoly
10. Opportunity, Cost, Specialization and Trade
11. Perfect Competition
12. Price Discrimination
13. Prisoner's Dilemma
14. Real and Nominal GDP
15. Reserves and Monetary Policy
16. Savings and Lending Version
17. Types of Elasticity

Graphing Tools

A series of basic and complex graphic questions are available within Connect® to aid students in their practice and development. These questions enable students to develop their graphical ability along with their calculating and plotting data skills.

Each question is auto-graded, available throughout the assignable content and are accompanied by immediate feedback to help guide students through the task.

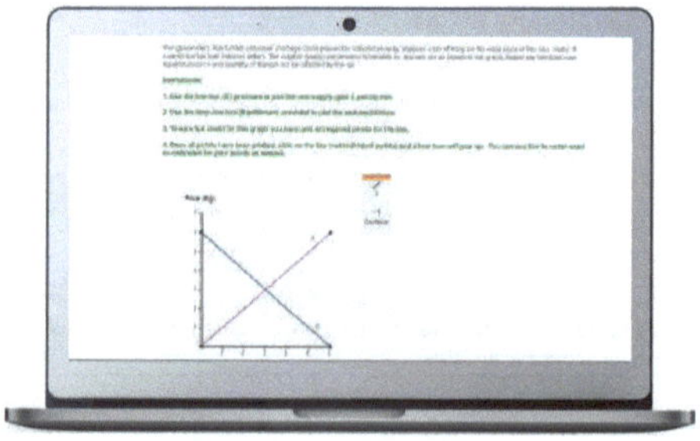

Smarter studying with

McGraw Hill SMARTBOOK®

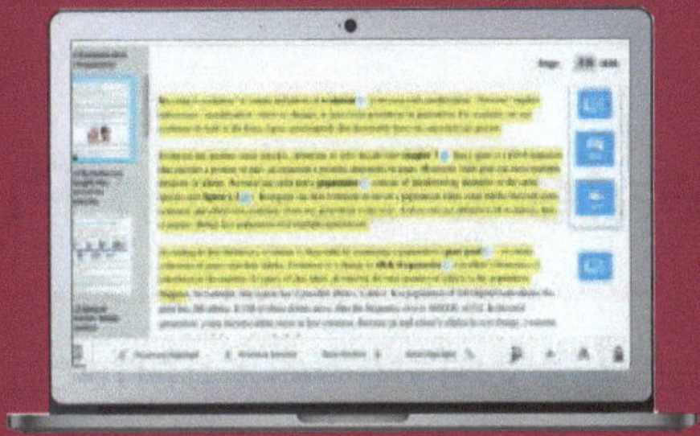

The **SmartBook®** tool integrated within Connect® maximizes learning by helping students study more efficiently, highlighting the most important points in the chapter, asking verification questions and indicating additional resources.

More Personalised

SmartBook® constantly adapts to students' needs, creating a personalised learning experience.

More Productive

SmartBook® creates an extremely productive learning experience, focusing students' attention on the concepts they need to learn.

More Prepared

SmartBook® helps students prepare for lessons, allowing you to use class time more dynamically

> "I liked the idea of continuous assessment online as it helped me to keep track of student performance while it freed up my time spent marking and meant I could focus on my research"
>
> **Alejandra Ramos, Trinity College Dublin, Ireland**

The ReadAnywhere App

To help you study anywhere, anytime! Gain mobile freedom to access your eBook anywhere, even offline, on your smartphone or tablet.

You can:

- Read offline and data-free by downloading the entire text or only the chapters you need
- Never lose an assignment, a note, or your place. ReadAnywhere includes the same functionality as the eBook offered in Connect® with auto-sync across both platforms
- Start studying anytime, anywhere

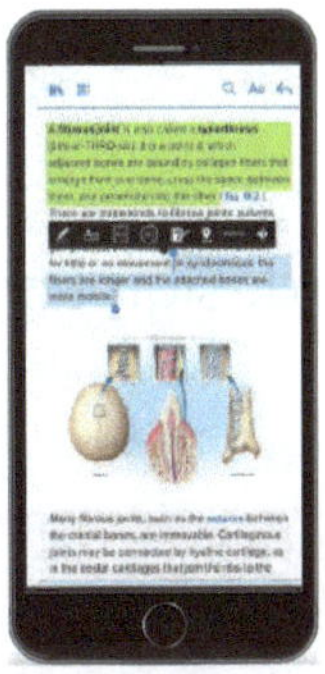

Available on:

App Store

Google Play

CHAPTER 1

Introduction

Chapter contents

At a Glance Introduction

The issue

How we define the subject area of macroeconomics? How can we use data to help us understand the workings of the economy? What does a macroeconomist do?

The understanding

This chapter helps develop a definition and understanding of the subject area of macroeconomics. We will look at an example of macroeconomic time series data and discuss the role of the macroeconomist. Finally, we look at how the profession presents ideas and policy advice to peers and policymakers.

The usefulness

Understanding the workings of the wider economy is central to developing useful economic policy; it is also useful to understand the macroeconomic climate when drawing up plans that require some estimate of the economic climate in the future, not only for policymakers, but also for firms and businesses.

1.1 An introduction to macroeconomics

The subject of macroeconomics provides us with the tools to develop our understanding of the wider economic changes within and across societies: why the economy expands and contracts over time, why economies experience rising and falling prices, and why the number of people employed in society fluctuates over time. Macroeconomics itself might not yet be considered an exact science; nevertheless it provides us with a robust framework to understand the driving factors of economic change. The subject makes use of evolving macroeconomic models that help to explain the latest economic thinking. Without these models we have no framework to base and judge our arguments and economic debate reverts to a simple exchange of opinion.

This book is motivated by a passion for teaching and my conscientious students. They have provided the encouragement to write a textbook that explains the subject of macroeconomics in a plain and simple, yet concise manner. I have included new subject areas from their interactions with me over the years in class, most reflected in the chapters on the wider financial system, sustainable growth and macroeconometrics.

I hope that you also find it fit for that purpose, and that you enjoy reading the book as much as I have enjoyed writing it. The text assumes very little previous knowledge of macroeconomics and is written in the context of a single economy. Focusing on the case of the United Kingdom, we benefit from consistency in explanation, though everything taught here could easily be applied to any other economies where characteristics might differ; the analysis remains universal. Each chapter in the book covers a key subject area, beginning with a more basic explanation and ending with a more technical one. Structured this way, the reader can choose a surface level understanding or a more in-depth and technical one.

The structure follows a market and model approach; after the introductory chapters on the scope of macroeconomics, we cover the three markets of finance, goods and labour. After the markets we take on the macroeconomic models individually, making a tailored chapter choice an easier task for the course convenor.

In the rest of this chapter, we will outline the scope of the subject of macroeconomics by providing some definitions and introducing five of the key macroeconomic concerns. We will learn about the role of a macroeconomist and the tools that provide insight into the relationships that connect these concerns and further our understanding of the macro economy. We will make basic interpretations and inference from macroeconomic data, presented in the form of macroeconomic time series. Finally we present a basic framework to begin the journey of understanding around the role and use of macroeconomic models, making use of a simple two-dimensional diagram that can be applied to the macroeconomic models that will be introduced in the following chapters.

Defining macroeconomics

Macroeconomics concerns itself with the higher-level economic workings of an individual society and is often referred to as the study of the aggregated economy, or the economy as a whole. We can contrast this with microeconomics, the branch of economics that concerns itself with the behaviour of the individual firm or that of a particular market place.

Macroeconomics is the study of the economy's condition measured using the values of macroeconomic indicators, or macroeconomic variables. These 'macro' variables – including output, economic growth, inflation and unemployment – are regularly reported by the media because they reflect important changes in the macroeconomy. The way that these variables interact and change over time is of interest to both economists and policymakers alike, and for this reason they are often referred to as 'macroeconomic issues' or 'macroeconomic concerns'.

The national public office of statistics will be the body responsible for collecting economic data and compiling macroeconomic variables, before they are published via media outlets such as televised news channels. You may recall hearing a news channel report the monthly inflation rate, which measures the change in the cost of living for consumers; something along the lines of: 'the office of national statistics has announced that the consumer price index (CPI) measure of inflation has increased to 5.2 per cent, up from 4.8 per cent the previous month'. To an individual who has not studied economics, announcements like these may have little meaning, perhaps because they are unaware of how a change in CPI inflation affects them personally.

The subject of macroeconomics gives us the tools to understand how the changes in the 'macro' variables occur and how they impact the fabric of society. Describing the way our economy works at the macro level is a complicated affair, with billions of transactions taking place every year between individuals, firms and public organizations. The relationships that explain the interconnections and changes in these transactions need to be explained easily, thus the need for economy-wide aggregated measures of activity and a simple understanding of the workings of the economy.

The macroeconomic issues are:

- **Output or income (the sum of all production)**
- **Economic growth (the change in production)**
- **Unemployment (the number of workers without jobs)**
- **Inflation (the change in the average price)**
- **International trade (production to and from abroad).**

An aggregated variable is either an average value (such as inflation) or an economy-wide level (such as output). For example, output is an aggregated variable that is calculated using the 'sum' of all revenues of final goods producers in the economy. The process of summing up, or averaging variables, is something we call the process of 'aggregation'. Macroeconomics concerns itself with the behaviour and search for meaningful relationships between these variables. Studying macroeconomics helps us to better understand certain realities not obvious to non-economists.

The role of the macroeconomist

To convey our understanding of the wider economy, and to communicate a theory of how the economy works, macroeconomists use simplified representations of the economy, called economic models. These models assist us with the complex task of describing our economy, without the addition of unnecessary detail, to those who are not specialists in the subject of economics.

One of the best examples of a 'non-specialist' is the media, who might unwittingly report variables in a misleading manner. For example, as far as the media are concerned, the CPI inflation rate is just the percentage change in the average consumer's cost of living, but in reality no one person is 'actually' average and consequently the measure is not 'actually' relevant to any particular individual. The media often fails to highlight or consider this. In the context of macroeconomics, inflation is just the change in the 'average' price.

A pensioner faces a very different inflation rate to a worker who commutes to work and so an aggregated inflation rate of 5.2 per cent is of little relevance to both those individuals who face quite different changes in their cost of living from the consumption decisions that they make. The job of a macroeconomist is to communicate the economy to non-specialists, study the relationships between the macroeconomic variables and invent new theories which will become useful to policymakers and in the interest of society as a whole.

Learning Outcomes

By the end of this chapter you should be able to:

- Define the subject area of macroeconomics as a subfield of economics.
- Describe the typical role of a macroeconomist interested in the higher workings of the financial interactions across a society.
- Interpret basic macroeconomic time series.
- Explain the purpose of a typical macroeconomic two-dimensional analysis.

1.2 The concept of macroeconomic time series

Keeping an official record of events across the economy is rather like an individual keeping a diary. At the time it doesn't seem more useful than a way to offload the events of the day, but over time this information becomes much more useful. A diary is a means to reflect and learn from the past and in the same way, keeping official economic records provides a policymaker with valuable information to analyse at a later date.

Time Series Data: A series of observations from a macroeconomic variable, constructed or collected by the Office of National Statistics. Data may be in the form of a level, an index or a percentage.

The public office of national statistics is the body responsible for the construction and measurement of the macroeconomic variables over time. To measure the variables it collates information, uses statistical technology to produce best estimates of the variables each month, and in doing so produces **time series data**. Of course, the individually collected macroeconomic variables change as time progresses, and those changes produce a profile for us to observe. The series of values for each variable over time are termed 'macroeconomic time series'. We can plot and view these profiles individually or together, especially if we consider that plotting variables together is of interest.

As an example, we might view the profile of the exchange rate together with the profile for international trade on the same graph. From a visual inspection of these profiles we might deduce that they tend to move in opposite directions; when the exchange rate is appreciating, international trade tends to decline and vice versa. This is an example of an economic observation that we can make from discussing macroeconomic times series – the exchange rate and international trade are negatively correlated.

Plotting and reading macroeconomic data

The easiest way to view economic time series is through plots of their values over time. We can instantly recognize a time series profile due to the fact that the 'variable of time' is positioned on the horizontal axis with the 'variable of interest' on the vertical axis. As an example, we can plot the variable of unemployment for the UK over the period 1997 to 2024, presented in Figure 1.1. The data plotted is the quarterly unemployment rate; defined as the percentage of the labour force actively seeking employment in any three-month period.

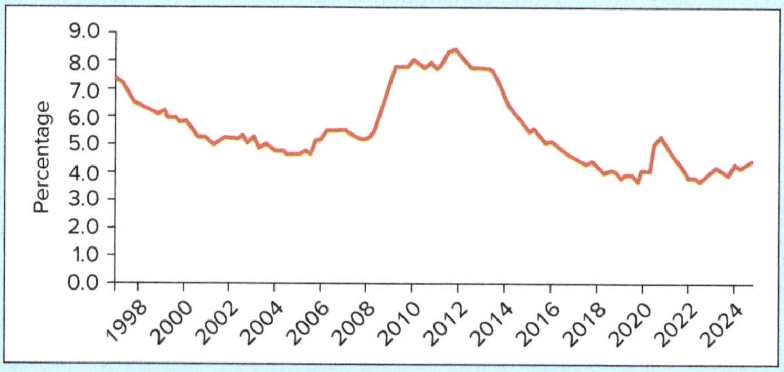

Figure 1.1 Unemployment rate in UK 1997–2024 (%)

Source: Office for National Statistics 2025. https://www.ons.gov.uk/employmentandlabourmarket/peoplenotinwork/unemployment/timeseries/mgsx/lms

Notice that the profile is slightly jagged, the degree of which is determined by the frequency of the data collected; generally speaking, the higher the frequency the less smooth will be the profile of the time series. An annual measurement of unemployment would produce a smoother profile than that from quarterly or monthly data.

The preliminary data analysis

From our plot of macroeconomic data we can make a visual inspection and a basic **preliminary data analysis**. Firstly, we can see that across the whole sample, UK unemployment ranges from around 4 per cent to 8 per cent and from this observation we might propose that a normal unemployment rate be in the region of 6 per cent. Further, we can see that there are prolonged periods where unemployment is either increasing or declining; these periods correspond to episodes in the general condition of the macroeconomy, such as economic activity or other economic and political factors. When output is declining during a recession, we would expect unemployment to be rising. From the profile of Figure 1.1, the most obvious example of this is during the financial crisis that began in 2008 where we witness a steep increase in the unemployment rate from nearly 5 per cent up to just over 8 per cent. We can also see a consistent recovery in the labour market from 2013 onwards, where unemployment falls to a historic low, just below 4 per cent in 2019. From this period forward we can see a jump in unemployment in 2021 caused by the COVID crisis before a fall back nearer to the historic lows, though this has been increasing more recently due to other geopolitical factors.

> **Preliminary Data Analysis:** An analysis, or visual inspection, that comes from the observation of a basic presentation of economic data. This may be in the form of summary statistics, or from the profiles and directions of the time series data itself.

We can now see the usefulness of plotting macroeconomic time series; from the profiles we can draw some basic economic inference using a visual inspection. These observations help to guide our ideas when developing new economic theory on the workings of the wider economy, though at this point we must add some caution – an observation from a basic visual inspection is not necessarily a fact. Facts also require proof through theoretical reasoning and economic research.

EXERCISE 1.1

An important characteristic of a macroeconomic series is the frequency in which it is presented. What key difference would you expect to see in the variance of a series presented in a quarterly frequency to that of an annual frequency?

1.3 The concept of economic modelling

The role of a macroeconomist involves the use of economic models, which we can think of as miniature representations of the economy that we use to explain economic linkages, and to predict the reactions of the economy to shocks and economic policy. Here we outline a simple explanation of the purpose and usefulness of a macroeconomic model.

What is an economic model?

An economic model is a simplified miniature of the economy; it can be represented in words as a description, a simple two-dimensional diagram, or a series of mathematical equations. None of these representation methods can be considered superior to another, but they can serve different purposes. A descriptive model is easy to understand, a diagrammatic model is easy to visualize and a mathematical model can be tested using macroeconomic data. What is clear is that the simpler models are probably the most useful, bearing in mind that the role of the macroeconomist is to communicate the economy to non-economists. A macroeconomist who can only communicate to other economists is a professional of limited usefulness.

It is also worth pointing out at this stage that there is no universally agreed way to model an economy, and this might lead some to conclude that the science of macroeconomics is somehow flawed or incomplete. We can split the many schools of thought into two categories: 'Keynesian type' schools that see prices moving more slowly and 'classical type' schools that see prices adjusting quickly. Traditionally, the debate between the two schools of economic thought centres on how prices move and the usefulness of economic policy. We discuss this in more detail in Chapter 4.

Even though we have yet to see a consensus between the two competing perspectives, many economists are beginning to accept the reality that some form of economic policy intervention is necessary during extreme or abnormal times. We can think of this emerging consensus as a neo-synthesis; policy is effective in the short run, but less so in the long run. Economic policy, especially demand side, has real economic impact in the presence of market inefficiencies, though the adjustment of prices undoes this in the long run. In other words, the use of fiscal and monetary policy is considered useful, but only in the short run.

An introduction to economic modelling

Schedule: A line or a curve in an economic model. The schedule reflects the behaviour of an agent inside the model; for example, the representative consumer or representative firm.

Economic models are often presented in the form of a two-dimensional graph, with two **schedules** (or curves); a downward sloping schedule and an upward sloping schedule. There are exceptions to this set up, as you will see in Chapter 4, but the purpose here is to understand how models work, rather than be over-definitive. The axis of the graph will include the variable of interest (often a quantity or outcome) on the horizontal axis and an adjusting mechanism (often a price) on the vertical axis.

The two schedules represent the behaviour of two economic agents in the model; the downward sloping schedule represents the agent who is demanding and the upward sloping schedule the agent who is supplying. As an example, and in the context of macroeconomics the two agents might be consumers (demanding) and firms (supplying).

In Figure 1.2, we present such a diagram showing a two-dimensional graph with two schedules imposed: the red agent supplying quantity and the blue agent demanding quantity. It is important to remember that the schedules are reflecting the behaviour of the agents in the model. Focusing on the demanding agent as an example, we see that at high prices the blue agent demands less quantity, but as the price falls the quantity demanded increases. Not all macroeconomic models have exactly two schedules (agents); sometimes there will be a third agent, such as a policymaker, or the schedules will be reflecting sectors of the economy instead of representative agents. For an example of a macroeconomic version of this generic model, we can use the labour market – replace the axis with the 'real wage' for price and the amount of labour employed for quantity, and the schedules with labour supply and labour demand.

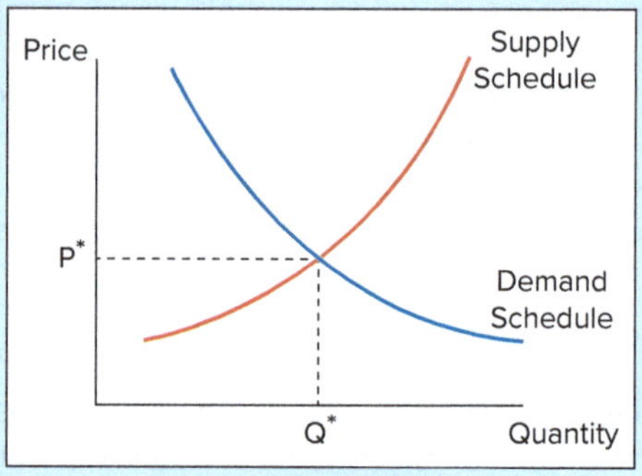

Figure 1.2 A typical example of an economic model

Equilibrium: An economic state where the economy is assumed to be 'settled' and no further change will take place without some movement in economic policy or shock. If we are not in equilibrium, then there is always a driving force back towards it, through the powers of excess supply and excess demand.

Now that we understand the composition of a model we can make some basic interpretation from our model. Notice that both agents behave the same at a particular value of price and quantity – the quantity demanded and the quantity supplied is exactly the same at price P^*. At this price there is agreement between the two agents and the market clears; here we are in a state of market **equilibrium**. At this price, the economy is considered at rest and there are no market forces at work.

The prices that we see every day as the outcome of interactions in efficient markets are equilibrium prices; for example, the prices we see changing in the stock market and currency markets are actually the equilibrium prices changing very frequently in real time.

From this basic analysis we can see that economic models make predictions; and here the prediction is that the market will clear at a particular equilibrium quantity and price. From economic models we can also make other kinds of predictions, for instance how the economy will behave after economic policy or after economic shocks. We will discuss these in more detail as we go through each model in turn, but for now we have a basic understanding of why macroeconomists use models and what purpose they serve.

EXERCISE 1.2

Imagine a scenario where the quantity demanded increases because of an exogenous increase in income, rather than a fall in price. Use the model presented in Figure 1.2 to explain the resulting effects on the equilibrium price and quantity.

Finally, we discuss the reaction of the model to changes in factors other than price or quantity. Both schedules reflect the behaviour of the buyer and seller in the dimensions of price and quantity; a change in the price will be reflected by a movement along the schedules, at the new price there is a new prediction for quantity.

The model assumes that all other factors outside of our analysis remain constant, something we refer to as the assumption of ***ceteris paribus***. Now imagine that something else that effects either agent does actually change, say an increase in income for the agent that represents demand. These changes are called exogenous changes because they are happening outside of the model; a decrease in income for the demanding agent will decrease demand at every price level, so the demand schedule shifts left to reflect this exogenous change.

Ceteris Paribus: A key assumption required for a typical 2 dimensional analysis. Everything that might affect the economic agents outside our space is assumed to remain constant; direct meaning 'all other things equal'.

EXAMPLE 1.1

Real world example: Relating the components of a model to the game of chess

Another way to see how a model works is to relate it to something we are familiar with in real life. Consider the components of an economic model and how they relate to a game of chess.

The landscape

The axes in an economic model are like the board in a game of chess; they are the economic space which frames the analysis and the space in which the game is played.

The operators

The agents in an economic model are similar to the players in a game of chess. The buyers and sellers in the model and the players in the game both interact.

Modus operandi

The schedules in the model map the behaviour of the agents in the same way that the players in a game choose moves.

Something else that you may have noticed about our example of an economic model – there is no account for changes in time. The model is considered 'static'; a picture taken at one point in time. Naturally we can include time as one of the external factors included in the assumption of *ceteris paribus*. Is it reasonable to apply this assumption for the case of time? Yes, if we can assume that the agent's behaviour does not change much over time. Otherwise we may need to enrich the model to account for these changes by including dynamic descriptions of the behaviour of the agents. Dynamic models are a more advanced species that we introduce in Chapter 7 and Chapter 17.

1.4 Chapter summary: Putting it all together

What have we learnt from this chapter? We have defined macroeconomics as the science of the economy – a branch of economics that interests itself with the measurement of the macroeconomic variables including output, growth, inflation, unemployment and international trade. The values of these aggregated variables are of concern to economists and policymakers who seek to understand and explain the linkages between them, and in doing so recommend economic policy that can produce positive or better macroeconomic outcomes.

To understand the higher workings of the economy we can make use of the profiles of macroeconomic variables in the form of time series plots. A visual inspection of these time series can give our economic research direction and motivation; if we can see that unemployment and output are negatively correlated then our theory should take this into account. A preliminary inspection of macroeconomic data should always precede good economic research.

A macroeconomist will communicate macroeconomic theory with an economic model. To familiarize ourselves with the models that will appear in later chapters, we have presented a bare bones economic model to understand the concepts of economic agents, *ceteris paribus* and equilibrium. Forward from here, this knowledge will be assumed, though we will highlight exceptions where schedules (curves) instead refer to sectors or dynamic differences.

Problems

EASY

1. How would you define macroeconomics?
2. Which of the following macroeconomic variables would be studied in relation to economic growth?
   a) The price level and inflation
   b) Output and its change over time
   c) Consumer spending and sentiment
   d) Exchange rate movements
   e) Government borrowing and debt

MEDIUM

3. What does a macroeconomist typically use to explain economic linkages and predict reactions to economic shocks?
4. What is a 'macroeconomic time series'?
5. Which would be an example of a negative correlation often observed in macroeconomic data?
6. Why are economic models said to be 'simplified' representations of the economy?

HARD

7. Explain the importance of time series data in macroeconomics. How can visual inspection of macroeconomic time series help economists develop new theories? Discuss the potential limitations of relying solely on visual inspections for economic analysis.

CHAPTER 2

Economic Activity – National Income and Growth

Chapter contents

At a Glance

Economic activity – National income and growth

The issue

In Chapter 1 we laid the context for the subject of macroeconomics and discussed the role of the macroeconomist. We now turn our attention to the field of operation – what are the key issues that concern the macroeconomist?

The understanding

This chapter introduces two key issues that help us to measure the performance of an economy. Both issues provide indicators of the direction of the economy in terms of economic activity. National income measures the size of the economy in terms of the sum of all production and economic growth measures how that income is progressing.

The usefulness

Both national income and economic growth are key indicators for the employment of resources in the economy. These indicators also help policymakers and commentators to compare economic activity across borders as a basic measure of economic performance.

2.1 Introduction

An obvious way to measure an economy is through its size, using the total value of all the transactions carried out in any year; the amount of economic activity taking place in a society gives us an immediate impression of a nation's well-being. It would be reasonable to predict that an economy with a higher level of output is a wealthy one with greater economic power, populated with healthy citizens that enjoy a higher standard of living. All perfectly reasonable assumptions, but not necessarily all true.

Our first lesson is that even though higher income and higher well-being tend to co-exist, one does not necessarily cause the other. For instance, the citizens of a fast-growing economy might also suffer higher levels of stress and have to breathe polluted air. Who can accurately determine if a self-sufficient island with a small economy has unhappy citizens, just from its macroeconomic indicators?

Where an economy sits in a league table of gross domestic product does not tell us everything; how long a worker has to work in years to be able to afford a house might be a better measure. An economy might appear to be growing, on the basis of an increase in the value of its economic transactions, but this increase might be due to rising prices rather than an increase in real activity. To help us make more harmonious comparisons across societies we can use measures that wash out the distortions created by price changes and use other variables that measure changes in economic activity rather than the absolute level.

In this chapter, we deepen our understanding of the first two of the main macroeconomic variables, national income and economic growth; both of these variables give us an indication of the condition of the economy. We will also come to understand the importance of distinguishing between a **real variable** and a **nominal variable** and discover why output, national income and expenditure are terms that we use interchangeably. We will also discuss one of the most important economic indicators for our policymakers, that of economic growth – how this macroeconomic variable is determined and influenced by economic policy in both the short-run and the long-run time horizon.

Real Variable: A variable that measures a physical quantity and is constructed with prices held fixed. Changes in real variables will only reflect changes in quantities as they are adjusted for inflation.
Nominal Variable: A variable presented at face value, and measured in current prices. These variables are not adjusted for inflation, so that changes in nominal variables can reflect both movements in prices and quantities.

Learning Outcomes

By the end of this chapter you should be able to:

- Describe how we measure national income using the production, income and expenditure methods.
- Understand the difference between real and nominal output in the measurement of economic activity, and why the difference is important.
- Identify the factors that influence a nation's rate of economic growth over the long-run time horizon.
- Classify the concept of economic growth into its short-run and long-run explanations.
- Explain how business cycles relate to fluctuations in economic activity.

2.2 National income, output and expenditure

Most macroeconomic variables are the result of a summing up or averaging, of individual transactions and prices. **Production** is the sum of the value-added revenues of firms in the economy, also known as 'output' or 'aggregate supply'. Total expenditure is the sum of all money spent, and national income is the sum of all money earned from transactions. For every single individual transaction in our economy, production will equal expenditure, will equal income.

Production: Production is the sum of the value-added revenues of firms in the economy, also known as 'output' or 'aggregate supply'.

EXAMPLE 2.1

Hypothetical example: Financial perspectives

Imagine a single economic transaction such as the sale of a £10.00 book. There are three financial perspectives of this transaction.

Income: To the book seller (or the owner of the shop) the sale represents income of £10.00.

Expenditure: To the buyer of the book this transaction represents an expense of £10.00.

Production: For the economy, the business turnover of £10 represents an increase of £10 to production.

In the context of this book, we can think of production, expenditure and national income, all representing the same economic activity. That is why we often see the terms national income and output (production) used interchangeably.

Gross domestic product (GDP)

Although there are several measures of national income and output, one of the most commonly used is called **gross domestic product (GDP)**. Gross, because it is measured using market prices, and domestic because it includes production carried out at home and not abroad. It is important to understand that we include the production of 'foreign owned' firms based in our own country, not just the production of our domestic producers 'owned domestically'. But how is gross domestic product calculated? Well, there are three main measurements; the production method, the expenditure method and the income method.

We start with the production method, but before we begin we need to make a distinction between two types of firms in the economy; those who produce final 'end user' goods and those who produce **intermediate goods** intended as contributing components in the production of **final goods**. As examples we can think of goods produced by component manufacturers or services provided by subcontractors.

The production method can be calculated in two ways; summing all final goods or summing all value-added across the economy:

1. The final goods approach simply sums up the production (revenue) of domestic final goods producers.
2. The value-added approach sums up the value that 'every' firm adds to the chain of production in the economy.

Gross Domestic Product (GDP): A measure of national income calculated by the summing up of domestic production (on home soil). There are three main methods to calculate GDP: the production method, expenditure method and income method.
Intermediate Goods: A good that is manufactured and intended for use as a component in an end-user good. An example of an intermediate good is a micro-chip inside of a laptop computer.
Final Goods: A finished product aimed at an end user, also one that is made up of components bought from intermediate goods producers. An example of a final good is a car sold in a showroom.

One thing to bear in mind here is that calculating GDP is not a simple task and not always clear what to include exactly. For instance, GDP also includes production where the goods and services are not sold at market prices, for example public health services. This element of GDP is estimated at cost, or imputed where this is not possible by the national office of statistics.

As an example of an imputed component of GDP, we can think of the nation's stock of housing. Citizens that own their own homes are providing a service to the economy by housing themselves, and so any calculation of GDP will include an estimated value for the contribution towards national income that comes from home ownership.

Whilst we are concerned of what to include in GDP we must also be mindful of what should not be included. The sale of a valuable painting from one individual to another is a transfer of an asset rather than the creation of a new one, and so some care is required. The sale of a car should be included but should we also include the sale of the engine from a supplier to the car manufacturer? The answer is no. If we include the sale of the engine to the manufacturer, then the creation of the engine will be included in the calculation of GDP twice. Including the sale of goods from intermediaries (suppliers) to final goods producers is called the 'problem of double counting'. We can address the problem of double counting by making use of the '**value-added** method' of calculating GDP, mentioned earlier.

Value Added: The value created by each contributing producer in the chain of production towards completion of a final good. If the production of a final good involves more than one company, the total value added of the final good is split between producers by contribution.

To help explain the difference between the final goods and value-added approaches of the production method of calculating GDP we can make use of an example that compares the two numerically. Imagine an economy where there are two producers, a fast food restaurant 'Twilight Snacks' and a food product supplier 'Haute Blend'. Haute Blend sells £100 worth of food products to Twilight Snacks, who then sell £1,000 worth of sandwiches to the public containing the products bought from Haute (Table 2.1).

Table 2.1 Final goods and value-added approaches

Producer Name	Value Added	Final Goods
Haute Blend	£100.00	£0.00
Twilight Snacks	£900.00	£1,000.00
Total GDP	£1,000.00	£1,000.00

Using the 'value-added' approach for calculating GDP we add up the value contribution to the chain of production by Haute Blend (£100.00) and the value added by Twilight Snacks (£900.00). For the final goods approach, we know that Twilight Snacks is a final goods producer and so we include this revenue (£1,000.00), but Haute Blend is an intermediary that does not produce final goods and so we enter zero for this supplier (£0.00). We can see from our table that both methods for calculating GDP are exactly equivalent (total GDP = £1,000.00).

Our second method of calculating GDP is the expenditure method. This involves the summing up of all the money 'spent' in the economy, as opposed to the production method that sums up firm revenues. It makes intuitive sense that all the money spent in the economy should equal the sum of production, and later we will discuss why this will always be the case. We can break down spending into categories of expenditure by consumers, firms, governments and through international trade.

We can see this more easily by using a mathematical expression called the income identity:

$$Y \equiv C + I + G + NX$$

If we split national income in terms of components of expenditure, then we can declare that the sum of those components 'must' be equal to national income; we call this kind of equation an identity. We can also think of this using an example; if we split an apple into two parts, then it follows that the sum of those parts 'must' be equal to the original apple. The expenditure method of calculating GDP involves collecting data on money spent by the four sectors (components) in the economy; consumers, firms, governments and foreign countries and summing up all these expenditures.

Our third, and last, measure of calculating GDP is the income method. Money spent is also someone else's income, so again it makes intuitive sense that we can sum up all income earned in the economy as a measure of GDP. A purchase in a shop will pay the wages of the staff, but it will also provide income for the shop owner in the form of dividend income from profits. So, for the income method of calculating GDP we simply add up all forms of income in the economy; mainly this will be made up of wages and profits.

One of the difficulties with using nominal output as a measure of the economy's performance is that it contains both quantity and price information. So far, we have calculated output as the sum of the value of transactions, in the form of production, expenditure and income. This measurement of economic activity is a 'nominal' measure, as the transactions are added up at face value using current prices. Whilst this nominal measure is totally valid, it can also mislead policymakers because changes in GDP can be for two reasons; changes in quantity and/or changes in prices. One way to control for these changes is by calculating a measure of national income called 'real' GDP. This measure washes out changes in price information so that increases can only be due to increases in quantities.

So an increase in output can be due to an increase in the quantity of goods sold or an increase in the price level. Obviously, a policymaker would prefer to see an increase in output due to an increase in quantity, and so economists tend to follow the 'real' level of output rather than the 'nominal' level; real output is a measure that washes out the noise created by changes in prices. Next we describe exactly how we go about controlling for price movements in the calculation of GDP.

Real GDP: The value of all goods and services measured using a fixed base year set of prices. This measure washes out the inflation element of the market value 'nominal' measure.
Nominal GDP: The market value, measured at current prices, of all goods and services produced by domestic producers in any one year. We can think of this measure as the 'value of transactions' (prices multiplied by the quantities)

Real vs nominal GDP

Real GDP is a measure of national income that is calculated using prices that are fixed at a base year, with the base year decided upon by the statistical office. This way, the calculation only measures the change in the quantities produced in the years ahead of the base year. In any particular year, the value of all transactions (the prices multiplied by the quantities) gives us a calculation for **nominal GDP**, or GDP at 'face value'.

EXERCISE 2.1

Fill in the blanks in the following:
If the quantity of goods and services produced in the domestic economy remains static, but the prices of those goods and services are rising, then ________ GDP will increase and ________ GDP will remain unchanged.

With real GDP calculated using base year prices, we have a measure that moves in line with changes in the quantities produced rather than when there is a movement in prices. Calculated in this way, real GDP gives us a more realistic measure of economic activity. Example 2.2 provides a simple explanation that helps us to distinguish between nominal and real GDP.

EXAMPLE 2.2

Worked example: Calculating real GDP

Table 2.2 provides us with data for output in an economy that produces only two goods: roses and guns. For each year the quantities are given for both goods along with the prices that they were sold for.

Table 2.2 **Guns and roses**

Year	Guns		Roses	
	Price	Quantity	Price	Quantity
2010	£10.00	1,200	£5.00	2,500
2011	£10.50	1,360	£5.10	3,200
2012	£11.70	1,400	£6.80	3,500

Start by multiplying the prices and quantities for each good and then adding up total production for each year. This will give the time series for nominal GDP.

Year	Calculation	Nominal GDP
2010	(£10.00 × 1,200) + (£5.00 × 2,500) =	£24,500
2011	(£10.50 × 1,360) + (£5.10 × 3,200) =	£30,600
2012	(£11.70 × 1,400) + (£6.80 × 3,500) =	£40,180

Now do the same again, only this time using the 'base year price' for each product with the correct quantities for each year:

Year	Calculation	Real GDP
2010	(£10.00 × 1,200) + (£5.00 × 2,500) =	£24,500
2011	(£10.00 × 1,360) + (£5.00 × 3,200) =	£29,600
2012	(£10.00 × 1,400) + (£5.00 × 3,500) =	£31,500

Now you have the calculation for nominal and real GDP for each year. Notice how, that in the base year of 2010, nominal GDP and real GDP are the same. This will always be the case because the prices and quantities are the same for nominal and real GDP in the base year.

You can see that real GDP rises more slowly than nominal GDP, but is that all you can see?

Perhaps you could take a closer look at the path of your calculated series for output and work out which year was the best one in terms of real activity.

Example 2.2 shows us the importance of reading the level of 'real' output before concluding whether or not an economy is growing. This is the reason why we often see the media reporting and discussing the real growth rate for the economy, rather than the growth in nominal output.

A point worth noting here is that calculated GDP may not always be the same over both methods in practice. The national office of statistics can never know exactly how much every single firm is producing in every period; this has to be estimated, and as a result there will be some measurement error. The office of statistics relies on sophisticated empirical methods to estimate the figures for output in each quarter from a very large number of firms so some error is inevitable; even though there exists a difference in practice, in theory both approaches should produce the same figure.

If the economy is growing, then it is also likely that the well-being of society is also increasing; output is reflecting this by increasing in its level (as calculated by the value of transactions) and unemployment tends to be falling. So a growing economy is consistent with other economic goals for the policymaker and one which we refer to as a positive macro outcome.

EXERCISE 2.2

1. Can you explain the difference between a nominal and a real variable?
2. In macroeconomics, we use aggregated variables. Can you think of any problems that may occur if a policymaker is formulating policy solely on the values of aggregated variables?

2.3 Economic growth

Economic growth is measured using the percentage change in the real level of output in the economy, or the one period change in real GDP. We use real rather than nominal output to ensure that the increases caused by rising prices are washed out and the data focuses on changes in economic activity. In this section, we will discuss the causes of growth in the short-run and long-run time dimensions. One of the benefits of this kind of time categorization is that we can also separate economic policy into those suitable for short-run and long-run time frames.

As an example of this time separation, a one-time increase in government expenditure aimed at increasing economic activity would be considered short run, as the effects of this policy would be relatively short-lived; whereas a policy that lowers taxation for an increase in investment might be viewed as having a longer-run positive effect. Long-run policies aimed at growth are considered to have fewer undesirable effects than those policies that are reacting to the short-run requirements of the economy. Figure 2.1 shows economic growth for the UK over 1997–2019, measured as the quarterly percentage change in UK real GDP.

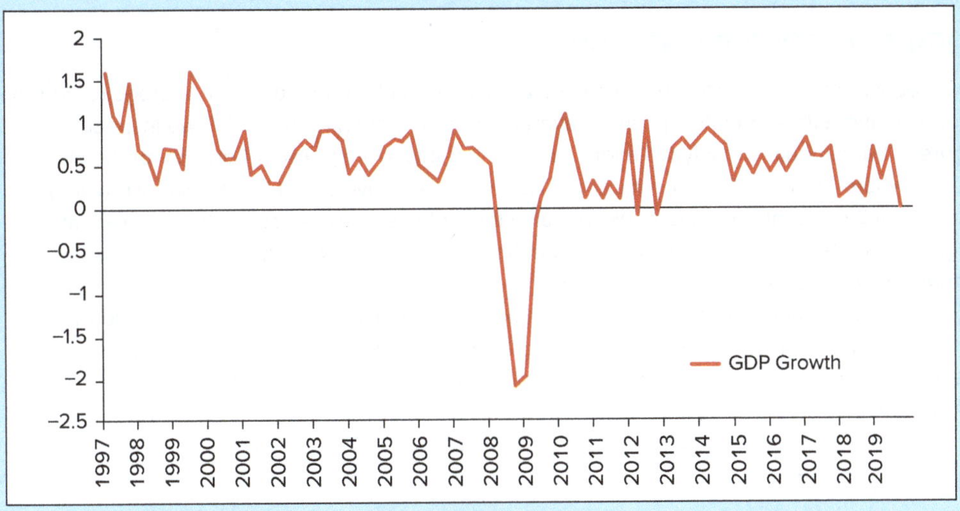

Figure 2.1 Quarterly change in UK GDP before the COVID-19 pandemic, 1997–2019 (%)
Source: World Bank Group. https://data.worldbank.org/

The data shown in Figure 2.1 is limited in scope to 1997–2019. The reason for this is that we can omit a major economic shock caused by the COVID crisis of 2019. The spike in the data from the COVID supply shock is so big that to include it in our sample would render the rest of the data as little more than a straight line.

EXERCISE 2.3

As a class exercise, you can find and plot the quarterly economic growth data for the UK between 1997 and 2024. You will see how the scope and scale of the data that we plot can change a storyline from a visual inspection of macroeconomic data. Notice how the magnitude of the spike caused by the massive supply interruption of COVID-19 mutes out the fluctuations from the preceding and proceeding periods. This outlier in the data makes a visual inspection of the whole sample more difficult.

From a visual inspection of the data in Figure 2.1 we can see that UK growth fluctuates consistently around an average rate of 0.5per cent per quarter (equivalent to 2 per cent per annum); this visual observation provides us with macroeconomic evidence that economic behaviour is cyclical in its nature. In fact, this characteristic is common across many developed economies, not just for the UK. Looking further at this profile we can observe that economic growth in the UK is largely above zero across the entire time horizon presented. Positive economic growth (increasing output) is an indication that the economy is in relatively good health, considering that we expect to see increases in output accompanied by increases in employment.

Further, from the profile provided in Figure 2.1 we can see a marked period of negative growth beginning 2008. This episode shows the UK economy shrank significantly during a period referred to as the Great Recession, a prolonged and severe economic slump triggered by the preceding financial crisis of 2008. Periods of declining output are classified as 'recessions' if they meet the technical criteria that growth is negative for at least two consecutive quarters (for at least 6 months). It is at times like these that we expect our policymakers – the central bank and the government – to intervene and manage the economy back towards a path of growth by using economic policy. A shrinking economy is politically undesirable for a number of reasons, not least because of the damaging effects of increases in unemployment – an issue discussed in Chapter 3. We further our discussion by looking at the long-run and short-run components of economic growth, starting with the long run.

Long-run economic growth

In our earlier example for the UK we see that growth is fluctuating around an average (or trend) over time; the data suggests a positive 'average' rate of growth for the UK. If we inspect Figure 2.1 again quite closely we might suggest that this average rate of growth for the UK is somewhere around 0.5 per cent per quarter, which is equivalent to the economy growing at a rate of 2 per cent per annum. We can also think of this average rate as the 'normal' rate of growth, a rate of growth considered to be the rate of growth we might expect across the longer-run time horizon or in normal times.

With the average rate in mind, a policymaker has a benchmark to gauge the performance of the economy from period to period. The government might 'aim' for this rate of growth over the long run and react with short-run economic policy when the growth rate is away from its normal level.

EXERCISE 2.4

Take a moment to find out how an annual growth rate of around 2 per cent (0.5 times 4 quarters) compares with the growth rate we see today in the UK and the US. You might also notice that UK and US rates are published in different ways. Discuss this difference.

We can think of the long run or 'normal' rate of growth as the expectation of the growth rate over the longer-run time horizon. Another way to view the normal rate of growth is as a longer-run average. In advanced economies this might be between 0 per cent and 3 per cent, and in developing economies between 4 per cent and 8 per cent. Bear in mind that the long-run rate of growth is not necessarily fixed; our normal rate of growth can change occasionally after a permanent shock, as the economy develops or after changes in the general level of competitiveness. These changes can often be found by breaking up the longer time frame into subsections and taking shorter-run averages to identify the movements in the long-run rate. Of course, a change in the normal rate might also drive a policymaker to attempt some influence using 'supply side' policies renowned for affecting the long-run growth rate. A common supply side policy used for this purpose is that of investment taxation, for instance increasing tax credits for firms prepared to make investments in long-term capacity.

- **Supply side policies: Lowering corporation tax, infrastructure investment, lower employment regulations, innovation grants.**
- **Demand side policies: Changing government expenditure, changing the money supply, changing taxation.**

Economic Slack: The difference between actual activity and the 'normal' rate of economic activity. In terms of the labour market we can think of labour market slack as the difference between the normal rate of unemployment and the actual rate of unemployment.

The observations of the growth rate from period to period can also be calculated as the difference away from the trend to provide a measure of **economic slack**. The slack increases/decreases as the economy moves towards or away from its maximum capacity. With our earlier estimate of 2 per cent for the UK long-run growth rate, we can say that a growth rate of 4 per cent (2 per cent above the normal rate) indicates the presence of excess demand (low economic slack) and a growth rate of 1 per cent (1 per cent below the normal rate) is a sign of demand deficiency (high economic slack). In the next section, we make a more detailed explanation of the deviations away from our natural rate in an explanation of the short-run economic fluctuations.

Economic fluctuations in the short run

In reality, we can see that economic growth is rarely based around its trend and actually follows a cyclical path above and below its trend. There are prolonged periods of increasing growth where unemployment is falling, followed by prolonged periods of slowing and even negative growth when unemployment is rising. These movements away from the natural rates in the economy are called short-run fluctuations. The oscillating pattern of these short-run fluctuations is something that we term the 'business cycle'.

Over the course of the **business cycle** we will see regular and prolonged periods of growth, booms, declines and recessions. In the UK, there has been an economic slowdown or recession every 10 years or so, and we call this kind of observation – one that comes from the macroeconomic data we collect – a **stylized fact**.

To react to these short-run fluctuations in economic activity our policymakers can use demand management policies aimed at returning the economy to its normal level in the short run. Imagine a policy scenario where growth is declining and has not only fallen below trend, but is approaching zero. The government and central bank will want to intervene in the economy to manage growth back upwards again to avoid the damaging consequences of a recession and rising unemployment.

Using **fiscal policy** and **monetary policy** to manage the economy in this way is considered 'short run' as it is reacting to the short-run movements in the economy and intended to have a more immediate effect on economic activity than a supply-side policy, that may take a lot longer. Fiscal policy is the use of changes in government expenditure G and taxation T, and monetary policy involves the change in the money supply M. All three variables – G, T and M – can change the level of demand in the economy and thus affect output in the short run. We look at these policies in more detail in Chapter 5 and Chapter 7, for monetary and fiscal policy respectively.

Economic policy can be both expansionary (increasing demand) and contractionary (decreasing demand) for economic activity. To give you an example of expansionary policy, imagine that the economy is shrinking and the government decides to intervene in the hope of reversing the fall in output by increasing government expenditure. The increase in expenditure increases aggregate demand generally and this drives suppliers to increase production. The effectiveness of economic policy is a widely debated and long-running topic of discussion in macroeconomics, with two mainstream schools of thought having opposite views on the usefulness of demand management. We will discuss these two economic schools of thought and economic policy in more detail in Chapter 4.

> **Business Cycle:** The oscillating pattern that we see in economic activity over the longer time horizon. Recessions and booms are a feature of this cycle, one that policymakers hope to influence through economic policy.
>
> **Stylized Facts:** The facts that we see reflected by the macroeconomic data. For example, the business cycle and the negative relationship between output and unemployment.
>
> **Fiscal Policy:** The use of taxation and government spending to make short-run impact on economic activity. An increase in government spending G will increase output.
>
> **Monetary Policy:** Changes in the money supply aimed at managing economic activity in the short run. An increase in the money supply M will increase output.

2.4 Chapter summary: Putting it all together

What have we learnt from this chapter? We have focused on the subject of economic activity and how we can measure that activity using three different methods; although in theory these measures are equivalent, in reality this might not necessarily be the case. In the same way that each transaction in the economy has three perspectives, so does the aggregated form of those transactions: production is equal to income is equal to expenditure.

We have also learned an important distinction between a nominal variable, which measures the value of transactions, and a real variable, which washes out the noise created by changes in prices in the economy; changes in real activity reflects the actual quantity changes in production. To adequately understand whether or not the economy is growing or shrinking policymakers need to follow real GDP. The same follows for any macroeconomic variable whose construction involves the use of a price.

Increases and decreases in national income are commonly measured through a country's growth rate, the percentage change in real GDP. Using the growth rate we can make better comparisons of macroeconomic performance across borders, compared to using levels, which can be complicated by changes in exchange rates. We have also understood the important distinction between the short-run growth rate that we observe from quarter to quarter, which can be influenced by policymakers in the short run, and the long-run rate of growth that can be influenced by macroeconomic structural factors and long-run economic policy.

Assessment Question

Economic activity can be measured using three different methods; the production method, the income method and the expenditure method. In theory, these three methods should produce exactly the same calculation. Explain:

a. Why this might not actually be the case in reality because of measurement error and time lags.

b. Why having three different ways of measuring the same variable might be a benefit when it has to be estimated.

Cases

Economic growth in the UK

Introduction

Economic growth refers to the increase in a country's output over time, typically measured by the rise in its gross domestic product (GDP). The UK, as one of the world's largest economies, has experienced varying rates of economic growth over recent decades. This case study examines the key drivers of economic growth in the UK, the challenges faced and the policy responses implemented by the government and the Bank of England.

Background

Over the past 30 years, the UK has seen periods of significant economic growth, particularly following the global financial crisis of 2007–2008. From 2010 to 2016, the UK experienced a recovery in GDP growth rates, often outperforming other European countries. However, this growth has been uneven, with some years of stagnation or contraction, especially during periods of economic uncertainty, such as the Brexit referendum in 2016 and the COVID-19 pandemic in 2020.

Key drivers of economic growth in the UK

1. **Investment in infrastructure and technology:** The UK government has consistently invested in infrastructure projects and technological advancements. From the HS2 rail project to the focus on digital infrastructure, these investments have helped drive productivity and long-term growth.
2. **Labour force and education:** The UK's strong labour force, supported by high levels of education and skills development, has contributed to its economic growth. The service sector, particularly in finance, technology, and professional services, remains a major contributor to GDP growth.
3. **Monetary and fiscal policies:** The Bank of England's monetary policy, including interest rate management and quantitative easing, has been central in stabilizing the economy. Fiscal policies such as government spending on public services and social welfare have also played a role in supporting demand during times of recession.
4. **Trade and global integration:** The UK's trade relations, particularly with the European Union, the United States, and emerging economies, have been vital to its growth. While Brexit has led to uncertainty regarding future trade agreements, the UK's historical trade networks have been an important growth factor.

Challenges to economic growth

1. **Brexit:** The decision to leave the European Union has created significant uncertainty around trade, investment and labour supply. The UK faces new barriers to trade with the EU, reduced access to the single market and challenges in attracting foreign investment.

2. **Productivity issues:** Despite steady GDP growth, the UK has struggled with stagnating productivity, particularly in comparison to other advanced economies. Low productivity growth can limit long-term economic potential and wage growth.
3. **Income inequality:** While overall growth has been strong, the benefits have not been evenly distributed. Income inequality has remained a persistent issue, with some regions and social groups benefiting more from economic growth than others.
4. **Ageing population:** Like many developed nations, the UK faces an ageing population, which places additional pressure on public finances and can slow down growth. The ageing population increases demand for healthcare and pensions, which could potentially divert resources away from other investments that fuel growth.

Recent developments

1. **COVID-19 pandemic:** The UK's economy was severely affected by the COVID-19 pandemic, with the country experiencing one of the deepest recessions among major economies in 2020. The government's fiscal stimulus measures, including furlough schemes and grants to businesses, helped mitigate some of the negative impacts.
2. **Post-COVID recovery:** Following the pandemic, the UK economy has been in recovery mode, with significant growth in the service sector. However, supply chain disruptions, inflation and labour shortages have hindered the full recovery.

Conclusion

The UK's economy has demonstrated resilience in the face of challenges such as the global financial crisis, Brexit and the COVID-19 pandemic. Moving forward, policies that encourage investment in innovation, improve productivity and address the challenges of an ageing population will be critical for sustaining long-term economic growth. Additionally, addressing regional inequalities and fostering a balanced economy will play a key role in ensuring that growth benefits all sections of society.

Questions

1. What are the key drivers of economic growth in the UK?
2. What challenges has the UK faced in terms of economic growth?
3. How did the COVID-19 pandemic affect the UK's economy?
4. What are some policy responses that could support future economic growth?

Problems

EASY

1. Define gross domestic product (GDP).
2. What does the term 'economic growth' primarily refer to?
   a) An increase in the inflation rate.
   b) An increase in the price level of goods and services.
   c) A sustained increase in a country's output of goods and services.
   d) A decrease in unemployment rates.
   e) An increase in the exchange rate of a country's currency.

MEDIUM

3. What is the difference between value-added goods and final goods?
4. Explain the difference between real GDP and nominal GDP.
5. What are some of the key features of a 'business cycle'?

6. Calculate the real GDP using the expenditure approach, given the following data:
   - Consumption (*C*): £600 billion
   - Investment (*I*): £200 billion
   - Government spending (*G*): £150 billion
   - Net exports (*NX*) (Exports – Imports): £50 billion
   - GDP deflator: 125

   Use the formula for nominal GDP:

   $$\text{Nominal GDP} = C + I + G + (X - M)$$

   Then, calculate real GDP using the formula:

   Real GDP = Nominal GDP / GDP Deflator × 100

HARD

7. How do we measure GDP? Discuss the different methods used to calculate GDP, including the expenditure approach, income approach and production approach, without using algebra.
8. Discuss the role of government policies, such as fiscal and monetary policies, in influencing economic growth.

CHAPTER 3

Unemployment, Inflation and International Trade

Chapter contents

At a Glance

Unemployment, inflation and international trade

The issue

In Chapter 2 we introduced the first two of five key macroeconomic variables. We now turn our attention to another three: unemployment, inflation and international trade. How important is unemployment? Why do we care about rising prices? What factors influence our trade across borders with our international trading partners?

The understanding

We introduce and discuss three key issues for the macroeconomist: the important condition of the domestic labour market is reflected by the level of unemployment; the prices that citizens pay for goods and services is reflected by the rate of inflation; and our international economic performance is reflected by our balance of trade.

The usefulness

Across Chapter 2 and Chapter 3 we open the conversation on the issues that face our policymakers and the concerns of the macroeconomist. Understanding these variables allows us to define the parameters of the field of macroeconomics.

3.1 Introduction

Aside from the measures of economic activity that have been introduced in Chapter 2, there are other important issues that macroeconomics concerns itself with. Another three closely followed economic indicators are the unemployment rate, the inflation rate and the exchange rate for the domestic currency.

The unemployment rate is probably the most important indicator because it directly reflects the condition and well-being of workers in the economy. Without a sufficient level of employment, the basic needs of society such as subsistence and housing are unfulfilled. We will learn how to use measures of the condition of the labour market, such as the unemployment and participation rates. To help us understand how the labour market changes, we break down unemployment into three categories, before highlighting the difference between quarter to quarter changes with those in the normal and long-run rate.

In terms of importance, the inflation rate is a close second; an explosive increase in prices across the economy will make day-to-day life extremely challenging for both consumers and producers, through the uncertainty that it creates. In this chapter we define the concept of inflation as the change in the level of prices in the economy and show how we can calculate this variable using the GDP deflator and the Consumer Price Index (CPI). As we construct our own inflation series arithmetically we also draw attention to the unreliability of this variable; inflation is not only an estimate, it is an average, and nothing more.

Finally, the movements in the rate at which the domestic currency exchanges for foreign currency matters for macroeconomic performance also – an increasing exchange rate will make domestically produced goods more expensive abroad at the same time as making foreign goods more attractive. We look at economic relationships when focusing on economic activity across borders; our trading partners bring much-needed expenditure from abroad and an opportunity to consume imported goods. We discuss how trade is affected by the level of the exchange rate and uncover the driving factors behind changes in the exchange rate itself.

Learning Outcomes

By the end of this chapter you should be able to:

- Identify the key components of the labour market as subsets of the working age population.
- Discuss common ways to measure the condition of the labour market.
- Compare two key methods for estimating the macroeconomic variable of inflation.
- Interpret local economic relationships with foreign trading partners and the importance of exchange rates for trade balance.
- Connect movements in the exchange rate to the workings of the market for foreign exchange.

3.2 Unemployment

More than any other macroeconomic variable, unemployment is probably the closest and most directly felt by the citizens of a society. The incidence of unemployment itself can be traumatic for workers, especially those with dependents. No surprise then, that this variable is widely reported and closely followed by policymakers, who are concerned with economic stability and the well-being of society. Here we look at the components and the key indictors used to describe this important part of the labour market.

The **workforce** of a society usually includes citizens of a working age, normally 16 to 65 years of age, who are 'willing and able' to work at the current wage rate. Only workers who are actively participating in the labour market are considered part of that workforce. With the **unemployment rate** defined as the proportion of the workforce without work, this means that in the context of macroeconomics, if a worker is without a job but not actively looking for one, then they are not considered unemployed. It is important to recognize that the unemployed do not include the portion of the working-age population that have left the workforce or who are not actively looking for a job.

Workforce: Also known as the labour force; the subset of the working age population willing and able to work at the current wage. Workers who retire or give up looking for work are no longer in the workforce.
Unemployment Rate: The percentage of the workforce that are without work but willing and able to work at the current wage rate.
Working Age Population: The set of individuals between the legal age for starting work and the age of retirement. For the UK, this is currently age 16 to 65.

By not including those leaving the workforce in the number of unemployed we are at risk of mismeasuring the changes in unemployment from period to period. Perhaps a worker has given up looking for work because they have been unemployed for too long, they therefore leave the workforce and are no longer considered to be unemployed, but in reality we know that this worker is not unemployed by choice. In a macroeconomic context, the number of unemployed workers in the economy can be defined as those of **working age** who are willing and able to work but without work, or 'the proportion of the workforce without work'.

Intuitively, we can predict that an increase in output will cause a decrease in unemployment as firms require more workers to produce that output. In fact, the data shows that output and unemployment are closely and negatively related to one another; the result follows intuition and is something we often refer to as a 'stylized fact'. Despite this close relationship, unemployment will naturally enjoy a higher weight in the list of concerns for the policymaker, being the most visible of the two variables to the economy's workers. Unemployment is another measure of the economy's success, with a decrease in unemployment seen as highly positive for economic and social well-being.

Measuring unemployment

The labour force is made up of two parts; the set of employed workers and the remaining set of unemployed workers, and so we can write:

$$Labour\ Force = Employed + Unemployed$$

remembering that those without work are only classified as unemployed if they are also part of the workforce. The unemployment rate is the proportion of unemployed workers within the labour force and is often quoted in percentage form in the media. We can calculate the 'unemployment rate' using the following:

$$Unemployment\ Rate = \frac{Unemployed}{Labour\ Force} \times 100$$

where the unemployment rate is quoted as a percentage. A decrease in unemployment can be for two reasons; an increase in economic activity or an increase in the number of people leaving the workforce. This highlights a problem with the unemployment rate as a measure of the condition of the labour market. The level or the rate of unemployment cannot tell you about the flows in and flows out of the work force, just the change.

LIMITATIONS OF THE UNEMPLOYMENT RATE

The rate of unemployment does not take account of the flows into and out of the workforce. A high unemployment rate is not so bad if there are many people in between jobs, 'separated' from existing employers and being 'hired' by new employers. In other words, if separations and hires are both higher.

If unemployment is higher in one country, it might not be as socially detrimental if there is still a good chance of getting a job.

Contrast the scenario given in the highlighted box, where the flow of separations and the new hires are both high, with one where the flows are low. With low separations and a low number of hires we might consider the labour market to be 'stagnant'; in this case, those out of work will have little chance of becoming re-employed. So we should be aware that the unemployment rate does not tell us a great deal about the health of the labour market.

Participation Rate: The percentage of the working-age population that are currently participating in the labour market.

Another ratio of interest to policymakers is the **participation rate** in the economy, or the proportion of the working-age population working or actively looking for work. Put more simply, the fraction of people willing to participate in the labour market, which we can write:

$$\textit{Participation Rate} = \frac{\textit{Labour Force}}{\textit{Working Age Population}}$$

The participation rate captures those leaving the workforce, having failed to find work (the non-employed) so that a drop in the unemployment rate 'not' caused by an increase in firm hires will show up as a drop in the participation rate. A drop in the participation rate might be seen as a negative indictor if workers have given up looking for work after a prolonged period of unemployment.

EXERCISE 3.1

Fill in the blanks in the following:

When graduating from university and entering the ______ for the first time, a student will immediately become ______ and cause a/an ______ in the unemployment rate.

Equilibrium unemployment

Equilibrium Unemployment: Similar in definition to the normal rate of unemployment, more exactly: the labour market clearing level of unemployment. Unwanted changes to equilibrium unemployment requires 'long-run' economic policy.

It is unlikely that unemployment will ever be eradicated altogether and so there will always be a certain level of unemployment. The efficient working of the labour market requires a pool of available workers and inevitably there will always be some proportion of the labour force unemployed at any one time. This minimum level of unemployment will exist even when the wage is at a level that would normally ensure that all those that wanted work equalled the number of vacancies posted by firms in the labour market. We call this type of unemployment **equilibrium unemployment** because despite the labour market being in equilibrium (labour supply is equal to labour demand) there is still some unemployment.

We can categorize equilibrium unemployment into three types:

1. Frictional unemployment (job search related)
2. Structural unemployment (infrastructure related)
3. Seasonal unemployment (due to the time of the year).

Unemployment will always exist due to workers being in between jobs because of the characteristics of the economy and because demand for labour varies across the seasons. If finding a job or being matched with an open vacancy in a particular country is difficult, we might classify this as unemployment caused by friction; a lack of jobs in a particular area caused by infrastructure problems is called structural unemployment; and where there is a lack of work at certain parts of the year, this is known as seasonal unemployment.

EXAMPLE 3.1

Real world example: Equilibrium unemployment

Equilibrium unemployment explains the 'always on' level of unemployment, even when the labour market clears.

Frictional unemployment

Labour markets differ across countries; for example, in the US it is easier to find a job than in France due to differences in labour laws.

Structural unemployment

A developing country like Nigeria will have a level of unemployment due to a lack of infrastructure across regions.

Seasonal unemployment

An ice cream seller will find it difficult to sell ice cream in the winter; unless that is, they are operating in Liverpool in the UK, where there is a market for ice cream in all weathers.

A macroeconomist will consider these types of unemployment part of the 'normal level' or the 'natural rate' of unemployment. We can observe these 'normal' unemployment rates for various countries around the world and make note of the considerable variance. In the UK, normal unemployment is typically around 5 per cent, whereas in Europe this is significantly higher due to the difference in the characteristics of the labour market in Europe, such as tighter labour laws.

Any particular actual rate of unemployment will be made up of the **normal rate of unemployment** and the deviation from that normal rate, which we can also think of as equilibrium unemployment and disequilibrium unemployment. As an example, if the observed rate of unemployment in the UK is 8 per cent we could say that this rate is 3 per cent higher than the normal rate of 5 per cent. The disequilibrium component (3 per cent) will be reflecting changes in economic activity, and is the component most likely to receive attention from the policymaker interested in the short-run economic cycle.

Normal Rate of Unemployment: The rate of unemployment that would exist in normal times or in the absence of economic shocks. The normal rate is sometimes referred to as the 'long-run' or 'natural' rate of unemployment.

The policymaker with eyes on both the short-run and long-run macroeconomic condition can use policy based on suitability for the time horizon under consideration. Short-run policy aims for a change to disequilibrium unemployment and long-run policy seeks to change equilibrium unemployment. In the short run the government could increase spending and/or the central bank may increase the money supply to react to an increase in disequilibrium unemployment. For the long run, new labour market policies provide a reaction or influence over the equilibrium (normal) rate of unemployment.

As an example, imagine that the government wants to lower normal unemployment because the current rate seems unsatisfactory or politically unpopular; they might consider policy that lowers 'frictional' unemployment, such as better job search facilities or an easier system for transfer of employment contracts. By lowering normal unemployment, the policymaker is also lowering the actual (observed) rate.

EXAMPLE 3.2

Real world example: Unemployment in the UK

Figure 3.1 shows the percentage of the workforce unemployed in the UK from 1997 to 2025, displayed as macroeconomic data time series.

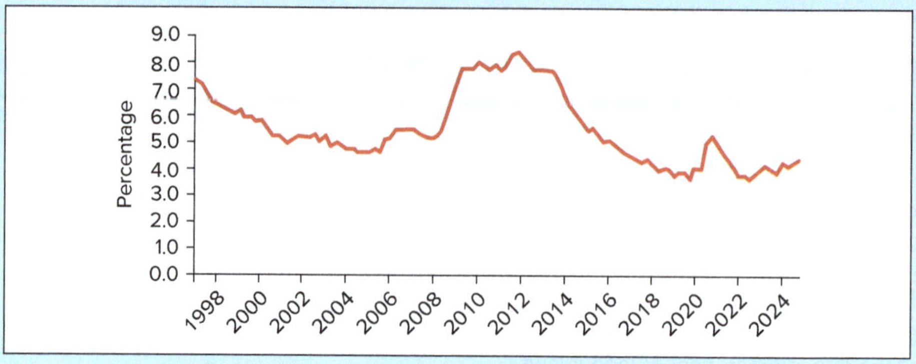

Figure 3.1 The UK unemployment rate, 1997–2025 (%)

Source: Office for National Statistics 2025. https://www.ons.gov.uk/employmentandlabourmarket/peoplenotinwork/unemployment/timeseries/mgsx/lms

Question:

a) Use the graph to discuss the evolution of unemployment in the UK since the late 1990s. Provide some basic economic commentary, such as episodes and trends.

b) Add another series for UK economic activity, perhaps that obtained from Exercise 2.3. Try to match periods of decreasing economic activity to increasing periods of unemployment.

Answer guideline:

a) For the United Kingdom, unemployment has been consistently around 4–8 per cent since the late 1990s, peaking in 2012 at around 8.5 per cent before falling back to nearer 4 per cent from 2014 onwards. Notice the spike in unemployment caused by the COVID crisis of 2019.

b) Using the data presented above and your plot of economic activity for the UK, you will see that unemployment began a steep incline while growth in output declined sharply around the beginning of the financial crisis. Coincidences like these are evidence of the countercyclical (running in opposite directions) relationship between output and unemployment that we expect to see from macroeconomic intuition – that when the economy is shrinking, unemployment is high or at least rising. This coincidence will be repeated clearly in the period surrounding the global pandemic of 2019. These observations provide us with empirical support for our earlier proposition that output and unemployment are negatively correlated.

3.3 Inflation

Inflation is an important macroeconomic variable that reflects the changes in the prices that we pay for goods and services sold in the economy. Of course, there are many prices used across the economy in any period, so which one should we use to help us find inflation? The answer is that we use the 'average' price across the economy because, as macroeconomists, we are also making use of other variables that are aggregated or averaged.

The task of finding the 'average' price is not a simple one; can you imagine contacting every single supplier every month to ask for all the prices of every good and service they have sold in that period? This is not possible, so inevitably the national office of statistics will make an estimate of the average price by contacting a 'sample' of firms in each period. The average price in the economy is also referred to as the '**price level**'.

Inflation: The measured change in the price level, also defined as 'the continuous rise in the price of goods and services sold in the economy'.
Price Level: A number estimated by the office of statistics, often in index form, that reflects movements in the average price in the economy.

Despite the fact that the reported inflation rate is estimated, this variable remains an important concern for the macroeconomist and the policymaker alike. Changes to the average price level give advanced warning of changing economic conditions ahead, such as economic booms or recessions.
The inflation rate can be defined exactly as the percentage change in the average price level in the economy. The word 'inflation' implies that prices are

rising as is normally the case, so it is worth noting that when prices are falling we instead have a macroeconomic condition called deflation.

In everyday life, we witness a moderate increase in prices over time as the economy continues to grow; it is something that we expect to see. So why is inflation considered a problem? Inflation is considered reasonable and easier to control while it remains within single figures (1–10 per cent), but above this figure there is a danger that inflation can increase at an exponential rate, or very quickly. Inflation has the potential to display a high level of volatility and for this reason, policymakers follow its movements quite closely.

When inflation is higher than 10 per cent and increasing at a fast pace, inflation can turn to high inflation very quickly, perhaps so quickly that inflation becomes 'hyperinflation' (prices rising very fast indeed) in a very short space of time. Hyperinflation is considered very costly to the economy because of the uncertainty it creates; a nation's producers can find this kind of environment one that is impossible to trade in. Sudden and unexpected price rises in a firm's inputs make sensible investment, hiring and inventory decisions very difficult to make. A period of hyperinflation will have a detrimental effect on economic activity and a most probable significant increase in unemployment. Needless to say, the volatile nature of inflation is the reason our policy makers will endeavour to keep inflation at a low level where it is easier to control.

EXERCISE 3.2

1. Define inflation and explain whether or not you consider it to be a positive or negative environment for economic activity?
2. Can you relate the reaction of two other macroeconomic variables, output and unemployment, to an episode of hyperinflation?

EXAMPLE 3.3

Real world example: Hyperinflation in Venezuela 2016–2023

A relatively recent example of an economy that is experiencing hyperinflation is Venezuela. The average annual inflation rate leapt to 254 per cent in 2016, and then peaked at 65,374 per cent in 2018, before dropping back to around 337 per cent in 2023. Inflation is still high, but no longer considered hyperinflation at the time of writing.

Inflation

At the height of the inflation crisis, prices were rising by between 1 per cent and 2 per cent every day. So Venezuela was facing the kind of inflation that most developed countries face in a year, but every day instead. Imagine a loaf of bread that cost 1 Venezuelan Bolivar at the beginning of the year rising to 640 Venezuelan Bolivar the following year.

Macroeconomic consequences

Venezuelan firms have suffered significantly – costs spiralled and customers struggled to find adequate funds to purchase goods and services. Firms reduced production and the economy contracted sharply. For the economy of Venezuela, the resulting negative effect is marked by a slump in real GDP of around 27 per cent in 2019 and a corresponding increase of 28 per cent in the number of unemployed.

Source: Statista 2025

The GDP deflator

Inflation is defined as the consistent rise in all prices of all goods and services in the economy. Naturally, this definition presents challenges such as successful data collection and accurate measurement of a single average for the change in prices for the economy. Choices have to be made on how to estimate this important variable in the best possible way. Those choices will involve how the data is sampled in its collection and the weighting of the relative importance of items included in the construction of the measure.

In macroeconomics we make regular use of two main standard measures of the price level. These two measures are the GDP deflator index and the consumer price index (CPI).

GDP Deflator Inflation: A measure of inflation that measures the change in the aggregate price level using the relative change between nominal and real GDP.

The GDP deflator is an index that reflects the changes in the price level using both nominal and real GDP time series data. These two data series are used to calculate an index that reflects price movements forward from a base year, set by the authority responsible for calculating the index. We can use the data provided earlier in Chapter 2, on calculating real GDP to form the GDP deflator index (Example 3.4).

EXAMPLE 3.4

Worked example: Calculating inflation using the GDP deflator

Remember the example for our imaginary economy where only two goods are produced, roses and guns. We can use our answers for nominal and real GDP in our calculation of the GDP deflator index:

Year	Nominal GDP	Real GDP
2023	£24,500	£24,500
2024	£30,600	£29,600
2025	£40,180	£31,500

With the following equation:

$$GDP\ Deflator = \frac{Nominal\ GDP}{Real\ GDP} \times 100$$

Using this equation, we can construct the GDP deflator index from our example economy:

Year	GDP Deflator Index
2023	100.00
2024	103.38
2025	127.56

Notice that in the base year nominal GDP and real GDP are the same and so the value of the index in the base year will always be exactly 100.00. Now that we have the values for the index we only need to calculate the percentage change in this index to obtain **GDP deflator inflation** for our economy. To calculate percentage change in any time series we can use:

$$\%\ Change = \frac{New\ Value - Old\ Value}{Old\ Value} \times 100$$

This gives us GDP inflation for 2024 and 2025:

Year	GDP Deflator Inflation
2024	3.38%
2025	23.39%

We can see that inflation was much higher in 2025 (23 per cent) than in 2024 (3 per cent), a fact which underpins our understanding how in nominal terms the increase in output was larger for 2025 but in real terms, the expansion of the economy was actually greater in 2024. You may remember that this is something you were asked to think about in the example on calculating real GDP, above.

An important characteristic of the GDP deflator measure of inflation is that it can only account for changes in the prices of goods and services produced domestically, it cannot account for imported inflation. If the price of an imported food product rises, this will push up the cost of living for the consumer, but the GDP deflator measure of inflation will not pick this up because it only measures the prices of goods produced domestically. Another issue arises for this measure when a new product comes to market further forward than the base year when it was not accounted for. Remember that, as with all measures, the GDP deflator measure of inflation is only an estimate as it is further based on estimates of nominal GDP.

The consumer price index (CPI)

Another commonly used measure of inflation is constructed from the change in the CPI, a measure closer to the cost of living that consumers face. A policymaker may prefer this measure over and above the GDP deflator measure of inflation because it better accounts for the change in the cost of living; accordingly this measure might be considered more policy relevant. Remember that GDP deflator inflation uses a 'base year' to calculate inflation, in other words, prices are held fixed. **CPI inflation** differs in that it is the 'basket of goods and services' or the quantities that are held fixed and the prices in each year allowed to vary in the calculation of inflation.

CPI Inflation: A measure of inflation that accounts for the change in the cost of living faced by the economy's consumers using an estimated and average fixed basket of goods.

The office responsible for calculating the CPI will make its best estimate of a representative basket of goods used to calculate the index. We can think of this basket as the estimated 'average' purchasing basket that the consumer faces over a period of time. For example, our representative consumer's basket might contain everything that we would expect the average individual to consume in an average month: six pizzas, half a bag of sugar, a month's supply of gas, two iTunes, and so on.

Once the basket is constructed (fixed) by the statistics office and considered representative (average) then the price of the basket is measured in each period to create the CPI. Using changes in the index, inflation is then calculated in the same way as in Example 3.4. A key difference for the CPI measure of inflation over the GDP deflator is that it accounts for inflation abroad, due to the fact that the consumer's representative basket contains imported goods (e.g., imported groceries). In Example 3.5, we show how to compute inflation from the consumer price index.

EXAMPLE 3.5

Worked example: Calculating inflation from the CPI

Imagine another economy where the representative consumer buys a typical basket of goods which is measured in terms of cost by the statistics office each year as follows:

Year (x)	Cost of Basket
2020	£21,000
2021	£21,840
2022	£22,495
2023	£23,957

If we use 2020 as our base year, then the CPI can be calculated using the following equation:

$$CPI = \frac{Cost\ of\ Basket\ in\ Yr\ (x)}{Cost\ of\ Basket\ in\ Yr\ (Base)} \times 100$$

For example, the CPI index for 2011 = £21,840 /£21,000 × 100 = 104. The CPI is calculated for 2022 and 2023 the same way:

Year (x)	CPI
2020	100.00
2021	104.00
2022	107.12
2023	114.08

With the index calculated we can use the equation for percentage change, just as we did for the GDP deflator example in Example 3.4:

Year	CPI Inflation
2021	4.0%
2022	3.0%
2023	6.5%

We can also provide some economic commentary now that we have the time series for inflation: 'Inflation fell to 3 per cent from 4 per cent in 2022, but increased to 6.5 per cent in 2023'.

GDP deflator or CPI?

Learn to highlight the main differences between GDP deflator inflation and CPI inflation. Remember that the two indexes are produced differently: the GDP deflator with fixed prices, fixed at the base year, and CPI with a fixed basket of goods – essentially the CPI uses fixed quantities instead of prices. It is also worth remembering that CPI inflation can account for changes in prices abroad whereas GDP deflator inflation cannot. The GDP deflator only measures changes in prices of goods and services produced domestically and the CPI measure will not include price rises for goods like factory equipment and machinery as they do not feature in the basket of the consumer.

Just as with the GDP deflator measure of inflation, the CPI inflation measure is exposed to inaccuracies which are impossible to avoid altogether. A sudden change in consumer tastes or introduction of new products will make the representative/basket an 'unrepresentative' one; goods in the basket will require re-weighting to accurately measure the change in the average consumer's cost of living. This regular updating of the series causes problems with consistency. A study that uses CPI inflation, which becomes updated in the future, will itself become outdated by the revision of the data used in the research.

EXERCISE 3.3

Using Example 3.5 on calculating CPI inflation, imagine that the cost of the representative basket was £25,650 in 2023 instead of £23,957. What change does this make to the CPI inflation rate for 2023?

3.4 International trade

Our economic relationship with the rest of the world is of paramount importance to our policymakers – our ability to trade with our foreign partners matters for national income and employment. Domestic firms will benefit from a landscape that enables the free movement of goods, so that they can export produce and increase revenue. In a similar way, open trade allows our consumers to benefit from a wider availability of goods and services imported from firms based abroad. Traditionally, trading agreements between countries have required arduous negotiations and the application of tariffs and quotas to ensure influence over the employment gains, but more recently we have seen the opening up of restriction-free trade in more and more partnerships across the globe – a phenomenon that has contributed towards globalization. Here we discuss trade in the context of the global economy and highlight the importance of our terms of trade with the rest of the world, reflected by our exchange rate.

The global economy

The global economy interconnects the markets for good and services beyond our physical borders, it encompasses international trade between many economies and makes an important contribution towards our own GDP. Global markets provide income to domestic exporters and employment for the workforce in the economy; the most obvious benefit from an increase in international trade being a reduction in domestic unemployment. This seems intuitive, if international trade can provide better macro outcomes then there is an implication that policymakers should always be looking to help firms to export. To understand how we can increase trade, we need to also understand what drives our trade balance with our trading partners.

Our foreign partners will be willing to trade with us, so long as we continue to provide value over and above existing domestic markets; normally this value can be thought of in terms of price. If our goods are less expensive, then there will be foreign demand for those goods. To provide goods competitively we need to operate with higher technology or lower costs– higher technology in terms of more modern machinery and lower costs in terms of wages. Indeed, a common criticism of globalization is the possibility of downward pressure on wages, as countries open borders with lower wage economies.

So, we cannot always think of trade as a win-win for both parties involved, though we now understand that competitiveness in price drives the amount of trade, which in turn contributes to our GDP. An obvious question arises as to what is determining the price at which we trade? As foreign transactions require a conversion of one currency into another, we can think of the exchange rate as an important part of the price at which that trade takes place. Movements in the exchange rate change the prices of imports priced in a foreign currency and exports priced in a domestic currency. Effectively the exchange rate is the 'price' of the domestic currency for an economy and an important part of our terms of trade.

The importance of the exchange rate

The quantities of goods and services exported and imported in an economy are determined by the price of those goods and services, and we have already mentioned that the exchange rate makes up an important part of that price. To show this we can begin with the trade balance *NX* which is exactly equal to the value of goods exported *X* minus the value of goods imported *M*.

$$NX = X - M$$

Further, note that the trade balance is directly driven by something we call the 'real' exchange rate, written mathematically as:

$$NX = NX(\varepsilon)$$

The trade balance *NX* is now written both in absolute terms and as a function of the real exchange rate $NX(\varepsilon)$. An increase in the real exchange rate will make exports more expensive and imports cheaper, giving us a definitive reduction in the trade balance *NX*. Conversely, a reduction in the real exchange rate will make exports cheaper and imports more expensive, driving a definitive increase in our trade balance. Our reasoning implies that there is a negative relationship between the real exchange rate and our trade balance, especially if we assume that export and import markets behave normally in reaction to a change in prices.

We can also write an expression for the real exchange rate in terms of the nominal rate and the relative price levels across trading borders.

$$\varepsilon = e \times \frac{P^h}{P^f}$$

The real exchange rate is made up of two parts: the nominal exchange rate **e** and the relative price level between the home country *h* and the importing country *f*. If the nominal exchange rate increases, this will raise the real exchange rate, and if prices increase in the home country this will also raise the real exchange rate. A qualification here – the nominal exchange rate is that which quotes the home (exporting) country's currency in terms of the importing country's currency. For example, for the case of the UK, we would use dollars/pound rather than pounds/dollar.

EXAMPLE 3.6

Real world example: The price of an imported good

When we buy an imported good we see one price – it is the price that we pay in domestic currency. Actually, there are two components to that price: the producer's price and the price of the exporter's domestic currency.

Imagine a £4.00 bunch of asparagus. We can break that down into the two prices of the producer's price and the price of the US dollar and calculate the final shelf price in the UK.

Producer's price

The producer prices goods in the exporting country's domestic currency. For our example, let's say that the US farmer has a domestic price of $5.00, available for international sale.

Currency price

An important factor of the UK sale price of £4.00 is the price of the US currency in the UK.

For our example of asparagus, let's imagine an exchange rate where £1.00 buys $1.25, meaning that USD/GBP = 0.80.

UK shelf price

UK shelf price of asparagus = US domestic price × USD/GBP

= $5.00 × 0.80 = £4.00

The market for foreign exchange

Another approach that helps us to explain the exchange rate uses the model of the market for foreign exchange (the forex market). The model uses a supply schedule and a demand schedule in two dimensions to show how the behaviour of suppliers of currency interact with buyers of currency to determine the equilibrium exchange rate. The market does not have any physical location but takes place virtually as part of a global network of many buyers and many sellers across international borders.

To keep our analysis simple, our explanation of the forex market will focus on the specific case of UK pounds sterling, so that our market for foreign exchange is the market for UK pounds. The demand schedule for UK pounds $£_d$ is made up of all the buyers in the marketplace and the supply schedule for UK pounds $£_s$ is made up of all the sellers in the marketplace. Now we can draw the foreign exchange market for the UK pounds in Figure 3.2.

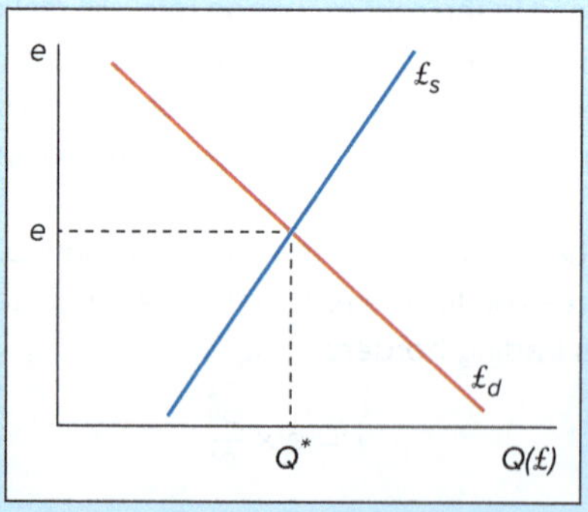

Figure 3.2 The foreign exchange market for UK pounds

Notice that the demand for UK pounds is downward sloping in the exchange rate, reflecting the fact that as the price of sterling (exchange rate) falls there is higher demand for the currency. The supply schedule for pounds is upward sloping, reflecting the fact that as the price of sterling rises more suppliers are willing to sell the currency, so supply increases. When there is a match in terms of supply and demand we have a price at which the market clears, this is the equilibrium exchange rate for the UK.

EXAMPLE 3.7

Real world example: French cheese is imported into the UK

A producer based in France agrees a sale of cheese to a British importer working on behalf of a domestic supermarket chain in the UK. Intuitively we can expect that the French producer will want to be paid in euros, and so to facilitate this the British importer will need to convert UK pounds into euros with which to pay the foreign supplier.

To complete the transaction, the importer will need to visit a bank to sell (supply) UK pounds and buy (demand) euros.

For the case of the UK forex market we see this reflected by an increase in supply of UK pounds. In our model, we will see the supply schedule $£_s$ shift right, applying downward pressure on the exchange rate for the UK.

We can relate this to the equilibrium in the market for international trade. All trade must be financed, thus:

$$Nx = NCO$$

(Trade in goods must be financed by net capital outflows [NCO].)

The export of cheese increases *NX* for France; consequently the Bank of France will accumulate pounds from selling euros to the importers. This accumulation of pounds is the result of the capital outflow from France to the UK.

The UK is holding the cheese, and France is holding UK debt, meaning that it has invested in the UK.

When a country exports, it has capital outflow – it is lending.

When a country imports, it has capital inflow – it is borrowing.

The model we have introduced here is a typical two agent macroeconomic model, which is similar in set-up to other markets in the macroeconomy such as the financial market and the labour market. Even though we discuss macroeconomic models in detail in Chapter 4, bear in mind that a change in the price variable (which always sits on the vertical axis) will give us a movement along the schedules but a change in anything else that affects the market will result in a shift of one of the schedules, as we have discussed in Chapter 1.

EXERCISE 3.4

Can you explain the effect on the market for the UK pound resulting from the export of car engine parts to Germany?

Now that we have introduced the market for foreign exchange we can also discuss the reaction of the market to a situation where the market exchange rate is away from its equilibrium value. The easiest way to see this is by making use of our diagram for the forex market (Figure 3.3).

We begin with the market away from equilibrium at e^1 and Q^1, the actual exchange rate is below the rate that would normally clear the market. Notice that, at this lower rate, the quantity demanded in the market is higher than that willing to be supplied; there is excess demand for

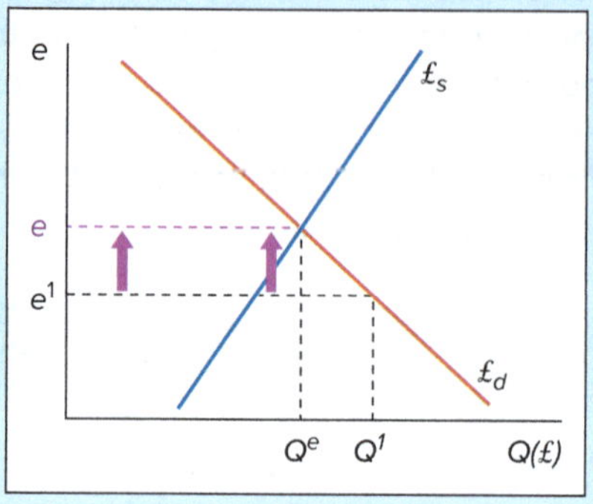

Figure 3.3 The foreign exchange market for UK pounds away from equilibrium

the currency. The shortage in the market will lead to the bidding up of the exchange rate by traders, eager to buy for their clients; the exchange rate will increase until it reaches its equilibrium rate where the number of UK pounds offered for sale is equal to the number of UK pounds demanded by buyers.

This exercise highlights our understanding of the natural forces in all markets where the price variable facilitates the return towards equilibrium after a change in supply or demand. Armed with this knowledge we might consider a policy such as a fixed exchange rate regime, where a country holds its currency rate fixed at a predetermined level, away from its equilibrium value.

Currency wars

Governments are sometimes accused of interfering in their own foreign exchange markets with the aim of keeping downward pressure on the exchange rate. One example of such a manipulation is selling a domestic currency in the open market at a lower rate than the current market clearing price (in our model this is equivalent to increasing supply and shifting the supply schedule right in the forex market). The price will drop and the equilibrium exchange rate will be lowered. With the rate at a lower level, exports will become cheaper and an advantage given to domestic suppliers over their foreign competitors.

However, this intervention comes at a cost; trading partners will not be pleased to see their own domestic suppliers become unemployed, caused by the exchange rate intervention of a foreign trading partner. There is also a cost to a central bank from selling a domestic currency at a price below the market equilibrium. Essentially there is an overpayment for foreign exchange, and when this is later resold in the open market it will be at a significant loss. But why is this a war? Intervention of this kind is costly for international trading partners who will lose out from the unfair terms of trade; employment will be transferred from abroad to a domestic economy. There might be a retaliation in the currency markets from the affected trading partner; If the currency fixer is holding reserves of expensive foreign exchange, that foreign exchange is also at risk of further devaluation by the future actions of a foreign trading partner, who might be suffering from unfair terms of trade.

We can think of a currency war as a lose–lose situation because both sides use up valuable foreign reserves to devalue their currencies. Nevertheless, the temptation to lower a currency is often very high because of the direct benefits it can bring to exporters and so it remains a modern global problem without an obvious solution in the future.

3.5 Chapter summary: Putting it all together

What have we learnt from this chapter? Unemployment is one of the most important economic indicators – changes in the variable directly reflect the experience and economic well-being of society. Inflation is a macroeconomic variable that reflects changes in the average price level in the economy and can be a concern to policymakers if it becomes too high; inflation can explode in value in a short space of time. Two of the most important measures of inflation are calculated from changes in the GDP deflator index and the consumer price index (CPI). GDP deflator inflation is of better use in circumstances that require the measurement of purely domestic inflation and CPI inflation of better use in circumstances that require knowledge of the price pressures facing the consumer.

In modern times economies increasingly find themselves operating on an international stage, where the exchange rate determines an important component of national income. At this early stage, we have discussed how the exchange rate affects our trade balance and further how the exchange rate itself is determined in the market for foreign exchange. With price stability now commonplace in developed economies and interest rates at historically low levels, it is the exchange rate that dominates as the subject of interest for our policymakers. Forward from here we will visit the subject of macroeconomic modelling, provide detail surrounding the financial markets, the goods market and the labour market before focusing on the most commonly used macroeconomic models.

Assessment Question

You have been appointed as the governor of a newly established central bank of a developing country that has recently experienced the economic problem of 'hyperinflation'. This explosive form of rising prices has caused economic damage to the country. The government is keen to ensure that in the future there will be an independent body who will oversee monetary policy to ensure price stability. One of your first tasks as governor will be to choose which measure of inflation the newly formed bank should follow. For this purpose, you should evaluate the choice between the CPI and GDP deflator measures of inflation. Write an essay on your choice of the two inflation measures you would recommend to the newly formed bank.

Cases

The impact of inflation on international trade in the UK

Background

Inflation, defined as the rate at which the general level of prices for goods and services rises, erodes the purchasing power of money. In the context of the UK economy, inflation can have significant effects on international trade – both exports and imports. In recent years, the UK has experienced fluctuations in inflation rates, which have impacted its trading relationships with other countries. This case study explores the effects of inflation on international trade, using data and trends from 2020 to 2024.

Inflation in the UK: A brief overview

The UK's inflation rate has seen notable volatility in the past few years. In 2020, due to the global COVID-19 pandemic, the UK's inflation rate dropped sharply to 0.8 per cent. However, as the economy began to recover in 2021, inflation surged. By 2022, inflation reached a 40-year high of 11.1 per cent before stabilizing to around 7 per cent in 2023. This increase in inflation was driven by various factors, including rising energy prices, supply chain disruptions and higher wage demands.

The impact of inflation on UK exports

1. Price competitiveness:
   - As UK inflation rises, the prices of domestically produced goods and services also increase. This makes UK exports more expensive relative to those of other countries. For example, if the UK's inflation rate is higher than its trading partners (such as the EU or the US), UK goods become less attractive to foreign buyers.
   - In 2022, the UK faced difficulties in exporting certain manufactured goods to European countries due to the higher costs of production. As a result, British exporters struggled to maintain competitiveness in global markets.

2. Exchange rate effects:
    - High inflation often leads to depreciation of a country's currency. If inflation in the UK outpaces that of its trading partners, the British pound (GBP) might weaken. A weaker pound can make UK exports cheaper in foreign markets, potentially boosting demand for UK goods.
    - However, the depreciation of the pound also increases the cost of imported raw materials and intermediate goods, leading to higher production costs for exporters. This creates a trade-off where the benefits of cheaper exports may be offset by higher input costs.

The impact of inflation on UK imports

1. Cost of imports:
    - Inflation in the UK means that import prices tend to rise, especially when the domestic currency weakens. For example, in 2022, the weakening of the pound due to rising inflation increased the cost of imported goods, such as energy and food.
    - The increased cost of imports puts pressure on businesses and consumers, leading to higher overall prices in the domestic economy. In the case of essential goods, such as fuel or electronics, this can lead to a rise in living costs, further impacting domestic inflation.
2. Import demand:
    - If the UK's inflation rate rises faster than its income growth, it can lead to a reduction in demand for imported goods. Consumers may cut back on discretionary spending as they face higher domestic prices. For instance, in 2022, rising inflation led to a decline in demand for high-end imported goods, as the UK household disposable income was squeezed.

Key factors influencing inflation and trade

- Exchange rate movements: The value of the pound is influenced by inflation rates. A higher inflation rate often leads to a weaker pound, which affects both imports and exports.
- Global supply chain disruptions: Events like the COVID-19 pandemic and geopolitical tensions (e.g., the Russia–Ukraine war) can exacerbate inflation and disrupt trade flows.
- Monetary policy: The Bank of England's response to inflation, such as increasing interest rates to control inflation, can affect both domestic demand and the value of the currency, which in turn impacts international trade.

Conclusion

In summary, inflation in the UK has both positive and negative effects on international trade. On the one hand, inflation can make UK exports more expensive and less competitive in global markets, whereas a weaker pound can make exports cheaper, which could benefit UK businesses. However, rising inflation also increases the cost of imports, impacting businesses and consumers. The net effect depends on the balance of these factors, as well as broader global economic conditions.

Questions

1. What is the relationship between inflation and the price competitiveness of UK exports?
2. How does inflation affect the exchange rate and UK exports?
3. What are the consequences of inflation on the cost of imports to the UK?
4. How does inflation impact the demand for imports in the UK?
5. What are the key factors influencing the relationship between inflation and international trade in the UK?

Problems

EASY

1. What is the most commonly used measure of inflation that accounts for the cost of living?
2. Inflationary pressures can be attributed to:
   a) A surge in energy prices.
   b) A decline in government spending.
   c) A reduction in the central bank's base rate.
   d) A rise in global agricultural production.
   e) A decrease in foreign investment.

MEDIUM

3. Define the natural rate of unemployment.
4. Which of the following is most likely to result in inflation in the UK?
   a) A rise in the Bank of England base interest rate.
   b) An increase in the supply of money in the economy.
   c) A decrease in consumer confidence.
   d) A significant rise in unemployment.
   e) A sharp decrease in consumer spending.
5. If the unemployment rate decreases significantly, which of the following could be a possible consequence?
   a) A decrease in inflation.
   b) An increase in inflation due to wage pressures.
   c) A decrease in consumer spending.
   d) A reduction in government debt.
   e) A fall in demand for imported goods.
6. The UK government reports that the country's unemployment rate is currently 5 per cent. The UK workforce consists of 35 million people, with 90 per cent of the workforce employed. How many individuals are unemployed? Additionally, if the government aims to reduce unemployment by 1 million, what would the new unemployment rate be?
7. Discuss the potential impact of rising inflation on the UK economy. Consider how inflation affects different sectors, including households, businesses and government policy.

HARD

8. What is the main distinction between 'disequilibrium' unemployment and 'structural' unemployment?
9. Analyse the relationship between international trade, unemployment and inflation in the UK, focusing on how trade imbalances and exchange rates can influence domestic inflationary pressures and unemployment levels.

CHAPTER 4

Macroeconomic Modelling

Chapter contents

At a Glance Macroeconomic modelling

The issue

A macroeconomist needs to present new theories and ideas to peers, policymakers and to those who want to study the science. In this chapter we can begin to connect the issues discussed in Chapter 2 and Chapter 3. How do we present current understanding on the workings of the macro economy?

The understanding

This chapter presents the tool of the macroeconomist in the form of the macroeconomic model. We first discuss the concept of modelling more generally – how can we use models to communicate in another subject? We apply our knowledge by discussing two key models in macroeconomics before discussing the differing opinions and debates across the science.

The usefulness

The ability to frame a problem by using or creating a model is a very useful one. A model can help us to frame a communication of ideas to team members and decision makers of an organization. In this chapter we also discuss 'how' we can model more generally – a skill we can apply across disciplines.

4.1 Introduction

In our practice of the science of macroeconomics we make use of miniature and simplified representations of the economy called macroeconomic 'models'. A model can take the form of a diagram, a set of equations or a collection of carefully selected categories. We can convey our model with a drawing, express it mathematically or in words. We can provide a simple example of this using the model of aggregate demand; in words, we can say that aggregate demand falls when the price level in the economy increases. We can even express our model mathematically so that output *Y* depends negatively on the price level *P* or we can use a two-dimensional diagram to display our model as a locus of points in *Y* and *P* space (Table 4.1).

Table 4.1 The model of aggregate demand

Model	Expression
In words	'Aggregate output demanded is negatively correlated to the average price level in the economy'. When prices rise we tend to witness a fall in demand for goods and services.
In maths	$Y = \left(\frac{M}{P}\right)^d$
In diagrams	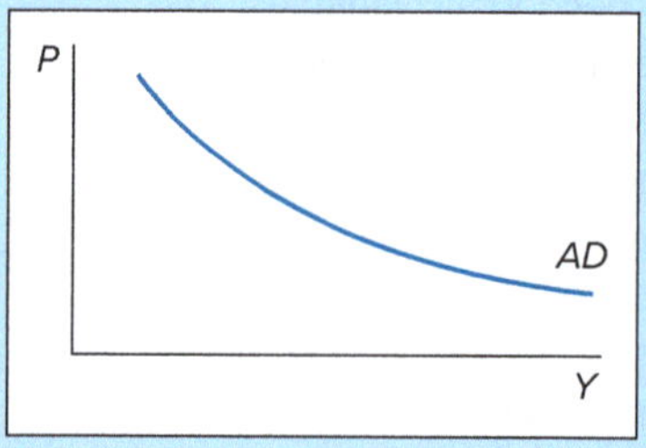

The model makes intuitive sense and is easy to explain since we can see for ourselves that in our day-to-day lives we are less likely to buy something at a higher price. Whichever way we choose to express our aggregate demand relationship we see the consistent prediction – that higher prices are associated with lower output. This prediction can also help us to think of how our model might provide some advice to a policymaker such as the government or the central bank.

In our example our advice to the central bank might be that 'inflation can be detrimental to economic growth', so the model has 'normative implications' or policy implications. The model is useful, not just because it can explain the economic reality but also because it provides us with policy advice. Another very good reason for making use of models in macroeconomics is that they provide us with a structure with which to focus our arguments. The formal framework helps the debate to progress in an ordered fashion, highlighting the assumptions we have made along the way to arrive at our conclusions.

Finally, the representation of the model provides us with a benchmark, or baseline, with which to compare our conclusions from both current economic thought and further advances in our area of interest. Naturally, an economy-wide attempt to capture the many complex relationships in all of our markets would require a model that is very large scale and burdensome. After all, there are many millions of economic agents reacting in many markets. To keep our message simple and easy to transmit we need to make use of something we call 'simplifying assumptions'. Some of the most useful models are the simplest, perhaps describing the economy as the interaction between just two economic agents in a single marketplace. When we analyse or compare our models we can review or criticize the assumptions made during its construction. This is often a matter for economic debate, but ultimately a model is tested on its ability to explain the past and to provide predictions to future changes in the economic environment.

What follows in this chapter is an introduction to some of the more commonly used macroeconomic models. We begin with a categorization of our economy into groups of agents and markets to capture the relations between them in a model called 'the circular flow', one of the most influential models in the subject area of macroeconomics. We then introduce two more iconic baseline models that show how income is determined in the economy, and also how firms and consumers react in a simple two-dimensional analysis using the price/income space (known as *P Y* space).

Finally, we take a brief look at the historic debate on macroeconomic modelling that represents two different views on how we should build our models – one school of thought that believes governments should intervene during episodes of economic decline and one that believes we should not.

Learning Outcomes

By the end of this chapter you should be able to:

- Understand why economists use models to explain their ideas and theories.
- Recognize how endogeneity and causality are used to interpret macroeconomic models.
- Use the circular flow model to explain a simple closed economy and apply this framework to model design more generally.
- Illustrate how income is determined in the economy using the Keynesian cross.
- Apply the aggregate demand and aggregate supply model to explain general equilibrium.
- Contrast and appraise the Keynesian and classical views in economic thought.

4.2 Modelling the macroeconomic variables

Now that we understand what a model is and what it is used for we can discuss macroeconomic modelling in a little more detail. To represent the economy a macroeconomic model will aim to show how the main macro variables are related to one another and predict how they will react to changes in other variables. As an example, let us imagine a two-sector model where output Y is simply equal to consumption C. By two sector we mean that there are just two sets of actors in our economy, firms and consumers.

Our model is very simple and can be written mathematically as:

$$Y = C$$

In words, if consumption increases we can see that output increases also, so output 'depends' on consumption. This result is quite intuitive; an increase in the consumption of goods and services will lead to an increase in production or output. In this case, we can say that output is 'determined' by consumption, or that output is 'endogenous' on consumption. In an economic model, the right-hand side variable is assumed to be driving the left-hand side variable.

As an example, for our equation above, we can say that 'consumption C is driving National Income Y'; or 'Y is dependent on C', 'Y is endogenous upon C', 'Y is determined by C'.

As a rule, we can call the right/left-hand side variables in the equation as follows:

- **Left-hand side – determined, endogenous, dependent**
- **Right-hand side – predetermined, exogenous, independent**.

In our two sector example above, it is output Y that we consider to be the determined or **endogenous variable** and consumption C that is considered the predetermined or **exogenous variable**. But would it be reasonable to object to this? Surely an increase in output or income causes an increase

Endogenous Variable: A macroeconomic variable that 'depends' on another variable in some way. Nearly all variables are dependent to some degree.
Exogenous Variable: A macroeconomic variable that is considered totally independent from other variables; we often call these variables 'fixed' or predetermined.

in consumption also. Which statement is correct? By asking these questions we want to know whether or not the variables are seated on the correct sides of the equation. Is consumption endogenous on income or is income endogenous on consumption? This issue, of accurately describing 'what causes what' is known as the issue of **causality**. The problem of causality is not a small one and in reality, the interdependencies between nearly all the macro variables are wide and complex. This problem is best shown by Example 4.1.

Causality: The issue of what is causing what, or the order in which macroeconomic variables determine or 'lead' each other.

EXAMPLE 4.1

Worked example: A simplified Keynesian model

Imagine a three-sector economy described by this simple model with two equations, the income identity and the consumption function:

$$Y = C + I$$
$$C = a + bY$$

The first equation describes income (or output) as determined by the sum of total consumption and total investment in the economy. The second equation tells us that consumption is partly determined by a fraction *b* of our income. As we have discussed, the left-hand side variables are classified as endogenous and the right-hand side variables as exogenous. The first equation is implying that a change in consumption *C* will 'cause' a change in output *Y*, but the second equation is implying the opposite. Both seem intuitively correct and make sense, but which is correct?

The unfortunate truth is that both equations are difficult to deny, and we have a case of 'dual' causality; output often rises when consumption rises and consumption often rises when income (output) rises. We can think of this as a 'feedback loop' where a change in one variable sets off an endless reaction between consumption and output. The problem of causality is one that we are forced to live with and our right-hand side variables have to be 'assumed' to be exogenous, rather than actually exogenous. In reality, nearly all variables are endogenous and if we were to account accurately for this we would not have any right-hand side variables at all for our models.

Can you think of any truly exogenous variables?

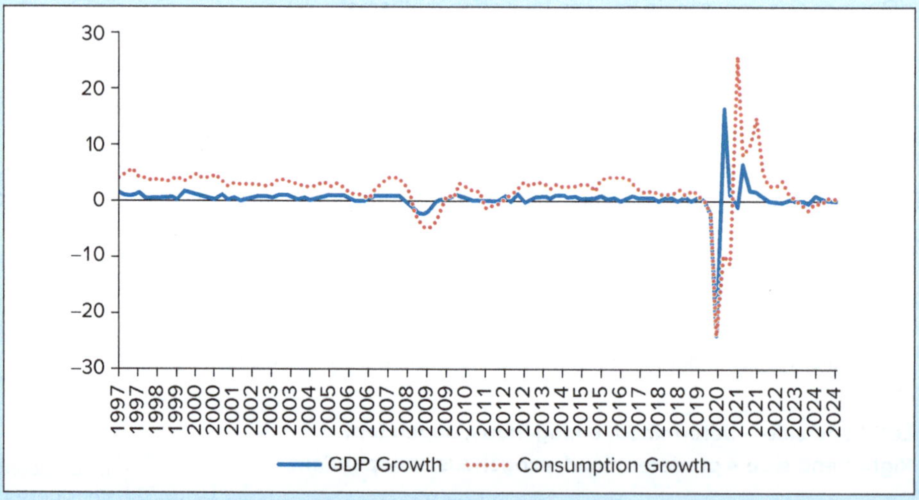

Figure 4.1 UK consumption and GDP growth 1997–2024

Source: Office for National Statistics 2025

Figure 4.1 shows us the time series for the quarterly growth in UK consumption and GDP plotted together for the United Kingdom between 1997 and 2024. As we can see, there is a close relationship between changes in consumption and national income. We can see that output and consumption are related but which variable is responsible for the movement in the other? In some periods consumption seems to lead output but in others, it is output that moves first; a visual observation that suggests that the causal relationship can also change over time.

The three agents and the three markets

To keep our economic models simple we often group individual consumers, firms and public bodies into 'representative agents'. So instead of 60 million individual consumers, we imagine one representative consumer who is considered the average consumer. Instead of many firms we imagine one representative or average firm. By making the representative agent assumption we are assuming that all consumers and firms are identical or will behave in exactly the same way.

So our first two agents are the representative consumer and the representative firm. Our third agent is the policymaker, who we associate with governance of the economy, whose role it is to react to certain economic conditions. In macroeconomic models there are normally two types of policymakers: the government carrying out fiscal policy and the central bank enacting monetary policy.

So our most simplified economy could be modelled using just three actors interacting in three markets as the title of this section suggests: consumers, firms and policymakers interacting in the labour market, the market for goods and services, and the financial market. Firms and consumers interact in both the labour market and the market for goods and services and our policymakers in the financial market and market for goods and services. We can begin to visualize how this might be modelled in the circular flow model, discussed in the following sections.

EXERCISE 4.1

1. Can you explain the difference between an exogenous variable and an endogenous one?
2. Can you name the three sets of economic actors in a closed economy? How do they interact with one another in the real world?

The use of representative agents

The use of representative agents inevitably attracts criticism towards the field of macroeconomic modelling. Is it reasonable to assume that we can group all consumers together into one representative, or average, consumer? An economist called Thomas Picketty (2015) has criticized their use, because they cannot be used to explain problems where there are groupings of consumers of firms that behave in different ways. While this is indeed true, most macroeconomic models are really interested in the higher level workings of the economy and tend to assume that these differences will 'wash' together when aggregated. So their use is valid where the questions being asked are appropriate or at an aggregated level of concern. Macroeconomic questions that cannot be solved using aggregated variables can be made richer, by splitting the agents into different categories – something we call 'controlling for heterogeneity'. So, Picketty's criticism is definitely valid, but certainly not damning to the science of macroeconomics; however, we must keep in mind that aggregate models should be used to ask macroeconomic questions.

The circular flow model

One of the most influential models in macroeconomics is the circular flow model of the macroeconomic economy. The model captures the behaviour of the agents and the markets where they interact in a simple flow chart type diagram. The success of this model is undoubtedly the simple way the economy is described as the 'flow' of income in exchange for tangibles between the two representative agents: households and firms.

Households and firms interact through flows between each other, so that:

FLOW OF INCOME: HOUSEHOLDS AND FIRMS

Households: *Supply labour to the firm and in return receive income in the form of money or wages.*

Firms: *Supply goods and services to the household and in return receive income in the form of household expenditure.*

The approach of modelling via financial and real flows can be taken in contrast to the model given previously in Example 4.1 that uses variables (*C*, *I* and *Y*) measured by their 'stock' value. One could argue that the stock approach is more problematic as there is a reliance on the measurement of variables at any particular time, making the business of taking the model to the data more difficult.

In macroeconomics, we often refer to the characteristics of the published data as 'stylized facts' and a good model should be able to replicate those facts. These facts can contain contamination from the effects of other variables at different points in time, rather like the endogeneity issues discussed before. To explain the differences between stock and flow models another way – it is sometimes easier to find a relationship between the changes, or flows, in variables than it is to find a relationship between their values at any one point in time.

The circular flow model can also be extended to encompass policymaking and to add a touch of reality. We can do this by moving away from the assumption of just two sectors, and adding more agents such as the financial and international markets.

EXERCISE 4.2

Fill in the blanks in the following:

A major lesson of the circular flow model is that one person's ________ is somebody else's ________?

As the circular flow is a diagrammatic model it is best explained with the use of a diagram (see Figure 4.2).

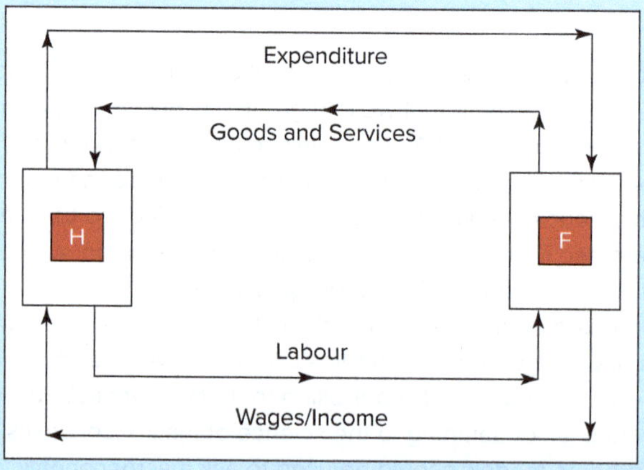

Figure 4.2 A two-sector version of the circular flow model

In its simplest form this two-sector circular flow model describes the economy as the interaction between households and firms. On the lower half of the diagram we see that households *H* are supplying labour to firms *F* and in return firms are paying wages, or income, to the households for their labour.

The upper half of the diagram explains how firms interact with households in the market for goods and services – firms supply goods and services to households and households pay for this in the form of expenditure. The lower half of the diagram explains how firms and households interact in the labour market, labour effort for wage income. Another feature of this model is the ability to differentiate between the real side and the monetary side of the economy as separate, equal and opposite flows.

The real flow in the economy measures the flow of tangibles (goods and labour), and the money flow measures the flow of income (wages and expenditure) around the economy. The flows are equal and opposite as for every real transaction there is an equal monetary transaction which flows in the opposite direction. For instance, the purchase of a car entails a real flow of engineered metal to the consumer and a purchase fee of equal value to the seller, the monetary flow.

Now we can extend the model to include a simple financial system by introducing a representative bank B. Adding a financial sector adds a further layer of reality to our model – banks collect savings (income not spent on expenditure) from the consumer and these funds are then used to lend to firms for investment (see Figure 4.3).

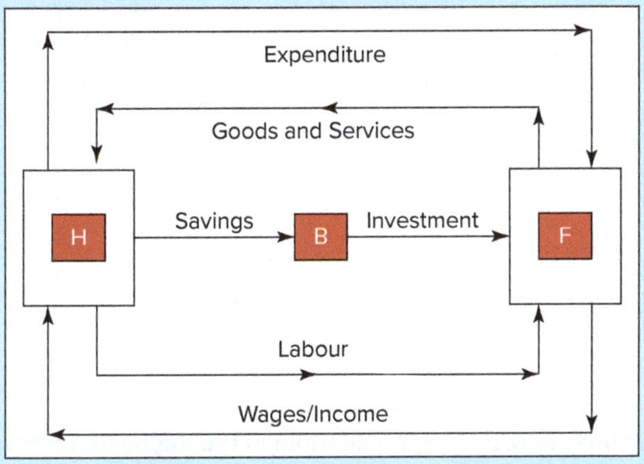

Figure 4.3 A three-sector version of the circular flow model

The new agent, in this case the representative bank, is shown as a new box that bypasses the flow of income; it can accept withdrawals from the flow and create injections back into the flow. Savings are a withdrawal from the flow where the consumer decides not to spend all of its income on goods and services. If the bank then invests this money by lending to firms this will cause an injection back into the flow. So long as the bank invests all of the funds deposited by savers then there will be no change in the flow of income.

We could extend this model further to include other agents, but we leave this as an exercise at this stage. When withdrawals are equal to injections the flow will not change and the economy is in equilibrium. Now let us imagine that we are not in equilibrium and the flow is changing – say, there is an increase in savings (withdrawals) and no change in investment (injections) – then money is being withdrawn overall and the flow will slow down (output will fall). So the flow changes when there is an unequal change in withdrawals or injection but is otherwise constant.

4.3 Two baseline models

In this section, we introduce another two macroeconomic models that describe the economy in entirely different ways to the circular flow: the model of income determination shows how the level of output is driven by **planned expenditure** or demand; and the AD/AS model describes the economy as the interaction between two representative agents in the economy – the supply side and the demand side.

Planned Expenditure: Expenditure that is anticipated or planned and assumed to be realized in the near future, also the forcing variable to drive changes in economic activity. We can think of planned expenditure as aggregate demand (AD).

A simple model of income determination

Aggregate Demand: Total output demanded, dependent on the prices faced by the representative consumer.
Equilibrium: An economic state where the economy is assumed to be 'settled' and no further change will take place without some movement in economic policy or shock. If we are not in equilibrium, then there is always a driving force back towards it, through the powers of excess supply and excess demand.

The model of income determination is drawn from the notion that output or income can be driven by the level of demand in the economy. This model is often referred to as the 'Keynesian cross' as it originates from the Keynesian school of economic thought. The cross is the intersection of two schedules that represent planned expenditure and actual expenditure. Here we use the two terms **aggregate demand** and planned expenditure interchangeably as they are much the same thing.

If aggregate demand increases, then intuitively the level of output will follow as firms increase production to meet that increase in demand. To begin with, we need two axes on a graph representing actual output (production) and aggregate demand (planned expenditure). In Figure 4.4 we draw a 45° line showing the locus of combinations where actual output is equal to aggregate demand. Along this line the economy is in **equilibrium**; in other words, the level of goods demanded is equal to the level of goods produced.

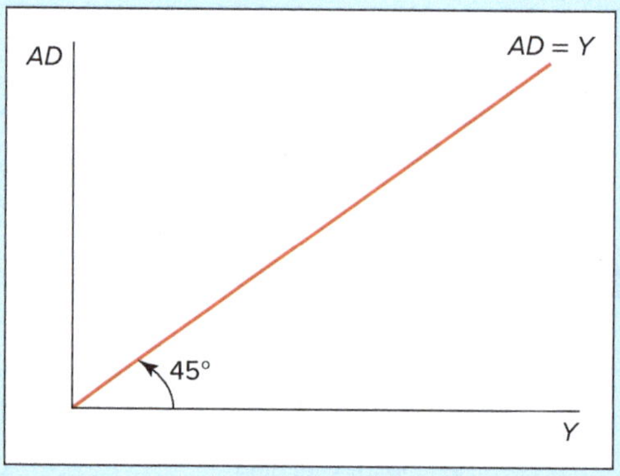

Figure 4.4 The 45° line representing equilibrium in the Keynesian cross

Our vertical axis measures aggregate demand *AD* (planned expenditure) and our horizontal axis is actual output (production). If we imagine that output is driven by aggregate demand then we can simply draw a schedule that represents aggregate demand, or planned expenditure, overlaid onto the same graph. In a two-sector economy, such as the one described in the simple form of the circular flow model, we can use our planned consumption function, in its mathematical form:

$$AD = C$$

Aggregate demand is equal to consumption, where consumption is given by the following equation:

$$C = a + bY$$

Consumption has an autonomous component a and is increasing in output by proportion b.

We combine the two equations (replace C in our first equation with the consumption function), so that:

$$AD = a + bY$$

This planned expenditure function was first introduced in Example 4.1. We can see that the expenditure function, or schedule, has an intercept a and a positive slope b that we can draw over the 45° line, shown in Figure 4.5, to see how output is determined on the model.

Where the 45° line and the demand schedule cross, the model predicts a determined level of equilibrium income in the economy. Now let us imagine that the economy has moved away from this determined level of Y^*. What are the driving forces that bring us back to equilibrium? When income Y is below the intersection of our two schedules, planned expenditure is greater than actual income and aggregate demand is greater than actual production.

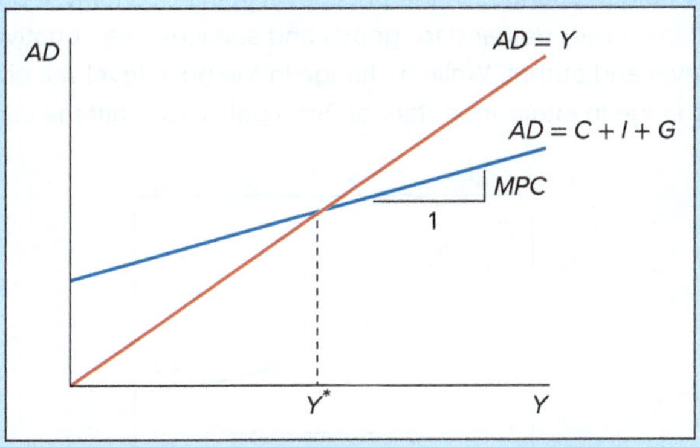

Figure 4.5 Model of income determination with investment and government

Firms see an unplanned reduction in stocks and, as a result, react by increasing production so that output increases. When income is above the intersection of the two schedules, actual output is greater than planned expenditure – firms see a build-up of stocks and react by reducing production so that output will fall. When output reaches the intersection itself we are in equilibrium; planned expenditure is equal to actual expenditure and there is nothing driving a change in output. The level of output that the model predicts is that for any given level of expenditure – in this case, consumption. If we want to incorporate the financial sector and government then we simply add this to the expenditure function so that $AD = C + I + G$, instead of $AD = C$.

The AS/AD model

The model of aggregate demand and **aggregate supply** also uses a two-dimensional equilibrium approach only this time the representative firm is added so that there are now two economic actors. The two representative agents react to changes in the price level and exogenous changes, or shocks, from outside the model. This model is only introduced here but a more detailed coverage and mathematical treatment can be found in Chapter 10.

Aggregate Supply: The schedule of aggregated supply decisions of the firm based on the level of prices in the economy.

The aggregate supply curve reflects the changes in the labour market and the aggregate demand curve reflects both the changes in the market for goods and services and the financial market. Because both schedules are represented as a two-dimensional analysis in prices and output the AS/AD model can also capture the dynamic change between the short run and the long run in the economy. The reason we can capture this change between the short-run and the long-run outcome is that the model is written in output/price space and the adjusting force between these two time periods is the price level.

ASSESSMENT ADVICE

It is important that you make clear your understanding of the importance of the price level in the economy as the adjusting mechanism between the short-run equilibrium in our models and the long-run equilibrium. The AS/AD model, and also the IS/LM model, described in Chapter 8, allow us to capture this change.

A change in economic policy will have a short-run real effect on output (policy will affect output) but it is generally agreed that the effect of policy is limited in duration. In the long run, policy is said to be neutral because prices adjust fully (policy will not affect output). We discuss this in more detail at the end of this chapter.

The aggregate demand schedule represents the collective reaction of all demand in the economy. We can simplify this relationship, in a two-sector economy, as the reaction of the representative household to changes in the price level in the economy. It predicts that a higher price level will result in a lower demand for goods and services or a negative relationship between the price level and output. While a change in the price level will give us a movement along this curve, a change in either monetary or fiscal policy will shift the curve (Figure 4.6).

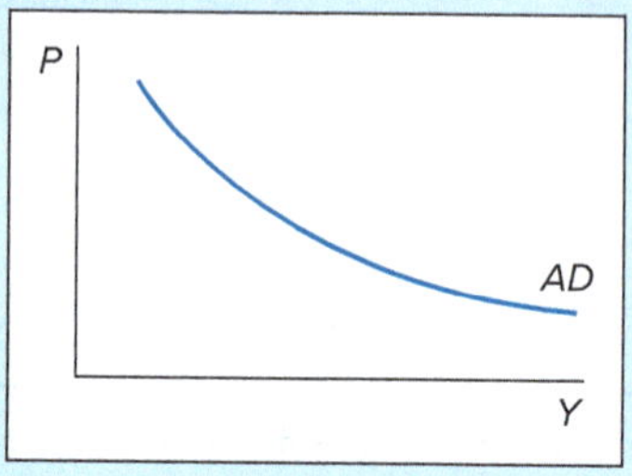

Figure 4.6 The aggregate demand schedule is downward sloping

The aggregate demand schedule is downward sloping, which reflects the fact that a higher price level is associated with lower levels of economic activity. To visualize this, imagine the central bank response to an increase in prices – an increase in interest rates will dampen consumer spending and in turn output.

Now that we have discussed the first agent in our model that represents the consumer, or demand side, we turn our attention to the supply side.

The aggregate supply curve represents the collective supply decision of all firms in the economy depending on the aggregate price level in the economy. This relationship predicts the reaction of the representative firm to changes in the price level. A lower price level will result in a lower willingness of the economy's firms to supply the market for goods and services. Figure 4.7 maps out the aggregate supply curve as the positive relationship between the price level and output, for the supply side of the economy.

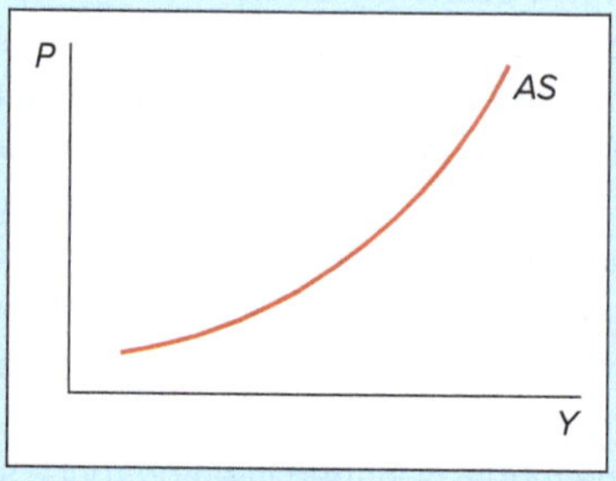

Figure 4.7 The aggregate supply schedule is upward sloping

Remember that a change in the price level will give us a movement along this curve but a change in the costs of operation or expected future prices will shift the curve. The aggregate supply curve is upward sloping, reflecting the fact that at higher prices firms are prepared to supply more goods and services, which is intuitive. Notice here that even though the aggregate supply curve is drawn upward sloping this may not always be the case.

Depending on the economic view of your taught material this curve could also be drawn in either of two extremes as vertically or horizontally. This difference is discussed toward the end of this chapter, but for now, we should continue towards a discussion of equilibrium in the model. As with all two equation models of this type, equilibrium is shown as the intersection of the two schedules: aggregate demand and aggregate supply (see Figure 4.8).

Where the aggregate demand curve and aggregate supply curve intersect the amount of goods and services that consumers demand is exactly the same as the amount of goods and services that firms are willing to supply. At this point, we have the general equilibrium in the economy with an equilibrium price level and equilibrium level of output Y^*.

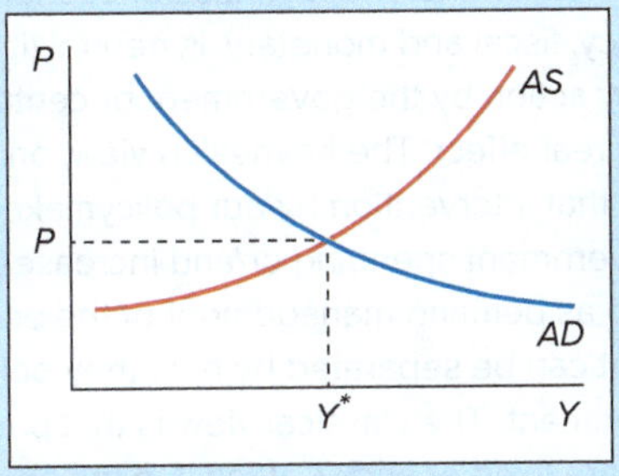

Figure 4.8 Equilibrium in the AS/AD model with upward-sloping AS curve

EXERCISE 4.3

Fill in the blanks in the following:

An increase in consumer confidence will lead to a/an ________ in the price level. This is shown by a/an ________ shift in the ________ curve in the AS/AD model.

Introducing economic policy

Up to now we have not mentioned economic policy; we have discussed the macroeconomic variables and the relations between them which we express with economic models. Models have policy implications which we can think of as messages to the policymaker. Aside from the messages that the models provide us with we can also use the models to 'show' policy. In other words, we can also model the act of policy within the model. We will then have a prediction from the model of how the economy will react to changes in these policies.

Two of the most basic forms of economic policy are fiscal policy and monetary policy. We will go into greater detail in Chapter 5 and Chapter 6 to describe these policies but for now, we can just describe them and show how we normally capture them in a macroeconomic model. Fiscal policy is commonly expressed as changes in the level of government expenditure and taxation, whereas monetary policy is commonly expressed as changes in the money supply.

To give a more explicit example of this, imagine an increase in government expenditure; this will set off a chain of reactions in the flow of income. The increase in expenditure increases revenues for firms, who in turn pass some of these revenues on to their workers in the form of wages. The workers complete the loop by spending some of their new income on goods and services, increasing revenue for firms and continuing the process of increasing output. Essentially the government has increased aggregate demand in the economy by spending more money.

Table 4.2 describes both fiscal policy and monetary and shows how they enter the model; as you will see it is nearly always via aggregate demand.

Table 4.2 Fiscal and monetary policy models

Policy Type	Detail	Modelled By
Fiscal policy	Changes to government expenditure and taxation: Variables G and T	Via aggregate demand $\Uparrow G \Rightarrow \Uparrow AD$ $\Uparrow T \Rightarrow \Downarrow AD$
Monetary policy	Changes to the money supply: Variable M	Via aggregate demand $\Uparrow M \Rightarrow \Uparrow AD$

4.4 The Keynesian and classical views

When we discussed aggregate supply in the previous section we made note that there is some disagreement about the schedules slope. There is a long and rich history on economic schools of thought and to cover this in any detail would be ambitious, but we can give a brief treatment by discussing the key differences in the two views.

Put simply, the two views differ on the effectiveness of economic policy. The classical dichotomy predicts that all policy, fiscal and monetary, is neutral (it has no effect on output, especially in the long run) – any action by the government or central bank to stabilize the economy is futile leading to no real effect. The Keynesian view, on the other hand, is opposite to this. Keynesian models predict that intervention by our policymakers *is* effective. Recessions can be avoided by increases in government spending or/and increases in the money supply by the central bank – often referred to as demand management of the economy.

The two schools of thought can be separated by how they believe prices will react to a change in the economic environment. The classical view is that prices are fully flexible while the Keynesians predict that prices are fixed or sticky, at least in the short run. In these two cases, we can use the slope of the aggregate supply curve to highlight the different predictions on the effectiveness of economic policy. So our discussion begins with the flexibility or 'stickiness' of the price level in the economy. The classical view, that prices are perfectly flexible, is intuitively correct if you agree that prices must eventually adjust to a change in the economic environment. After all, in real life we see prices change all the time.

We can show this in Figure 4.9 where output is fixed in the long run by the fixed factors of production, capital and labour. To capture the long-run position of output we draw the long-run aggregate supply (*LRAS*) curve vertically; long-run output is fixed. The model begins in equilibrium where the original aggregate demand curve *AD* and the long-run aggregate supply curve *LRAS* intersect at *Y** and *P*. An increase in aggregate demand shifts the *AD* curve outwards to *AD'*; output remains at *Y** but prices have increased to *P'*.

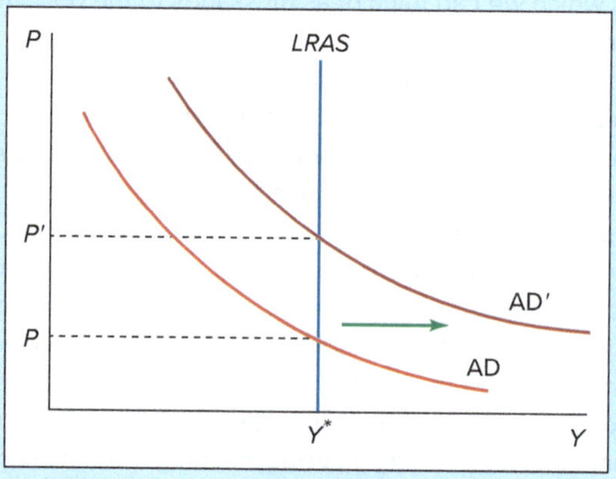

Figure 4.9 Long-run aggregate supply and expansionary economic policy

So despite an increase in aggregate demand, output remains unchanged. The only effect of policy is an increase in prices. The vertical supply curve provides us with the classical view that economic policy is ineffective.

By contrast, the Keynesian view is that the aggregate supply curve should reflect sticky, or fixed, prices. Accordingly, the Keynesian view lends itself to the AS/AD model drawn with the aggregate supply curve *AS* upward sloping (see Figure 4.10). Our initial equilibrium begins where the original AD curve intersects with the short-run aggregate supply curve (*SRAS*) at price level *P* and output at *Y*.

An increase in aggregate demand caused by expansionary economic policy shifts the *AD* curve outwards just as before. With the upwards sloping aggregate supply curve we see that the reaction of the economy is different; output increases to *Y'* and prices *P'*. Economic policy is now said to be effective as output has increased.

Although this is a rather simplistic way to describe the difference between the two schools of thought, it is also a clear one – the classical model and the Keynesian model give opposite policy implications. Our classical model predicts that policy intervention is futile, whereas the Keynesian model predicts that intervention is effective; the economy can be stabilized by demand management through fiscal or monetary policy. An obvious question arises at this point as to which model, or school of thought, is correct?

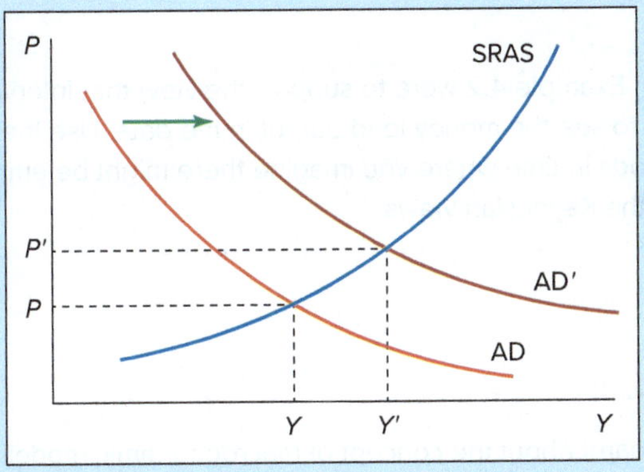

Figure 4.10 Short-run aggregate supply and expansionary economic policy

The current consensus among economists is that the true explanation of the supply side lies somewhere in between the short run and the long run. In the short run, we will see real effects (output will increase) but after a while prices will increase also and output will fall back again to the long - position. Policy is then effective only in the short run.

EXAMPLE 4.2

Real world example: Policy effectiveness – the relationship between money and output

The argument that has dominated economics for a long time is that of whether or not economic policy has any real effect on the economy – the Classical view is that policy intervention is futile, while the Keynesian view is that policy is not only effective but can also be welfare enhancing. The following graph shows how growth in output (real GDP) and the money supply (M1) move together over time in the UK between 1997 and 2024. So here we can ask the question from the data; does money lead output?

From a visual inspection, there appears to be some relation (co-movement), though this is far from clear. There are periods where an increase in the growth of money coincides with an increase in economic growth, but also periods where growth and money are negatively related (early 2000s). One thing is certain, the relationship changes over time – sometimes output leads money and at other times the converse is true. The data gives us a mixed picture, at least for the UK.

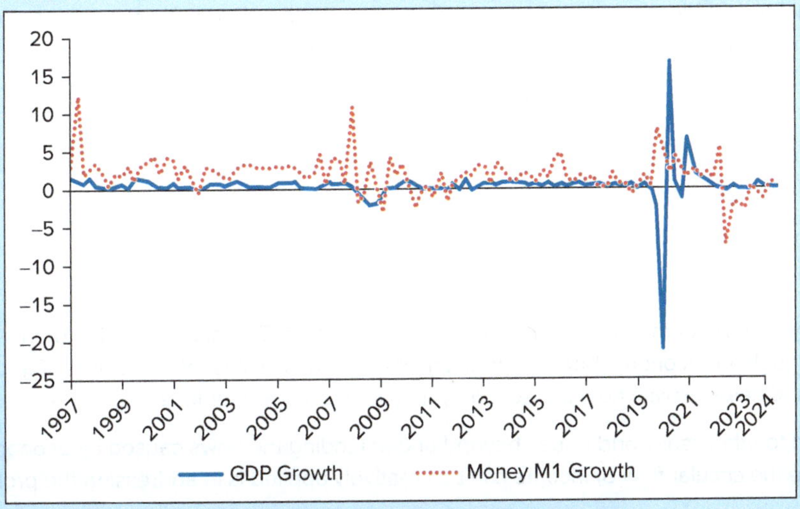

Source: Office for National Statistics 2025. https://www.ons.gov.uk/

EXERCISE 4.4

If the data presented in Example 4.2 were to support the view that intervention is effective then you might expect to see the money lead output in the data. Use the graph in the example to match periods in time where you imagine there might be empirical support for both the classical and the Keynesian views.

4.5 Chapter summary: Putting it all together

In this chapter, we have learnt about the concept of macroeconomic modelling and the important issues of endogeneity and causality. We have also discussed the importance of using models that can predict the reaction of the economy to economic policy and external shocks. In terms of simplifying assumptions we have discussed the validity of reducing the economy to representative agents, and why we must be careful about exactly which questions we ask of a model.

A model requires the correct identification of variables; between the determined (endogenous) variables and the predetermined (exogenous) variables. Endogenous variables are caused by exogenous variables, but it is not always exactly clear which variables lead or which are truly exogenous. We demonstrated through the simple example of the relationship between consumption and income that causality can run in two/both directions; we must be cautious about how we specify a model.

We have introduced three important models – the circular flow, the Keynesian cross and the AS/AD model – which provide the basis or 'benchmarks' from which many other models have been developed up to the current modern larger-scale models. The circular flow models the economy as a set of financial and real flows between two or more agents, while the Keynesian cross and AS/AD models provide a static picture of equilibrium best used to explain policy as a movement from one equilibrium to another.

Lastly, we have learnt a simplified explanation of the differences between the two competing schools of economics using the slope of the aggregate supply curve – the classical view of policy ineffectiveness and the Keynesian view that policy can provide us with real effects (movements in output). We will revisit the Keynesian cross in more detail in Chapter 6 and the AS/AD model in Chapter 10, when we can use them for the purpose of economic policy analysis.

Assessment Question

Extend the circular flow model to include the public sector and government, and in doing so predict the effects of expansionary fiscal policy, what we call an increase in government expenditure.

Cases

The circular flow of income and environmental sustainability

Context

In this chapter on modelling, you have learned about the circular flow of income. This simple version of this model shows how money moves through the economy between households and firms. It illustrates the flow of goods and services, as well as income, and helps explain how the economy functions at a broader level.

But can this model be applied to other real-world issues beyond understanding the flows caused by economic activity? One such area where the circular flow of income can be creatively applied is in addressing the problem of environmental sustainability.

Scenario

The UK government is considering implementing new policies to promote sustainable development and reduce carbon emissions. The goal is to shift the economy towards greener, more sustainable practices, such as renewable energy, carbon pricing and reduced consumption of non-renewable resources.

To understand the implications of such policies on the broader economy, the government decides to apply the circular flow of income model, adding the public sector and environmental factors into the analysis. The model will help predict the impact of changes in government spending (such as subsidies for green technologies) and shifts in household spending (such as increased demand for eco-friendly products) on economic activity.

Questions

1. How could the circular flow of income model be adapted to encompass environmental sustainability?
   a) Consider how spending on renewable energy or green technologies might affect the flow of income between households, firms and the government.
   b) What impact might a shift in consumer preferences towards sustainable goods and services have on the economy?
2. a) What are the potential effects of government spending on green initiatives (such as subsidies or tax incentives for green businesses) on the circular flow of income?
   b) How might these policies influence business investment, household consumption and income distribution?
3. a) How could the environmental sector be incorporated into the flow of income?
   b) Could the environmental sector (e.g., renewable energy firms, recycling industries) be treated as a new participant in the circular flow? How might their presence affect overall economic activity?
4. What might the longer-term effects be if households and firms consistently shift towards more sustainable consumption and production patterns?
   a) Consider how this could affect GDP growth, unemployment and inflation.
   b) How might this transition influence external trade, as the UK could become a leader in green technologies?
5. In what ways could the circular flow of income model help policymakers assess the broader impact of environmental policies on the UK economy?

Problems

EASY

1. Which of the following is an example of a representative agent in a macroeconomic model?
   a) A single firm in the market.
   b) A household representing average consumer behaviour.
   c) A government budget constraint.
   d) A specific group of consumers with different preferences.
   e) A country's central bank setting.
2. Which of the following is a key difference between Keynesian and classical macroeconomic views?
   a) Keynesians believe that markets are always in equilibrium, whereas classical economists do not.
   b) Classical economists believe in the importance of government intervention, whereas Keynesians do not.
   c) Keynesians emphasize the role of aggregate demand in the economy, while classical economists stress the role of supply.
   d) Keynesians see wages as fully flexible, while classical economists see wages as sticky.
   e) Classical economists support a high level of government spending, while Keynesians oppose this.

MEDIUM

3. What is the primary purpose of a macroeconomic model?
4. Why do macroeconomists use economic models despite their simplifications of reality?
5. How does the Keynesian cross model relate to the circular flow of income in the economy?
6. In the context of macroeconomic time series data, which of the following best describes a potential use of a macroeconomic model?
   a) To predict short-term fluctuations in a single market.
   b) To estimate the future path of economic indicators like GDP, unemployment and inflation.
   c) To analyse the history of one specific firm's production output.
   d) To evaluate the impact of global trade on a single country's economy.
   e) To model individual spending behaviour of consumers.
7. Suppose the economy is represented by the following simple Keynesian model, where the consumption function is given by:
   $C = 100 + 0.8\, Y^d$
   where C is consumption, Y^d is disposable income, and the marginal propensity to consume is 0.8.
   The total amount of government spending is $G = 200$ and taxes $T = 50$.
   If the level of income Y in the economy is 500, calculate the level of consumption C and the equilibrium income.

HARD

8. Discuss the importance of representative agents in macroeconomic models. How do they help simplify the analysis of aggregate economic behaviour, and what are the limitations of using such a concept in real-world analysis?
9. Compare and contrast the Keynesian and classical views of macroeconomics. In your answer, focus on their respective perspectives on government intervention, the role of aggregate demand, and the flexibility of wages and prices.

CHAPTER 5

Financial System I – The Market for Money

Chapter contents

At a Glance

Financial system I – The market for money

The issue

Money is an asset to those who hold it and a liability to those who issue it. What is money, what purpose does it serve and how does it come into existence?

The understanding

In the same way that an accountant views a single balance sheet transaction, we can use the concept of money to help us see multiple perspectives of every single economic transaction that takes place in the economy. This is the first chapter of two on the subject of money and finance. We start by developing our understanding of a concept that exists to facilitate the trade in goods and services.

The usefulness

Money is often included in its own right on the list of important macroeconomic variables or even as a leading indicator. It is valuable to appreciate the proposition that it acts instead as a reflection of the economic activity that it represents.

5.1 Introduction

The money supply is an important macroeconomic variable made up of a number of financial assets that range in terms of liquidity, from high powered central bank money, to deposits and savings to financial instruments. In our everyday lives, we accept income in the form of money and use it to carry out our necessary expenditures in the form of purchases. The receipt of money in the form of wages and the consequential expenditure is captured neatly in the circular flow model that we discussed in Chapter 4. The reason for the use of money in society might appear rather obvious – it helps us to carry out economic transactions – but do we ever stop to think what money actually is, or how it comes to be in existence?

Quite simply, money can be defined as an asset that acts as a medium of exchange, used to facilitate the 'real' transactions in the circular flow, our labour at work and our consumption of goods and services. Any financial asset can be used to serve as money, so long as it is accepted to purchase goods and services universally across society. Because we use money to make purchases abroad, we can also think of money as a form of national debt, or even as an 'I owe you'. If I receive a good or service from a producer, I can pay for that good using anything, so long as the producer will accept it and that they also can then use it for their own needs. In this context we can refer to money as a means of deferred payment; a payment is made to a worker in the form of income, but the value of that money is not realized until it is used by the worker to make their own purchase. The value is only received when we go forward and use our money. Money is a deferred means of payment.

Aside from its usefulness as a medium of exchange, money is also an important macroeconomic variable of particular interest to economists and policymakers. In Chapter 4, we discussed the two different schools of economic thought: the Keynesians who believe that economic policy is effective and the classical school arguing the opposite. If monetary policy is indeed effective then a change in the supply of money will bring about a change in economic activity, or a change in output. It is intuitive that an increase in the amount of money available in the economy can bring about an increase in demand for the goods and services produced in the economy and then an increase in the level of aggregate output. So if changes in the money supply produce changes in economic activity, then money can be used as a tool to manage aggregate demand in the economy, to avoid recessions and also to prevent the economy from overheating. The use of money to control the fluctuations in output is something that we call monetary policy and is carried out by the central bank.

The following two chapters introduce students to the financial system of an economy as a whole. Where the money market is traditionally taught using the money market for high power money in isolation, this book uses an approach that explains the whole system of finance across the economy. The financial system is made up of three main sections: financial institutions, financial markets and financial instruments.

In this chapter, we focus on financial institutions and the role of central bank money in our economy. How the central bank changes the amount of money in the economy and how commercial banks use deposits to create money is discussed here. Bringing together the supply and the demand for central bank money we will lay out a simple model of the market for money, where the economy-wide interest rate is determined. Finally, we will use our knowledge on the determinants in the money market to help us to understand the mechanics of monetary policy and to explain the financial crisis of 2008.

Learning Outcomes

By the end of this chapter you should be able to:

- Define the concept of money and explain its importance as a macroeconomic variable.
- Illustrate how the money supply is controlled by the central bank and how the interest rate is determined.
- Relate the theory of liquidity preference to the traditional explanation of the demand for money.
- Connect the financial and real flows caused by economic activity using the quantity theory of money.
- Appraise the role of commercial bank money creation, and the liquidity ratio in the macroeconomic event known as the 2008 financial crisis.

5.2 The supply of money

At any one time, there is a quantity of real money balances in the economy which, according to the traditional model of the financial markets, is determined by the supply and demand for these balances. In our model of the financial markets, the **money** supply is set by the central banking authority and the demand for money by firms and consumers.

The money supply is normally modelled as exogenously set by the central bank and money demand as endogenous on economic factors such as output and the interest rate. We will first look at the supply side in the money markets by briefly discussing the definition of the money supply, the role of money in the economy and the categories of the money supply before going on to discuss money demand.

Money: A financial asset that can be used to facilitate the purchase of any good or service or to pay wages. An asset needs to meet three conditions to be considered as money: 1) it should be universally accepted for the purpose of transactions; 2) it should help us to measure value of goods and services; 3) it should keep its value stable over time.

The role of money and the types of money

The role of money in society is to provide us with an account to trade our labour and goods and services that we produce in a convenient manner. Without money, transactions would be very complicated indeed – we would have to rely instead on a physical system of barter. Life would probably have to revert to a simplified world of trading our own goods for a small selection of others. Imagine life as a baker trying to top up a mobile phone with half a loaf of freshly baked bread at the iPhone store!

Our day-to-day lives have become quite complicated and the need for a medium of exchange is quite obvious. So money is at the very least a medium of exchange but what qualifies our coins and notes as money? The truth is that money does not necessarily have to take the form of the coins and notes that we are used to; in fact, anything can be used as money so long it meets the following conditions. Money needs to act as a:

- **medium of exchange**
- **unit of account**
- **store of value.**

To act as a medium of exchange money must be universally accepted as a means of payment for all economic transactions amongst the community it is meant to serve. In a small community such as a prison where traditional money is disallowed, cigarettes have been known to act as a form of money because they are universally accepted to carry out transactions.

Money must also operate as a unit of account by enabling us to measure the value of the good or service that we wish to purchase; we expect the price of a shirt in a fashion outfit to be higher than the one available in a discount store. We might expect a shirt worth £100.00 to be of better quality than one priced at £10.00.

Finally, money must keep its value steady over time and not be subject to sudden movements in its purchasing power. If we keep a stock of money in the form of savings, then we would like to know with certainty that it will have the same purchasing power in the future. In a country where there is a risk of a currency devaluation, we may prefer to keep our wealth in the denomination of another currency such as the dollar whose future value is more certain over time.

Now that we have defined the role of money in the economy we need to explain how we measure money and what types of assets are included in the money supply. A problem we face is that money is not easily defined; it can take more than one form in any economy and in order to compare monies across borders we need a system of definition. What should be included in the money supply is not clear; we understand that coins and notes should be included, but what about bank deposits, savings accounts, corporate shares, bonds and other types of wealth held in investment accounts?

All of these forms of money can be used to make purchases even if they have to be converted into cash first, so should we include everything? Because of this complication we 'band' money into different definitions according to the speed in which the monetary asset can be turned into cash or made 'liquid'. The most liquid forms of money, such as cash and deposits, are included in the band we call 'narrow money' and the less liquid forms, such as savings or other interest-bearing assets, are added to form the broader measures. For example, in Europe some commonly used measures are as follows:

- **M1 – Monetary Base (the monetary 'base': cash + overnight deposits)**
- **M2 – Narrow Money (M1 plus deposits with longer maturity notice)**
- **M3 – Broad Money (M2 plus money market funds).**

The narrowest and most liquid measure, M1, includes cash in circulation and overnight deposits that can be converted instantly for cash transactions. M2 encompasses M1 and adds deposits/savings that require notice for withdrawal and M3 further broadens the measure by including financial instruments such as government bonds etc.

Control over the money supply

The market for money balances in the economy is normally represented by a two-dimensional model showing the interaction between the money supply and money demand schedules. The intersection of these two schedules provides us with the equilibrium interest rate in the economy. As with most models of this type, we would expect to see some form of price on the vertical axis and for this reason, the vertical axis in the money market represents the change in the interest rate, which we also term the price of money.

It is quite common to model the money market with the assumption that the money supply is solely controlled, or set, by the central bank. The central bank decides the amount of real money balances, so in the economy, we can say that the money supply is assumed to be exogenous. For this reason, the money supply schedule is often drawn vertical; though this assumption is refuted by those who believe that the money supply is endogenous.

The idea that the money supply is actually endogenous is becoming more popular. If money is endogenous then it will be driven by money demand as opposed to being exogenously set by the central bank. It is not surprising that central banks tend to agree with this explanation as it conveniently points the finger of blame for seigniorage back towards the financial markets and the government. **Seigniorage** is the act of printing new money and is seen negatively for its tendency to devalue the existing money stock.

> **Seigniorage:** The profit made by the government when increasing the amount of money in circulation, also known as 'printing money'. Adding to the money stock can devalue that money already in circulation by causing prices to rise.

There is a tenuous connection between seigniorage and the now popular measure of quantitative easing. The advertised definition of quantitative easing relates to the purchasing of bonds from commercial banks and other financial institutions. Essentially, bonds are being replaced with Tier 1 cash; if those bonds are not AAA rated assets, then there is a case that the term 'quantitative easing' could be used to disguise the act of seigniorage in a crisis.

For now, we continue to assume that the money supply is set exogenously and this is represented in Figure 5.1 with the money supply drawn vertical in the interest rate–real money balances space. Notice the disconnection between the interest rate and the amount of money supplied; the money supply is set or fixed by the central bank, regardless of the interest rate.

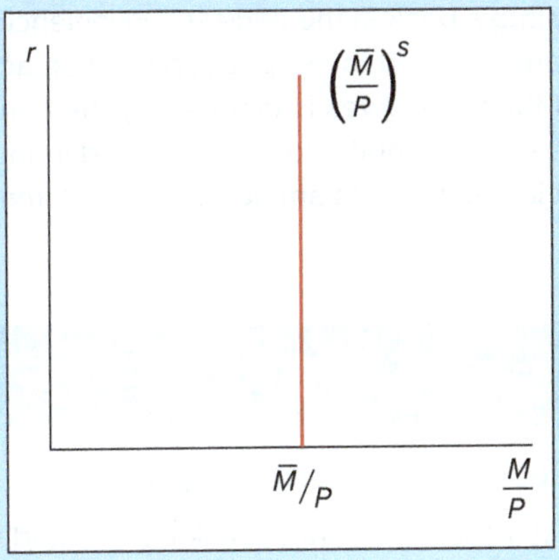

Figure 5.1 The money market showing exogenously set money supply

By assuming that the central bank has sole influence over the money supply in this way we are also assuming that the only type of money in the economy is cash in circulation and reserves held by commercial banks, that is, that there are no deposit accounts. As a result, the market for money is more formally a market for high powered, or central bank, money. In reality, commercial banks also create money by issuing loans from the balances that they hold in the form of deposits.

We will revisit this in the section on money creation below, but for now, this complication does not matter in our understanding of how the interest rate is determined in the money market. It is sufficient to say that the central bank sets the money supply independently of the interest rate.

Money creation and the money multiplier

There are two main actors in the creation of the money supply in the economy: the central bank and the commercial banks. That is why it is important to distinguish between money created by the central bank and that by the commercial banks. The central bank can create money in the form of cash in circulation and reserves (high-powered money) and the commercial banks can create money in the form of deposits. Although the central bank has total control over the amount of high-powered money, it has only indirect control in the level of deposits created in the economy. Remember that one of our commonly used measures of money, M2, contains cash in circulation *and* deposits.

If the central bank wants to increase the amount of cash in circulation it can simply print more money and distribute it by buying financial assets such as bonds from the private sector. The central bank may also be required to accept bonds issued by the government when the government wants to borrow money. Imagine the government wants to increase spending but does not have the cash to do so, it will raise the cash by issuing government bonds (or IOUs) to the central bank.

If the central bank holds onto these bonds the government will have increased the money supply just by spending money that it did not have. Essentially the government has created money by the act of borrowing when the bonds are issued (printed). If the central bank wants to reverse this creation of money it will have to sell the bonds on to the private sector. The bonds end up in the hands of the public and money is returned to the central bank, reducing the money supply back to its original level. Figure 5.1 gives a diagrammatic representation of the money supply schedule in the money market. If there is an increase in the money supply the vertical schedule shifts to the right and vice versa.

The commercial banks are also licensed to create money in the form of deposits; loans are issued to the public by converting a proportion of its deposits into reserves for new loans. This type of money creation is unaccounted for in our simple model of the market for central bank high-powered money. Let us begin our description of commercial bank money creation by imagining a simple economy where the only financial assets are cash in circulation and deposit accounts. Let us also assume that the population chooses not to hold money back and instead prefers to deposit all money into a bank at the earliest convenience.

All commercial banks are required to keep reserves in an account held at the central bank, the minimum level of these reserves is dictated by the announced reserve ratio. Reserves are held to insure against capital losses from bad loans and thus possible bankruptcy of the commercial banks. In Example 5.1, we will imagine that the reserve ratio is set at 10 per cent.

EXAMPLE 5.1

Hypothetical example: Money creation by a commercial bank

We begin by imagining that a country's central bank has created some £1,000 of new money by buying a bond in the financial market and that this new money is deposited in the country's one representative commercial bank, Vin de L'eau (VdL) Bank plc. This is the first deposit at VdL and, consequently, we can show the balance sheet of the country's sole commercial bank:

VdL Bank plc			
Liabilities	**£s**	**Assets**	**£s**
Deposits	1,000	Cash Reserves	1,000

The bank has liabilities of £1,000 because it owes this much to its depositor and also £1,000 in assets as it is now holding this money in the form of reserves. Financial regulations, however, stipulate that the bank need only hold 10 per cent of its assets as cash reserves, the rest can be lent out so that the bank can earn income in the form of interest.

We can assume that the amount of interest is negligible and so we will ignore these accumulated earnings on the balance sheet. VdL Bank lends out £900 (90 per cent of its assets) to a firm called Acorn. Acorn needs to invest in some machinery from another firm, Bravo Ltd, and so the money passes on from Acorn to Bravo. Bravo deposits this income into the only available bank, VdL. The balance sheet of the bank will now look like this:

VdL Bank plc			
Liabilities	**£s**	**Assets**	**£s**
Deposits	1,000	Cash Reserves – (Loan to Acorn)	100
		Loan to Acorn	900
Deposit from Bravo Ltd	900	New Cash Reserves	900
Total Liabilities	**1,900**	**Total Assets**	**1,900**

Notice that the liabilities and assets of VdL have grown by £900 as the result of the money created by its loan to Acorn; the money lent out has come back in the form of a new deposit by Bravo Ltd. This creates further reserves with which the bank can use to lend out even more money. In fact, VdL can lend another 90 per cent of these new cash reserves, a further

£810 to another company, the funds for which will come back again as a new deposit. Each time the deposit comes back the bank can lend out another 90 per cent of the new reserves. The only constraint to the bank, known as the leakage from the process of money creation, is the reserve ratio of 10 per cent.

So the process of money creation is endless but diminishing each time by the reserve requirement set by the central bank. We have seen by example that the only influence the central bank has over this type of money creation is via the reserve ratio requirement.

In fact, we can write out the path of money creation from our example where the reserve ratio is 10 per cent and the initial deposit is £1,000. The first round of money creation is 90 per cent of the initial deposit or (0.9) × £1,000 in the form of a loan. When the loan funds come back in the form of another deposit, 90 per cent of that new deposit can be loaned out again (0.9) × £900, and so on.

The path is as follows:

$$\text{Money created incl. initial deposit} = £1{,}000 + £900 + £810 + £729 + \text{and so on}$$

or

$$\text{Money created incl. initial deposit} = (£1{,}000) + 0.9(£1{,}000) + (0.9)^2(£1{,}000) + \ldots + (0.9)^n(£1{,}000)$$

This is a geometric progression that we can write mathematically, replacing 90 per cent (0.9) with 100 per cent – 10 per cent or (1 – *RR*), where *RR* is the reserve ratio:

$$Money\ created = \sum_{n=0}^{\infty} £1{,}000\,(1 - RR)^n$$

or

$$Money\ created = £10{,}000 = \frac{£1{,}000}{RR}$$

So in the case of 'no' money kept back by the public, all loans are returned as deposits and the bank multiplier can be written as:

$$M^B = \frac{1}{RR}$$

Now we have understood the bank multiplier let us again consider that there is some further leakage from the process where the population decides to hold back some of the money created in the form of cash. We can think of an example where somebody puts some money under the mattress instead of returning it as a deposit to the bank. If money is kept in circulation and not redeposited into our representative commercial bank, then this reduces the amount of money that can be created by the bank in each round. Our new money multiplier M^M becomes:

$$M^M = \frac{1 + c}{(c + RR)}$$

where *c* represents the cash held back from the process of money creation. We call this parameter the cash to deposits ratio and can think of this as the propensity of the population to hold cash. Let us consider an extreme case in Example 5.2.

EXAMPLE 5.2

Hypothetical example: A closed example with zero cash in circulation

If the population decides not to hold any cash and instead returns all money, then $c = 0$ and the bank multiplier reverts to $\frac{1}{RR}$. In other words, with the cash to deposits ratio at zero the money multiplier is equal to the bank multiplier as per our previous example (Example 5.1), where all money is kept in the form of deposits.

With this in mind we can see that if there is an economic shock to the economy that affects the desire of the population to hold more cash, this will have a direct effect on money creation by commercial banks. A recapitalization of the commercial bank's balance sheets (increases in the **liquidity** ratio RR) or a propensity by the population to hold more cash can lead to a reduction in the money created via the money multiplier. Our simplified version of the money market given earlier in the chapter cannot account for this type of money creation and destruction.

Liquidity: The speed at which a financial asset can be converted into its most liquid form: money in the form of cash.

EXERCISE 5.1

1. With a reserve ratio of 20 per cent, calculate the bank multiplier. How does this compare to the bank multiplier in our VdL Bank example?
2. If the cash to deposits ratio c is 50 per cent, how does this affect the amount of money created in the economy by commercial banks?

5.3 The demand for money

Most markets in macroeconomics require both a demand schedule and supply schedule and the market for central bank money is no different; in the labour market we can visualize who will supply labour (workers) and who will demand it (firms), we can even intuitively understand why a firm will demand labour and why a worker will supply labour. In the money market the need for a demand side presents us with a problem; it is not obvious who will demand money and even less obvious as to why. Do consumers demand money or just accept its existence? The need for a convincing demand side in the money market prompted Keynes' 'theory of liquidity preference'.

Keynes' theory of liquidity preference

Keynes' theory of liquidity preference provides us with an intuitive foundation for the quantity of money demanded in the economy. In short, the theory gives us three reasons to hold or demand money:

- **Transactions – (money to carry out our economic transactions)**
- **Precaution – (money held to insure against an unexpected expense)**
- **Speculation – (money held to buy speculative assets)**.

We demand money to carry out our day-to-day purchases in the form of transactions demand, as a precaution for unseen events, or with which to speculate. If national income increases, then the transaction demand for money will also increase as a consequence; economic activity and the transactions demand for money are closely correlated. The precautionary motive for money demand comes from our desire to hold back some cash for unexpected expenditures – think of money put aside for a rainy day. Precautionary demand for money can also be driven by other factors; for instance, a change in sentiment or a lack of certainty about the future – during a financial crisis we may want to hold more cash due to mistrust in the banking system. Our motive for holding balances for speculative motives depends on the return we could have made otherwise by banking our money in an alternative interest-bearing account; in other words, the opportunity cost of holding money in the form of cash.

Money demand is positively correlated to nominal income (as income goes up we will demand more money) and negatively correlated to the nominal interest rate (as the interest rate rises we will demand less money). Remember that money held as cash does not earn us income in the form of interest, so as the interest rate rises we may prefer to transfer our holdings into interest bearing accounts at the bank.

Money Demand: The demand for central bank money, or base money, dependent on the interest rate (negative) and income (positive).

What we have just discussed is actually our preference for liquidity. It is our preference for liquidity that gives us a reason to hold money for these three motives against tying up our money in a savings account. At a low interest rate, we would rather keep more money in the form of cash as the opportunity cost of holding money is low (we are not losing much income in the form of interest). We can now include our money demand schedule into the money market that shows how money demanded in the economy is negatively related to the interest rate (see Figure 5.2).

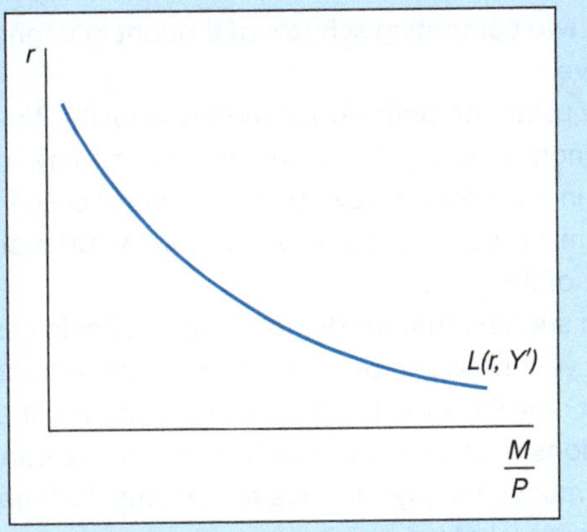

Figure 5.2 Money demand is downward sloping in the interest rate

Notice that, as the interest rate falls, there is a higher preference to hold real money balances; in this case, interest-bearing accounts have become less attractive. We can formally express the money demand function as:

$$\left(\frac{M}{P}\right)^d = L(r, Y')$$

where the left-hand side represents real money (money divided by the price level) demanded and the function L tells us that money demand is a function of the interest rate r and income Y'. In fact, money demand is negative in the interest rate and positive in income; an increase in the interest rate will give us a movement left along the money demand curve and, because in our analysis we are holding income constant (it isn't on the axis), an increase in income will give us a rightwards shift in the money demand function (see Figure 5.3).

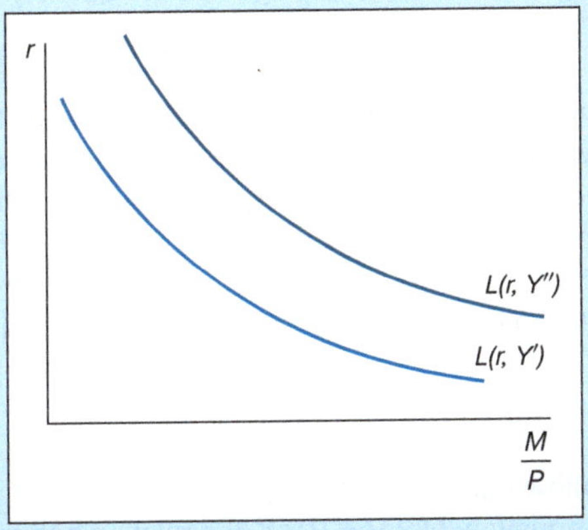

Figure 5.3 A rightward shift in the money demand function after an increase in income

An increase in income from Y' to Y'' will give us an increase in money demand for any given level of interest rates due to the need for cash to carry out the additional transactions. We will come to see later, that with the **money supply** set exogenously, the increase in income also leads to a rise in the interest rate in the economy as banks have to try harder to attract cash.

Money Supply: The supply of money set by the central bank; this is independent of the interest rate and drawn vertically in the money market.

The quantity theory of money

Another theoretical approach that provides us with an explanation for money demand is through the quantity theory of money. This theory also helps us to understand how an increase in the money supply leads us to an increase in either output or the price level and to briefly revisit the argument between the two competing schools of thought in economics. It is simple to understand and also intuitive.

We build our model by using the definition of money velocity. We can think of money velocity as the speed at which the money supply flows around the economy. In order to carry out all the economic transactions in the economy every year we need cash in circulation. Imagine an economy where the economic transactions in one year total £100m and that the transactions are carried out over the course of the year.

It seems reasonable to suggest that we do not need £100m in cash as money will be 'passed around' during the year between people carrying out the transactions. It is also reasonable to consider that only £10m will be required to carry out the £100m worth of transactions each year. In order to cover all the transactions, we can also say that the money supply will have to circulate 10 times each year. This rate of circulation is what we call the **velocity of money** and in our example has a value of 10.

> **Velocity of Money:** The speed at which money flows around the economy. The higher the speed the less demand there will be for real money balances.

Using our explanation above we can derive the quantity equation by writing our description of velocity in mathematical terms:

$$\textit{Velocity}, V = \frac{\textit{Value of Transactions}\ (£100\text{m})}{\textit{Money Supply}\ (£10\text{m})} = 10$$

or we can write:

$$V = \frac{T}{M}$$

Note also that the **value of transactions** T is equivalent to nominal GDP and so we can replace T with an expression for nominal GDP ($P \times Y$) where Y is real GDP.

> **Value of Transactions:** The total sum value of the sale prices multiplied by the sale quantities of all goods and services sold in any year. This variable is equivalent to the nominal value of gross domestic product.

Now we have:

$$V = \frac{P \times Y}{M}$$

Multiplying both sides by M will give us the quantity equation:

$$M \times V = P \times Y$$

The quantity equation helps us to explain the connection between the real and monetary sides of the economy or how the money market and the market for goods and services are interrelated. For example, we can use the quantity equation to predict the reaction of the variable's prices and output to an increase in the money supply. We can see that if M increases then this must be met with an increase in prices or real output or both, we can say that the quantity theory of money tells us that the relation between the money supply and the price level is positive.

EXERCISE 5.2

Fill in the blanks in the following:

According to the quantity equation, $M \times V = P \times Y$, the relation between the money supply and output is ________ and the relation between output and prices is ________.

Finally, we can rearrange our quantity equation to provide another expression for money demand and show how it is related to output. Rearrange our quantity equation by dividing both sides by P and V to get:

$$\frac{M}{P} = \left(\frac{1}{V}\right) \times Y$$

In words, real money balances demanded are equal to a fraction of real income. Compare this to our previous equation for money demand given above and you see that both forms of the money demand function predict that money demand will increase if output increases. This prediction from the theory is highly intuitive.

EXAMPLE 5.3

Worked example: Working with an explicit form of the money demand function

$$\left(\frac{M}{P}\right)^d = L(r, Y') = Y(0.8 - r)$$

Question:

This function represents the economy-wide reaction of money demand to changes in income and the nominal interest rate.

1. Describe the money demand equation in words.
2. If national income is £800bn what is the change in money demand if the interest rate rises from 2 per cent to 5 per cent?

Answer guideline:

1. Money demanded in the economy is a function (*L*) of both interest rates and national income. More explicitly, we can say that money demand is positively related to income and negatively to interest rates; here, the proportion of income demanded as money is 80 per cent minus the current interest rate.
2. First, calculate money demand for both interest rates:

$$\text{For r} = 2\% \quad \left(\frac{M^d}{P}\right) = L(r, Y) = £800\text{bn}(0.8 - 0.02) = £624\text{bn}$$

$$\text{For r} = 5\% \quad \left(\frac{M^d}{P}\right) = L(r, Y) = £800\text{bn}(0.8 - 0.05) = £600\text{bn}$$

To calculate the change in money demand we take the difference of the above two figures for money demanded, so we can see that, after the rise in the interest rate, money demand falls by (£624bn – £600bn) = £24bn.

Equilibrium in the money market and monetary policy

To complete our discussion on the money market we need to bring both the demand for money and the supply of money together in one marketplace where the economy-wide interest rate is determined. The interest rate can also be thought of as the opportunity cost of holding money in cash form; in other words, the income we would have received from our money if we had placed it in an interest bearing account. So the interest rate is the 'price' of money and this is consistent with the interest rate sitting on the vertical axis, normally the price axis.

Our financial system in its most basic form is another two-dimensional analysis between the interest rate and the quantity of money balances held. The interaction considered by our analysis is between those that demand money and the policymaker that supplies it. In Figure 5.4 on the next page we see a typical depiction of the money market.

Now we can more clearly see how the interest rate reacts to changes in monetary policy or a change in money demand; an increase (right shift) in money demand will lead to a higher interest rate and an increase (right shift) in the money supply will lead to a reduction in the equilibrium interest rate. In Figure 5.5 (also overleaf), we give a detailed account of how a reduction in the money supply leads to an increase in the interest rate.

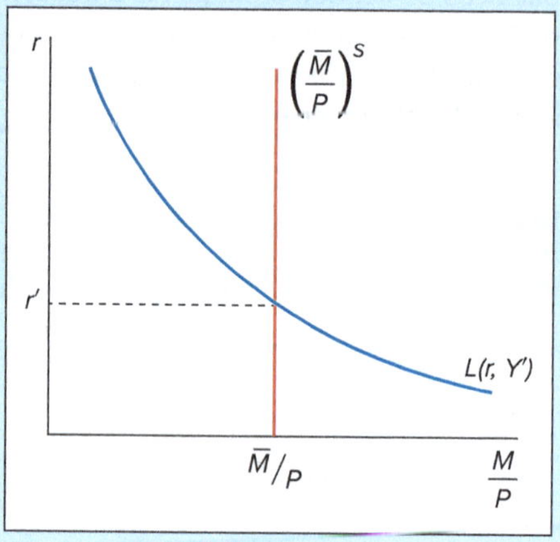

Figure 5.4 Equilibrium in the money market

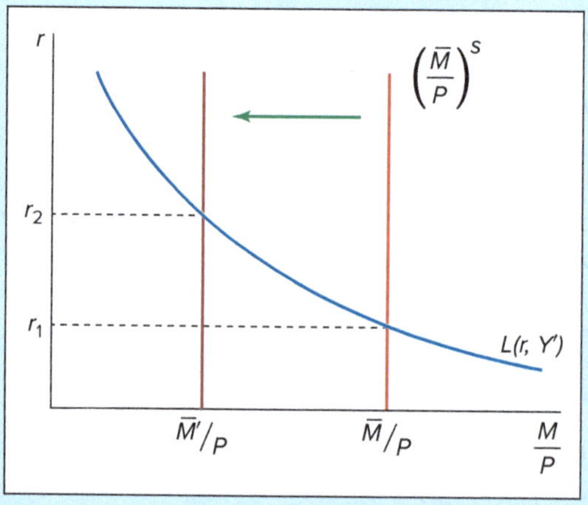

Figure 5.5 The money market showing the reaction of the interest rate to a reduction in the money supply

EXERCISE 5.3

1. How will an increase in the money supply affect the equilibrium interest rate in the money market?
2. How will an increase in national income affect the equilibrium interest rate in the money market?

A reduction in the money supply from $\frac{\overline{M}}{P}$ to $\frac{\overline{M}'}{P}$ causes excess money demand at the old interest rate r_1. In order to attract money into interest bearing accounts, commercial banks will have to offer higher interest rates. This competitive force drives up the interest rate and moves us from the original equilibrium backwards along the money demand function until we reach the new equilibrium interest rate r_2. Remember that the purpose of monetary policy is to manage demand in the economy with the primary aim of keeping prices stable; a decrease in the money supply will increase the price of money (the interest rate), making investment less attractive and reducing aggregate demand.

The liquidity trap

Finally, we need to highlight a couple of difficulties that a central bank faces in its business of economy-wide price stability. The most obvious limitation for monetary policy is that the interest rate cannot go below zero; although ironically 7 years after the financial crisis, we have seen some central banks announce negative interest rates for the first time, with the aim of encouraging commercial banks to lend. In normal times we would not expect or be able to maintain a negative interest rate.

Remember that the interest rate is also the opportunity cost of holding money; if money is held as cash balances it is not gaining interest, so the cost of holding money is the interest foregone. As the interest rate approaches zero those demanding money in the money market become indifferent between holding money (the value they place on liquidity) and banking it in interest bearing accounts. If this happens the bank can reduce the money supply, but people may not be induced to bank it to earn interest. The reason for this is that the opportunity cost of holding money has fallen below the value of liquidity itself. This liquidity indifference will make it difficult for the central bank to initiate the intended rise in the interest rate, a reduction in the money supply will not increase the interest rate. In this situation the money demand curve has become flat and movements in the money supply will leave the interest rate unchanged. The monetary authority has become ineffective and we are facing a liquidity trap.

5.4 The money market in practice

The mechanics of monetary policy

The purpose of monetary policy is to manage economic activity and a natural tool to use for this purpose is the interest rate. We have already seen how the money supply is negatively correlated with the interest rate in the money market. We can take the case of a momentary contraction; in order to cool economic activity the central bank will have to increase the interest rate that producers and consumers pay for borrowing and investing. It can achieve this through a reduction in the money supply.

We follow the case of a monetary contraction pursued by the central bank. Remember that the money market is drawn in interest rate–real money balances space. For those demanding money, the choice is between interest bearing and non-interest bearing assets. At a higher interest rate, agents will want to switch from non-interest bearing assets (such as cash) to interest bearing assets (such as savings accounts), so that the return from the new interest rate can be exploited. The interest rate r_1 equates the money demand and supply schedules, before the policy to contract the economy by the central bank. To achieve a contraction, the central bank reduces the money supply. From Figure 5.6, we can see that with the reduced money supply and money demand constant, at the old interest rate there is now excess demand for non-interest bearing assets; we can also say that there is an excess demand for liquidity. As a reaction to this the banks, offering interest bearing assets such as savings, will have to increase the interest rate to attract investors to overcome the excess demand for cash. The interest rate rises to rate r_2, and equilibrium is restored in the money market.

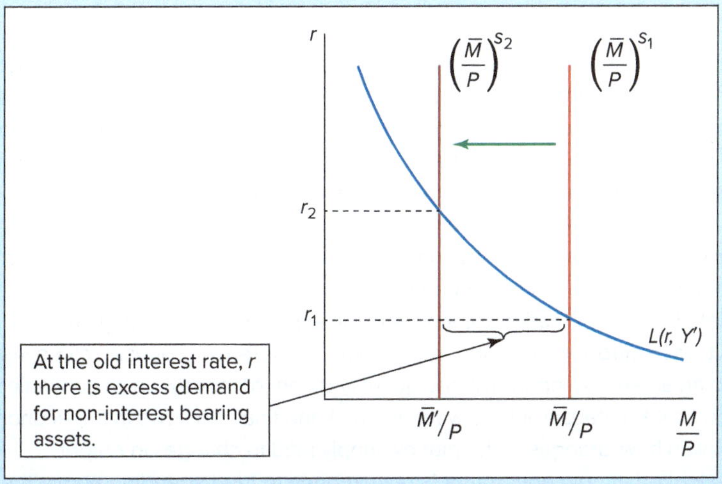

Figure 5.6 Contractionary monetary policy and how the interest rate changes

Quantitative easing by the central bank

In a major economic event, the central bank may need to continue to raise the supply of money, even after the interest rate has been set to a level of zero. Of course, an interest rate cannot be set at a negative value; so how does the bank continue to stimulate the economy even after interest rates have reached this lower bound?

The answer lies in a central bank tool called quantitative easing. The central bank can buy assets from financial institutions using newly created money; this is particularly useful to financial institutions that have assets to sell, but no way of selling them in a time of financial turbulence. The central bank will provide tier one cash to financial institutions in return for bonds of varying creditworthiness to help to free up capital that can be used to make loans into the economy, as in normal times. Remember that in a recession, an increase in loan defaults will leave holes in the balance sheets of commercial banks and this will impede vital lending required by consumers and producers.

However, this practice does leave the central bank in the position of holding more assets while increasing the money supply more generally. It is important that the assets purchased are not only liquid, but highly rated. Should the central bank relax this requirement it could stand accused of seigniorage; increasing the money supply by more than that required to maintain economic activity, and risk an unnecessary bout of inflation. To reverse this position the bank will have to reverse the purchases by selling the bonds once the financial crisis is over; the act of selling the accrued bonds is referred to as quantitative tightening (QT).

EXERCISE 5.4

1. Why did central banks struggle to stimulate demand in reaction to the economic slowdown caused by the financial crisis in 2008?
2. **Fill in the blank in the following:**
   Commercial banks react to loan defaults by ______ the amount of loans available to rebuild reserves.

It is worth mentioning that it is not universally agreed upon that the central bank actually controls the interest rate through the money supply, rather that the interest rate is changed by the simple act of changing the bank rate, the rate charged or applied to reserves held at the central bank. This position implies that the money supply sets itself. Here, we avoid this debate about the source of changes in the money supply and assume that the money supply is set exogenously. It is fixed or set by the central bank, whether directly or indirectly, and is drawn vertically in the money market.

5.5 Chapter summary: Putting it all together

What have we learnt from this chapter? We have discussed the meaning and the purpose of money, how money is created both by the central bank and the commercial banks, and how the central bank has a role to play in both types of money creation. We have built up a model of the market for central bank (high-powered) money where the supply of money is set by the central bank exogenously. We could also have explained the evolution of the money supply as endogenous on the demand for loans, though this book refrains from doing so. The explanation for the money creation cycle is immune to this criticism, meaning that liquidity ratios matter for the amount of money created in the economy.

To complete the money market we also need an explanation for money demand, and to achieve this we have introduced the theory of liquidity preference proposed by Keynes. We have also discussed an alternative approach, the quantity theory of money which conveniently provides us with a theoretical and causal link between the real and financial flows in the economy. With this link we can explain how changes in the money supply lead to changes in output.

Lastly, we looked at how governments raise money to fund spending above the level of tax receipts (government borrowing) in the financial markets. The price of bonds can explain the connection between changes in the money supply and changes in the interest rate. With the overview of the financial system complete, our knowledge of bank reserves and economic policy has helped to build a basic narrative for the global financial crisis that began in 2008, a recession exasperated by the position of central banks and governments in the period leading up to the crisis.

Up until now, governments have taken innovative and sensible fiscal steps to mitigate the negative impact on employment – for instance, the furlough scheme in the UK, introduced to prevent a collapse in demand after the COVID crisis of 2019 – a concern forward from here is the ability of governments to continue to service debt levels in the face of such unprecedented increases in government expenditure. The ability of governments to avoid a repeat of the austerity measures, like those witnessed through the 2010s, will depend on the reaction of international financial markets and credit rating agencies to the increases in debt to GDP ratios for affected nations.

There is a key difference between the debts accrued during the financial crisis of 2008 to that of 2019, in that in the former the debt to GDP levels have increased more globally. Accordingly international capital imbalances across nations have been less severe. Capital movements between debtor to lending nations in 2008, have been replaced by capital movements between asset types in 2020 onwards; what we may see instead of austerity is more volatility in equity and commodity markets.

Assessment Question

Since the financial crisis that started in 2008, central banks across the world have lowered interest rates to levels close to zero in a bid to avoid stagnating economies. Explain in words and using diagrams how the central banks went about lowering interest rates and highlight any challenges they may face tightening monetary policy in the future.

Cases

The UK money market and its role in the economy

This case study highlights the dynamic nature of the UK money market and how various players, especially the Bank of England, interact to influence economic stability.

Introduction

The money market plays a crucial role in the UK economy by facilitating the short-term borrowing and lending of funds. It helps maintain liquidity in the financial system and supports the broader economy through its influence on interest rates and monetary policy. Understanding how the money market operates is essential for evaluating how the Bank of England manages inflation, economic growth and financial stability.

Key players in the UK money market

1. The Bank of England: The central bank controls monetary policy in the UK, using tools like interest rates and quantitative easing (QE) to influence the money market. The Bank of England's Monetary Policy Committee (MPC) sets the official Bank Rate, which impacts short-term interest rates across the market.
2. Commercial banks: These banks are major participants in the money market, borrowing and lending short-term funds to each other, often using overnight loans. Banks use the money market to ensure they have sufficient reserves to meet their daily obligations.
3. Financial institutions and corporations: Non-bank financial institutions and large corporations also engage in the money market to manage their liquidity and to meet short-term financing needs.
4. Government: The UK government participates in the money market by issuing short-term securities like Treasury bills. These instruments help manage the government's liquidity needs.

The role of the Bank of England in the money market

The Bank of England is the primary institution influencing the UK money market. One of its main tools is setting the Bank Rate, which affects the cost of borrowing and the return on savings in the economy. When the Bank Rate rises, borrowing becomes more expensive, and when it falls, borrowing becomes cheaper.

Another significant role the Bank of England plays in the money market is through open market operations (OMOs). These operations involve the Bank buying or selling government securities to regulate the money supply. For example, if the Bank wants to increase liquidity in the market, it may buy government bonds from commercial banks, which injects money into the system and lowers short-term interest rates.

Example: The impact of the Bank of England's monetary policy on the money market

In 2020, during the COVID-19 pandemic, the Bank of England reduced the Bank Rate to a historic low of 0.1 per cent to help stimulate economic activity and support the financial system. As a result, borrowing became cheaper, which encouraged businesses and individuals to take loans and spend more, boosting demand in the economy. This intervention also helped ensure that banks could meet their liquidity needs despite the uncertain economic environment.

The UK money market and interest rates

Interest rates in the money market are closely tied to the overall economy. When the economy is growing too fast and inflation begins to rise, the Bank of England may decide to increase interest rates to reduce borrowing and slow down inflation. Conversely, if the economy is in a recession or facing low inflation, the Bank may lower interest rates to stimulate economic activity.

In the case of rising inflation, such as in 2021 when inflation rates began to climb due to supply chain issues and rising energy prices, the Bank of England may respond by increasing interest rates to cool down the economy.

Challenges and risks in the UK money market

1. Liquidity risk: In times of financial stress, commercial banks may be unwilling to lend to each other, causing a liquidity shortage. This can lead to higher interest rates and potentially a credit crunch, where businesses and consumers cannot borrow as easily.
2. Inflation and interest rate risks: While low interest rates can stimulate economic growth, they can also fuel inflation if the economy overheats. The Bank of England must balance the need to stimulate growth with the risk of rising prices.
3. External shocks: Events like Brexit or global economic crises can lead to uncertainty in the money market, impacting the flow of funds and the stability of interest rates.

Questions

1. What is the money market, and why is it important for the UK economy?
2. Who are the key players in the UK money market?
3. How does the Bank of England influence the money market?
4. What happened in 2020 regarding the Bank of England's monetary policy?
5. What are the potential risks in the UK money market?

Problems

EASY

1. In the UK, the market for central bank money involves:
   a) Commercial banks borrowing from each other
   b) The buying and selling of government bonds between banks
   c) The Bank of England lending to commercial banks
   d) The purchase of foreign currencies by the Bank of England
   e) The trading of shares in the stock market

2. In the context of money creation, which of the following best explains how banks create money in the UK?
   a) By printing currency notes
   b) Through the government's issuance of Treasury bills
   c) Through lending activities that increase the money supply
   d) By purchasing foreign currency in the foreign exchange market
   e) Through the Bank of England's purchases of gold
3. According to Keynes' theory of liquidity preference, the demand for money is influenced by:
   a) The level of government spending
   b) The amount of money in circulation
   c) The interest rate and national income
   d) The rate of return on physical capital
   e) The level of exports and imports
4. The Quantity Theory of Money ($MV = PY$) suggests that:
   a) An increase in the money supply will always lead to an increase in real GDP
   b) The velocity of money is constant and determines the level of prices
   c) The money supply and price level are inversely related
   d) Changes in the money supply have no impact on inflation
   e) The money supply affects real output more than the price level
5. Which of the following represents an equilibrium situation in the money market?
   a) When the demand for money equals the supply of money
   b) When the money supply exceeds the demand for money
   c) When interest rates are higher than the equilibrium level
   d) When commercial banks have excess reserves
   e) When the government sets a fixed interest rate for loans
6. Quantitative easing (QE) in the UK involves:
   a) Raising interest rates to reduce inflation
   b) Selling government bonds to commercial banks
   c) The Bank of England purchasing government bonds to increase the money supply
   d) Increasing taxes to reduce the amount of money in circulation
   e) Encouraging private banks to issue new loans

MEDIUM

7. Explain how the market for central bank money operates in the UK. Discuss the role of the Bank of England in providing liquidity to commercial banks and its impact on the economy.
8. Discuss the effectiveness of quantitative easing (QE) as a tool for stimulating economic activity in the UK, particularly in the context of post-financial crisis monetary policy.
9. We have seen that in a financial crisis, the leveraging of banks plays an important role in the amplitude of the effect on economic activity. In the context of the financial crisis, discuss the connection between commercial bank money creation and the Great Recession of 2008.

HARD

10. The Bank of England conducts quantitative easing by purchasing £50 billion in government bonds from commercial banks. If the reserve ratio is 10 per cent, what is the maximum potential increase in the money supply?

CHAPTER 6

Financial System II – Financial Markets and Financial Instruments

Chapter contents

At a Glance

Financial system II – Financial markets and financial instruments

The issue

How do we connect our understanding of the market for central bank money to the wider financial system? How are the returns for interest bearing assets connected to the returns for other monetary assets? How can we connect the wider financial system to the pathology of the financial crisis of 2008?

The understanding

In Chapter 5 we introduced the concept of money, the traditional macroeconomic concept of the money market. We discussed the major players in the money market and how they helped to create the money needed to facilitate economic activity. In this chapter we widen our understanding of the financial system in an economy, to include the financial markets and the market for more exotic monetary assets.

The usefulness

Understanding where the money market sits in the wider financial system in an economy is key to connecting concepts normally taught separately on courses in macroeconomics and in finance. In this chapter we piece together the separate concepts to develop an understanding of the financial system as a whole, forwards from the money market to include financial innovations and instruments.

6.1 Introduction

In a developed economy, the financial system that facilitates the financial needs from trade will be made up of several important sectors. Here we use three categories to capture these sectors of the financial system as a whole; financial institutions, financial markets and financial instruments (Table 6.1). In the subject area of macroeconomics it is traditional to explain the financial system using the first two categories, and to see the material related to the third category taught on a course specializing in the area of finance. Pulling together all three, helps us to explain the 'whole' financial system, and for students to see the connections between the components of the financial system as a whole, normally taught separately.

Table 6.1 The complete financial system

Sector	Components
Financial institutions	Central banks, commercial banks and insurance companies
Financial markets	Platform for the buying and selling of all types of tradable financial assets, including and not limited to bonds, equities and mutual funds
Financial instruments	Monetary assets including derivatives, assets born from debt-based financial contracts between two financial entities

Monetary Asset: An asset that could be used as money or as a form of security that ranges in liquidity from the most narrow to the most broad.

Most developed economies use a wide variety of licensed assets as part of the broader money supply. The money supply itself ranges from narrow high-powered money, such as cash and deposits, to broader types of **monetary assets**, such as bonds, equities and financial instruments. While the focus of Chapter 5 centred on the more liquid assets and high-powered money provided by the central bank, here we complete a representation of the financial system using a more detailed look at financial markets that can facilitate the trade in the more traditional assets like bonds and equities termed cash instruments, to the trade of more exotic forms of money such as derivative instruments.

Cash instruments that represent more traditional monetary assets exist to facilitate the transfer of funds from investors (lenders) to institutions that need to borrow money (borrowers). These debt-based assets include government and commercial bonds, shares in publicly quoted companies and mutual funds. As an example: The central bank is the bank for the government, providing funds as required to meet the expenditure needs of the government when tax receipts will not suffice. In return for those funds the government will issue bonds, which will include a redemption value and a coupon payment to encourage investors to part with the cash that the government needs to service its debts. Once issued by an institution, a bond can be traded openly in the financial markets; the value of which can change on a daily basis just like any other commodity. An increase in demand for bonds by investors will lead to an increase in the traded price and because bonds promise a fixed income for investors, the price directly affects the return that an investor can hope to receive upon redemption, something also known as a **bond yield**.

> **Bond Yield:** The distance between the face value and market price of a bond as a proportion of the market price. Normally quoted as a percentage so that it can be compared to the interest rate.

Beyond the trade in traditional financial assets such as stocks and bonds, financial markets will also facilitate the trade of more exotic forms of money known as financial derivative instruments. A derivative instrument is more explicitly defined as made up of one or more underlying contracts between two financial entities and will include more modern types of financial innovation: assets such as options, futures, collateralized debt obligations, credit default swaps and other exotic financial derivatives. As an example of how a derivative might come into being, an individual can borrow money to make a purchase; in return for the funds the lending bank will issue a contract that enforces the repayment of those funds. The contract can then be traded between institutional investors as part of a financial derivative instrument. The contract or promise to repay has become a financial asset in itself.

In this chapter, we learn more about the trade of traditional cash instruments in the financial markets, starting with the role of the central bank and the connection between bond yields and interest rates. In doing so, we highlight an important fact about the relationship between all financial assets in general. We go on to extend the traditional macroeconomic view of the money supply and financial markets by considering the role of both cash and derivative instruments. Finally, we will use our knowledge on the determinants of the money market, how money is created and the role of financial instruments in the financial system to help us to explain the financial crisis and subsequent great recession of 2008.

Learning Outcomes

By the end of this chapter you should be able to:

- Understand the concept of and key role played by financial markets.
- Connect the relationship between bond yields and interest rates to the relationship between all financial assets.
- Describe the role of the central bank in relation to the bond market.
- Distinguish between traditional cash instruments and financial derivative instruments.
- Discuss the economic conditions surrounding the financial crisis and great recession of 2008.

6.2 The financial markets

Financial markets exist to facilitate the trade in financial assets such as bonds, equities, derivatives and financial innovations. These markets also provide a facility for political institutions, such as the central bank and government, to go about economic policy, for example the sale and purchase of government debt in the form of government bonds. The financial markets also allow companies to raise capital and those buying and selling capital to transfer risk.

A key category of monetary asset traded in financial markets is that of the financial bond, a distinguishing feature of which is the fixed income nature included in the return for investors. Bonds have a 'fixed' face value that will be guaranteed by the issuing institution when the asset reaches maturity, and the money is repaid to investors. The relative difference between the face value and the market value for these **security** types is known as the yield.

Government issued bonds specifically are a type of security that help us to understand the mechanics of **monetary policy**. We have already learnt in Chapter 5 that the central bank has control over the monetary base that circulates the economy and facilitates economic activity, but how is this done in practice?

> **Security:** A financial instrument that can be traded between two financial entities, for example bonds, stocks, exchange traded funds (ETFs), options, futures, derivatives and other financial innovations. A security represents 'ownership'.
> **Monetary Policy:** Actions taken by the central bank to achieve stability in price movements, avoiding episodes of high inflation and the economic uncertainty that comes with it.

Monetary policy and bonds

In many modern economies, a central bank is licensed to print and issue the money required to facilitate the trade of goods and services. Until the early 1970s, however, central bank notes came with a printed promise to bear value, as a guarantee to those left holding it. The value of money was underwritten by tangible assets, such as gold and silver. This 'backing' of sovereign debt was effective until the limited supply of such metals proved to be a constraint to the requirement to facilitate ever-increasing economic activity.

By removing this backing for tender, we now see that money is backed by little more than the credibility of its issuing authority. For instance, the US dollar, once redeemable for a quantity of gold, is now underwritten by little more than the creditworthiness of the US government; people are prepared to hold the dollar because they believe that it will hold its value until they need to spend it. So the money we accept as income is backed by little more than the credibility of the issuing authority. We call this type of money, with no intrinsic (asset) backing, **fiat money**. Further to this, the central bank is required to provide the government with the funds needed to maintain public expenditures and simultaneously maintain an environment of price and financial stability.

Fiat Money: A monetary base that has no tangible backing. The notes issued by the central bank are underwritten by the credibility of the issuing authority.

The central bank uses open market operations to buy and sell government debt in its bid to manipulate the supply of money in the economy, itself with a view to manipulating aggregate demand. Selling government bonds in the financial markets will have the effect of reducing the money supply; buying the debt back will have the opposite effect on the money supply. For instance, if the central bank sells government debt in the form of bonds then it will be releasing securities with a face value to the public and in return receive money in the form of cash. The flow of cash into the central bank reduces the supply of money.

The reduction of the money supply applies downward pressure on aggregate demand and may relieve inflationary pressures. Bear in mind that we have assumed in our money market above that the only type of money in the economy is high-powered money and that the tool to control the cash in circulation is the trading of bonds in the open financial market. Including the money supply created by commercial banks, described above, and the demand for deposit accounts would require an extension to our model. Nevertheless, if we allow for money creation by the commercial banks then the central bank can also control the money supply by changing the reserve ratio (RR).

Remember that the amount of money created in the economy is given by the bank/ deposit multiplier:

$$M = \frac{1}{RR}$$

If the central bank increases the reserve ratio we can see that this has the effect of reducing the amount of money created by the multiplier, as the money supply and the reserve ratio are inversely related. Again, a reduction in the money supply through an increase in the reserve ratio will have the effect of reducing aggregate demand. One other way for the central bank to control the money supply is through the interest rate the central bank charges the commercial banks to save or borrow money for the purposes of maintaining the reserve position on the balance sheet; this interest rate is referred to as the 'bank' rate.

Bond prices and interest rates

Now that we understand the purpose of an issued bond and its importance as a vehicle to control the money supply we can discuss the relationship between the price of bonds and the interest rate in the financial markets. We start by imagining a bond issued by the central bank; it has a face value and a current value. The face value is equivalent to a promise to pay the holder of the bond a redemption upon **maturity**. For simplicity we ignore any complication presented by the inclusion of a 'coupon' attached to the bonds which is a separate incentive in the form of an interest payment to attract investors; the inclusion of which would have helped us address the issue of 'time to maturity'.

Bond Maturity: The term for which the bond is issued and this can vary considerably. The term of the bond also dictates which interest rate the bond yield would align to; for instance, a GILT bond would be related to the long-term interest rate.

For a simplified example, imagine a bond whose current value price is £100.00 but face value, or promise to pay, is £110.00 in one year's time. It is not difficult to see that the return on the bond is £10.00, which makes up 10 per cent of the face value. This return is something that we call the bond 'yield' because it measures the return from the difference between the face value and the market value at any time. Movements in bond yields will affect the demand for other monetary assets and also be a factor determining the economy-wide interest rate.

EXAMPLE 6.1

Real world example: The effect of a change in bond prices

We can also write an expression for our bond example mathematically and show what happens when the current price of the bond changes.

The return on a bond, *B*, can be written:

$$Return\ (B) = \frac{Face\ Value\ (B) - Current\ Price\ (B)}{Current\ Price\ (B)} \times 100$$

In our example, above, we can demonstrate the effect of a fall in the bond price on the interest rate. To start with we use the figures: *Face Value* (*B*) = 110 and *Current Price* (*B*) = 100

$$Return\ (B) = \frac{110 - 100}{100} = 0.1\ or\ 10\%$$

Now let's see what happens when the bond price falls to, say £95. How does this affect the return?

$$Return\ (B) = \frac{110 - 95}{95} = 0.16\ or\ 16\%$$

In the above example, we see that a decrease in the market value of bonds will increase the yield on a bond; in turn this increase will put upward pressure on the interest rate, as banks offering interest bearing accounts have to compete with the bond returns to attract investors' funds. Note that interest rates and bond prices flow in the opposite direction. If there is an expectation that bond prices will fall, as in our example, then there will be upward pressure on the interest rate and vice versa. So how do we connect up the interest rate and the price of bonds in the context of monetary policy? To increase the money supply the central bank can buy bonds as part of its open market operations, this increases the demand for bonds, putting upward pressure on bond prices and thereby decreasing the bond yield and the interest rate together. The money market we have presented above reflects exactly this, where we see an increase in the money supply associated with a lower equilibrium interest rate.

6.3 Financial instruments and derivatives

A financial instrument is defined by international standards as any tradeable contract between financial entities that gives rise to a financial asset. A financial instrument can be securitized by being given a monetary value and traded in a public exchange, though it is worth remembering that not all instruments are necessarily securities and are sold privately between financial institutions.

The promise or contract to repay a loan can itself be part of the broader money supply by being absorbed into a financial derivative. The special nature of how a derivative instrument is derived allows the creation of monetary assets from items such as contracts and agreements about the future. Contracts to repay a loan or agreements to insure future values of commodities can be repackaged as securities by institutions that hold a special licence to do so. These institutions are called special pool vehicles and can themselves add to the broader money supply through the creation of new assets.

Assets born from contracts

So far, in this chapter we have discussed the financial institutions and the financial markets where we have related the buying and selling of bonds to movements in the interest rate. Bonds themselves are a type of financial instrument; they are issued in return for funds borrowed as part of a financial contract, whose value derives from agreements between the two financial entities – in this instance, investors, financial traders and institutions that require lending. It is important to remember that a financial instrument is created from a financial contract, such as a promise to repay a debt or agreement to sell a commodity at a predetermined price. Consequently we see how the contract of a bond between lender and borrower provides a perfect example of a cash instrument.

Financial instruments can be split into two classes: cash instruments such as equities, bonds and mutual funds whose value can be ascertained in financial markets; and derivative instruments which are more complex innovations whose value is derived from a group of underlying assets. The value of a derivative instrument can be determined in both open markets and privately between institutions. The derivative can also be divided up, sold in part or sold in tranches based on risk, in a similar fashion to the way equities are traded. Examples of derivatives are forward contracts, futures and options on financial prices of other types of assets. One particularly interesting derivative instrument is that of the collateralized debt obligation, which groups all kinds of assets including debt-based contracts to be sold to institutional investors in tranches categorized by risk.

Collateralized debt obligations

One financial innovation that stands out as a contributing factor for the global financial crisis and great recession of 2008, is that of the collateralized debt obligation (CDO). The CDO is a financial derivative instrument that brings together a whole range of financial assets – including various types of debt including other cash instruments – into one financial asset that can be traded between institutions. The contents of the CDO will vary in terms of security; meaning that some highly secure debt will be mixed with low security debt. We can also think of a CDO as a soup of different financial assets. The key for this innovation is that it contains tranches of debt ranked by seniority, with the most senior being AAA-rated assets and the most junior in the form of BB or lower-rated (junk) debt. The cash collected by the CDO is prioritized to the senior tranches, meaning that those holding the junior tranches are the first to lose from default of loans within the CDO itself. CDOs are normally only purchased by financial institutions looking for higher returns than that paid by bonds, to pass on to their own investors.

6.4 The 2008 financial crisis

Now that we understand more about money creation and the financial markets we have an opportunity to discuss the 2008 financial crisis, a relatively recent and severe economic event that caused a deep and pronounced global recession. The episode began in 2008, after a long period of positive growth that lasted nearly two decades, probably the longest in recent history for the UK.

Liquidity ratios and the macroeconomic environment in 2008

Policymakers had begun to believe in the mantra that the business cycle had been tamed through successful application of economic policy. Price stability had been achieved through the introduction of independent central banks and the chance of another recession was perceived as highly unlikely. Some policymakers had even taken the bold step of suggesting that the business cycle had been conquered – 'no more boom and bust'.

Accompanying the success of the independent central banks we witness significant deregulation of financial markets, especially in the UK and the USA, that had taken place from the 1980s onwards. Financial innovations such as credit cards and new types of business finance blurred the categorization and definition of money. Further, increased competition from a globalizing banking industry had increased the flow of funds into international capital markets. Commercial banks had become more leveraged and exposed to possible financial collapse, meaning that banks were being allowed to lend with smaller and smaller reserves (as we have learnt in the example of money creation; normally reserves act to underpin losses in the case of widespread loan default).

The higher availability of funds fuelled over-optimism in the housing market with house prices in the USA and the UK growing at much faster rates since the turn of the millennium. When asset prices are growing at a faster rate than normal, we might consider this an episode termed an 'asset price bubble'. House prices were driven higher still by historically low long-run interest rates caused by financial deregulation and an increased willingness to lend. When prices increase we might expect central banks to react by increasing the interest rate but during this period interest rates remained largely static; central banks rarely follow house price inflation and this was no exception in 2008. The 'over exuberance' in the housing market led to loans being offered to US citizens who did not pass the usual requirements of a regular income, assets or employment. This type of mortgage, debt without securitization, was later classified as 'sub-prime' debt.

The consistent house price inflation spilled over into price levels more generally and central banks began to react, albeit belatedly. In the normal course of monetary policy Alan Greenspan, the then chairman of the US Federal Reserve, began to increase US interest rates, steadily and significantly. Increasing mortgage payments for those without income led to large scale default in the 'sub-prime' debt market in the USA. These defaults would not normally have caused such a large global problem, but the worldwide banking system had become interconnected and highly leveraged (essentially the bank's reserves had become too low to absorb the shock of a significant loan default).

The contribution of financial innovations towards the crisis

The availability of 'loose money' was further compounded by the evolution of new financial innovations – assets such as CDOs which contained subprime debt were being rated as AAA and replacing cash on the reserves of commercial banks. Effectively the liquidity ratio was being reduced to close to zero, meaning that money creation was totally unhindered. Accordingly, confidence in the already illiquid banking system collapsed and the financial crisis was underway. Banks whose balance sheets were over-exposed to losses began rebuilding balance sheets by withdrawing lending; this loss of credit for consumers and firms caused a large-scale recession across the globe.

Central banks, who would normally increase aggregate demand through expansionary monetary policy during times like this, could do very little as interest rates were already historically low. Eventually, central banks introduced another financial stimulus called 'quantitative easing', where the central bank offered tier 1 assets (cash) in return for the junk bonds held by commercial banks as reserves. This further stimulus was not a complete success – although it shored up the banking sector, protecting it from collapse, the money did not find its way into the real economy.

Governments who would normally increase government spending to increase aggregate demand during periods of economic slump were also inhibited by the overspending in the run-up to the crisis and proved to be over-indebted themselves. The global economy, without sufficient stimulus from policymakers, entered a severe slowdown, as we can see displayed in Figure 6.1, which shows the percentage growth in real GDP for France, Germany, Italy and worldwide.

EXERCISE 6.1

1. Why did central banks struggle to stimulate demand in reaction to the economic slowdown caused by the financial crisis in 2008?
2. Commercial banks react to loan defaults by ______ the amount of loans available to rebuild reserves.

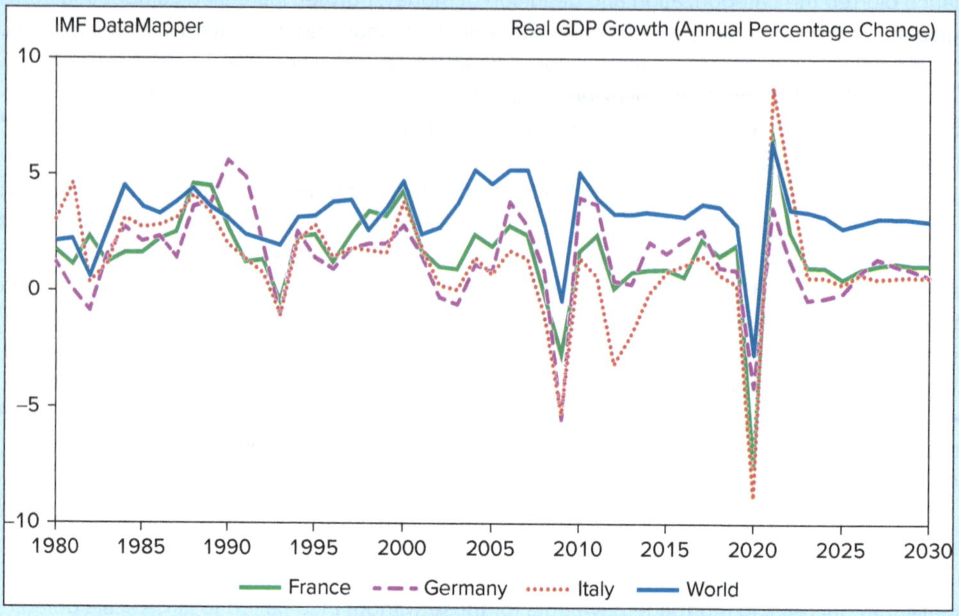

Figure 6.1 Real GDP growth (annual percentage change) for France, Germany, Italy and world, 1980–2030

Source: International Monetary Fund, Real GDP Growth

6.5 Chapter summary: Putting it all together

Chapter 5 and Chapter 6 describe the economy-wide financial system using three distinct areas: financial institutions, financial markets and financial instruments. Explaining the financial system in this way helps to describe the meaning and usefulness of money from the perspectives of the macroeconomist and the financier. Financial markets help us to understand the link between the return on bonds and the interest rate; this exercise is useful because it also helps us to understand how the return from all financial assets are linked by the need to compete for investors' funds.

Our introduction to financial instruments also helps to reinforce our understanding of a property shared by all financial assets. All money is born from the existence of a contract – for financial instruments, this can be an entitlement to a share in collateralized debt, and for central bank money this is the promise to the bearer of notes issued by the central bank.

Finally we have completed our description of the financial crisis of 2008; from Chapter 5 we learnt how low reserves created a crisis of liquidity in the banking system and in this chapter, how the ratings on poorly constructed instruments exacerbated the panic in financial markets, around the same time.

Assessment Question

Discuss the following assertion: 'Money is an illusion: a social construct that relies upon little more than the credibility of the authority that issues it.'

Cases

The financial impact of the COVID-19 pandemic on the UK financial system

Introduction

The COVID-19 pandemic, which began in early 2020, triggered a global economic downturn and significantly disrupted financial markets worldwide. In the UK, the pandemic led to an economic contraction, widespread uncertainty and a shift in investment behaviour. The government's fiscal response, the Bank of England's monetary policy interventions and the economic slowdown all contributed to changes in investor behaviour and affected the performance of various financial assets.

This case study examines the financial impacts of the pandemic on the UK financial system, focusing on investor choices and the movement between different types of financial assets in response to the crisis.

Impact on the UK financial system

1. Economic contraction and financial volatility: The UK economy contracted sharply in 2020 as businesses shut down, unemployment rates rose, and consumer confidence dropped. Financial markets reacted with extreme volatility, as investors scrambled to reassess risks. The FTSE 100 index, a benchmark for the largest UK-listed companies, saw significant declines, falling by nearly 30 per cent from its pre-pandemic highs in early 2020. The pandemic caused investors to reconsider the risk of equities, leading many to shift from more volatile assets like stocks to safer investments, such as government bonds and gold.
2. Government response: The UK government introduced a range of measures to support the economy, including the furlough scheme, grants to businesses and low-interest loans. The Bank of England also cut interest rates to a historic low of 0.1 per cent and introduced large-scale asset purchases through its quantitative easing programme. These actions were aimed at stabilizing financial markets, lowering borrowing costs, and maintaining liquidity in the system. These measures created a favourable environment for certain types of financial assets. The low-interest-rate environment meant that fixed-income assets, such as government bonds, became more attractive, as their yields were relatively higher compared to other low-risk alternatives.
3. Shifts in investor choices between financial assets:
   - *Bonds:* As government bonds became more attractive due to lower interest rates, many investors flocked to these safer assets. The Bank of England's bond-buying programme provided additional liquidity to the bond market, making it an appealing option for investors seeking stability during the uncertainty of the pandemic.
   - *Equities:* The stock market experienced extreme volatility during the early stages of the pandemic. Many sectors, particularly those dependent on physical interactions (e.g., travel, hospitality, retail), saw massive declines in stock prices. In contrast, technology and healthcare sectors (e.g., pharmaceuticals, online services) saw growth as they were viewed as essential during the crisis. As a result, some investors shifted from traditional industries to companies positioned to benefit from pandemic-related trends, such as remote working and healthcare innovation.
   - *Gold and precious metals:* Gold, traditionally viewed as a 'safe haven' asset during times of crisis, saw a significant increase in demand. Investors turned to gold as a store of value amid growing concerns about inflation and the long-term economic impact of the pandemic. The price of gold rose significantly in 2020, reaching its highest levels in nearly a decade.
   - *Real estate:* The real estate market in the UK saw an initial dip in prices due to the uncertainty brought on by the pandemic. However, the government's stamp duty holiday (introduced in July 2020) incentivized buyers, particularly in the housing market, leading to a rapid recovery and even a surge in house prices by the end of 2020 and into 2021.
4. The role of financial derivatives: As the pandemic increased market uncertainty, the use of financial derivatives, such as options and futures, rose. Investors used these tools to hedge against market declines or to speculate

on future market movements. In particular, the volatility index (VIX) saw a sharp rise, reflecting the heightened level of risk in the market. Derivatives markets allowed investors to manage the uncertainty and adjust their portfolios more flexibly.

Conclusion

The COVID-19 pandemic had a profound effect on the UK financial system, creating both challenges and opportunities for investors. The crisis led to a shift in investor preferences, with many moving from equities and more volatile assets to safer assets such as government bonds, gold and certain real estate sectors. Central bank and government interventions helped stabilize the financial system, but the pandemic also highlighted the increasing importance of diversification and risk management in an environment marked by heightened uncertainty.

Questions

1. How did the COVID-19 pandemic affect the performance of the FTSE 100 in early 2020?
2. What role did government interventions, such as the furlough scheme and quantitative easing, play in stabilizing the UK financial system?
3. In what ways did investor choices between different financial assets change as a result of the pandemic?
4. How did the Bank of England's monetary policy, particularly interest rate cuts and asset purchases, influence investor behaviour in financial markets?
5. What role did gold play in the financial system during the pandemic, and why did it see increased demand?
6. How did the real estate market in the UK react to the pandemic, and what government measures helped stimulate recovery in this sector?
7. What role did financial derivatives play during the pandemic, and how did investors use them to manage risk?

Problems

EASY

1. Which of the following is the primary effect of an increase in interest rates on the price of bonds?
   a) Bond prices rise
   b) Bond prices fall
   c) Bond prices remain unchanged
   d) Bond prices fluctuate unpredictably
   e) The interest rate on bonds increases
2. In the context of monetary policy, what is the typical effect of an increase in the central bank's policy rate on the bond market?
   a) Bond yields fall
   b) The price of existing bonds rises
   c) The price of existing bonds falls
   d) Bonds become less liquid
   e) Short-term bonds become riskier

MEDIUM

3. Which of the following distinguishes traditional cash instruments from financial derivative instruments?
    a) Cash instruments derive their value from an underlying asset, while derivatives are independent contracts with no link to an underlying asset
    b) Cash instruments represent direct ownership or debt, while derivative instruments derive their value from the price movements of underlying assets
    c) Cash instruments are primarily used for short-term investment, while derivatives are long-term investment tools
    d) Derivative instruments are used only by central banks, while cash instruments are used by private investors
    e) Cash instruments do not involve any risk, while derivatives are highly risk-averse
4. Which of the following best describes a collateralized debt obligation (CDO)?
    a) A government bond that is backed by real estate
    b) A complex financial instrument that pools various forms of debt and divides it into tranches
    c) A savings account for high-net-worth individuals
    d) A short-term loan issued by a central bank
    e) A type of insurance policy against defaults on corporate bonds
5. The global financial crisis of 2008 was partly attributed to which of the following?
    a) The collapse of oil prices
    b) The widespread use of CDOs and the mispricing of risk
    c) High levels of inflation in emerging markets
    d) A dramatic increase in the price of gold
    e) The collapse of stock market indices
6. How important are liquidity ratios for ensuring financial stability in banks and other financial institutions?
    a) Liquidity ratios are not important, as they do not impact financial stability
    b) Liquidity ratios are crucial in ensuring that institutions can meet short-term obligations and avoid insolvency, especially in times of market stress
    c) Liquidity ratios are only relevant for long-term investments, not for financial stability
    d) High liquidity ratios always indicate that a bank is financially stable
    e) Liquidity ratios are not monitored by regulatory authorities
7. Suppose an investor purchases a bond with a face value of £1,000 that pays a coupon rate of 6 per cent annually. The investor holds the bond for one year, and at the end of the year, the bond price has risen to £1,050. What is the investor's total return on the bond over the one-year period?

    (Assume the bond pays a coupon of £60 for the year, calculated as 6 per cent of £1,000. And that the return is calculated as the proportional total return on the initial investment.)

HARD

8. Explain how changes in monetary policy, particularly changes in interest rates, can affect the price and yield of government bonds. How does this relationship impact the wider economy, particularly consumer spending and investment?
9. Discuss the role of CDOs in the 2008 financial crisis. How did the widespread use and mismanagement of CDOs contribute to the global economic downturn?

CHAPTER 7

The Market for Goods and Services I

Chapter contents

At a Glance The market for goods and services I

The issue

In Chapter 4, in our overview of macroeconomic modelling, we introduced the circular flow model. This model describes the economy in terms of opposite and equal flows: the monetary flow and the real flow. The goods market discussed in the following two chapters concerns itself with the real flow of goods and services around the economy.

The understanding

In this chapter we use the categories of expenditure to model the market for goods and services, the real flow in the economy. Combined with John Maynard's proposition that the economy is demand driven, we build the Keynesian cross model. In turn, this model helps us to explain how fiscal policy transmits to the real economy. Combining this with the market for money we can make an important analysis of the financial effects of government policy choices.

The usefulness

Understanding the difference between the financial and real flows in the economy helps us to delineate the analysis of economic policy. By introducing the market for goods and services, we begin to see how macroeconomics as a science presents perspectives on economic activity: the money perspective, the goods perspective and the labour perspective.

7.1 Introduction

The model of the goods market makes use of the Keynesian idea that changes in activity can be driven by aggregate demand. This model provides us with our first explanation of the short-run deviations in output from its trend. In order to build this model, we will need to assume that prices are fixed so that economic policy can provide real effects (changes in output). Given that central banks have achieved relative price stability in developed economies more recently this seems to be a reasonable assumption. Even if (in reality) prices are not fixed then we can at least think of them as adjusting slowly, or sticky. Sticky prices imply an upward sloping aggregate supply schedule and as such a prediction of policy effectiveness (a policy-led change in aggregate demand leads to a change in output).

In the circular flow model, we learnt that the flow of money was equal and opposite to the real flow in the economy; imbalances between the withdrawals and injections led to a change in the flow of goods and services. Increases in the real flow must be met by equal and opposite changes in the flow of money. The concept of sticky prices allows us to explain something that the circular flow cannot – that a change in the money supply can also lead to change in the real sector, an idea first shown in the quantity equation in Chapter 5, where we connected the money and goods market.

What exactly do we mean by goods and services? The answer is the aggregated sum of all goods and services bought by consumers or produced by firms in the economy. Remember that two ways of describing GDP are the sum of money spent on goods and services (expenditure) and the sum of products actually produced. The two are equivalent in equilibrium, but otherwise we can think of the difference as the change in the firm's level of inventories. If expenditure is lower than actual production then the firm will accumulate higher stock levels. The Keynesian view is that this change in inventories is a driving force behind changes in the real economy, the change in stock levels is classified as inventory investment; it encapsulates demand.

Planned expenditure represents aggregate demand and provides the driving force for output in this model. The split of GDP into its components helps us to explain both actual and planned expenditure with the condition that expenditure equals output in equilibrium. With aggregate demand explained in this way, we can revisit the Keynesian Cross model that shows how output is determined through the equilibrium condition that aggregate supply should at least eventually equal aggregate demand. We can also show how the predictions of this model are equivalent to the model of the market for loanable funds.

In this chapter, we introduce the market for goods and services and learn more about how the government can manage economic activity through **fiscal policy**. We measure the magnitude of these effects on the real economy using a concept called **the multiplier**. We will also present the classical argument once more that policy is ineffective using the concept of

Fiscal Policy: The action taken by the government to stabilize the economy using changes in the levels of government expenditure or taxation.
The Multiplier: the factor by which an increase in government expenditure will increase output. This factor depends on the marginal propensity to consume.

crowding out and use the loanable funds market to underpin this. Later we extend our model to encompass the reality of international trade in a small open economy and show how the exchange rate, determined in the market for foreign exchange, also has real effects. Finally, we can use our knowledge to discuss the pathology and modern problem of global imbalances in international trade.

Learning Outcomes

By the end of this chapter you should be able to:

- Categorize gross domestic product into the components of expenditure.
- Explain the implications of fiscal policy by applying the Keynesian cross model.
- Illustrate the government purchases multiplier and the crowding out effect.
- Modify the market for goods and services to encompass the open economy.
- Evaluate the economic pathology of global trade imbalances.

7.2 The components of gross domestic product

As we have mentioned in the introduction, the role of the model we call the 'market for goods and services' is to provide an explanation for short-run fluctuations in output. The model simply requires that we separate the components of GDP into three or four categories; three in the case of a closed economy and four in the case of an open economy. An open economy trades with outside economies via the sale of exports and purchase of imports; a closed economy does not engage in international trade.

EXAMPLE 7.1

Real world example: How true to life is the closed economy?

In the subject of macroeconomics we often refer to a baseline class of models called closed economy versions. The closed economy is one that does not trade across borders. This baseline simplification is convenient for macroeconomic modelling because it avoids the complication surrounding exchange rate movements.

In reality there are fewer and fewer examples of such economics and so you might ask what relevance to real life, or what purpose, can this type of model offer?

One way to think about this and bring this baseline model class back to modern day relevance is to view the closed economy as the 'global economy'. The increasing amount of international trade that now takes place across the world means that countries and domestic business cycles are becoming more aligned.

This is an interesting proposition for a classroom discussion. Can we think of the global economy as our real life example of the closed economy?

Consumption, investment and government spending

To help us model the market for goods and services we can make use of a simple categorization. We can split aggregate expenditure three ways into consumption, investment and government spending. This allows us to present expenditure as an identity made up of its individual parts. Our first component of gross domestic product is consumption, and this is modelled by the **consumption function**. To model consumption is quite simple, we can say that consumption depends on household disposable income. This statement requires little further foundation as it is quite intuitive (the more money we have the more we are likely to spend).

Consumption Function: The behavioural equation that describes consumption as linearly dependent on disposable income ($Y - T$).

In this model, there is an assumption that the functional form for consumption is linear and always positive. The consumption function captures the behaviour of consumers and we will often see it simply expressed as:

$$C = a + b(Y - T)$$

where C is aggregate consumption, a is autonomous consumption (our minimum consumption regardless of income), Y is income, T is taxation and b represents the fraction of disposable income $(Y - T)$ that is consumed. What is not consumed is saved and deposited into banks, who in turn can invest the funds into firms who require investment. The parameter b is also quite special – it is the slope of the consumption function but also a parameter that we call the marginal propensity to consume (MPC). We can see immediately by inspection of the functional form above, that consumption C is positively related to disposable income $(Y - T)$. In Figure 7.1 we see this graphically.

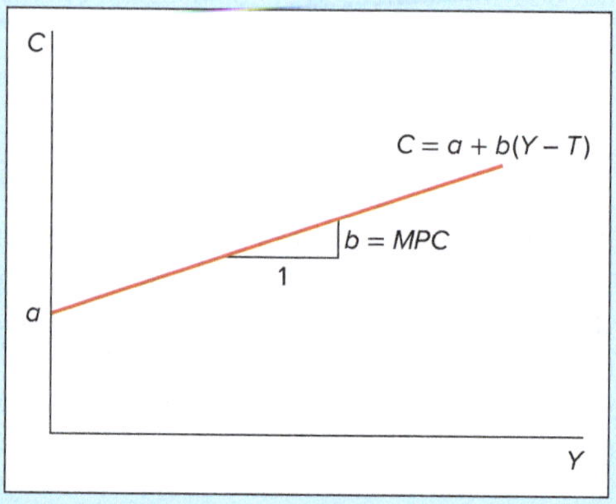

Figure 7.1 The consumption function showing the positive relation between goods and services consumed by households and disposable income

Even with disposable income $(Y - T)$ at zero, we can see from our figure that there is always some autonomous consumption, as indicated by a, and that as disposable income increases so does consumption. This autonomous consumption is funded by borrowing, or dissaving. The rate at which our consumption increases as income increases is given by the slope of the consumption function – the MPC – and is a key structural parameter in the model.

Investment Function: The behavioural equation that describes non-residential and residential investment as dependent positively on output and negatively on the interest rate.

The second component of GDP is investment, and this is modelled using the **investment function**. Intuitively we associate investment with the type of expenditure that will bring us higher income in the future. Remember that investment is not the same as saving, purchasing a financial product at the bank is often termed as such but in economics, we make a distinction; we do not include these types of 'financial investments' within our definition. Think of investment as something we 'borrow' to do; firms and households borrow in order to invest. When consumers buy financial products (even those labelled as investments), they are saving in the context of macroeconomics, and this saving is money not spent from income.

A typical form for the investment function is shown below:

$$I = c - d(r)$$

From the negative sign in front of $d(r)$ we can see that investment is downward sloping in the interest rate, reflecting the reality that higher interest rates deter firms and households from investing (or borrowing to invest) in plant, machinery and housing.

There are three types of investment:

- **Non-residential investment – firms buying plant and machinery with production in mind**
- **Residential investment – households buying buildings to be used as dwellings/homes**
- **Inventory investment – firms producing more than they are selling; building up stocks for sale later.**

Importantly we do not include inventory investment in the components of GDP; instead this type of investment helps us to account for other macroeconomic realities such as the difference between sales and production. We can even think of inventory investment as reflecting changes in aggregate demand, or as representing the transition of aggregate demand into actual production. Figure 7.2 is a graphical representation of a typical investment function.

The investment function in Figure 7.2 shows investment as downward sloping in the interest rate, in a similar fashion to our mathematical expression above. Notice here that the investment function $I(Y, r)$ is drawn non-linear and expressed implicitly as depending on the interest rate *and* output. This is because in reality investment is driven by both; when sales of firms are higher investment is higher and when interest rates are higher investment is lower. It is quite common to see investment assumed as exogenous (written $\bar{I}$) but you should keep in mind that it is a variable dependent on both Y and r. In macroeconomics, we often use a bar on top of a variable to indicate that it is assumed exogenous or fixed.

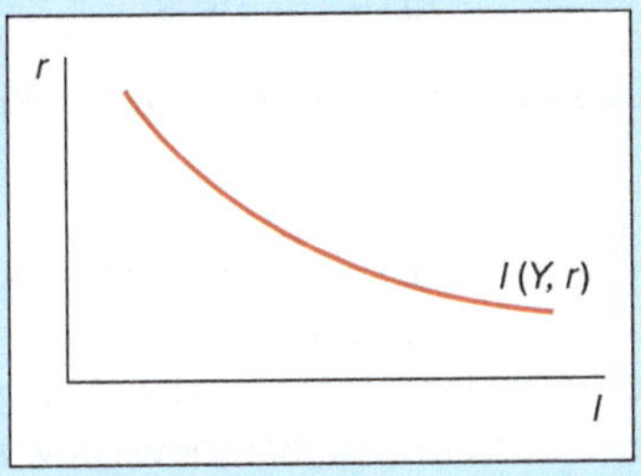

Figure 7.2 The investment function showing the negative relation between investment and the interest rate

Government Expenditure: The amount that the government spends on goods and services excluding transfer payments. We use changes in this exogenous variable to measure the effects of policy in our model.

The third component of gross domestic product is **government expenditure**, which is simply the amount spent by government on goods and services. In most cases it is assumed exogenous – in other words, set by government independently – and thus we write it as $\bar{G}$, Perhaps, in reality, government spending may be cyclical (depending on the level of economic activity), but this is not normally modelled as such, especially in smaller-scale models. Assuming government spending is set this way is convenient in that it enables us to use this variable to measure the model's prediction from changes in government expenditure, or government spending shocks.

There are, however, a couple of important identifying assumptions for this component of expenditure – government spending does *not* include transfers such as social welfare payments and also does not include the interest payments on government debt. Lastly, we also specify taxes exogenous in the same way as government spending and write taxation simply as $\bar{T}$. The variables for government spending $\bar{G}$ alongside taxation $\bar{T}$ make up the two exogenous policy variables which combine to describe fiscal policy, as we will see later.

Now that we have described the three components of expenditure in this way we can write out an identity that must hold by design – that total demand in the economy must be equal to the sum of its individual parts:

$$AD = C + I + G$$

In words: aggregate demand (planned aggregate expenditure) is equal to the sum of consumption, investment and government expenditure.

EXERCISE 7.1

1. How does an increase in income affect consumption in our model?
2. By what percentage does consumption change in Question 1 when income increases?

Equilibrium in the goods market

To complete the model, we need only specify the condition that aggregate supply is equal to aggregate demand in equilibrium. The proposition that firms will supply the amount demanded in the market is highly intuitive; if a supplier of electrical equipment sees that their shelves are emptying quicker, they will soon learn to stock more goods. As a real life example, we can think of the period in the run-up to the annual seasonal holidays such as Christmas when suppliers anticipate a rise in demand.

We can model aggregate supply using the production function, which is a commonly used explanation of aggregate supply in the economy. The production function predicts that total supply will be determined by the factors of production, labour and capital, that exist in the economy.

An increase in capital or labour enable an increase in production:

$$Y = F(K, L)$$

and aggregate demand:

$$AD = C + I + G$$

Then by equating aggregate supply with demand we have an equilibrium condition:

$$Y = C + I + G$$

Remember that this equilibrium condition assumes that firms follow demand immediately; there are no dynamics of adjustment in this model. Let us now view a graphical representation of this model and discuss the dynamic adjustment via the model of the Keynesian cross that we first discussed in Chapter 4. The Keynesian cross model shows how aggregate demand determines equilibrium output in the economy.

This model is framed in a two-dimensional analysis between actual output Y and aggregate demand AD. We have learnt how demand 'drives' output, so where the aggregate demand curve (which represent the components of GDP) crosses the equilibrium line $AD = Y$ is where demand will push suppliers to produce in equilibrium at Y^*. In this model, adjustment from one equilibrium to another is assumed to be instantaneous but in reality we know that it is not.

Imagine the case that actual output is in fact to the left of the equilibrium at Y^*; this scenario is mapped by the red line in Figure 7.3. At this level of output we see that demand in the economy is above actual output (blue line is above black line). There is excess demand in the economy and stock is being purchased from shelves faster than firms have anticipated. Firms experience an unanticipated drop in stocks (there is a drop in inventory investment) and so react by increasing aggregate supply; output rises until it reaches the equilibrium predicted in our graph – notice that there is a natural driving force towards equilibrium (the difference between demand and actual output). Inventory investment is the reaction to this difference; firms build up and run down stock levels and this drives changes in production. Using the aggregate demand identity, we can also take a first look at the reaction of the economy to an increase in government expenditure, also known as fiscal policy:

$$(\uparrow AD) = C + I + (\uparrow G)$$

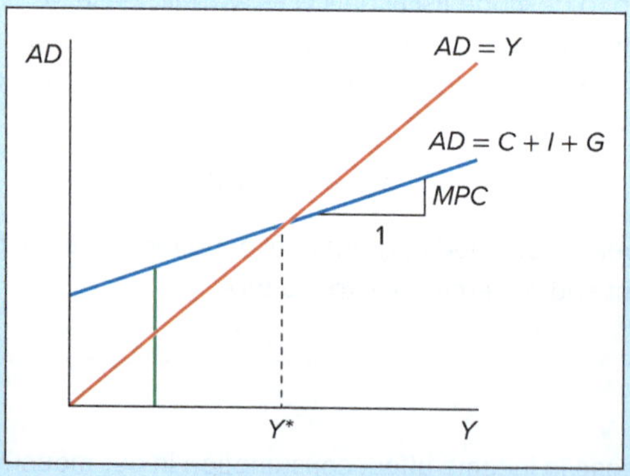

Figure 7.3 The Keynesian cross model explains how the economy moves towards equilibrium output

Using the aggregate demand identity, we can see that an increase in G leads to an increase in aggregate demand which, using our model, must lead to an increase in output toward equilibrium.

In Figure 7.4 we see this prediction in more detail. The economy begins initially in equilibrium with output at Y_1^* where the aggregate demand function crosses the equilibrium line. An increase in government expenditure from G_1 to G_2 shifts the aggregate demand line upwards (to blue line). Now we see that the Keynesian cross model predicts that an increase in government spending leads to an increase in output. The same scenario applies for exogenous increases in consumption and investment; that is, increases in consumption and investment not caused by changes in Y.

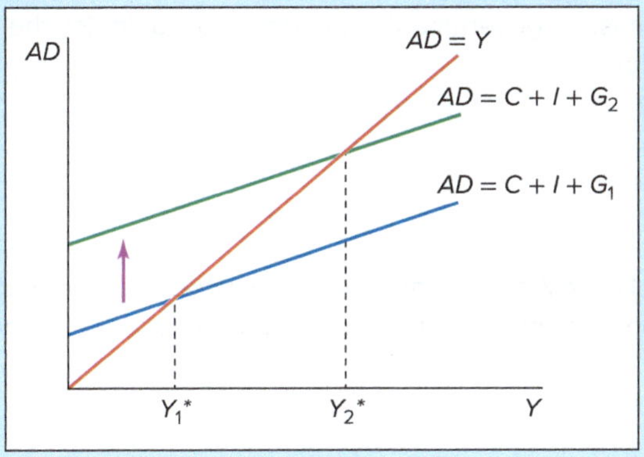

Figure 7.4 The Keynesian cross model and an increase in government expenditure

7.3 Fiscal policy and the multiplier

Two key roles governments play in society are the provision of public goods and services and a maintenance of economic stability, the latter being something we can think of as demand management. The government manages aggregate demand with the aim of smoothing economic fluctuations so that at least recessions might be avoided. In this section, we will focus on the purpose of macroeconomic stabilization via fiscal policy.

A lack of intervention of some kind during an economic slowdown can lead to a loss of confidence in financial markets, an ensuing withdrawal of loanable funds and a sharp reduction in output; this downward spiral can fuel a further loss of available credit leading to an even deeper recession. When fear grips the economy in this way we need some resort or ultimate intervention to stop the panicked self-defeating actions of economic agents acting in their own interest rather than society's interest.

It is intuitive to understand that in the event of a fire we need a fire marshal and in the same way government stabilization exists to intervene in extraordinary times. The view that intervention is useful to smooth out economic activity is not universally agreed upon, however. We have already discussed in Chapter 4 the two views of economic thought and we are revisiting this in more detail.

Fiscal policy

Fiscal policy can be defined as the actions taken by a government to actively manage aggregate demand. This involves using the two exogenous variables of government spending G and taxation T, with the aim of smoothing fluctuations in output and unemployment. These fluctuations are something that we call the economic business cycle; where economic growth fluctuates around its average, driven by unpredictable demand- and supply-side shocks. Without intervention, these shocks produce oscillations in output that can be damaging to the economy, leading to unwanted recessions and economic booms. However, the use of fiscal policy in the management of the economy is not without its problems. There is:

- **a question of fiscal policy effectiveness**
- **a problem of identifying the origin of shocks (supply or demand side)**
- **an unpredictability of the lag between policy and realized effect.**

The question of fiscal policy effectiveness is central in the debate between our two competing schools of economic thought discussed in Chapter 4 (the Keynesian and classical views). If prices are flexible, then fiscal policy is ineffective and an increase in aggregate demand leads to no change in output; whereas if prices are fixed then policy will lead to an increase in output (a real effect). So, the justification of fiscal policy relies on the predictions of economic models such as the Keynesian cross.

The second problem for a policymaker is posed by the problem of identification – is a sudden observed movement in output caused by a supply-side shock or a demand-side shock? Policymakers should only resort to demand-side policy if the economy is hit by a demand-side shock. Reacting to a negative supply shock – such as an increase in the global oil price – with an increase in government expenditure G would risk the long-run unintended outcome of high inflation.

EXERCISE 7.2

Use the AD/AS model described in Chapter 4 to show the predicted outcome of expansionary fiscal policy after a negative supply shock has hit the economy.

The third problem for policymakers is the problem of policy lags. For instance, how long does it take for an increase in government expenditure to effect output as intended? You might reasonably consider that if the lag between policy and effect is known then the government can take this into account when deciding on the correct policy choice.

The reality is that the exact length of lag can only be approximated and, even then, the reaction of output can be dynamic in itself; the government policy shock may have a short *and* long-term effect – in this case, we say that the shock has persistence. Even if the lag is predictable and the government takes this into account, the future path of output is entirely unpredictable. As an example, imagine that output is falling and the government is reacting by increasing expenditure to reverse an economic decline; given a policy lag of six months, it is reasonable to guess that the government should stop increasing expenditure six months before the economy starts to expand again.

The problem is that the government can only guess when the downturn in economic activity will appear in the future and so will actually carry on increasing expenditure right up and until the economy reverses. The economy will have unnecessary stimulus and this will then lead to output growing faster than needed. This is an example of how demand management can distort the economy rather than stabilize it. Of course, the problem of lags and distortionary policy is not limited to the enactment of fiscal policy; it is also a problem for the central bank (another policymaker involved in demand management).

When we model fiscal policy, we do so with government expenditure G assumed fixed or exogenous; it is a variable that we can use to shock the economy from one equilibrium to another. Taxation is normally treated the same way, though we can also specify taxation as endogenously dependent on income to give our model a more realistic specification. When we specify tax as endogenous on output/income we write it as:

$$T = t(Y) = tY$$

Taxation T is a function of income, normally income multiplied by the tax rate, t.

Exogenous taxation, also known as lump sum taxation, is set by the government and can be written:

$$T = \overline{T}.$$

From this point forward we can maintain some simplicity by using lump sum taxation in our description of the government.

The government purchases multiplier

So far we have explained that an increase in government expenditure will lead to an increase in output, but we have not explained by how much output will change. The one-for-one change in output predicted by the aggregate demand identity neglects the reaction of consumption to the new level of income in the economy. In fact, the increase in government expenditure set off a chain reaction in the circular flow. Let us look again at the system of equations that make up the model for our economy and make the simplifying assumption that investment I, government expenditure G and taxation T are exogenously set:

$$Y = C + I + G$$
$$C = a + b(Y - T)$$

where $I = \bar{I}$ and $G = \bar{G}$ and $T = \bar{T}$.

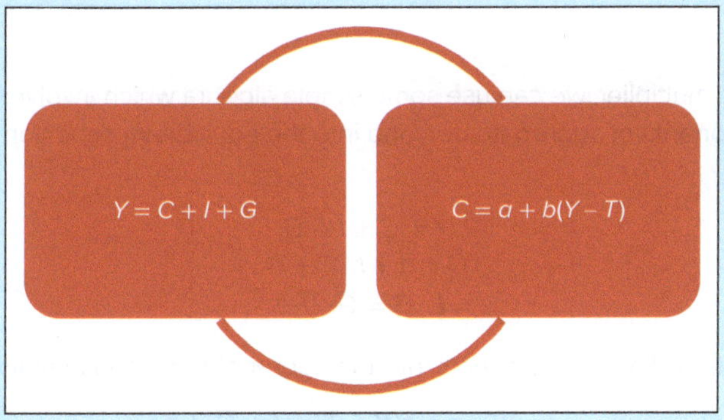

Figure 7.5 Fiscal policy and the multiplier

You will notice that in the first two equations output Y and consumption C are both right- and left-hand side variables. There is no clear causality here as the first equation tells us that consumption drives output and the second that output drives consumption. So which is correct? Actually, in our model both are correct – an increase in consumption C will cause an increase in output Y, but this will increase consumption further, which will then increase output again. You may have noticed an everlasting loop and the reason that output does not increase one for one with an increase in government spending G.

We will now take a closer look.

As an example, we can use the case of expansionary fiscal policy (an increase in G). The initial increase in government spending will lead to a one-for-one increase in output (by the aggregate demand identity). However, this increase in income will also lead to an increase in consumption (by the consumption function). This process continues endlessly – except the amount that consumption increases is not one for one in each period, it is reduced each time by the parameter b (as $0 < b < 1$). Remember that b is the marginal propensity to consume (MPC).

When consumption increases by the proportion b, the following increase in output is always smaller than the previous. So each time output increases, it does so by a lesser amount until the increases are eventually zero and it reaches the new equilibrium. To see this another way, it may be good to use a numerical example, as in Example 7.2.

EXAMPLE 7.2

Worked example: A numerical example of the multiplier in practice

We begin with the following economic system:

Equation 7.1: $Y = C + I + G$

Equation 7.2: $C = 100 + 0.5(Y)$

where $I = 50$ and $G = 100$

Imagine that G increases from 100 to 120, what will be the change in output?

Round 1 Y increases by 20 (Eq. 7.1) and consumption increases by 0.5(20) = 10 (Eq. 7.2)

Round 2 Y increases by 10 (Eq. 7.1) and consumption increases by 0.5(10) = 5 (Eq. 7.2)

Round 3 Y increases by 5 (Eq. 7.1) and consumption increases by 0.5(5) = 2.5 (Eq. 7.2)

Round 3 Y increases by 2.5 (Eq. 7.1) and consumption increases by 0.5(2.5) = 1.25 (Eq. 7.2)

The process continues with the increase in Y becoming smaller and smaller. In fact, the increases will eventually become very close to zero, so that in the limit we can say that the increase will stop as we reach the new equilibrium. But even though we understand the path of the increase in output how can we calculate it exactly?

To calculate the multiplier, we can use some simple algebra which involves substituting the individual components of aggregate demand into the equilibrium condition and solving for output.

$$Y = C + I + G$$
$$C = a + b(Y - T)$$
$$I = \bar{I} \quad G = \bar{G} \quad T = \bar{T}$$

We start by substituting all the components into the aggregate demand identity:

$$Y = a + b(Y - \bar{T}) + \bar{I} + \bar{G}$$

Multiplying the consumption function out gives:

$$Y = a + bY - b\bar{T} + \bar{I} + \bar{G}$$

Moving terms in Y to the left-hand side (LHS):

$$Y - bY = a - b\bar{T} + \bar{I} + \bar{G}$$

Using Y as a common factor on the LHS:

$$(1 - b)Y = a - b\bar{T} + \bar{I} + \bar{G}$$

Dividing through by $(1 - b)$ solves our system for output:

$$Y = (a - b\bar{T} + \bar{I} + \bar{G})\frac{1}{(1 - b)}$$

This is the solution for equilibrium output in our economic system but it also helps us to see the algebraic expression in terms of the multiplier. It is easier now to see how much output changes when government spending changes: it is by the factor $\frac{1}{(1 - b)}$.

As b is also the MPC, we can write the multiplier as:

$$\frac{1}{1 - MPC}$$

This expression for the government expenditure multiplier assumes exogenous (or lump sum) taxation.

EXERCISE 7.3

As an exercise replace lump sum taxation with endogenous taxation and calculate the adapted expression for the multiplier.

7.4 Allowing for the open economy

A simple way to capture the open economy in the market for goods and services is to extend our income identity for the open economy. We can do this simply by adding a fourth category of expenditure: net exports (*NX*).

Net exports and net capital outflow

Including international trade as a component of GDP means that we can extend our aggregate demand identity as follows:

$$Y = C + I + G + NX$$

$$\text{where } NX = (X - M).$$

GDP can be split into total consumption, investment, government expenditure and net exports (exports minus imports). It matters to policymakers whether or not net exports are positive or negative just as it would to a private business if sales were greater than costs. If exports are greater than imports, then the country is running a **trade surplus** and vice versa for a deficit.

> **Trade Surplus:** Net exports are positive because exports are greater than imports.

We can use the differentiation between the real side and the money side of the economy to help us represent international trade in terms of the flows of funds (capital) instead of goods. When we are exporting, we consider that we are saving, as we send goods and receive foreign currency in return, and when we are importing we can imagine that we are investing. To reconcile this, we will take a more detailed look in Example 7.3 at the actual transactions involved with trade.

EXAMPLE 7.3

Real world example: Why exports are considered as saving and imports as investment

Saving (lending)

When we 'export' we supply goods to foreign consumers who will need to buy our currency to pay for them. To do that they will have to supply their own currency, which is a form of debt. We accumulate foreign currency – other countries owe us money and we are said to be saving.

Investing (borrowing)

When we 'import' we purchase goods from foreign producers and supply our domestic currency to purchase foreign exchange as a means of payment in return. We are supplying our own currency (our debt) and borrowing from other countries who will now hold our currency – in this case we are said to be investing.

Trade between China and the USA

China exports goods to the USA and in return imports a much smaller amount of goods from the USA. When a Chinese producer sells to an American he will want to be paid in yuan (not dollars). To pay for the goods the American must first exchange dollars for yuan.

The Bank of China will accumulate dollars during this transaction, selling yuan to the American in return for dollars. Ultimately the goods have arrived in the USA and dollars have arrived in China. As the dollars are just US debt we can say that America is borrowing from China by this transaction. China is 'saving' while the US is 'investing' (it is borrowing money to invest).

In the closed economy, savings were equal to investment and the interest rate adjusted to ensure this in the loanable funds model. In the open economy, the interest rate is fixed at r^* and the difference between saving and investment is something that we can term the 'international flow of funds', which we call net capital outflow (*NCO*):

$$NCO = S - I$$

Net capital outflow is the difference between national saving and national investment. This is a good opportunity to revisit our understanding – that the real flow of goods is always equal and opposite to the flow of money – and we can demonstrate this starting from the goods market and focusing on the relationship between net exports (real flow) and net capital outflow (monetary flow).

We know from the aggregate demand identity that:

$$Y = C + I + G + NX$$

which we can rearrange in terms of net exports:

$$NX = Y - (C + I + G)$$

or

$$NX = (Y - C - G) - I$$

Also, remember that national saving is equal to income minus consumption by households and government:

$$S = (Y - C - G)$$

which we can substitute into the previous equation to write:

$$NX = S - I$$

and given that savings minus investment is actually net capital outflow:

$$NX = NCO$$

Trade Deficit: Net exports are negative because imports are greater than exports.

The net balance of international trade in goods and services is equal to the net balance of the flow of international funds. We can see that if a country is running a **trade deficit** then this will require a net capital 'inflow'. A country that is running a persistent trade deficit will end up as a debtor nation (a borrowing nation) and a country running a persistent surplus (a lending nation). The existence of these persistent surpluses and deficits is the cause for imbalances in world trade, which we refer to as 'global imbalances', discussed in the next section.

EXERCISE 7.4

Check for yourself that national saving is equal to income minus consumption minus government expenditure, in other words that: $S = (Y - C - G)$.

Use the equation for national saving given earlier in the section on crowding out: $S = S(p) + S(g)$, remembering that public saving $S(g) = T - G$.

7.5 Global imbalances

We have seen that the trade balance is driven by changes in the exchange rate and that the exchange rate itself is driven by changes in macroeconomic performance. The export and import of goods and services are also reflected by the level of savings and investment in an economy. We can also consider the international effects of these changes. If a country is more competitive in terms of the price for a good, then normally there will be a flow of goods from the more competitive country to the less competitive one and an opposite and equal flow of capital in the other direction. If this continues one way, then surely this must lead to a global imbalance of capital around the world?

The answer is yes, except that there is a global balancing mechanism which we have already discussed – the exchange rate. If a country is more competitive then it will attract capital, but this will have a positive effect on its exchange rate, which will – in turn – have a dampening effect on the trade balance (exports will start to fall back and imports will start to rise). This is the natural correction for world trade – the exchange rate has a natural levelling effect between trading partners.

In reality, this is a little more complicated. What if a country does not allow its exchange rate to be freely determined in the international foreign exchange market? How can this rebalancing take place if the currency rate is fixed? What if the government forces its central bank to intervene (sell and buy currency) in a bid to keep the rate of exchange artificially low to remain competitive for longer? If the exchange rate is not allowed to adjust freely then a country can maintain a competitive advantage. Maintaining competitiveness is highly desirable from a political perspective; domestic producers will have higher revenue, unemployment will be low and income higher.

With these incentives ingrained, global imbalances exist and are hard to overcome; with active intervention in foreign exchange markets, a currency can be manipulated to ensure that trade flows one way and capital the other. Global imbalances are caused where the exchange rate is kept artificially low by a government and are a common issue for such institutions as the World Trade Organization (WTO), whose purpose it is to address these imbalances through negotiations. Let us recap using our knowledge so far, to picture how global imbalances come about.

In the example in Figure 7.6 we can see how Country A, which starts as more competitive, maintains its advantage over Country B by manipulating its currency. Of course, we have imagined that Country B cannot retaliate by manipulating its own currency in return.

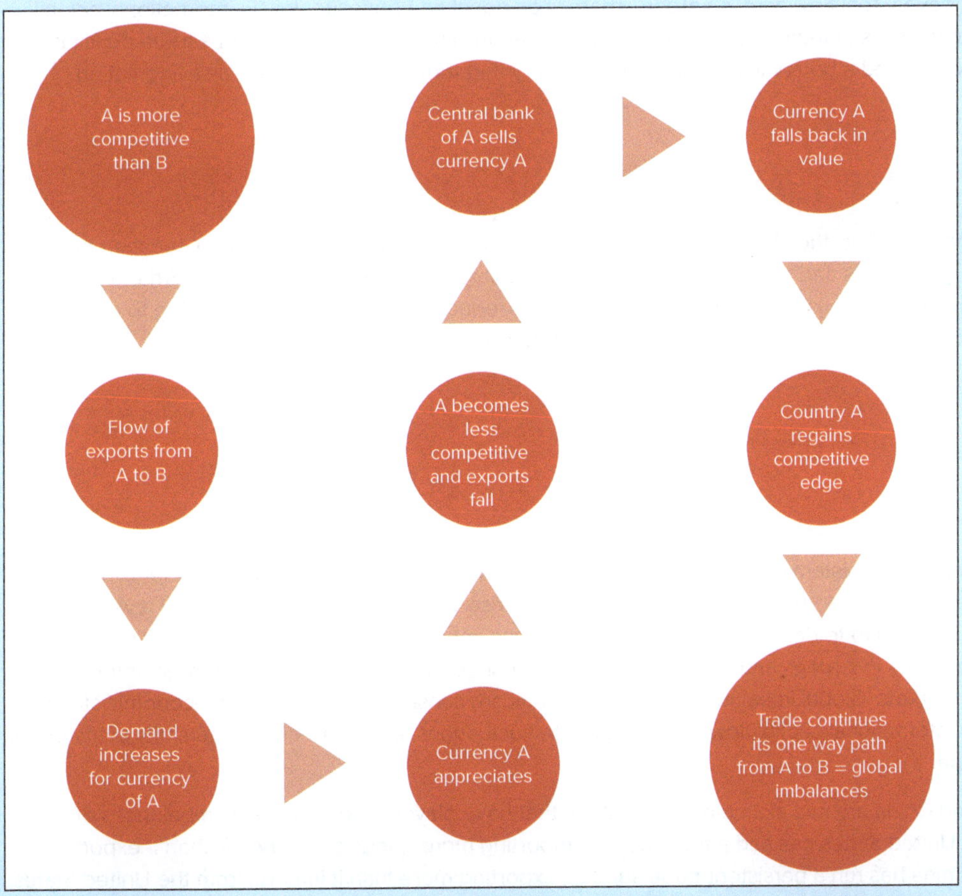

Figure 7.6 A flow chart showing how Country A might maintain competitive advantage over Country B

We call the scenario of countries intervening in currency markets (maybe retaliating for one another's interventions) a 'currency war'. Countries fight to keep their real exchange rates low in a bid to keep a bigger slice of international trade. In a globalized world the relative share of international trade as a component of GDP is also increasing and policymakers are applying a greater attention to international trade policy.

7.6 Chapter summary: Putting it all together

In this chapter, we have learnt about the market for goods and services and the monetary equivalent version of the model called the loanable funds market. The market for goods and services relies on the ability to distinguish between the components of gross domestic product; consumption, investment, government spending and net exports. One of the easiest ways to model any variable is by expressing it in terms of its components – a simple but totally valid way to model almost anything. The loanable funds market version makes use of investment and savings to explain the monetary effects of changes in the goods market.

Splitting expenditure into its components has allowed us to discuss the difference between demand and actual output and to learn the advanced monetary effects of fiscal policy. The model for the goods market helps us to understand the concept of the government expenditure multiplier. Understanding how net exports contributes towards the makeup of GDP has enabled us to offer an early understanding of the open economy and further this by describing the driving forces behind the trade balance.

Finally, we have introduced a basic understanding of the real world pathology of global imbalances brought about by the unequal distribution of international trade. Remembering that: for every real flow across borders, there is an equal and opposite flow in international capital; imbalances in trade cause imbalances in a nations finances; a country with a trade deficit is considered a borrowing nation, and a country that runs a trade surplus is a saving nation.

Assessment Question

During the recent financial crisis, the ability of governments to service their debt was called into question by financial market rating agencies and led to the downgrade of credit ratings for various countries. Write an essay on whether governments should use an increase in taxation or a reduction in government spending to address a budget deficit in a bid to calm the financial markets that service its debt.

Cases

Global imbalances between China and the United States

Global imbalances refer to persistent disparities in international trade between global trading partners. In the context of the market for goods and services, these imbalances arise when countries have unequal levels of exports and imports, leading to trade surpluses and deficits. These imbalances are often the result of various factors, such as differences in savings and investment rates, exchange rate policies and government interventions in foreign exchange markets. Global imbalances can have significant consequences for global economic stability, including volatility in international capital flows, exchange rate fluctuations, economic crises and shifts in the global geopolitical landscape.

The United States and China are two examples of countries that have played a central role in imbalances of trade. For years, the United States has had a trade deficit, importing more goods and services than it exports to China. By contrast, China has run a persistent trade surplus, exporting more than it imports from the United States. This imbalance has been partially driven by the United States' high consumption levels and China's low domestic consumption combined with its role as a global manufacturing hub.

The consequences of these imbalances are felt in various ways. For the United States, a trade deficit can lead to an accumulation of foreign debt, affecting the value of the dollar and the country's economic policies. On the other hand, China's trade surplus results in large foreign reserves, particularly in US denominated assets, influencing its currency policies and contributing to global flows of capital.

These imbalances are not without risks. Persistent trade deficits can weaken a country's currency and lead to higher borrowing costs because of lower demand for government bonds, while trade surpluses may cause inflationary pressures and trade tensions. Efforts to address global imbalances often involve adjustments in exchange rates, fiscal policies and trade agreement negotiations.

Questions

1. What is meant by 'global imbalances' in the context of the market for goods and services?
2. Why do countries like the United States and China experience different trade balances?
3. What are some of the economic consequences of persistent global imbalances?
4. How can trade deficits lead to changes in exchange rates and foreign debt?
5. What policy tools could countries use to address global imbalances in trade?

Problems

EASY

1. Which of the following is NOT a component of national expenditure in the Keynesian cross model?
   a) Consumption (C)
   b) Investment (I)
   c) Government spending (G)
   d) Exports (X)
   e) Savings (S)
2. The marginal propensity to consume (MPC) is defined as:
   a) The change in government spending divided by the change in national income.
   b) The ratio of consumption to income at any given point in time.
   c) The change in consumption divided by the change in income.
   d) The portion of income saved rather than spent.
   e) The total amount of goods and services consumed by the economy.
3. What is the longer run effect of a country experiencing a net capital inflow from its net exports?
   a) Net exports increase.
   b) Net exports decrease.
   c) Net exports remain unchanged.
   d) Net exports initially decrease but later increase.
   e) There is no relationship between net capital inflow and net exports.

MEDIUM

4. The Keynesian cross model assumes that in the short run, prices:
   a) Are flexible and can adjust quickly.
   b) Are sticky and do not adjust to changes in aggregate demand.
   c) Will immediately rise if there is an increase in aggregate demand.
   d) Can only fall, not rise, in the short run.
   e) Are irrelevant to the model's analysis.

5. Which of the following is a global imbalance in the context of macroeconomics?
   a) A balance between government spending and tax revenues.
   b) A sustained deficit in a country's current account, paired with a surplus in the capital account.
   c) A perfectly balanced market for goods and services.
   d) A situation where all nations have identical inflation rates.
   e) A balanced exchange rate for all currencies worldwide.
6. The multiplier effect describes how:
   a) An increase in taxes decreases overall national income.
   b) A small increase in government spending can lead to a larger increase in national income.
   c) The money supply controls inflation.
   d) Higher interest rates lead to lower investments.
   e) A decrease in consumer confidence results in a proportional decrease in output.
7. Suppose that the marginal propensity to consume (MPC) in an economy is 0.8. If the government increases its spending by £500 million, calculate the total change in national income (Y) using the Keynesian multiplier formula.
8. Explain the relationship between net exports and net capital outflow. How do changes in one of these variables affect the other, and what does this mean for the overall economy?

HARD

9. Discuss the causes and implications of global imbalances. How do persistent current account deficits in one country and surpluses in another affect global economic stability?

CHAPTER 8

The Market for Goods and Services II

Chapter contents

At a Glance — The market for goods and services II

The issue

In Chapter 7 we introduced the concept of the market for goods and services, which exists to represent the real side of economic activity, modelled with the Keynesian cross. How else can we model the goods market? Can we enrich our explanation so that the financial effects of policy are captured more directly? Can we think about public sector dynamics?

The understanding

This time we employ the market for loanable funds to present a financial reflection of the market for goods and services. The loanable funds model is useful for two reasons; firstly we have the interest rate as the adjusting mechanism in the model, allowing us to see the financial effects of fiscal policy directly; and secondly because we can extend the loanable funds model to build a simple understanding of international capital flows in the context of the small open economy.

The usefulness

Fiscal policy has far-reaching implications for the economy, both internally and externally. Here we will learn both the immediate financial consequences of fiscal policy and the longer-term intergenerational ones.

8.1 Introduction

In this chapter, we extend our explanation of the market for goods and services and learn more about the financial disturbances caused by fiscal policy, both internally and externally. We begin by laying out the market for loanable funds where the supply of loanable funds comes from unspent income and the demand for loanable funds from borrowers looking to invest. In equilibrium we have the familiar condition that savings will be equal to investment at a prevailing economy-wide equilibrium interest rate. Where this differs from our explanation in Chapter 7 is that the loanable funds model makes use of the interest rate as an adjusting mechanism. This allows us to measure financial impacts from disturbances to the level of investment and savings, and to introduce the theory of crowding out. Government spending can create tensions in financial markets, which in turn can negatively impact investment.

Later we extend our model to encompass the reality of international trade in a small open economy and show how the exchange rate, determined in the market for foreign exchange, effects the level of exports and imports. We can then connect the real and financial flows that result from exporting to abroad and importing from abroad, by considering the capital flows that are also required to facilitate international trade. Finally, we can use our knowledge to discuss the pathology and modern problem of global imbalances caused by international trade.

Learning Outcomes

By the end of this chapter you should be able to:

- Apply the loanable funds model to explain the market for goods and services.
- Understand the crowding out of investment caused by fiscal policy.
- Extend the loanable funds model to encompass international trade in a small open economy.
- Explain how the demand for our currency can be combined with the loanable funds market to present the market for foreign exchange.

8.2 The market for loanable funds

We have already seen how the components of expenditure combine to make up the standard model for the market for goods and services. The loanable funds model is an alternative financial perspective on the same proposition, founded on the concept of equilibrium between investment and savings in the economy.

The supply and demand for loanable funds

The loanable funds market is an equivalent and an alternative approach to general equilibrium but focusing on the relationship between investment and savings. We can think of the loanable funds model as the financial explanation of the economy, or as representing the financial markets.

Although the model presented here uses the standard explanation for aggregate demand, a notable difference is that aggregate supply is determined solely by the factors of production: capital and labour. Effectively this leaves output fixed at the potential level of output in the economy. Output, *Y*, is fixed and exogenous changes in demand are counteracted by investment through the interest rate.

There are two agents – those demanding funds and those supplying them. The loanable funds market concerns itself with a broader array of money forms (credit and loans) than the money market from Chapter 5 which considered only high-powered money.

Because this model is two dimensional in interest rate/loanable funds space it also helps us to understand the 'monetary or interest rate effects' of fiscal policy, as we will see later. The model uses the concept that in equilibrium savings in the economy will equal investment, that the supply of loanable funds (given by savings) will be equal to the demand for loanable funds (for investment). To build the model, we begin with the components of national saving before combining with the investment function given earlier.

There are two types of savings, private saving and public saving. The expression for private saving $S(p)$ is given by:

$$S(p) = Y - T - C$$

Here, economy-wide private savings are national income minus taxation and consumption (what we spend).

Public saving $S(g)$ is given by:

$$S(g) = T - G$$

Public saving is simply the difference between government income and government spending, or taxation T minus government spending G.

To calculate total national saving, we can simply add private and public saving.

$$S = S(p) + S(g)$$

Total saving equals private saving by households and public saving by the government. Another way to express savings is by expanding the right-hand sides of the two components of total savings:

$$S = S(p) + S(g) = (Y - T - C) + (T - G) = (Y - C - G)$$

or

$$S = (Y - C - G)$$

To complete the loanable funds model we can specify investment as a downward sloping function in the interest rate as before:

$$I = c - d(r)$$

Remember that the investment function is downward sloping in the interest rate as shown in Figure 8.1.

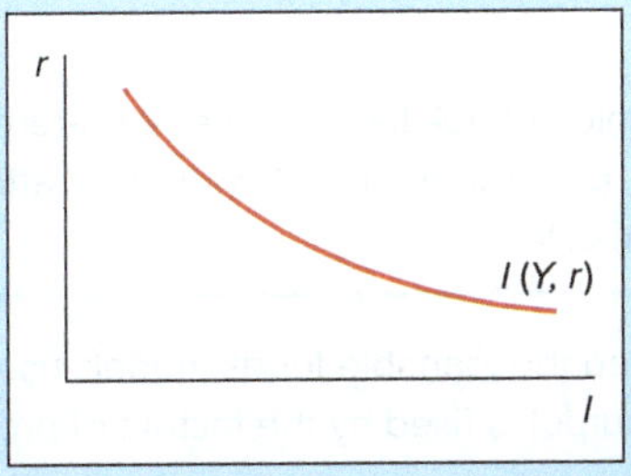

Figure 8.1 The demand for loanable funds is represented by the investment function

Equilibrium in the market for loanable funds

Now we can bring the two schedules together in the market for loanable funds; savings are equivalent to the supply of loanable funds and investment is equivalent to the demand for loanable funds. Figure 8.2 is a graphical representation of the market for loanable funds.

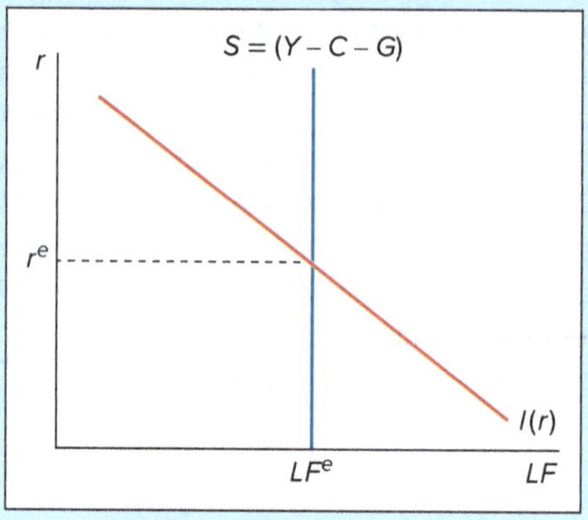

Figure 8.2 The market for loanable funds

It is important to notice that the supply of loanable funds (savings) is drawn vertical because its components, the variables Y, C and G, are exogenous or independent of the interest rate. The demand for loanable funds (investment) is drawn downward sloping in interest rate loanable funds space, as investment is lower at higher interest rates. The equilibrium interest rate is given at the intersection, where the supply of loanable funds is equal to the demand for loanable funds (r^e). This model is quite useful because it can also help us to understand the monetary effects of fiscal policy more directly than the Keynesian cross discussed in Chapter 7.

As an example, we can use the case of the UK during the sovereign debt crisis of 2010, where the UK government felt pressured into enacting fiscal discipline (later known as austerity), in order to calm financial markets (Example 8.1).

EXAMPLE 8.1

Real world example: Austerity in the UK, 2010

Like many governments around the world, the UK government spent heavily during the financial crisis of 2008, mainly on recapitalizing the financial system, propping up over-leveraged commercial banks. Europe as a whole suffered a similar fate in what was to become known as the European sovereign debt crisis beginning in 2009.

Financial market response

Credit ratings agencies became increasingly concerned about the ability of the UK government to meet its financial obligations. Although the UK maintained its credit rating of AAA throughout the crisis, the trajectory was generally predicted as downward. In fact the UK credit rating did drop in 2013.

Reaction of the interest rate

The downgrade in the economic outlook led to higher long-term interest rates payable on UK government national debt; government bonds were less attractive and yields had to increase to reflect the higher risk level.

Both the Keynesian cross and the loanable funds models use exactly the same components, though as we have discussed, output is fixed by the factors of production.

- The Keynesian cross uses the equilibrium condition: $Y = C + I + G$
- The loanable funds market is a rearrangement: $I = (Y - C - G) = S$

EXERCISE 8.1

Using the loanable funds market, explain how the equilibrium interest rate reacts to an exogenous increase in investment, something Keynes has referred to as 'animal spirits'.

8.3 Fiscal policy and its financial effects

With the loanable funds model under our belt we can now look at another concept that surrounds fiscal policy – the financial effects of fiscal policy, which we can think of as the reverberations that impact the financial markets in the aftermath of spending by the government.

The dynamics of fiscal policy

In Chapter 7 we have already discussed the problem of the timing lag between policy enactment and impact on the real economy. In order to capture these lags, we really need to move away from a static explanation and replace it with a dynamic one.

To address this, the behaviour of the government can be modelled using the government budget and the accumulation of these budgets, government debt. For this purpose, we will need to add time subscripts to our variables so that T_t and G_t become that level of taxation and government expenditure at time t. The government budget is simply the difference between government spending and taxation, written:

$$\textit{Government Budget} = T_t - G_t$$

If taxation is greater than expenditure, then the government is running a surplus and if expenditure is greater than taxation then the government is running a deficit. The government budget deficit is referred to as the public sector borrowing requirement (PSBCR) or the public sector net cash requirement (PSNCR).

To further our understanding of government finances we need to consider the accumulation of these borrowings by modelling the path of the accumulated debt. To do this we can write a budget constraint for the government that shows us how the level of government debt B_t changes in each period:

$$B_t - B_{t-1} = rB_{t-1} + G_t - T_t$$

which can be rewritten:

$$\Delta B_t = rB_{t-1} + G_t - T_t$$

In words, the change in government debt (or the government's borrowing requirement) ΔB_t is equal to the interest payable on the previous level of debt rB_{t-1} plus the difference between government spending G_t and government receipt of taxes T_t. To cut the overall level of public debt the government can either reduce G_t or increase T_t, else negotiate a better interest rate it pays to service its debt r.

Of course, we can use government debt as a performance indicator to compare economies across the world but this may be a little misleading. Suppose that a small country like Ireland has a much lower debt than that of the USA. Are we to infer that Ireland is a more fiscally responsible country? The USA has a much larger economy than Ireland so perhaps we should expect to see the USA borrowing larger amounts.

To overcome this problem of relative measurement, economists also use the debt-to-GDP ratio when comparing a country's performance in the area of fiscal responsibility. We can write this mathematically by writing our equation above in terms of output (dividing by Y_t):

$$\Delta\frac{B_t}{Y_t} = (r - g)\frac{B_{t-1}}{Y_{t-1}} + \frac{G_t - T_t}{Y_t}$$

where Y_t is real output and g is the rate at which Y_t grows. Intuitively, higher output will reduce the debt-to-GDP ratio. We see this reflected by the negative sign in front of the growth rate in output g in our equation, and also by the fact that Y_t is on the denominator in our equation above. The government can now address the debt-to-GDP ratio in the same way as above but also this time by allowing the economy to grow faster than the rate of interest, that is, $(r < g)$. You might want to know how to derive this equation in more detail and to help with this we have provided more detail in the example box below.

To summarize, fiscal policy is the action of the government aimed at stabilizing the economy using the tools of government expenditure and taxation. When there is a recession, governments will attempt fiscal expansion to smooth the path of output and vice versa for an economic boom.

EXAMPLE 8.2

Worked example: Debt-to-GDP debt accumulation equation

We can derive the debt-to-GDP debt accumulation equation from the standard government borrowing constraint and although this is complicated to do exactly, most of the steps are provided below. We start from one of the equations above that explains the change in government borrowing, B_t:

$$B_t - B_{t-1} = rB_{t=1} + G_t - T_t$$

Borrowing depends on past debt, the interest that it pays on that debt, and the government spending budget. Rearrange this:

$$B_t = B_{t-1} + rB_{t-1} + G_t - T_t$$

Collecting terms on the right-hand side:

$$B_t = (1 + r)B_{t-1} + G_t - T_t$$

To account for the debt-to-GDP ratio we divide through by Y_t:

$$\frac{B_t}{Y_t} = (1 + r)\frac{B_{t-1}}{Y_t} + \frac{G_t - T_t}{Y_t}$$

Multiply top and bottom of the first term on the right-hand side by Y_{t-1}:

$$\frac{B_t}{Y_t} = (1 + r)\frac{Y_{t-1}}{Y_t}\frac{B_{t-1}}{Y_{t-1}} + \frac{G_t - T_t}{Y_t}$$

Now write the growth rate of output, g, and rearrange:

$$g = \frac{Y_t - Y_{t-1}}{Y_t} \quad or \quad \frac{1}{(1 + g)} = \frac{Y_{t-1}}{Y_t}$$

Using the second equation for the growth rate into our debt-to-GDP ratio:

$$\frac{B_t}{Y_t} = (1 + r)\frac{1}{(1 + g)}\frac{B_{t-1}}{Y_{t-1}} + \frac{G_t - T_t}{Y_t}$$

Now, for small values of r and g, we can use a log linear approximation that $\frac{(1+r)}{(1+g)} \approx (1 + r - g)$:

$$\frac{B_t}{Y_t} = (1 + r - g)\frac{B_{t-1}}{Y_{t-1}} + \frac{G_t - T_t}{Y_t}$$

Now we bring the 1 over to the left-hand side and use this to make up the change in the debt-to-GDP ratio:

$$\frac{B_t}{Y_t} - \frac{B_{t-1}}{Y_{t-1}} = (r - g)\frac{B_{t-1}}{Y_{t-1}} + \frac{G_t - T_t}{Y_t}$$

Home and dry! The left-hand side is the growth rate in the debt-to-GDP ratio:

$$\Delta \frac{B_t}{Y_t} = (r - g)\, \frac{B_{t-1}}{Y_{t-1}} + \frac{G_t - T_t}{Y_t}$$

This equation is the one described in the text above; the path of the public debt-to-GDP ratio is driven by the interest rate, the growth rate, the debt-to-GDP ratio in the past and the budget of the government.

The crowding out effect

Perhaps – after reading the previous section on the government multiplier – you have become rather suspicious of the result, that an increase in *G* will not only increase output but increase it by a multiple factor! This implication might lead us to the opinion that there is an incentive for a policymaker to continue spending endlessly; in reality, the government also faces some monetary costs when it increases expenditure and these costs can act as a counteracting force to the multiplier effect.

To explain the 'crowding out' effect we can make use of the market for loanable funds model introduced in Section 8.2. An increase in government expenditure leads to a fall in national saving; remember that:

$$\textit{Public Saving } S(g) = T - G$$

Public saving is equal to government receipts in the form of taxation minus government expenditure. It is easy to see here that if expenditure increases, and taxation remains the same, then public saving will fall. If public saving falls then so too does national saving:

$$\textit{National Saving: } S = S(p) + S(g)$$

A fall in national saving will shift the savings schedule to the left in the market for loanable funds (Figure 8.3).

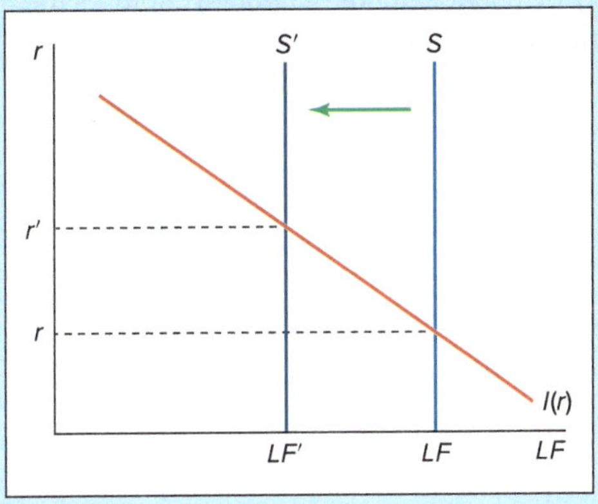

Figure 8.3 The market for loanable funds showing the reaction of the interest rate to a fiscal expansion (an increase in G)

An increase in government spending does not increase output in this model, but lowers the level of national saving and causes the savings schedule to shift to the left. The leftward shift in the savings schedule means that at the old interest rate there is excess demand for loanable funds; in reaction to the increase in demand banks charge higher interest rates and the interest rate increases from *r* to *r'*.

The increase in the interest rate lowers investment in the economy (remember that investment and the interest rate are related negatively), and so by the aggregate demand identity output falls back again. The crowding out effect is total, rendering fiscal policy ineffective (an implication that would support the classical view of macroeconomics).

We can also use the loanable funds model to explain monetary policy – an increase in the money supply will shift the supply of loanable funds to the right. The predicted response from the loanable funds model is an increase in the level of investment and a fall in the interest rate. This result is consistent with our explanation for monetary policy in Chapter 5, though there is no account for money demand or for liquidity preferences. In this respect the role of the central bank is simplified.

8.4 A small open economy

So far in this chapter the models for the goods market and loanable funds market have both been presented under the assumption that the economy is closed; in other words, there are no international transactions. We can relax this by adding a further component to the split in GDP called net exports, the balance between the goods exported to foreign countries and goods imported from foreign countries. Another key assumption we need to make to help us control for international trade is that the economy we are modelling is small and as such the interest rate is 'fixed' at the world interest rate.

$$r = r^*$$

Fixing the interest rate in this way is convenient as it allows us to replace the adjusting mechanism (the interest rate) with the exchange rate. After all, a model that cannot show the effect of changes in the exchange rate would be of little use in the analysis of an economy's international transactions. Remember that in our loanable funds market, it was the interest rate that adjusted to ensure that savings were always equal to investment. Now that the interest rate is fixed at the world interest rate we allow a scenario where savings are no longer necessarily equal to investment.

The open economy version of the loanable funds model

We can now use the loanable funds market to visualize the open economy where the difference between investment (represented by the demand for loanable funds schedule) and savings (represented by the supply of loanable funds schedule) captures the flow of capital in and out of the country required for international trade.

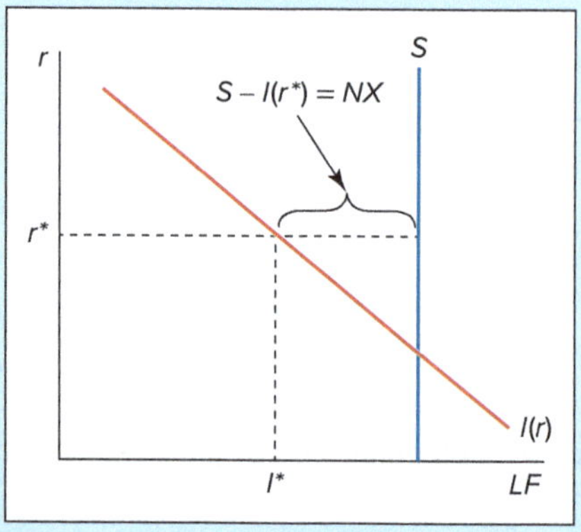

Figure 8.4 Using the loanable funds market to capture the difference between investment and savings at the world interest rate

We can see that at r^* (the fixed world interest rate) the loanable funds market is in disequilibrium and there is a difference between investment (determined by r^* at I^*) and savings. This difference is equal to the funds diverted for international transactions, which we call net capital outflow (*NCO*). Through the balance of payments the difference can also be labelled as the balance of trade, net exports (*NX*). We can also see here that if the world interest rate drops enough, a lack of competitiveness will cause a trade surplus to convert into a trade deficit accompanied by a net capital inflow.

The market for foreign exchange

In this section, we discuss in more detail the mechanics of international trade. Every transaction requires a medium of exchange and internationally that means that local currencies will need to be traded for one another. A foreign trader will require payment in their own currency (a Chinese exporter will want to be paid in yuan, not in dollars, so an American importer will need to exchange their dollars into yuan first).

The rate at which the currencies are exchanged is determined in the market for foreign exchange and called the nominal exchange rate. As the exchange rate changes, the price of exports and imports changes (if the pound sterling falls in value then we will need more of them to buy a car priced in euros) and in turn the quantities demanded changes. In fact, there are two driving forces behind the quantity of exports and imports demanded: first, the nominal exchange rate, and secondly, the domestic prices of the goods traded themselves.

To allow for these two driving factors we can use the real exchange rate which controls for changes between the changing price levels in two trading partners. Another way to view the real exchange rate is the relative price of domestic goods in terms of foreign goods. The real exchange rate ε can be written:

$$\varepsilon = \frac{E \times P}{P^*}$$

where E is the nominal exchange rate, P is the home price level and P^* is the foreign price level. It is worth noting that the biggest contributor to movements in the real exchange rate is the nominal exchange rate, which can be quite volatile. Working towards our market for foreign exchange we need to discuss the relationship between net exports (the trade balance) and the real exchange rate, which we can show with the aid of Figure 8.5.

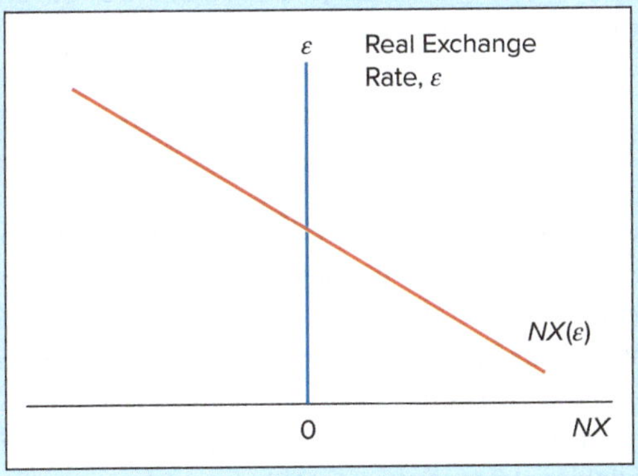

Figure 8.5 The net exports schedule shows the relationship between the trade balance and the real exchange rate

If the real exchange rate increases (e.g., the pound becomes more valuable) then exports become more expensive for foreigners; exports will fall. Similarly, the home currency can purchase more foreign currency and so imports cost domestic consumers less; imports will rise. So, a rise in the real exchange rate leads to a fall in exports and a rise in imports which will give us an unambiguous fall in net exports, and a resulting fall in output.

Thus, net exports and the real exchange rate are negatively correlated, and our net exports schedule is downward sloping to reflect this. Specified this way our net exports function also makes up a schedule for the demand for foreign exchange, as currency is demanded to buy exports. We turn to capital flows for a description of the supply schedule for foreign exchange. The supply of foreign exchange comes from the financial dealings required to facilitate trade, which involves the sales of currencies by central banks in a similar fashion to that given in our China/US example above. Using net capital outflow as the 'supply' of foreign currency completes the market for foreign exchange shown in Figure 8.6.

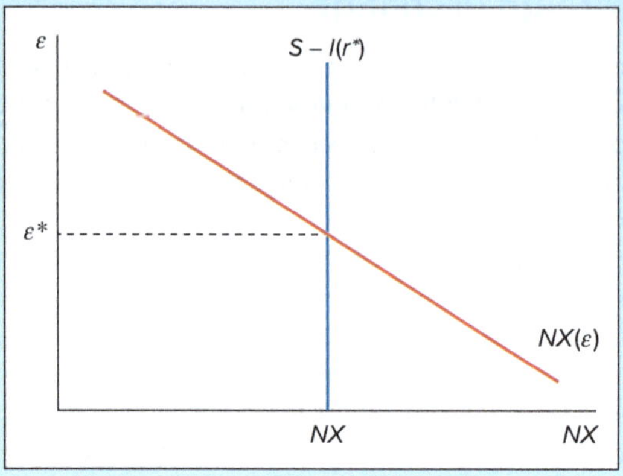

Figure 8.6 The market for foreign exchange showing how the exchange rate is determined

Notice that net capital outflow $S - I(r^*)$ is independent of the exchange rate (savings are exogenous and investment is only dependent on the world interest rate) and for this reason is drawn vertically. Notice also that the demand for foreign currency is downward sloping and reflects that, at a higher real exchange rate, the trade balance is lower.

EXERCISE 8.2

Using the market for foreign exchange

Imagine an increase in net exports caused by an increase in competitiveness in certain industries. Use the market for foreign exchange to predict the effect on the exchange rate and discuss how this will affect the economy in the longer run.

8.5 Chapter summary: Putting it all together

In this chapter, we have learnt about the market for goods and services and the monetary equivalent version of the model called the loanable funds market. The loanable funds market version makes use of investment and savings to explain the monetary effects of changes in the goods market. The loanable funds market provides the channel to understand the concept of crowding out, where increases in government expenditure lead to increases in the interest rate and lower investment. The crowding out of investment reminds us that increases in government spending come with an additional financial cost, aside from the original expenditure.

Understanding how net exports contribute towards the makeup of GDP has enabled us to offer an early understanding of the small open economy and further this by describing the driving forces behind the trade balance. We have also learnt to use the foreign exchange market to explain the movements in the exchange rate. An increase in the price paid by foreign consumers for our exports can be for two reasons: a change in the exchange rate itself; and due to an increase in prices domestically.

Assessment Question

The level of government debt is often measured using the debt-to-GDP ratio. This measure helps us to compare macroeconomic performance across countries controlling for the size of the economy. Discuss what economic policies might be employed to lower the debt-to-GDP ratio in an economy over the short run and the long run.

Cases

The market for foreign exchange in a small open economy

In a small open economy, the exchange rate plays a crucial role in determining the flow of goods and services between countries. The economy's trade balance (exports minus imports) is affected by the value of its domestic currency in the foreign exchange market. When the domestic currency appreciates, foreign goods become cheaper, leading to an increase in imports, while domestic goods become more expensive for foreign consumers, potentially reducing exports. Conversely, a depreciation of the domestic currency makes imports more expensive and exports cheaper, improving the trade balance.

The government in this economy has been running a budget deficit, borrowing from both domestic and international sources to finance its expenditures. As the government increases borrowing, interest rates rise, attracting foreign investment and leading to an appreciation of the currency. However, this appreciation could negatively impact exports, as foreign consumers find the country's goods more expensive. At the same time, higher interest rates might reduce domestic consumption and investment in the short run, further influencing the trade balance.

For the goods and services market, a strong currency may harm the competitiveness of domestic industries, especially those that rely heavily on exports. The trade balance becomes an important consideration for policymakers who seek to manage both the exchange rate and domestic economic growth.

Questions

1. What is the relationship between the exchange rate and the trade balance in a small, open economy?
2. How does a change in the interest rate affect the exchange rate in an open economy?
3. Explain how an appreciation of the domestic currency can affect the export sector.
4. What is the role of government borrowing in influencing the foreign exchange market?
5. In the context of this case study, what could be some potential consequences of a currency appreciation on the goods and services market?

Problems

EASY

1. The market for loanable funds refers to:
   a) the market where firms borrow money to fund their investment projects
   b) the market where consumers borrow money for consumption purposes
   c) the market where the government borrows funds to finance its deficit
   d) the market for saving, where the supply of funds comes from savings and the demand comes from investment
   e) a market with only long-term loan contracts
2. Which of the following factors would most likely lead to a crowding-out effect?
   a) an increase in government spending financed by borrowing
   b) a decrease in private sector investment
   c) a rise in consumer savings
   d) a decrease in the domestic interest rate
   e) a reduction in government tax rates

MEDIUM

3. What is the effect of an increase in government spending on national income in terms of the crowding out effect?
   a) it has no effect on national income as it is entirely offset by higher interest rates
   b) it increases national income as government spending stimulates private investment
   c) it leads to a higher national income due to a rise in the money supply
   d) it decreases national income because higher government spending reduces private investment
   e) it leads to a permanent increase in national income without any long-term effects
4. The government budget constraint states that:
   a) government spending must always equal tax revenues
   b) the government must finance its deficit by borrowing or creating money
   c) the government can finance any deficit through printing money
   d) the government can only increase spending by reducing taxes
   e) the government must always balance its budget without borrowing
5. Which of the following best describes the relationship between the market for loanable funds in an open economy and the exchange rate?
   a) a rise in the interest rate will lead to a depreciation of the currency
   b) a rise in the interest rate will lead to an appreciation of the currency due to capital inflows
   c) a rise in government spending will increase the exchange rate immediately
   d) exchange rates are unaffected by the loanable funds market in an open economy
   e) a higher interest rate has no impact on the foreign exchange market

HARD

6. In the market for foreign exchange, an increase in a country's interest rates relative to foreign rates will likely lead to:
   a) a depreciation of the domestic currency
   b) a capital outflow and a depreciation of the domestic currency
   c) a rise in inflation and a depreciation of the domestic currency
   d) an appreciation of the domestic currency
   e) a decrease in exports and an appreciation of the domestic currency
7. Assume the domestic interest rate is 4 per cent, while the world interest rate is 3 per cent. If the country's capital account is balanced and it is a small open economy, how would an increase in the domestic interest rate to 5 per cent affect the country's net capital flows and exchange rate?
8. Explain the crowding-out effect and discuss how it can potentially reduce the effectiveness of government fiscal policy. Provide examples of situations where crowding out could be significant.
9. Discuss the role of the loanable funds market in determining the equilibrium interest rate in an open economy. How do international capital flows influence the domestic interest rate and exchange rates?

CHAPTER 9

The Labour Market I

Chapter contents

At a Glance — The labour market I

The issue

The labour market is a close reflection of the goods market that we covered in Chapter 7 and Chapter 8. It reverses the role of the consumer from the agent that demands goods and services to that of a supplier. The labour market is also more relatable to real life than that of the aggregate demand aggregate supply model. What approaches can we employ to analyse the important area of labour market policy?

The understanding

In this chapter, the first of two on the labour market, we lay out the standard static explanations of the labour market; first, the price setting/wage setting model; and then the labour supply/labour demand model. The former will helps us to go beyond labour market policy and provide our first explanation for equilibrium unemployment.

The usefulness

The labour supply/labour demand model allows us to demonstrate and evaluate the normative implications of market intervention. We learn, by example, how to use a macroeconomic model to make a detailed analysis of a labour market policy.

9.1 Introduction

The labour market is a model where households that supply labour and firms that hire labour can interact to determine both the average wage rate and the level of employment in the economy. The higher the level of employment the lower the level of unemployment – remember that the incidence of becoming unemployed can be highly negative for an individual worker. It is for this reason that unemployment is a macroeconomic variable of strong significance to policymakers and why the labour market is an important consideration in macroeconomics. Recall from Chapter 3 that we can measure the condition of the labour market using various indicators and we outline those again as a reminder in Table 9.1.

Table 9.1 Labour market definitions

Measure	Meaning
The working age population	All those of working age (normally 16–65)
The labour force	The portion of the working age population willing and able to work at any given wage
The unemployed	The portion of the labour force without work
The (un)employment rate	The percentage of the labour force (un)employed
The participation rate	The portion of the working-age population in the labour force

The labour market is a model most commonly taught in two dimensions with the usual two schedules representing two agents. Typically, these two agents are either the household and the firm, or price setters and wage setters. In this chapter, we will cover both models so that you can compare the two approaches and understand the difference between them. Up to now, we have seen our two representative agents (households and firms) interact through the model of aggregate supply and aggregate demand, in order to determine the price level in the economy.

With the addition of the labour market, we have an alternative explanation for the determination of economic activity but in terms of labour instead of production. In this way, the labour market acts like a mirror of the market for goods and services, one that helps to explain activity through employment. Remember that output and unemployment are closely related macroeconomic variables; when output is rising, we expect unemployment to fall and vice versa. The labour market is a tool that we can use to enrich models that are lacking an explanation of persistent unemployment. We know that the issue of unemployment is of key concern to macroeconomists and policymakers alike, and so it is important that macroeconomic models can help to capture this and predict the reaction of employment to economic policy.

One popular and simple measure to rank the short-run success of economies around the world is through the unemployment rate, that is, the proportion of the workforce out of work. Even though rates of unemployment can range from around 5 per cent to as high as 80 per cent, it is not necessarily the unemployment rate that measures the distress or lack of well-being in an economy. What matters more than the level is the change in unemployment or the speed in which the unemployment rate is increasing. In other words, unemployment is probably most painful to those in the process of moving out of work against their wishes. The labour market itself does not need to sit inside a fully specified general equilibrium model as it can be presented as a stand-alone model to explain economic activity. In this chapter, we describe the labour market in a variety of ways: the more traditional mainstream static views and also a view that captures the flows in and out of unemployment and the workforce.

We begin by outlining the long-run wage and price setting model before moving on to the model for the supply and demand for labour, a short-run view. The latter model explains unemployment through disequilibrium in the market, a scenario we can think of as the presence of 'market inefficiencies'. We then introduce the labour market in terms of employment flows – flows in and out of the workforce due to hires and separations (or exits) from the labour force. This flow approach allows us to offer a more dynamic view of the labour market that captures these important movements otherwise ignored by the static explanations. Finally, we describe the relationship between unemployment and inflation that has become known as the Phillips curve. The Phillips curve helps us to understand how supply-side factors in the economy or changes to a firm's cost base drives the inflation of prices, and also provides us with a policy analysis tool for those policymakers interested in the stabilization of prices in the economy.

Learning Outcomes

By the end of this chapter you should be able to:

- Explain the concept of the labour market.
- Relate two differing explanations of the labour market using the static approach.
- Explain the impact of equilibrium in the labour market.
- Use the labour market to evaluate and make predictions about the minimum wage.
- Connect the macroeconomic variables of inflation and unemployment using the theory of the Phillips relation.

9.2 Static explanations of the labour market

Now that we understand the reason for modelling the labour market and why it matters to macroeconomists and policymakers, we can discuss the different ways in which the market is modelled. The approaches can be categorized by the way they treat time; that is, into static and dynamic explanations. By static we mean that the model cannot account for changes across time in the variables, and by dynamic we mean that variables can take on different values as time progresses. The standard static approach is convenient in that we can model the labour market in a two-dimensional diagram and from this make a static comparison. By static comparison, we mean that we can show how the model reacts to shocks (normally seen as shifts in the curves or schedules) away from market equilibrium.

The static views of the labour market are:

- **Price setting/wage setting – market clears, long-run view**
- **Labour demand/labour supply – firms vs households, short-run view.**

Labour Demand: The total number of working hours demanded by firms at the current wage rate.
Labour Supply: The total number of all working hours willing to be supplied by households at the current wage rate.

In the price setting/wage setting model, prices are decided by the set of firms in the economy and wages are decided by both unions and firms. In the labour demand/labour supply model, there are those that supply labour (workers) and those that demand labour (firms). One of the most obvious differences between the two approaches is that in the price setting/wage setting model the labour market always clears and for this reason, it is thought of as representing a long-run perspective where unemployment is always at its natural rate. In the labour supply/labour demand approach, unemployment can also be included by setting the wage 'away' from the equilibrium wage using the concept of an excess supply of labour.

We can think of the price setting/wage setting model as a long-run model and the labour supply/labour demand model as a short-run explanation. Next, we take a look at the two approaches to modelling the labour market in more detail.

The wage setting and price setting model

The wage and price setting model uses two agents interacting in real wage and unemployment space with the real wage drawn on the vertical axis and unemployment drawn on the horizontal axis. This market determines the **natural rate of unemployment**, which we can also think of as the long-run rate of unemployment. The two agents in our model are wage setters and price setters. Wage setters such as firms and unions set the wage depending on their current economic environment, made up of factors such as the unemployment rate and union power etc.

Natural Rate of Unemployment: The level of unemployment that would prevail when the labour market is in equilibrium.

At higher levels of unemployment, workers have less power to bargain up their wage and so the real wage is lower. It also follows intuitively, that when unemployment is high the real wage will be low and vice versa. Thus, the wage-setting curve (*WS*) is drawn downward sloping in the real wage as we can see, diagrammatically, in Figure 9.1.

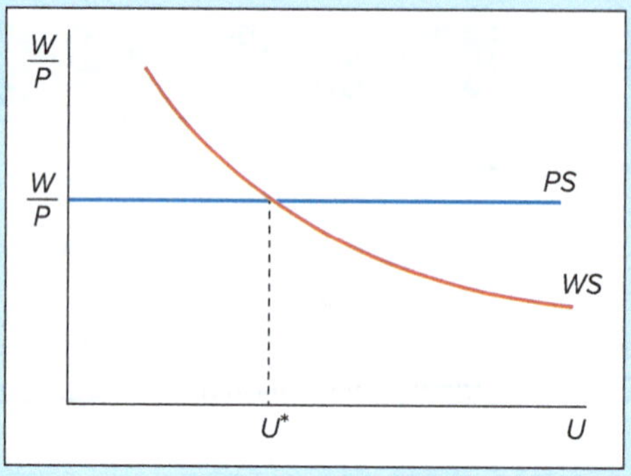

Figure 9.1 The price and wage setting model of the labour market

Our second agent is the price setter, who we can think of as the firm setting prices based on a mark-up over direct costs. If wages are higher or there is a decrease in the level of competition in the economy there will be an increase in prices – an intuitive outcome. As prices do not depend on unemployment, the price setting curve is drawn horizontal in real wage/unemployment space. Both of our agents interact in the market to determine the natural rate of unemployment in market equilibrium; if prices are higher than wages, to the right of *U**, then the firm will hire more labour due to the increase in profits, and unemployment will fall back to its long-run natural rate. Conversely, if we are to the left of *U** with wages higher than prices then the firm will cut back on workers and unemployment will rise back until it reaches *U** once more.

As an exercise, we can see the prediction of our model to a change in labour market policy, such as an increase in unemployment benefits. An increase in the amount of money paid to the unemployed will make it harder for firms to find workers. This change pressures the firm to offer a higher wage, shifting the wage curve right, or outwards, as we see in Figure 9.2.

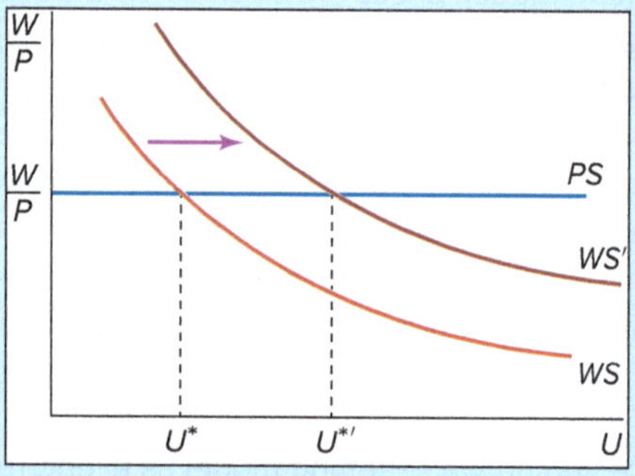

Figure 9.2 The price and wage setting model showing an increase in unemployment benefits

Our model predicts that with the outward/right shift in the wage-setting curve that unemployment will increase from *U** to *U*'* – but why is this? The increase in benefits puts upward pressure on wages as firms struggle to hire, with fewer households willing to work, but this wage is higher than firms are willing to pay so firms reduce hiring instead and the unemployment rate rises. The price/wage setting model predicts that an increase in benefits will have a negative impact on our labour market.

The model of labour supply and labour demand

Our next model of the labour market is based on the proposition that the equilibrium wage is determined by the interaction between those who supply and those who demand labour, in contrast to the price/wage setting model. This setup is similar to the AD/AS model of income determination in that it also delineates between households and firms. The labour demand schedule represents the demand for hours by firms and is downward sloping in the wage rate, reflecting the negative relationship between costs (wages) for firms and the demand for hours to carry out production. Now we can draw the labour demand schedule with a negative slope as shown Figure 9.3.

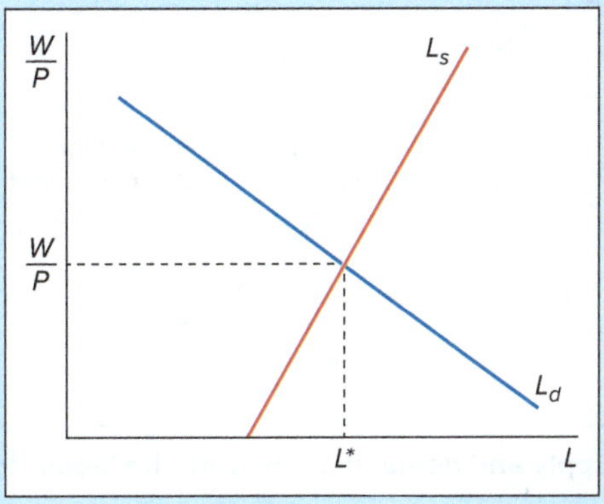

Figure 9.3 The labour demand and supply model in real wage, employment space

To understand why the labour demand curve is downward sloping imagine a case where there is an increase in the real wage. Firms will demand less labour, because of the higher cost, and output supplied by the firm will consequentially be lower; thus higher wages are associated with lower labour demand. The labour supply schedule represents the willingness of the household to supply labour at different wage rates so this relationship can be thought of as a positive one. The labour supply curve is drawn sloping upwards reflecting the presumption that higher wage rates will induce more households to provide more hours of work to firms. Where the two schedules intersect the model predicts an equilibrium real wage and equilibrium level of employment, L^*, in the economy.

Remember that a change in the wage rate will give us movements along these schedules but any exogenous change to the market may shift the schedules – for example, an increase in technological progress, or an increase in workers entering the workforce. In our previous model we looked at the scenario of an increase in unemployment benefits; clearly this affects our market for labour, but in an exogenous way (the variable changing is not on the axis). In this model an increase in unemployment benefits could be shown as a leftwards shift in the labour supply schedule as households find work less attractive.

EXERCISE 9.1

1. Can you explain the difference between the two approaches to modelling the labour market in a simple way?
2. Try to imagine a scenario where the labour demand schedule has been caused to shift left and another where the labour supply schedule shifts right. What effect will this have on the real wage?

Equilibrium and disequilibrium in the labour market

To help us to explain unemployment we can use both the price and wage setting model and the labour demand and supply approach. The first model assumes that the labour market always clears and as such is associated with a long-run view; it is an explanation of the natural rate of unemployment. Our second model allows us to explain the short-run deviation of employment from its equilibrium level; here unemployment comes from disequilibrium.

Let us begin by looking again at Figure 9.3, but this time adding another schedule which represents the actual labour force (those willing and able to work at any given real wage). By adding a labour force schedule we can include those workers participating in the labour market but find themselves without work (Figure 9.4).

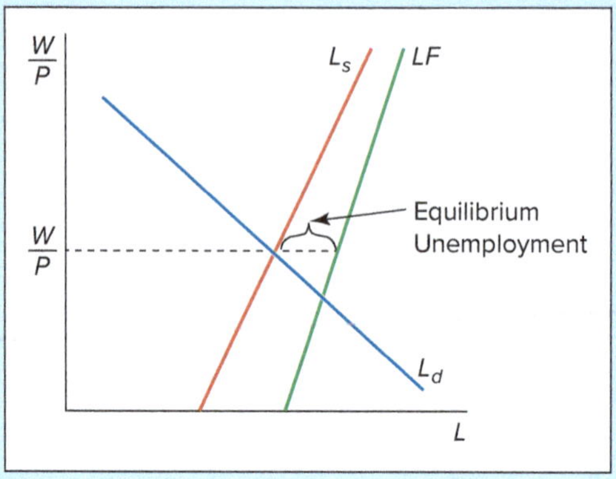

Figure 9.4 The labour supply and demand model with the labour force schedule

As we have already discussed, where the labour demand and labour supply schedules intersect, the labour market clears at the equilibrium real wage, with zero unemployment. In reality, however, we witness that the labour market does not clear and there is always some unemployment; whenever do we hear that unemployment is zero per cent? The inclusion of the labour force *LF* schedule in our figure helps us to explain the element of our workforce that are persistently unemployed. The *LF* schedule gives us an explanation for unemployment even when our labour market is in equilibrium; we can measure this as the horizontal distance between our *LF* schedule and our labour supply schedule at the equilibrium wage rate. Notice that our LF schedule is slightly steeper than our labour supply schedule. The reason for this is that as employment increases the labour market tightens; as wages increase the proportion of households supplying labour increases.

Now that we have described this 'core' of unemployment that exists in normal times we can also use this model to show unemployment when the economy is away from its equilibrium, in other words 'disequilibrium unemployment'. You might question under what conditions the labour market might ever be away from equilibrium, or indeed why it might stay that way for any length of time. From our knowledge of macroeconomic modelling we understand that, should any market be at a point away from equilibrium there always exists a force drawing us back again, for example, the driving force of excess demand. When market forces act, the adjusting mechanism will restore equilibrium; in the case of the labour market, this is the real wage.

Evidence has shown that the average real wage changes slowly over time. So if the labour market fails to adjust to a change in fundamentals then it can be away from equilibrium for longer periods. This market 'inefficiency' has been termed a real wage rigidity, where the wage is too rigid to allow the labour market to return to equilibrium in a short space of time. Figure 9.5 shows a real wage higher than the equilibrium wage, which might be for the reason discussed above or through labour market policy such as minimum wage legislation. We can also think of this policy as a 'wage floor' below which the wage cannot fall.

At $\frac{W^{Min}}{P}$ the wage is set above the equilibrium wage and consequently we can see that our model predicts that at the minimum wage there will be excess supply of labour, in other words, unemployment. We term this type of unemployment caused by a deviation of the market wage from equilibrium, 'disequilibrium unemployment'. Our *LF* schedule accounts for the unemployment that continues to exist in all states of the market and so we see now that at the minimum wage there exists two types of unemployment: equilibrium unemployment and disequilibrium unemployment.

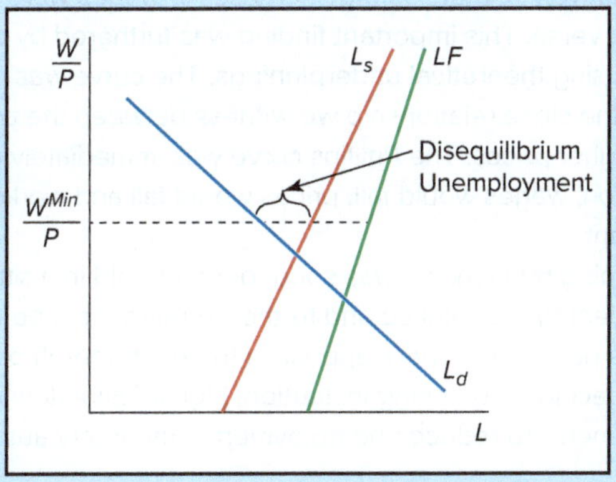

Figure 9.5 **The labour demand and supply model with a minimum wage**

EXAMPLE 9.1

Real world example: Minimum wage

Now that we have represented the minimum wage in our static model we can discuss the policy in a little more detail. As we might expect in normal times, and certainly when the policy is first announced, that the minimum wage is above the wage that would prevail in a free market. We also see that with the minimum wage higher than the market clearing wage, the model predicts the existence of unemployment, as a consequence of this policy. In any market where the price is higher than equilibrium, there must exist excess supply. The only way to counter this argument is to deny the prediction of the model or claim that the model is mis-specified in some way, perhaps that it fails to account for the well-being created by the minimum wage for those still employed.

If we feel that the assumptions that support the model are reasonable and that its prediction is accurate, this leaves us to question the suitability of this labour market policy altogether. Another problem for the minimum wage is that once the wage floor has been set we are no longer able to see the market clearing wage, which can only reveal itself in a free market. If we are unable to see the market clearing wage, then over time we are no longer aware whether or not the equilibrium wage is above or below the minimum wage. If the minimum wage is below the market clearing wage this presents an even bigger problem.

The discussion and debate over the minimum wage could take up a book of its own, the success or otherwise of this policy is a matter of fierce debate among economists and for good reason, it is vitally important to reduce unemployment and just as important to protect the poor in society. The discussion also demonstrates that economic models can be very useful as a framework for our arguments about important economic policies.

9.3 An introduction to the Phillips curve

Now that we have discussed the determination of unemployment in some detail we can also reflect upon our earlier discussion on inflation from Chapter 3. In a typical macroeconomic model, the price level in the economy is indirectly dependent on the decision of the representative firm. The firm takes into account prevailing economic conditions before making its price decision in each period. One model that captures the price-setting behaviour of firms at the macroeconomic level is the Phillips curve – but first some history on this relationship between inflation and economic activity.

The history of the Phillips curve

In 1958 an economist called William Phillips discovered a relationship between the movement in wages and unemployment. Observations taken from the UK from both macroeconomic variables appeared negatively related, so that increases in wages were associated with lower unemployment and vice versa. This important finding was furthered by other economists who formalized the relation using theoretical underpinnings. The curve was rewritten in terms of price inflation, mainly due to the close relationship we witness between the two types of inflation – higher wages lead to higher prices. The Phillips curve was immediately popular due to its intuitive predictions; in a recession, wages would fall, prices would fall and workers would be laid off, increasing unemployment.

This downward-sloping relationship was soon found to hold in a similar way for other countries leading to widening acceptance and further formalization, before being taken up by policymakers as a policy tool. There appeared to be a trade-off between two of the macroeconomic issues facing a governing institution; high inflation/low unemployment or low inflation/high unemployment. To reduce unemployment a monetary authority would simply have to create inflation.

The Phillips curve drawn in Figure 9.6 is shown as a downward-sloping function in inflation/unemployment space; when unemployment is high, perhaps during a recession, we expect wage inflation to be lower. The slope of the Phillips curve, α, is the sensitivity of unemployment to change in wage inflation. In an economic boom, we expect prices to be rising more quickly and unemployment to be low.

Faced with higher inflation in an economic boom a policymaker might make use of the Phillips curve which predicts that lower inflation can be achieved through an increase in unemployment. The Phillips curve was indeed adopted for use by policymakers in the 1980s; they forced interest rates up to increase unemployment with a view to controlling rising inflation. Nowadays, this tool is seen as rather a blunt one; increasing unemployment is less acceptable politically and theoretical advancements deem this unnecessary in any case. Credibility in monetary policy is far more effective for price stability.

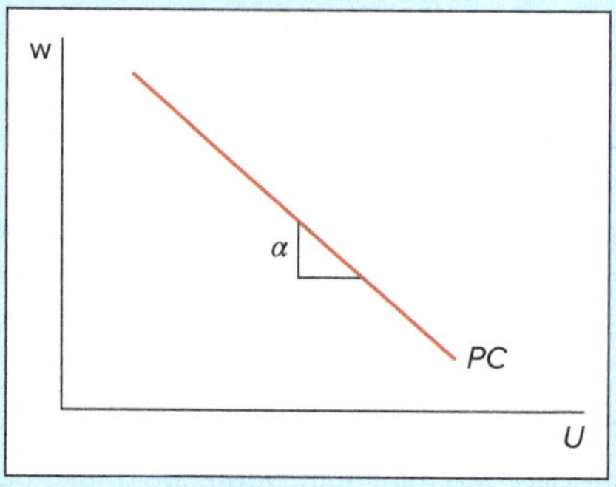

Figure 9.6 The Phillips curve (*PC*) in unemployment inflation space

Accounting for expectations and the natural rate

The Phillips curve may have been supported by the economic data in the 1960s, but in the 1970s and onwards, countries have experienced coincidences of high inflation and high unemployment. The data that led to its construction now denied the stable negative relationship. This denial by the observed fact has led economists to rethink the Phillips curve with a general consensus that the curve might hold in the short run, but perhaps not necessarily in the long run. This caveat is convenient because it means that the curve remains a key structural equation in many macro models today; also that a valuable and intuitive policy tool is not lost to the problems posed by the data of the 1970s and later.

Expectations: The expected value of an economic variable in the future. If inflation turns out as expected, then unemployment and output would be at their natural rates.

To help us understand how the Philips curve can be adapted to allow for shifts across time periods we need to introduce the concepts of the natural rate of unemployment and inflation **expectations**. The concept of a natural rate was first introduced by Milton Freidman in his Natural Rate Hypothesis in 1968. In a simple way, we can think of this special value of economic activity as applicable to the 'long run' or the rate of economic activity (here unemployment) that would prevail in the absence of shocks to the economy. Another way to think of the natural rate of unemployment is as our average rate over time. In any period, unemployment will be above or below our natural rate, as it moves through the ups and downs of its natural cycle.

In 1956, an economist called Phillip Cagan wrote an influential paper, introducing the idea of using expected values of variables within macroeconomic models. To extend our Phillips curve model we can make use of expected inflation, which we can think of as the aggregate prediction of inflation for the following period. To demonstrate by example, one simple prediction for expected inflation might be to make use of the previous period; if we have witnessed two years of 2 per cent inflation then it is reasonable for our expectation of inflation for the following year to be the same, that is, 2 per cent.

We can write this simple example of inflation expectations:

$$\pi_t^e = \pi_{t-1} \text{ or } \pi^e = \pi_{-1}$$

In words: the expectation of inflation is assumed to be equal to the value it took in the previous period. The only difference between the two equations above being the type of notation you might see.

We can see the short-run version of the Philips curve (*SRPC*) in diagrammatic form in Figure 9.7.

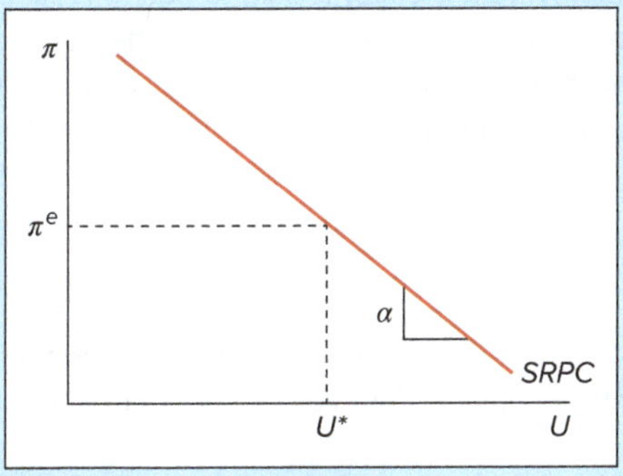

Figure 9.7 The short-run Phillips curve (*SRPC*)

Notice now that unemployment can take values below and above the natural rate of unemployment U^*; also, that the curve passes through the point where unemployment is at its natural rate and where inflation is at its expected level. If inflation is as 'we expect' at π^e there are no shocks and unemployment will be at its natural rate. On the other hand, if inflation is above that expected then the Phillips curve predicts that unemployment will fall and vice versa. To explain an incidence of high inflation and high unemployment together we can now imagine that the *SRPC* has shifted outward (to the right), rather than bent upwards to account for the unusual observation so that at any level of inflation we have a higher associated level of unemployment. We can write the Philips curve mathematically as:

$$\pi = \pi^e - a(U - U^*)$$

In words, inflation is determined jointly by the expectation of inflation itself and some measure of excess demand; in this case, the difference between the actual rate of unemployment and the natural rate of unemployment, with a sensitivity of α. This particular version of the Phillips curve is also known as the 'expectations-augmented Phillips curve' because it now accounts for expectations in the determination of inflation.

We now take a more detailed look at the *SRPC* and show how it is used to explain the labour reaction to economic policy in the short run and in the long run. In Figure 9.8 (on the next page) we can see how a policymaker might use this tool to reduce unemployment.

The central bank wants to reduce unemployment to below its natural rate and so increase the money supply in an unanticipated (unexpected) way. Inflation will be higher than expected and (via the *SRPC*) we see that the economy moves along the Phillips curve following the red line and unemployment is reduced. However, this effect is only short run because in the following

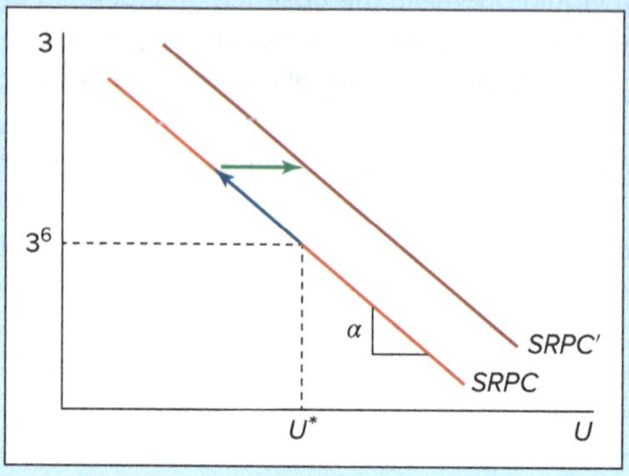

Figure 9.8 The *SRPC* prediction of policy, short run through to long run

period the expected price level will be higher (people adjust) and so the *SRPC* shift out to *SRPC*' to reflect this. Even at the higher expected rate of inflation, unemployment rises back again to U^*.

So in the short run the central bank has reduced unemployment, but in the long run, unemployment has returned to its natural rate. The outcome, in the long run, is just higher prices and no increase in employment – policy is said to be ineffective. You may recall that we had a similar discussion over the effectiveness of policy in Chapter 4. Just as the slope of the aggregate supply curve dictates the effectiveness of policy, so does the existence of a long-run Phillips curve (a vertical line up from the natural rate of unemployment in our diagrams).

EXERCISE 9.2

Use Figure 9.8, adding a long-run Phillips curve (*LRPC*), to show the effects of a policy introduced to decrease inflation just as Paul Volker, chairman of the US Federal Reserve (FED) did in the 1980s.

Unemployment to output using Okun's law

Output Gap: The difference between the actual and potential output. This difference can be in the levels or measured as a proportional deviation. If the output gap is positive, it is thought to be inflationary.
Unemployment Gap: The difference between the actual rate of unemployment and the natural rate of unemployment. We can think of this gap as the short-run deviation from the long run.

In 1962 an economist named Arthur Okun found an empirical relation between two common measures of excess demand: the **output gap** and the **unemployment gap**. The output gap is measured as the difference between actual output and the natural rate Y^* and the unemployment gap as the difference between actual unemployment and the natural rate of unemployment U^*, specifically defined as:

$$Y_{gap} = Y - Y^* \text{ and } U_{gap} = U - U^*$$

We can see why these measures or gaps represent excess demand in the economy. Imagine that output is rising above its normal level – we might be in an economic boom where there is excess demand in the economy. If output is below its normal level, there is demand 'deficiency' in the economy; we could think of an example such as a recession. Using data for the United States, Okun found a linear relationship of the form:

$$U_{gap} = -\theta Y_{gap}$$

The first thing to notice is that the relationship is negative or downward sloping, reinforcing our understanding that output and unemployment are close to equal and opposite partners, they are both highly correlated representatives of economic activity. The value for θ is thought to be between 1/2 and 1/3 so that a 1 per cent increase in unemployment is associated with a 2–3 per cent decline in output. Now that we understand the close relation between output and unemployment we can use it to develop an aggregate supply curve from our expectations-augmented version of the Phillips curve. In doing so, we bring together the short-run Phillips curve and Okun's law.

The expectations-augmented Phillips curve:

$$\pi = \pi^e - a(U - U^*)$$

which we can rewrite in terms of the unemployment gap:

$$\pi = \pi^e - a(U_{gap})$$

Okun's law from earlier states that:

$$U_{gap} = -\theta Y_{gap}$$

Combining the second Phillips curve with Okun's law gives:

$$\pi = \pi^e - a(-\theta Y_{gap})$$

Rewriting with the proportional deviation version of the output gap:

$$\pi = \pi^e + a\theta(Y - Y^*)$$

and rearranging in terms of Y:

$$Y = Y^* + \frac{1}{a\theta}(\pi - \pi^e)$$

and finally removing the dynamics from inflation (adding and subtracting P_{-1} inside the brackets) we have a version of an aggregate supply curve:

$$Y = Y^* + \delta(P - P^e) \text{ where } \delta = \frac{1}{a\theta}$$

According to the relation for aggregate supply above, output depends on potential output and some proportion δ of the deviation in prices from their expected level. If prices are higher than expected, suppliers will increase production. This exercise is very useful because it helps us to see why the Phillips curve is often referred to as the supply side relationship. We will discuss this functional form for the supply side in greater detail in Chapter 13.

9.4 Chapter summary: Putting it all together

In this chapter, we have learnt about the differing approaches to modelling the labour market. We have discussed in detail the static approaches through the long-run price setting/wage setting model, and the labour supply/labour demand model. The latter enables us to distinguish between equilibrium and disequilibrium unemployment in the short run. Recognizing the disequilibrium component of unemployment helps us to make an analysis of the labour market policy called the minimum wage; the protection that this policy provides is not always cost free.

We have introduced the Phillips curve, also known as the inflation equation, and used this theory to question the success of labour market policy aimed at reducing unemployment in the short run. We have also discovered the close relationship between output and unemployment using Okun's law and used this to connect the Phillips curve model to the aggregate supply curve. Developing the curve in this way leads us nicely into Chapter 10, where we will introduce the supply curve in more detail alongside the aggregate demand curve, to show how we can explain movements in output via the aggregate supply/aggregate demand model.

Assessment Question

Use the labour supply and demand schedules to provide some explanation and predictions of the effects of introducing a minimum wage in an economy where wages have been historically lower in comparison to international trading partners. Is the concept of an equilibrium wage a reasonable one?

Cases

The impact of the minimum wage on the labour market in the UK

Context

In 1999, the UK introduced the national minimum wage (NMW) policy, a labour market policy designed to protect low-paid workers by ensuring that employers pay their employees a minimum wage per hour. The policy was part of the then Labour government's broader commitment to reducing poverty and promoting fairness in the labour market.

Since its introduction, the minimum wage has been periodically increased, with the introduction of the national living wage (NLW) in 2016, aimed specifically at workers aged 25 and above. The government argues that the minimum wage policy ensures that workers receive a fair compensation for their labour, increases living standards, and can reduce income inequality. However, economists and policymakers continue to debate the potential side effects of such interventions.

Theoretical background

In a perfectly competitive labour market, the equilibrium wage is determined by the market forces of supply and demand. The market-clearing wage ensures that the quantity of labour supplied equals the quantity of labour demanded. However, when the government sets a minimum wage above the equilibrium wage, it can lead to wage distortions. This may cause:

- Unemployment: Employers may not hire as many workers because they cannot afford to pay a higher wage, and mechanical means of production becomes more attractive.
- Inefficient allocation of resources: With the wage floor set above equilibrium, some workers may find it difficult to secure jobs, while others may benefit from higher pay, but the market is no longer clearing.

Critics argue that this policy has unintended consequences, including potential job losses, especially for younger or less skilled workers. Conversely, supporters argue that the minimum wage helps reduce poverty, increases workers' purchasing power, and supports the economy by enhancing consumer demand.

Real-world data and impact

The UK has raised the minimum wage numerous times since 1999, normally as part of the chancellor's budget statement. As of 2025, the national minimum wage for workers aged 23 and over is £10.42 per hour. The government monitors the impact of the minimum wage on employment levels, poverty rates and overall economic performance from the office of the Low Pay Commission (LPC).

Research studies have shown mixed results. Some studies suggest that while the minimum wage increases the income of low-paid workers, it may also lead to reduced hours or job losses, particularly in sectors that rely on low-wage workers, such as hospitality and retail.

Key issues in the labour market policy of the minimum wage

1. Market distortions: Setting the minimum wage too high can distort the labour market, leading to unemployment among the least skilled workers.
2. Unintended effects on employment: The imposition of a minimum wage may reduce the number of jobs available, especially for younger workers or those with fewer qualifications.
3. Policy efficiency: While the minimum wage may lift some workers out of poverty, it does not necessarily target the most vulnerable, and could lead to inefficiency in the allocation of labour.
4. Regional discrepancies: The national minimum wage applies across the entire UK, but cost-of-living differences across regions can mean that a single wage rate may not be appropriate in all areas.
5. The role of employers: Employers may respond to the minimum wage by reducing employee hours or substituting workers with technology or automation.

Questions

1. Explain the basic economic theory behind the concept of a minimum wage in the context of a labour market.
2. Discuss the potential consequences of imposing a minimum wage above the market-clearing wage, particularly in relation to unemployment and job market inefficiencies.
3. What are some of the possible unintended consequences of the minimum wage policy in the UK, especially in relation to young workers and those with lower skill levels?
4. How does the minimum wage policy affect the supply and demand for labour? What are the potential consequences for employers and workers?
5. What role do regional disparities in living costs play in the effectiveness of the national minimum wage? How might the minimum wage policy fail to address such disparities?
6. In the context of the UK, assess whether the minimum wage has successfully reduced poverty or income inequality, or whether it has led to inefficiency in the labour market.

Problems

EASY

1. Which of the following best describes equilibrium in the labour market?
   a) The wage rate is determined by government policy, not by labour supply or demand.
   b) The labour market is always in a state of disequilibrium in the short run.
   c) The quantity of labour demanded exceeds the quantity of labour supplied at the prevailing wage rate.
   d) The quantity of labour supplied equals the quantity of labour demanded at the prevailing wage rate.
   e) The quantity of labour supplied exceeds the quantity of labour demanded at the prevailing wage rate.
2. According to the Phillips curve, what is the expected relationship between inflation and unemployment in the short run?
   a) Unemployment and inflation move in opposite directions in the long run.
   b) As unemployment rises, inflation falls.
   c) There is no theoretical relationship between inflation and unemployment.
   d) As unemployment falls, inflation rises.
   e) As unemployment rises, inflation rises.
3. In the context of the expectations-augmented Phillips curve, which factor can shift the curve upwards in the short run?
   a) A reduction in the level of government spending.
   b) A decrease in the money supply.
   c) A drop in the level of aggregate demand.
   d) An increase in the expected rate of inflation.
   e) A decrease in the level of unemployment.

MEDIUM

4. Which of the following statements best describes Okun's law?
   a) Okun's law suggests that unemployment and inflation are inversely related in the long run.
   b) It predicts that the government can use fiscal policy to decrease unemployment.
   c) It shows how changes in inflation rates affect unemployment in the short run.
   d) For every 1 per cent increase in the unemployment rate, a country's GDP will fall by approximately 2 per cent.
   e) Okun's law is a theory explaining the relationship between real wage levels and productivity.

5. In a situation of disequilibrium unemployment, which of the following might occur?
   a) Aggregate demand will exceed aggregate supply.
   b) Wage rates may fail to adjust, preventing the labour market from clearing.
   c) All unemployed workers become less willing to work at the prevailing wage.
   d) The labour market will return to equilibrium at full employment in the short run.
   e) Labour supply always exceeds labour demand, resulting in higher inflation.
6. Suppose the natural rate of unemployment in an economy is 5 per cent. If the actual unemployment rate is 8 per cent, and Okun's law holds with a coefficient of 2, calculate the approximate resulting loss in GDP as a percentage.
7. Discuss the relationship between the Phillips curve and the aggregate supply curve. How do shifts in the Phillips curve in turn affect aggregate supply, and what role do expectations play in this relationship?

HARD

8. Evaluate the role of the expectations-augmented Phillips curve in explaining long-run inflation-unemployment trade-offs. How does the concept of expectations impact the behaviour of inflation and unemployment over time?

CHAPTER 10

The Labour Market II

Chapter contents

At a Glance The labour market II

The issue

The static models of the labour market are useful for explaining and analysing pathologies such as the minimum wage and concepts such as disequilibrium unemployment. In reality, though, the labour market does not clear; unemployment is a reflection of economic activity which is itself a cyclical macroeconomic variable. How do we explain fluctuations in unemployment and the reality of labour market frictions?

The understanding

Following on from Chapter 9, we introduce labour market dynamic so that we can take account of the flows between the components of the labour market. We take a simplistic approach to explaining the flows before introducing a labour market matching efficiency model capable of capturing real life labour market behaviours.

The usefulness

Measures of the labour market such as the unemployment rate are fundamentally flawed; worse still, the media use these figures to comment on the state of the labour market and the economy more generally. Understanding the importance of taking into account the richer dynamics of the labour market enables us to provide more accurate economic analysis.

10.1 Introduction

In Chapter 9 we laid out the traditional static explanations of the labour market, using the price setting/wage setting model and the market for labour supply and labour demand. These models are useful to explain concepts such as equilibrium and disequilibrium unemployment and even to analyse labour market pathologies such as the minimum wage. In this chapter we take a richer view of the labour market to capture the realities of labour market flows. Models with dynamics can capture such realities that highlight problems with labour market measures, such as the unemployment rate, which is flawed by the absence of account for those workers exiting the labour force.

We begin by defining the flows or workers that move in and out of the labour force and the inter movements between the pool of the employed and unemployed. These flows give us a deeper understanding of how the labour market takes shape over time. Adding the dimension of time allows us to measure unemployment duration, a reflection of the flexibility of a labour market and allows better comparison of labour markets across countries. Finally we build a labour market matching model that captures the path of unemployment using the job finding and vacancy filling rates that workers and firms experience in the real world. Unemployment dynamics allow us to explore fluctuations in unemployment and help us to measure labour market rigidity and mobility in society.

Learning Outcomes

By the end of this chapter you should be able to:

- Explain labour market flows between the components of the labour market.
- Discuss dynamic explanations for unemployment and the concept of unemployment duration.
- Connect the concepts of unemployment duration and long-term unemployed.
- Evaluate the conditions for equilibrium in the labour market matching model.

10.2 A dynamic approach for the labour market

A common cause of criticism for the static explanation of the labour market is a failure to account for important labour market behavioural characteristics. To explain this simply; our two static models presented in Chapter 9 were able to predict the level of employment at a particular wage level, but little else. If we are comparing the labour market in a country across two years, we could use the change in the level of unemployment to make a better judgement; perhaps that an unemployment level of 2 million is better than 3 million in the previous year.

Now imagine that in the previous year a lower number of workers were leaving the labour force. It is possible that the drop in unemployment was actually caused by workers 'leaving' the workforce rather than being fired. Which year is better, now that we have more detail? Here we look at the dynamic explanation of the labour market so that we can measure the changes below the surface statistics for the labour market.

Unemployment explained in terms of flows

To begin with, we can use a model that uses stocks and flows to explain the labour market. The level of unemployment in our model is a stock variable and when workers are fired there is a flow into the stock and when workers are hired, a flow out.

The two diagrams in Figure 10.1 represent the labour market pictured over two periods, say periods 1 and 2. In both diagrams the labour market is split into three components: The biggest (outer) circle represents the working age population, typically those between the ages of 16 and retirement age. Within the outer circle is another circle which represents the labour force or those willing and able to work at any given wage rate. This labour force is made up of two parts: the proportion employed and the proportion unemployed. Here we have drawn the labour market with its three components across two periods to demonstrate the flows between the components.

Figure 10.1 Over time there are flows into and out of employment and unemployment

We can see that in period 2 unemployment has decreased, and based purely on this observation we could say that economic conditions have improved – but have they? Unemployment has fallen in the second period but so has the workforce. One reason for this might be that workers have given up looking for jobs, instead of being hired. In other words, it is possible that employment has not grown at all and what we are actually seeing is a worsening of macroeconomic conditions. The dynamic approach shows us a 'fuller' picture when we control for the flows between the components. In the next section, we discuss the flows in more detail.

The flows and the duration of unemployment

We can categorize the flows in the labour market using our three components: the unemployed can find jobs (hired) or leave the labour force (discouraged); the employed can become separated from their jobs (fired/quit); or can leave the labour force (retire). The remainder of the working age population (those outside the workforce) can move straight into employment or unemployment should they decide to participate in the labour market. Additionally, we can define three concepts using these flows:

- **Separations – a movement from employment to unemployment**
- **Hires – a movement from unemployment to employment**
- **Exits – leaving the labour force from unemployment.**

Notice that the labour market hires and separations only include movements between the components within the labour force, that is, between employment and unemployment. Also, that exits are specifically defined as an exit from unemployment to outside the workforce – as an example, we can think of these as discouraged workers. From these flows, we can now calculate a measure of 'fluidity' for the labour market – known as the 'duration of unemployment' – so that an economy with a high duration of unemployment is seen as sclerotic (rigid) and associated with an inefficient labour market where workers take a longer time to find jobs. If we define h as the proportion of the labour force being hired in any period and e as the proportion exiting from unemployment, then the average duration of unemployment equals the inverse of the sum of these two proportions:

$$\textit{Duration of Unemployment} = \frac{1}{h + e}$$

The average duration of unemployment equals the inverse of the probability of leaving the pool of unemployment in any period. Figure 10.2 gives an example of how the pattern of unemployment changes over time. Notice that for our case of the UK, the number of those unemployed for more than one year tends to increase during recessions, as we might expect. Here we see that those considered as long-term unemployed peaked around 2014 and spiked more recently during the COVID crisis.

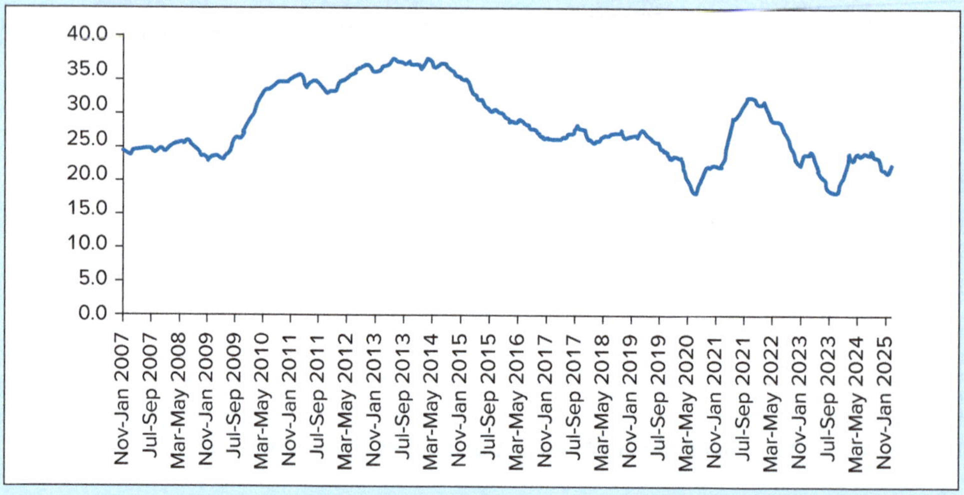

Figure 10.2 Percentage of unemployed, without work for more than one year in the UK (2007–2025)

Source: Office for National Statistics 2025. https://www.ons.gov.uk/employmentandlabourmarket/peoplenotinwork/unemployment/timeseries/mgsx/lms

EXERCISE 10.1

In any month in the UK there is a probability of 30 per cent of an unemployed worker finding a job and at the same time a 20 per cent probability of an unemployed worker giving up looking for a job. What is the average duration of unemployment in the UK in terms of months?

10.3 The matching function in the labour market

The traditional explanation of the labour market is that there is a simplifying assumption that all workers and the jobs that they seek are identical to each other. Although this is convenient, it overlooks important levels of heterogeneity in the behaviour of firms and workers and the challenges they come across in the process of matching worker to vacancy. In real life there are also important imperfections to information availability, and these are assumed away in traditional representations of the labour market.

A matching model of the labour market describes how workers are matched together, leading to employment. It explains the process of how unemployed workers find jobs and how firms find the right employees. Key components of the model include labour supply by households, labour demand by firms facing the costs of searching for jobs and the matching of jobs.

Key assumptions of the model are that there exist labour market frictions, whereby there are costs to searching for and finding jobs, that the matching process depends on the number of vacancies and the level of unemployment, and that firms make the hiring decision based on labour market conditions; job creation is endogenous.

We can specify a matching function:

$$M = \lambda(U, V)$$

Matching is described as a function of the number of unemployed U and the number of vacancies V. The functional form displays diminishing marginal returns to unemployment and vacancies. We can think of a Cobb Douglas-type structure to suit our purposes.

$$M = A(U^{\alpha}, V^{\beta})$$

where M is the number of successful matches; A is a constant reflecting labour market characteristics; and the elasticities α and β are the returns of increasing unemployment and returns to vacancies, respectively – both values are typically less than one, reflecting decreasing returns.

EXAMPLE 10.1

Real world example: The US labour market

After the financial crisis of 2008, unemployment in the US labour market rose sharply and despite rising vacancies in 2010, remained stubbornly high. This highlighted new labour market imperfections, or frictions, that existed in the market for workers. Structural changes had brought new inefficiencies in the matching process between workers and firms.

Labour market imperfections

A significant percentage of workers had skills in declining industries such as construction, whereas new industries in healthcare and technology faced a lack of available skilled workers. This made it more difficult to make successful job matches between unemployed workers and vacancies.

Active labour market policy

To address this problem, US policymakers introduced new active labour market policies aimed at improving the matching process. These policies included investment in retraining workers with new skills and increasing incentives to improve labour market mobility.

Job finding and vacancy filling

Two key parameters in the matching model are provided by the job finding rate and the **vacancy filling rate**. These key parameters provide a richness to our labour market model that can reflect the rigidity of individual labour markets. A more flexible labour market, perhaps one displayed by countries with similar labour market regulations to that of the US, can be captured here. We can specify these more exactly using the following functions:

> **Vacancy Filling Rate:** The rate at which job vacancies are filled by workers looking for jobs. A higher vacancy filling rate is associated with a more flexible labour market.

$$\textit{Job Finding Rate} = \frac{M}{U}$$

The job finding rate for unemployed workers depends on the ratio of the number of successful matches to the number of unemployed. Notice that the job finding rate is also the probability of an unemployed worker finding a job in this labour market.

$$\textit{Vacancy Filling Rate} = \frac{M}{V}$$

The vacancy filling rate for firms depends on the ratio of the number of successful matches to the number of vacancies. The vacancy filling rate is also the probability of a firm filling a vacancy.

We can use the concepts of the job finding rate and the vacancy filling rate to discuss another measure of the condition of the labour market, that of labour market fluidity. Labour market fluidity is reflected by the concept of labour market tightness; how flexible the labour market is in terms of workers being matched with jobs. Labour markets that are less tight (or slack) tend to be associated with more tightly regulated labour protection laws, so that they are less fluid.

$$\text{Labour Market Tightness} = \frac{V}{U}$$

Labour market tightness can be defined using the ratio of vacancies to unemployed workers. The job finding rate increases with higher labour market tightness, as an increase in the number of vacancies per unemployed will make it easier for individuals to find jobs. The vacancy filling rate decreases with higher labour market tightness as there are relatively fewer unemployed workers per vacancy, making it harder for firms to find workers.

Unemployment dynamics and equilibrium in the matching model

To introduce dynamics into the model we can make use of a process for the path of unemployment. Given our framework here, we can make use of the difference between the number of losing jobs and the number of new hires from the matching process. We capture this formally after introducing the concept of labour market separations.

The **separation rate**, *S*, measures the in-flows into the pool of unemployed workers. Think of workers being fired, but this is not the whole story; separations from employment include workers being fired, workers quitting their jobs and jobs themselves disappearing.

> **Separation Rate:** The rate at which employed workers lose their jobs, flowing from employment into unemployment. All fires are separations, but not all separations are fires.

Define the number of separations in the labour market, *S*, as equal to the number of employed workers losing their jobs at rate *s*:

$$S = (1 - U)s$$

Then the change in unemployment can be written:

$$\Delta U = S - M$$

The change in unemployment is equal to the number of separations from job losses, *S*, minus the number of successful matches, *M*, in the labour market.

Basic equilibrium is reached when the number of vacancies and the number of workers unemployed are in balance. Firms will create job vacancies up until the cost of creating vacancies is equal to the benefit of creating that vacancy. The matching model of the labour market helps us to capture the dynamics and labour market frictions that we see in real life macroeconomy.

10.4 Chapter summary: Putting it all together

In this chapter, we have developed our understanding of how we can model the labour market in macroeconomics. Focusing on dynamic processes and flows, we have shown how we can bring a sense of realism to the explanation of how unemployment can exist in the presence of labour market imperfections. The flows between the components give us a deeper understanding of the shortcomings of the traditional measurements of the condition of the labour market. For instance, the flow approach helps us to identify the underlying causes for changes in the unemployment rate; a drop in unemployment does not always reflect an improving macroeconomic performance.

We can also use the flows to draw down deeper metrics that can help us to form policy aimed at specific sections of the labour force, using the concept of the duration of unemployment. Further to this, we have outlined a fully specified model that can help us to explain why some labour markets are more flexible than others. The matching efficiency model takes into account the labour market flows and fluctuations in unemployment that we witness in the macroeconomic data.

Assessment Question

Evaluate the equilibrium relationship between the number of unemployed workers (*U*) and the number of job vacancies (*V*) in a simplified matching model of the labour market. Discuss how job creation, matching efficiency and labour market dynamics influence this equilibrium.

Cases

Labour market flows in the United States after COVID-19

In 2020, the COVID-19 pandemic caused an unprecedented shock to the US labour market. Within weeks, millions of workers lost their jobs due to lockdowns and forced business closures. As the economy reopened over time, hiring resumed once more, but the labour market was much slower to recover than expected. Economists and policymakers have used the framework of labour market flows, specifically the job finding rate and separation rate, to understand the dynamics of the recovery in terms of employment over this episode.

Labour market snapshot (approximate monthly averages during 2021):

- Labour force: approximately 160 million
- Unemployed persons: approximately 9 million
- Employed persons: approximately 151 million
- On average, around 6 million people were hired per month.
- Around 5.5 million people were separated from their jobs each month (voluntarily or involuntarily).

Key concepts:

- Job finding rate (f): the proportion of unemployed individuals who find a job in a given month.
- Separation rate (s): the proportion of employed individuals who lose or leave their jobs in a given month.

Observations:

- Despite high levels of hiring, the unemployment rate declined slowly at first.
- The so-called 'Great Resignation' saw record levels of voluntary quits, contributing to high separation rates.
- Policymakers were not unanimous in how to support a faster and more stable recovery in the job market.

Questions

1. What do the job finding rate and separation rate tell us about the US labour market during the pandemic recovery?
2. Why did unemployment remain relatively high at times even though millions of people were being hired monthly?
3. How might the 'Great Resignation' have influenced the separation rate and labour market recovery?
4. If the job finding rate increases but the separation rate remains high, what is the most likely impact on the unemployment rate?
5. What kinds of policy responses did (or could) the US government implement to influence these labour market flows?

Problems

EASY

1. In a standard labour market flow model, which of the following represents a worker moving from unemployment to employment?
   a) separation rate
   b) job finding rate
   c) vacancy posting rate
   d) matching efficiency
   e) wage-setting rate
2. An increase in the job separation rate, holding all other labour market flows constant, would initially lead to:
   a) lower unemployment
   b) higher employment
   c) higher unemployment

d) more vacancies
e) lower labour force participation

3. In a matching function, which of the following would be considered a labour market friction?
   a) perfect information about all available jobs
   b) immediate relocation of workers
   c) delay in finding a suitable job
   d) faster wage negotiation between unions and employers
   e) a lack of separation from jobs

MEDIUM

4. Suppose the number of matches *M* depends on unemployment *U* and vacancies *V*. If unemployment rises while vacancies remain constant, what is the likely short-run effect on the number of matches?
   a) matches will fall
   b) matches will stay the same
   c) matches will increase
   d) matches will double
   e) matches will be unaffected if matching efficiency falls
5. Which of the following labour market characteristics is most directly linked to the average duration of unemployment?
   a) the job separation rate
   b) the efficiency of wage bargaining
   c) the job finding rate
   d) the elasticity of labour supply
   e) the number of vacancies posted
6. The labour market matching function is often assumed to have constant returns to scale. This means that:
   a) doubling unemployment and vacancies halves matches
   b) doubling unemployment and vacancies doubles matches
   c) increasing vacancies reduces unemployment at a decreasing rate
   d) matches depend only on unemployment
   e) matches are unrelated to the number of unemployed or vacancies

HARD

7. In Econland:
   - The labour force is 10 million people.
   - In a given month, 300,000 unemployed individuals are hired.
   - An additional 50,000 unemployed individuals exit the labour force (e.g., become discouraged workers).

   a) What is the monthly proportion of the labour force hired from unemployment, *h*?
   b) What is the monthly proportion of the labour force exiting unemployment, *e*?
   c) Using the formula in the text, calculate the average duration of unemployment (in months) in Econland.
   d) Suppose policy reforms reduce the number of exits from unemployment to 20,000 per month, while hiring remains unchanged. What is the new duration of unemployment?
   e) What does this tell us about the relationship between fluidity and unemployment duration?
8. Explain how changes in the separation rate and the job finding rate in an economy can affect the steady-state rate of unemployment. How might labour market policy interventions affect these rates?
9. Discuss the role of search frictions in labour markets. How do they justify the use of a matching function rather than a simple supply and demand model?

CHAPTER 11

The IS/LM Model

Chapter contents

At a Glance — The IS/LM model

The issue

This chapter introduces the closed economy version of the general equilibrium IS/LM model. How does the economy behave in the short run when prices are slow to adjust?

The understanding

Making the extreme assumption that prices are fixed, we analyse how the goods and money market react to economic fluctuations and changes in economic policy. With the goods market and money market represented simultaneously we can account for the multiplier effect and the crowding out effect as part of the adjustment process from one equilibrium to another.

The usefulness

The IS/LM model is the workhorse framework for professional economists around the world. While not without its own limitations, this model underlies the reasoning behind much commentary in the profession of economic analysis.

11.1 Introduction

The Investment Savings/Liquidity Money (IS/LM) model evolved from attempts by an economist called John Hicks to formalize John Maynard Keynes' general theory of employment, interest and money in 1937. The model proposes an interrelationship between the money market and the goods market via two schedules in one general economy wide market place. The interest rate is used as the adjusting mechanism that can equilibrate both markets simultaneously, in doing so providing a general equilibrium prediction for the level of output in the economy.

One of the most important assumptions behind the IS/LM model is that prices are held fixed – a convenience that makes space for a two-dimensional analysis between output and the interest rate. This simplifying assumption is why the model is termed a 'short-run' model; given that in the long run we assume that prices are flexible. The model is useful because we can use it to make predictions about how the economy will react to disturbances and economic policy in both real and financial terms simultaneously. As an example, we can consider the use of expansionary fiscal policy – after an increase in government spending, the model allows us to analyse the two after-effects: the multiplier effect and the crowding out of investment.

EXAMPLE 11.1

Real world example: The multiplier and crowding out effects after COVID-19

During the COVID-19 pandemic, governments across the world implemented substantial fiscal expansions to revive sectors of the economy that had been adversely affected by forced shutdowns. The US American Rescue Plan Act 2021 provided direct transfers to households and extended social security and aid to local government.

The multiplier effect

Lower income consumers spent this money directly on household essentials, boosting demand and employment across the economy, amplifying the original spend and setting off a chain reaction of economic activity.

The crowding out effect

As the US economy recovered, crowding out took place; massive increases in government spending combined with supply chain constraints contributed towards higher inflation between 2021 and 2022. Increases in interest rates by the Federal Reserve made borrowing more expensive for households and firms, leading to a slowing of investment across the economy.

It is because of the policy implications and the simplicity in terms of set up, that nearly 80 years after its conception the model is still widely referred to by practising economists across the globe. The model provides an easy framework to base arguments over economic policy and its implications.

In this chapter, we will build the IS/LM model by making use of our knowledge from earlier chapters in the book. In Chapter 6, we learnt how to build the Keynesian Cross using the individual components of aggregate expenditure, to predict the determination of income. From these 'goods market' components we will derive the investment savings schedule, also referred to as the IS curve. We will also turn to our knowledge of the money market from Chapter 5, where money supply and money demand come together to determine the interest rate in the economy. From these 'money market' components we will derive the liquidity preference money schedule, also called the LM curve. The two schedules combine to provide us with a 'general equilibrium' in the economy where the goods and money markets are simultaneously equilibrated with one level of output and one interest rate.

The chapter begins by deriving the IS/LM model using the diagrams of the Keynesian cross and the money market, before bringing the two schedules together in one diagram, so that we can then make use of the model to analyse and predict the effects of economic disturbances and policy. The model is later laid out using a more formal approach, solving the IS/LM model mathematically. In order to do this, we will make use of the explicit functional forms of the components of aggregate expenditure (consumption, investment and government expenditure), given in Chapter 6 and the money supply and demand functions, given in Chapter 5 before solving the model for general equilibrium.

Learning Outcomes

By the end of this chapter you should be able to:

- Build the IS curve from the model of the goods market.
- Build the LM curve from the money market.
- Discuss the effects and economic consequences of economic policy using the IS and LM schedules.
- Appraise the short- and long-run effects of economic shocks using the IS and LM schedules.
- Solve the IS/LM model mathematically from individual explicit functional forms for the goods market and money market.

11.2 Building the IS/LM model diagrammatically

The IS/LM model is the simultaneous representation of the goods and money markets together in one two-dimensional setting, where output is determined by the intersection of the IS and LM schedules, and the interest rate adjusts to ensure equilibrium is maintained across both markets. With the interest rate r on the vertical axis and output Y on the horizontal axis, we hold all other macroeconomic variables constant for this analysis, an assumption we commonly call '*ceteris paribus*'.

The assumption of *ceteris paribus* might seem like an over-simplification, but a benefit of this is the ability to use variables like government spending G and the money supply M as policy or shock variables. With this set-up we can show the use of policy as exogenous changes that shift the appropriate schedules left and right and visualize the effect of the policy on economic activity. What follows is the diagrammatic derivation of the investment savings schedule (**IS curve**), which represents the real side of the economy, and the liquidity preference schedule (**LM curve**), which represents the financial side. Once we have built the model diagrammatically we can then use the curves to analyse economic policy and other economic disturbances.

IS Curve: The schedule (locus) of different combinations of r and Y that represent equilibrium in the goods market. The IS curve is built via the Keynesian cross.

LM Curve: The schedule (locus) of different combinations of r and Y that represent equilibrium in the money market, given by the intersection of the money supply and money demand schedules.

The savings and investment schedule (IS curve)

The Keynesian cross, that we introduced in Chapter 4 and discussed further in Chapter 7, is a two-dimensional model between actual output and planned aggregate expenditure that enables us to visualize the proposition by Keynes that the economy is driven by demand. The model is drawn for a given interest rate (where the interest rate is assumed fixed); in which case, investment *I*, which naturally depends on the interest rate, is also assumed fixed or exogenous. The other components of **aggregate demand** are consumption *C*, which depends on national income, and government expenditure *G*, also assumed exogenous – in other words, fixed by the government.

Aggregate Demand: A force that drives economic activity, not to be confused with economic activity (or output) itself. Aggregate demand drives changes in production and becomes output at the point of transaction.
Goods Market: The real side of the economy where goods and services are exchanged for domestic expenditure. We can think in terms of suppliers producing goods and consumers providing revenue to the firms in return.

If we allow the interest rate to change, we obtain a new level of investment and a new equilibrium level of output in the **goods market**. The IS schedule is the locus of these equilibrium sets of interest rate and output combinations for the goods market. Put another way, we can think of the IS schedule as representing all the combinations of output *Y* and interest rate *r* for which the goods market is in equilibrium.

To begin with, let us recall the goods market from Chapter 7, where we learnt that aggregate expenditure can be split into its individual components:

$$E = C + I + G$$

This key equation is also an identity, being constructed using the sum of its own parts; in the same way that when we divide an apple, the sum of the slices must be equal to the original apple before it was split. Now we can borrow the message from Keynes – that changes in planned expenditure, which we can also think of as aggregate demand, will lead to changes in economic activity (output). Given the Keynesian proposition, we can also write the aggregate identity as:

$$AD = C + I + G$$

To underpin the idea that the economy is demand-led the Keynesian cross is drawn in two dimensions between aggregate demand *AD* and output *Y*.

Notice that with the model drawn in aggregate demand/output space, the AD schedule is upward sloping in output; as output increases, consumption also increases through higher income. In Figure 11.1 we can see that the rate at which the aggregate demand schedule is sloping upwards is given by the marginal propensity to consume (MPC); as income increases only a proportion is spent on firms and the rest is saved, meaning that aggregate demand increases less than one for one with increases in income. As the only component of aggregate demand that is dependent on output is consumption, the slope of the consumption function is also the slope of the aggregate demand schedule, the MPC.

Investment *I* and government expenditure *G* are fixed for this analysis (they are just numbers, as you will see in our numerical example later); they make up part of exogenous expenditure along with autonomous consumption. These exogenous elements come together to make up the

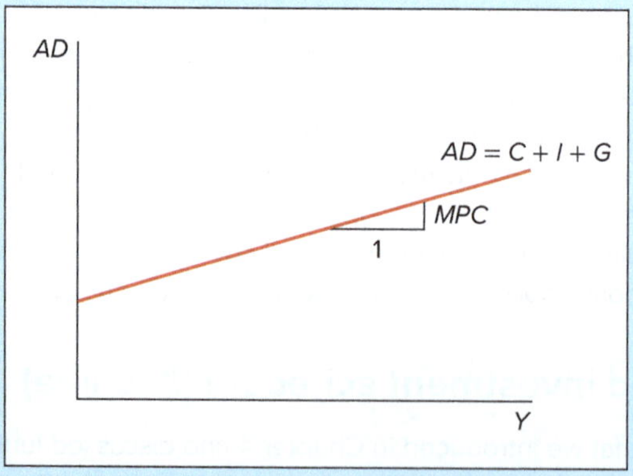

Figure 11.1 The aggregate demand schedule showing how AD increases with higher output *Y*

intercept of the AD schedule as they are all independent of the level of output. Now that we have plotted the AD line, we can also use it to show us how income is determined in equilibrium using a 45° line (Figure 11.2).

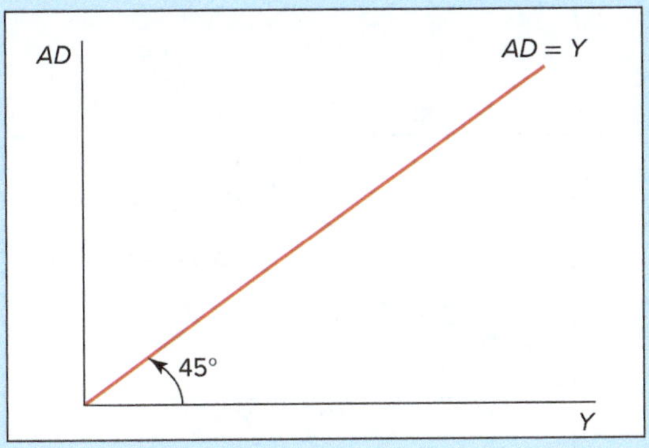

Figure 11.2 The 45° line, showing where aggregate demand equals output

Anywhere along the 45° line, **aggregate demand** is equal to output, or in other words the amount of output demanded is exactly equal to the amount of output supplied. As demand is met exactly, suppliers have no need to change production to meet existing demand (we are in a state of equilibrium). The 45° line provides us with an equilibrium condition that we can combine with the aggregate demand schedule to construct the Keynesian cross.

Aggregate Demand: The anticipated level of spending in the economy that provides the driving force for movements in output. Output demanded is negatively related to the price level.

Combining the equilibrium condition and the aggregate demand function in Figure 11.3 we see how income is determined in the economy. Given any different level of expenditure in the economy the Keynesian cross model will predict an equilibrium level of output at the intersection of both lines. Remember that this Keynesian cross is drawn for a specific level of investment, which is dependent itself on an exogenously set interest rate.

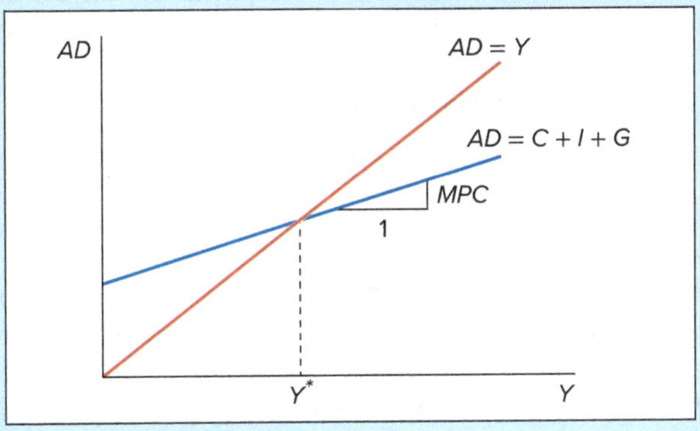

Figure 11.3 Building the Keynesian cross

At any specific interest rate our cross will predict a corresponding equilibrium level of output, which together make up a single goods **market equilibrium** and one single point on our IS schedule. If we change the interest rate, there will be a different corresponding level of equilibrium output which will give us another point on the IS schedule. The IS schedule, then, is the locus of equilibriums that come from the Keynesian cross given different rates of interest – or put another way, the corresponding combinations of interest rate and output from equilibriums in the goods market.

Market Equilibrium: A unique outcome where the natural driving forces of the market come to an end. After a disturbance in the market, changes in the market price will drive the economy back towards equilibrium. In equilibrium, the price clears the market, ending the process of adjustment.

In Figure 11.4 we see how changes in the interest rate affect investment and in turn the AD schedule, leading to a new equilibrium level of income and a corresponding co-ordinate for our IS schedule. We begin with the interest rate at r' where our Keynesian cross predicts an initial equilibrium level of output, Y' (red dot). This combination of interest rate and output gives us our first co-ordinate for our IS schedule at (r', Y').

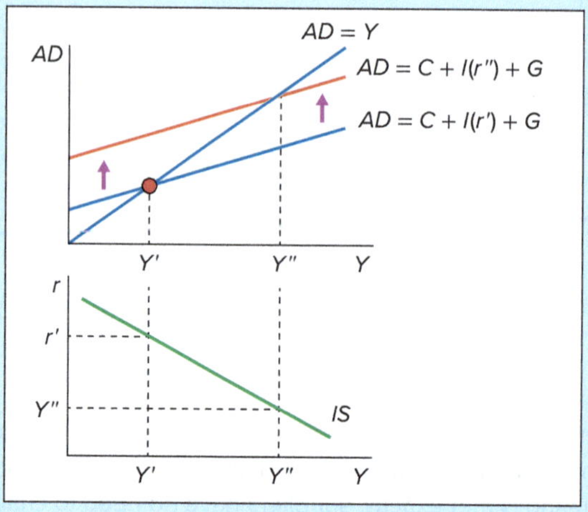

Figure 11.4 Using the Keynesian cross to plot the IS curve

Now imagine that the interest rate decreases to r''; remember from Chapter 6 that the interest rate and investment are negatively correlated; investment will increase when firms realize their ability to borrow more to invest; higher investment increases aggregate demand and so the AD schedule shifts upwards. The AD line shifts upwards providing us with a new predicted equilibrium level of output at Y''. This new combination of interest rate and output gives us our second point on the IS schedule (r'', Y''). In fact, for every value of r there is a unique equilibrium level of output in the goods market and these combinations give us the locus of co-ordinates for our IS schedule.

We can now write the IS curve mathematically, as:

$$Y = C + I(r) + G$$

Notice the similarity to our equation for the goods market in Chapter 6. A change in Y or a change in r will provide us with a movement along the IS curve, and a change in anything else (for example, a change in government expenditure) will shift the IS curve left or right. The IS curve is downward sloping in Y reflecting the prediction that at higher rates of interest we will have lower levels of investment and thus lower levels of output.

A key characteristic of the IS/LM model is the slope of the *IS* schedule itself; this is dependent on the sensitivity of investment to changes in the interest rate – the more investment changes after a change in the interest rate the flatter the IS schedule will be in interest rate r output Y space.

EXERCISE 11.1

1 How would the IS schedule react to an exogenous increase in investment? (In other words, a change in investment *not* brought about by a change in the interest rate.)

2 Can you discuss why the reaction of the IS schedule is different for an exogenous and an endogenous change in investment.

The liquidity preference money schedule (LM curve)

Money Market: The monetary side of the economy where the money supply is set by the central bank and money is demanded to facilitate the transactions taking place in the goods market.

The key elements that make up the **money market** were introduced in Chapter 5; the money supply set by the central bank and money demand dependent on the choice between holding money balances or interest-bearing assets (savings accounts), with the economy-wide interest rate reacting to that choice. In a similar way to the IS schedule, the LM schedule represents a locus of combinations of output and interest rates for which the money market is in equilibrium, and so we begin our explanation with the individual elements of the money market, starting with money demand.

The demand for money can be explained using Keynes' theory of liquidity preference, first introduced in Chapter 5. Money demand can be categorized into three types: *transactions demand* for economic activity; *precautionary demand* for money kept to one side; and *speculative demand* to invest in assets that bear a return. All three types of money demand depend negatively on the interest rate and positively on output and so we can simplify the schedule for money demand into one curve, just as we have for $L(r, Y)$ in Figure 11.5.

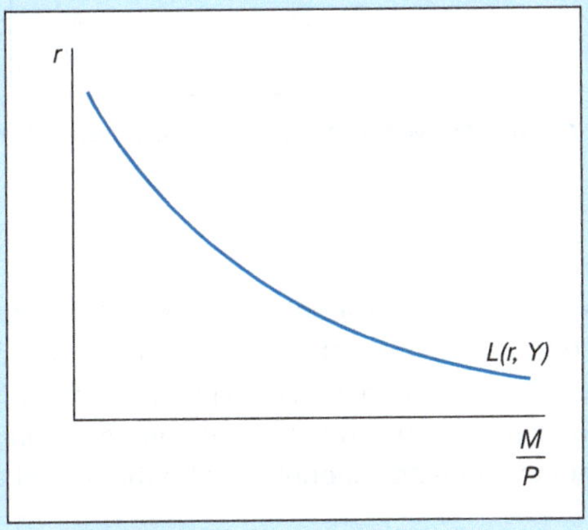

Figure 11.5 The money demand schedule in the money market

The money market is drawn in interest rate r real money balances $\left(\frac{M}{P}\right)$ space, with money demand $L(r, Y)$ dependent on the interest rate and the level of output. Changes in output will shift the curve up or down; for instance, higher output will result in a higher demand for money at every interest rate to facilitate the additional transactions from the additional output. Notice that the curve is downward sloping, reflecting the fact that at higher interest rates money is attracted into interest-bearing accounts, reducing demand for real money balances.

We can write money demand mathematically as:

$$M^d = L\ (r, Y)$$

which helps us to see mathematically that the demand for money M^d depends on the interest rate r and the level of income in the economy Y (the variables in the brackets). The supply of money in the money market is normally assumed to be exogenously set by the central bank, though it is also worth noting here that this assumption/understanding is a contentious one. In fact, a growing number of commentators believe that the money supply is endogenous, driven purely by the demand for loans. Rather than the bank setting the money supply, the money supply expands and contracts in reaction to the changes in demand.

While this argument over the determination of the stock of money in the economy continues unabated, it is not entirely essential for our understanding of the money market. Accordingly, we will continue with an explanation that assumes that the money supply is decided by the central bank, in other words set exogenously. We can combine the money supply schedule with money demand in a market for central bank money to see a clear picture of how the stock of money in the economy is determined. The money supply schedule is drawn vertically in interest rate r real money balances $\left(\frac{M}{P}\right)$ space in Figure 11.6.

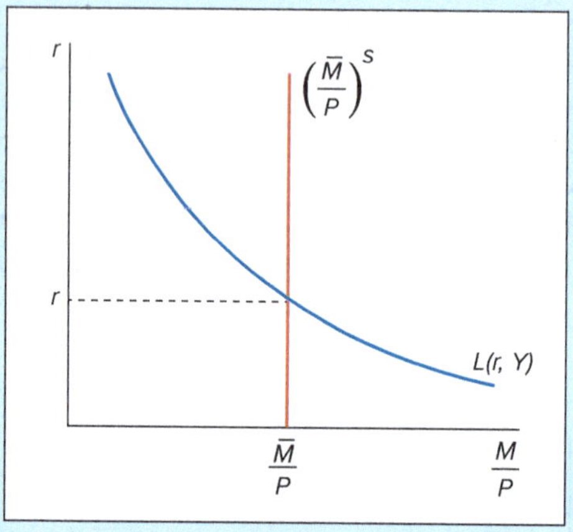

Figure 11.6 The money market showing the money supply and demand schedules

Where the demand for money and the supply of money intersect, the money market predicts an economy wide equilibrium interest rate r and level of real money balances. The equilibrium interest rate can be thought of as the price of money in the economy, or the opportunity cost of holding money instead of placing money in an interest-bearing bank account; the slope of the money demand schedule can be thought of as our economy wide preference for liquidity.

Notice that we write the money supply schedule mathematically as:

$$M^S = \left(\frac{\bar{M}}{P}\right)$$

where the money stock is set by the central bank for the purposes of monetary policy. Notice that the money stock is divided by the price level P to specify money in real terms. Increases in the price level erode the purchasing power of the money supply, lowering real money balances. Below, we use the money market to explain the locus of equilibriums that make up the LM curve. We begin by drawing two graphs, aligned horizontally, with the money market on the left and another graph in (r, Y) space on the right (Figure 11.7). Notice that the interest rate features on both vertical axes.

In the money market there is an initial level of output (Y') with a corresponding level of money demand $L(r, Y')$ and the money supply set by the central bank; we can see that the money market predicts an initial equilibrium interest rate of (r'). This combination of output and interest rates from money market equilibrium provides us with our first co-ordinate on the LM curve (r', Y') in our diagram on the right, bearing in mind that all points on the LM curve represent different money market equilibriums.

If output increases to (Y'') there will be an increase in the demand for money to carry out the additional transactions from the additional production; there is an increase in money demand at every interest rate and the money demand function will shift up to $L(r, Y'')$ to reflect this. With higher money demand, the money market will predict a new higher equilibrium interest rate (r''). Together the higher level of output and higher interest rate gives us the second point on the LM curve (r'', Y'').

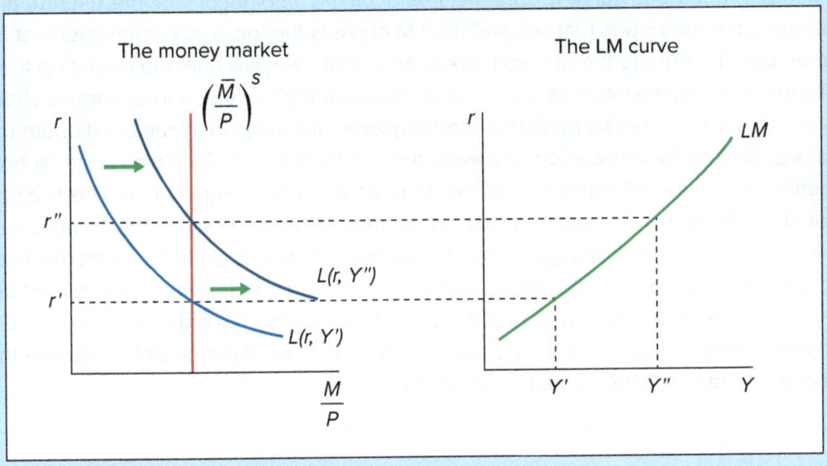

Figure 11.7 Plotting the LM curve from the money market

An event that begins with a change in the interest rate or a change in output will be reflected by a movement along the LM curve, but a change in anything else that affects the money market will result in a shift of the curve. The LM curve shifts after exogenous changes to the money supply, exogenous changes to money demand, and after changes in the price level.

We can now write the LM curve mathematically as:

$$L(r, Y) = \frac{\bar{M}}{P}$$

where money demanded in the economy is equal to the money supplied. Money demand is a function of the interest rate and output and money supply is set exogenously by the central bank. Notice that the LM curve is upward sloping, reflecting the prediction that a higher level of income causes higher demand for money and thus higher rates of interest. A key characteristic of the IS/LM model is the slope of the LM schedule itself, this is dependent on the sensitivity of money demand to changes in the interest rate and the sensitivity of money demand to changes in output. The more that money demand changes after a change in the interest rate the flatter the LM schedule will be in interest rate r output Y space.

General equilibrium in the IS/LM model

Now that we have derived the IS and LM schedules in diagrams separately, we can now plot them together in a unified general equilibrium model of the economy; the intersection of the IS and LM schedules provides the interest rate r^e and level of income Y^e that simultaneously equilibrate the real and monetary sides of the economy. Figure 11.8 shows the two schedules together in general equilibrium.

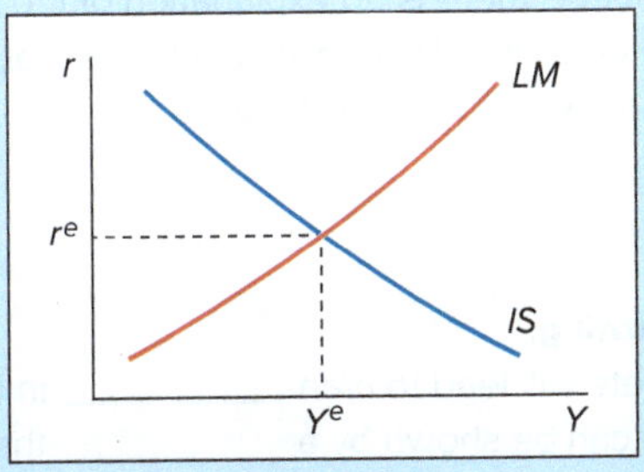

Figure 11.8 General equilibrium in the IS/LM model

Remember that the IS curve represents the locus of combinations of interest rate and output that equate the goods market, and the LM curve is the locus of combinations of interest rate and output that equate the money market. Now that we have built the model up from the two individual markets we can use it to predict the economy's reaction to economic shocks and economic policy; these shocks push the economy away from any long-run equilibrium to a new short-run equilibrium. With the economy away from its long-run position we will show how market forces combine with the adjustment of prices to restore long-run equilibrium. This is a static model, so there is no exact description of how we move from one equilibrium to another.

To overcome this shortcoming completely, we would need a larger-scale model and an exact specification showing how the dynamics of each variable and their interactions are related across time periods. We will discuss how the model uses these 'jumps' to explain shocks and economic policy in more detail in the next section, and how we can extend the model to capture the real life impacts of international trade in the following chapter.

EXERCISE 11.2

1 How would you expect the money demand function to react to a decrease in output?
2 Does this change provide us with 'a movement along' or 'a shift' in the LM schedule?

ASSESSMENT ADVICE

It would be impressive to highlight your understanding that only interest rate led changes can lead us to movements along the IS curve. Other exogenous changes, such as a change in government expenditure and exogenous changes in consumer confidence, will shift the curve. In an exam, it would be quite impressive to show that you have grasped this distinction.

Now that we have built the IS/LM model using diagrams of the goods market and the money market, we can also express the model mathematically. The economy can now be described by two equations, the IS curve and the LM curve, with the interest rate adjusting to ensure equilibrium in both the goods and money markets. We can see this by the presence of the variable r in both equations:

$$Y = C + I(r) + G \qquad \textit{The IS Curve}$$

where aggregate supply Y equals the sum of the components of expenditure; consumption C, investment $I(r)$ and government expenditure G.

$$L(r, Y) = \_M \ \_P \qquad \textit{The LM Curve}$$

where money demand $L(r, Y)$ is equal to the exogenously set money supply $\frac{M}{P}$.

The model helps us to analyse the short-run fluctuations of the business cycle where prices are held fixed. Although the interest rate adjusts to ensure equilibrium, it is the change in the price level that can help us to explain movements from one equilibrium to another. Remember that P is normally held fixed by assumption and that prices only adjust if we want to explain the movement 'across' equilibriums. As there is no explanation of the movement in prices (inflation), the model cannot capture the detail of inflationary effects of fiscal or monetary policy between policy enactment and the changes in the interest rate.

EXERCISE 11.3

Fill in the blanks in the following:

An increase in the interest rate will lead to a/an __________ in investment and a/an __________ in output. This can be shown by a __________ the __________ curve in the IS/LM model.

11.3 Fiscal and monetary policy analysis using the IS/LM model

As we have learnt in Chapter 4 and Chapter 5, economic policy is an action by the policymaker to manipulate economic conditions or activity, often with the intention of avoiding unwanted changes in the level of output or in the price level. We most commonly associate fiscal policy with the actions of the government and monetary policy with the actions of the central bank. Throughout this text, we will assume that fiscal policy is conducted by the government only and monetary policy by an independent central bank only. Although this particular set-up is popular in many developed economies, it may vary depending on geo-political differences.

Fiscal policy is a simple exogenous change in government spending (G) or taxation (T) and **monetary policy** is an exogenous change in the money supply (M). In terms of the IS/LM model, fiscal policy is shown through the changes in the IS curve and monetary policy through changes in the LM curve. We can see this clearly from the two equations for the IS and LM:

> **Fiscal Policy:** The use of a change in government spending or taxation revenue, in order to manipulate economic activity through changes in aggregate demand.
> **Monetary Policy:** The use of a change in the money supply, in order to manipulate economic activity through changes in aggregate demand.

$$Y = C + I(r) + G \qquad \textit{The IS Curve}$$

and

$$L(r, Y) = \_M\ \_P \qquad \textit{The LM Curve}$$

Notice that the IS equation contains both fiscal variables G and T (included in consumption) and that the LM equation contains the monetary variable M. We now turn our attention to policy analysis using the IS/LM model.

Policy-led changes to the IS and LM schedules and exogenous economic shocks are modelled as short-run changes, in other words, the effects are assumed to be short-lived. Immediately after a policy change or economic shock, the economy will move away from long-run equilibrium to a new short-run equilibrium. From this short-run position, the economy will begin its move back towards the long run again via the adjustment of prices. Remember that under normal circumstances prices are assumed fixed in the IS/LM model, so we can use this variable as an **adjusting mechanism** to explain a movement from the short run to the long run.

As the price level adjusts, the economy begins a movement back towards the long-run equilibrium and we see the LM curve shift to reflect this, just as we have discussed in the previous section. The LM curve will shift up or down as prices adjust until the economy returns to its original long-run position. Notice that the equation for the LM curve, above, is the only one affected by changes in the price level. In the next section, we show this adjustment process in more detail.

> **Adjusting Mechanism:** The variable that changes to restore equilibrium in our model. This is normally the variable on the vertical axis. In the AS/AD the adjusting mechanism is the price level. If output is above its natural rate, prices will rise, if output is below the natural rate, prices will fall. If the economy is in equilibrium, no adjustment is necessary.

Fiscal policy in the IS/LM model

Fiscal policy is a change in government spending G or taxation T and can be either expansionary (expand economic activity) or contractionary (shrink economic activity). An increase in government spending is expansionary and is, more or less, equivalent to a reduction in taxation. Thus, an increase in government expenditure (or a reduction in taxation) will be shown much the same diagrammatically in the IS/LM model. Remember from earlier in this chapter that changes in the variables G or T affect the aggregate demand schedule in the Keynesian cross model, shifting it up when there is expansionary policy and down when there is contractionary policy. As an example, we will discuss the case of expansionary fiscal policy using Figure 11.9.

An increase in government expenditure from (G') to (G'') shifts the AD schedule upwards in the Keynesian cross, resulting in an increase in equilibrium output from (Y') to (Y''). Notice, though, that despite the increase in output, the interest rate remains unchanged in the expenditure line; there is higher output at the existing interest rate. In fact, there is a higher output at every level of the interest rate. In interest rate/output space the IS curve shifts to the right, or outwards, to reflect this. For the case of contractionary fiscal policy, the argument is the

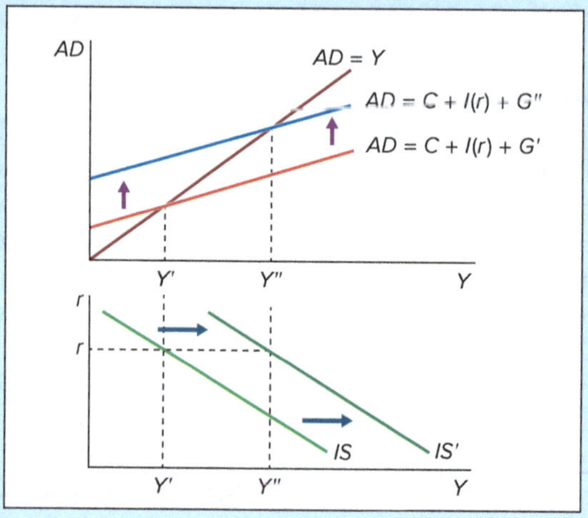

Figure 11.9 **An increase in government expenditure shifts the IS curve right**

same but in reverse – an increase in *T* will shift the expenditure line down from the lower level of consumption that will ensue from the tax rise; there is lower output at every interest rate and the IS curve will shift left, or inwards to reflect this.

Monetary policy in the IS/LM model

In the context of the IS/LM model, monetary policy is a change in the money supply by the central bank and, in a similar fashion to fiscal policy, can be classified as expansionary or contractionary. Changes in the money supply affect the liquidity preference money schedule (LM curve) shifting it down/right when there is expansionary policy and up/left when there is contractionary policy.

For example, if the central bank aims to reduce inflation caused by excess demand it would need to decrease the money supply to cool the economy (action considered contractionary). The decrease in the money supply will result in a leftward shift of the LM curve due to the lower real money balances in the economy. In detail: a decrease in the money supply will produce a higher interest rate via the money market, but with output unchanged, the LM curve will shift left to match the increase in interest rates at the same level of output. Figure 11.10 shows how the reduction in the money supply feeds through to the shift in the LM curve.

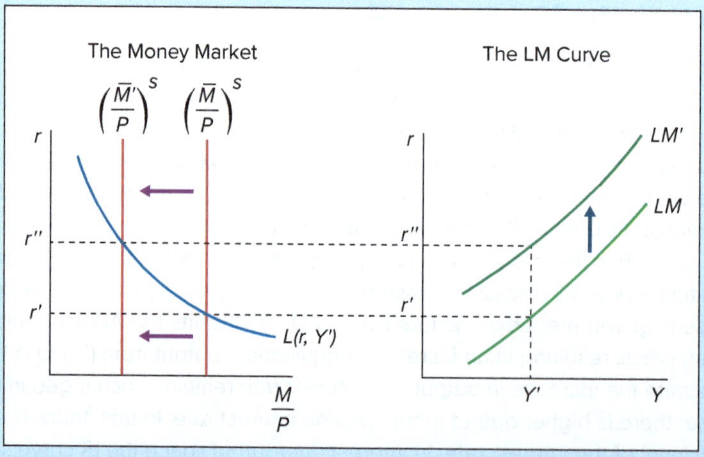

Figure 11.10 **Contractionary monetary policy leads to a leftward shift in the LM curve**

We begin in the money market with the original money supply at $\left(\frac{M}{P}\right)^S$ and money demand at $L(r, Y')$. To reduce inflation the central bank reduces the money supply. The money supply schedule shifts leftwards, and money market equilibrium predicts a higher interest rate, up from r' to r''. Because the change was initiated by a change in the money supply and because this variable is not on the axis of our IS/LM model, right of Figure 11.10, the LM curve will shift. It results in the shift of the LM curve to LM′ where lower real money balances reflect a reduction in aggregate demand and higher interest rates at every level of output.

EXERCISE 11.4

Fill in the blanks in the following:

An increase in the money supply will lead to a/an ___________ in the interest rate in the ___________ market. This can be shown by a ___________ shift in the ___________ curve.

Economic shocks and stabilization policy

We have now seen how economic policy can shift the IS and LM schedules which take us from one equilibrium to another. We can think of policy as taking us from what might be a long-run equilibrium position to a new short-run equilibrium, but it is not just policy that can move the economy in this way. Other changes that can take us away from the long-run equilibrium include exogenous shocks to the economy, such as supply and demand shocks. We can categorize these shocks into IS shocks that affect the economy through the goods market and LM shocks that effect the economy through the money market. We can also take this opportunity to show diagrammatically how the IS/LM model can capture the movement of the economy from a short-run position to the long-run equilibrium via the adjustment of prices, that we mentioned earlier.

Let us take an example of a negative LM shock, such as a sudden increase in the global oil price. The increase in the price level that results from the higher global oil price will lower real money balances in the economy and to reflect this the LM schedule will shift left or up – remember that it is only the LM curve that contains the price level variable P (on the denominator). Figure 11.11 shows the new short-run equilibrium after a negative LM shock.

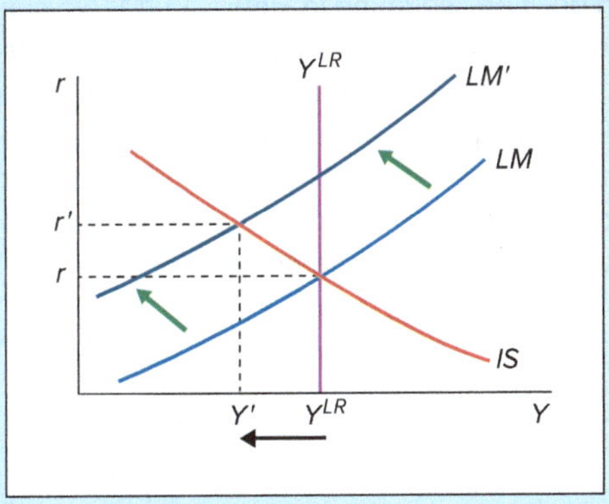

Figure 11.11 The short-run equilibrium after a negative LM shock

IS/LM Long-Run Equilibrium: The equilibrium in the IS/LM model where the economy returns to after a short-run change in the model from economic policy or a shock. The return to equilibrium is explained by the adjustment of prices. The level of output in long-run equilibrium is shown by the LRAS curve at Y^{LR}.

We begin with the original IS and LM schedules in **long-run equilibrium** at interest rate r and output Y^{LR}. Note that the vertical line drawn upwards from Y^{LR} is also known as the long-run aggregate supply schedule (LRAS). This curve represents potential or normal output in the long run when prices can adjust fully. The oil price shock pushes up the price level, which in turn reduces real money balances $\left(\frac{M}{P}\right)$ and the LM curve reflects this by shifting left/up towards LM'. Interest rates rise in reaction to the lower real money balances and output falls in reaction to the higher interest rates, so that the economy now sits at the new short-run equilibrium at (r', Y'). Notice now that the new short-run equilibrium is to the left of the long-run equilibrium and output is below its long-run rate. The short-run outcome of the oil price shock is one of increased equilibrium interest rates and reduced equilibrium output.

Here is a list of typical shocks and the IS/LM reaction:

- **Introduction of contactless payment: Positive LM shock – LM right**
- **Oil price spike: Negative LM shock – LM left**
- **Increase in investors' optimism: Positive IS shock – IS right**
- **Credit crunch: Negative IS shock – IS left**

Exogenous Shock: A sudden or unanticipated change to a variable, *not* caused by a change in a variable on the axis of our two-dimensional model. An exogenous shock comes from outside the model.

Finally, we need to discuss in more detail exactly how the economy adjusts after a disturbance caused by economic policy or an **exogenous shock**; in other words, how the economy moves back from a new short-run position towards long-run equilibrium where output is at its long-run (or normal) rate. To do this we make use of the long-run supply curve (LRAS), the vertical line in Figure 11.11, comparing the levels of output between the short-run and long-run equilibriums, and discuss the adjustment process in the box below.

THE PRICE AS AN ADJUSTMENT MECHANISM

In the IS/LM model the price level is assumed fixed, but in between the short-run equilibrium and the long-run equilibrium we can use the price as an adjusting mechanism reacting to market forces:

- **If output is below its long-run rate, prices will fall (economic slump)**
- **If output is at its long-run rate, prices will remain static (long-run equilibrium)**
- **If output is above its long-run rate, prices will rise (economic boom)**

From the new short-run position, we found in Figure 11.11, we can now imagine exactly how the economy will return to long-run equilibrium through natural market forces. We begin by noting that the new short-run equilibrium is to the left of the long-run equilibrium marked by the LRAS schedule. If we make the important assumption that authorities remain passive, in other words refrain from intervention, we can show how the economy returns to its long-run position. Figure 11.12 depicts this scenario; output is below its long-run rate after a negative LM shock, the economy is contracting, and prices will begin to adjust downwards.

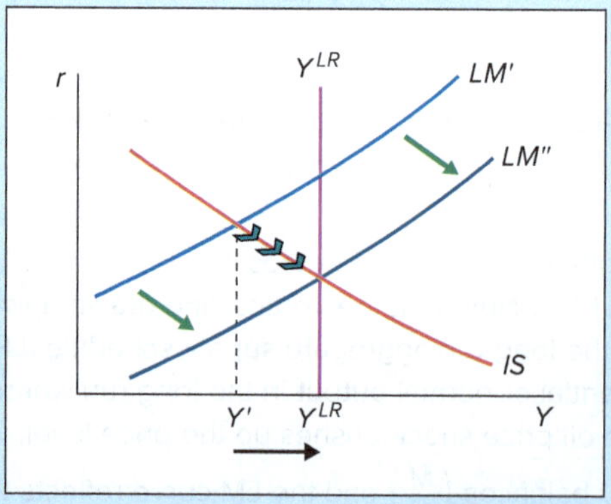

Figure 11.12 The transition from the short run to the long run in the IS/LM model

After the shock, and because output is below its long-run rate, the price level begins to fall due to a general demand deficiency. As the price level falls the LM schedule begins to shift right to reflect the increases in real money balances – $\left(\frac{M}{P}\right)$ is higher with the lower price level. The adjustment continues with the LM curve shifting right until output returns to the long-run rate at Y^{LR} where the price adjustment process ends.

At this point you might well ask the question: How long will the adjustment process take to return the economy back to its 'normal' levels? This question is not an easy one to answer, because the time it takes for the economy to adjust is dependent on many factors that change over time. This presents our policymakers with a dilemma: if there is no way to tell how long the economy will take to return to equilibrium it might be better to intervene/manage the economy back rather than wait. We will begin our analysis again (from the negative LM shock) and compare the two outcomes between leaving the economy to return to normal naturally, and by force with demand side policy.

In our diagram on the left of Figure 11.13, we see that the economy is hit by a negative LM shock, such as a significant hike in the minimum wage; the firm's costs will rise, and this will lead to an increase in the overall price level. The increase in prices, with money supply constant, will result in lower real money balances; the LM curve will shift left to reflect this and the economy moves from Y^{LR} to Y'. The policymaker now faces a choice: either allow the economy to return to its normal level naturally, else intervene to avoid an increase in unemployment.

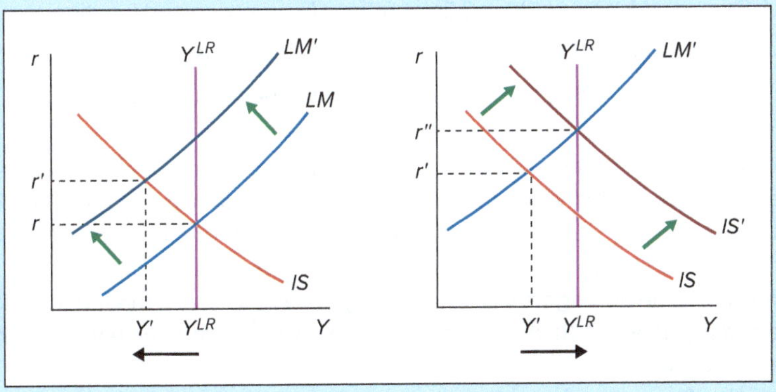

Figure 11.13 Managing the economy back to normal after a negative LM shock

If the economy is left to adjust naturally, prices will fall due to the reduction in economic activity from Y^{LR} to Y'. With prices falling, the LM curve will shift back right to its original position, moving the economy back to normal after the shock. Alternatively, looking at the diagram on the right of Figure 11.3, the policymaker can use expansionary economic policy, perhaps using an increase in demand though the market for goods and services, to force the economy back to its normal level. Expansionary fiscal policy, say an increase in government expenditure, will increase aggregate demand and the IS curve will shift right to reflect this – output will return from Y' to Y^{LR}.

At first sight, it seems that the most obvious path to follow each time is to intervene during a recession, but on further inspection we see that the outcomes are not quite the same. In the case of intervention, the economy is left with higher interest rates than the case of a natural return to long-run equilibrium. The higher resulting interest rates are the cost of policymaker intervention.

We have now considered the reaction of the IS/LM model to economic policy and to economic shocks; the immediate position after policy or a shock is considered a 'short-run' position from which the economy will return back to its 'long-run' position, in a natural manner if left to its own devices. This will happen through the adjustment process of a change in the price level. In the last section, we will show how we can solve the IS and LM curves mathematically for the equilibrium price level and equilibrium output.

EXERCISE 11.5

1 Using the IS/LM diagram, explain the IS/LM prediction of the economic effects of a decrease in government expenditure.
2 After a positive IS shock, equilibrium output will be away from the long-run level of output. Explain how the economy will return to its long-run equilibrium.

11.4 The mathematics of the IS/LM model

Rather than provide you with less intuitive implicit functional form algebra we can use an explicit form example and show how to solve a closed economy IS/LM model, in a similar fashion to a typical assessment.

Imagine a closed economy described by the following equations:

(Equation 11.1)	$Y = C + I + G$	(aggregate demand identity)
(Equation 11.2)	$C = 200 + 0.75(Y - T)$	(consumption function)
(Equation 11.3)	$I = 325 - 25r$	(investment function)
(Equation 11.4)	$T = 500$	(exogenous lump sum taxes)
(Equation 11.5)	$G = 500$	(exogenous government spending)
(Equation 11.6)	$Md/P = L(r, Y) = 0.5Y - 50r$	(money demand function)
(Equation 11.7)	$Ms = 1000$	(exogenous money supply)
(Equation 11.8)	$Ms = Md$	(money market equilibrium)

In our example, we can start by assuming a value for the price level; let $P = 2$, remembering that this is a fixed price model. With this information, we can derive the IS and LM curves of the economy, expressing Y as a function of r for both schedules. After this we can calculate the short-run equilibrium values of Y and r.

Equation (11.1), the aggregate demand identity, provides us with the framework to derive the IS curve and Equation (11.8), the money market equilibrium, the framework for the LM curve.

Proceed as follows:

To derive the IS equation, insert Equations (11.2) to (11.5) into (11.1) and solve for Y:

$$Y = 2600 - 100r \qquad \text{(IS equation)}$$

To derive the LM equation, set Equation (11.7) = Equation (11.6) and solve for Y:

$$Y = \frac{2000}{P} + 100r \qquad \text{(LM equation)}$$

Now set, by assumption, $P = 2$:

$$Y = 1000 + 100r \qquad \text{(LM equation)}$$

To calculate the equilibrium level of output, you first need to rewrite the LM equation with the rate of interest on the left side and everything else on the right:

$$r = 0.01Y - \frac{20}{P} \qquad \text{(LM equation in terms of } r\text{)}$$

Now insert the LM equation into the IS equation and solve for output:

$$Y = 1300 + \frac{1000}{P} \qquad (AD \text{ equation in } Y/P \text{ space})$$

Note: This is the aggregate demand function (*AD*), in case you are asked to derive it.
Now set, by assumption, $P = 2$ and substitute into the *AD*:

$Y = 1800$ (short-run equilibrium level of output)

Now insert the short-run equilibrium level of output into either the *IS* or *LM* equations and solve for the rate of interest to calculate its equilibrium value:

$r = 8$ per cent (short-run equilibrium interest rate)

11.5 Chapter summary: Putting it all together

In this chapter, we have learnt about the IS/LM model which uses the concept of a general equilibrium between the market for goods and the money market in one two-dimensional diagram. The model predicts an equilibrium level of output and economy-wide interest rate that simultaneously satisfies both goods and financial markets together.

We have built the investment savings *IS* schedule which is derived from the market for goods and services both diagrammatically and mathematically. The *IS* curve is downward sloping reflecting that at lower interest rates, investment will be higher and this will lead to higher output. Similarly, we have built a liquidity money *LM* schedule that represents money market equilibrium which is upward sloping, reflecting the fact that at higher levels of output, money demand is higher and this will lead to higher interest rates.

The IS/LM model is intuitive and universally accepted as a benchmark by professional economists in the private sector, but it is not without its critics. The model uses non-trivial simplifying assumptions such as fixed prices, and also the debated concept of a 'general equilibrium' where one interest rate resolves all markets simultaneously. The model is normally drawn with the intersection of the *IS* and *LM* schedules coinciding at the level of output given by the long-run aggregate supply curve (*LRAS*) or Y^{LR}. From this position, economic shocks and policy disturb the model so that the *IS* and *LM* intersection moves away from the *LRAS* to a new short-run equilibrium. Over time the economy will naturally move back to the long run making use of a movement in the price level to explain the jump between short-run and long-run equilibriums.

Assessment question

Using the IS/LM model, show the effects on the equilibrium interest rate and output of an increase in government spending in the goods market. Provide some critical analysis on the economic predictions of the model.

Cases

The UK and the global financial crisis (2008–2009)

Applying the IS/LM model to a real economic shock

Introduction

The UK was significantly affected by the 2008 global financial crisis, with a sharp fall in GDP, plummeting consumer confidence and a near-collapse of the banking system. Major UK banks became over-leveraged and as a result required government bailouts to repair balance sheets. The lack of liquidity in the banking system resulted in a major negative demand shock.

In response, the UK government launched a fiscal stimulus, and the Bank of England cut interest rates aggressively and began quantitative easing in early 2009 – buying government bonds to increase the money supply.

IS/LM analysis context

The IS/LM model provides a useful framework for interpreting the short-run policy response to the financial crisis:

- The IS curve shifted left due to a collapse in private investment and consumer spending.
- The LM curve flattened due to near-zero interest rates and increased liquidity preference.
- Expansionary fiscal policy (temporary VAT cuts, increased infrastructure spending) and monetary easing were utilized in an effort to restore demand.

Key data (UK, 2008–2009)

Indicator	Value/change
GDP growth (2009)	−4.2%
Unemployment rate (2009)	7.9%
Bank of England base rate	Cut from 5.0% to 0.5% (November 2008–March 2009)
Government spending	£20 billion fiscal stimulus (1.5% of GDP)
Quantitative easing (QE1)	£200 billion in asset purchases (from March 2009)

Questions

1. Using the IS/LM model, describe what happened to output and interest rates in the UK following the crisis. What caused the IS curve to shift inward?
2. Evaluate the effectiveness of the Bank of England's monetary policy during this period. What does a flat LM curve suggest for the impact of future changes in the money supply?
3. Explain how a fiscal stimulus (e.g. VAT cuts, infrastructure investment) affected the IS/LM equilibrium. Could the government have offset the fall in private demand?
4. What limitations does the IS/LM model have in explaining the full range of economic outcomes in the UK during the crisis?

Problems

EASY

1. In the IS/LM model, the IS curve represents:
   a) equilibrium in the market for liquidity and money
   b) combinations of interest rates and output that satisfy the goods market equilibrium
   c) the demand for money as a function of income and interest rates
   d) all combinations of income and interest rates where government spending equals taxation
   e) the monetary policy response to increases in the price level
2. In the IS/LM framework, if the central bank increases the money supply, the:
   a) LM curve will shift left
   b) IS curve will shift right
   c) interest rate falls and income rises
   d) interest rate rises and income falls
   e) IS curve will become steeper

MEDIUM

3. A rightward shift in the IS curve can be caused by:
   a) a decrease in the money supply
   b) an increase in the interest rate
   c) an increase in government spending
   d) a fall in the demand for investment
   e) a decrease in marginal propensity to consume
4. If the economy is operating at the intersection of the IS and LM curves, which of the following is true?
   a) The goods market is in disequilibrium
   b) The money market is not in equilibrium
   c) There is involuntary unemployment
   d) Both the goods and money markets are in equilibrium
   e) The interest rate is at its long-run level
5. Consider an economy where:
   - Consumption $C = 100 + 0.8Y$
   - Investment $I = 150 - 10r$
   - Government spending $G = 250$
   - Taxes $T = 200$
   - The real money demand is $L = 0.25Y - 20r$
   - The nominal money supply $M = 600$
   - The price level $P = 2$

   a) Derive the IS and LM relations in terms of output Y.
   b) Find the equilibrium values of output Y and the interest rate r.
6. Explain the impact of an increase in government spending using the IS/LM model in the short run. What happens to the equilibrium interest rate and output? Discuss the potential for the crowding-out effect to occur.

HARD

7. The LM curve becomes flatter when:
   a) the sensitivity of money demand to interest rates increases
   b) the central bank increases reserve requirements
   c) investment becomes less sensitive to interest rates
   d) the marginal propensity to consume rises
   e) the government increases the tax rate
8. In the IS/LM model, a liquidity trap is illustrated by:
   a) a vertical IS curve
   b) a downward-sloping LM curve
   c) a flat LM curve
   d) a leftward shift of the IS curve
   e) a vertical LM curve
9. Critically evaluate the effectiveness of monetary policy when the economy is in a liquidity trap. Use the IS/LM framework to support your answer.

CHAPTER 12

The Open Economy IS/LM/BP Model

Chapter contents

At a Glance The open economy IS/LM/BP model

The issue

The IS/LM model from the previous chapter is a very useful way to present an economy, with both the financial and real flows in the economy shown together in one diagram and with the interest rate adjusting to restore equilibrium after a disturbance. However, two major real life features are missing – both international trade and capital movements across borders are ignored.

The understanding

In this chapter we correct this omission. The investment savings, liquidity money and balance of payments (IS/LM/BP) model is a small open economy model that allows a deeper understanding of an economy that engages in trade across economic borders. The international trade in goods and services is facilitated by movements of foreign and domestic capital, and this allows us to capture the important contribution of the exchange rate.

The usefulness

Being able to explain the outflows and inflows of international capital brings a richer understanding to our commentary on the challenges facing a real life economy. The exchange rate matters for our domestic producers who rely on exports for employment and consumers who need to buy foreign produce.

12.1 Introduction

In Chapter 11, we introduced the Investment Savings and Liquidity Money (IS/LM) model, developed by the economist John Hicks in his interpretation of Keynes' General Theory. This general equilibrium model allows the analysis of both the goods and financial markets together in a single diagram with one economy-wide equilibrium interest rate and one equilibrium level of national income that satisfy both markets simultaneously.

This property is convenient, in that we are able to see the reaction of the whole economy to economic policy and shocks and also to analyse policy interactions. What we did not cover in Chapter 11, however, is how the model might be adapted to account for the real world feature of the open economy. More economies are now open to international trade and the international movement of capital than ever before. Politicians have become more focused on the topic of cross-border commerce and economists more interested in the role of the exchange rate transmission mechanism that supports it.

With recent successes in macroeconomic policy, in terms of price and interest rate stability, what can policymakers do to influence the domestic business cycle? The answer lies in the exchange rate – it is the exchange rate that determines the price that foreign consumers will pay for our exports and also what we will pay for our imports from abroad. It might be worth spending some time to revisit our discussion on the importance of the exchange rate for the business cycle in Chapter 3.

Up until now, we have assumed that the economy is closed and therefore we have been unable to consider international macroeconomic variables or impacts from abroad. The IS/LM/BP model proposed by Marcus Mundell and Robert Fleming in the early 1960s is an attempt to incorporate international effects in a general equilibrium model that can be used to highlight the important relationship between economic policy, international capital flows and exchange rates. The main difference between the IS/LM/BP model and its closed economy IS/LM counterpart is the more detailed consideration of the exchange rate and the balance of payments as policy filters through to the real economy.

In a similar fashion to its closed economy counterpart, the economy is drawn in interest rate/output space to allow us to consider the open economy impacts of policy on the market for goods and market for money together. The open economy IS/LM/BP model has two important assumptions: that the interest rate is now fixed at the world interest rate and that there is perfect capital mobility to and from abroad:

- **The interest rate is fixed at the world interest rate.**
- **The movement of capital is unrestricted to facilitate trade.**

In this chapter, we will build the IS/LM/BP by making use of our knowledge from earlier chapters in the book. In Chapter 11, we learnt how the IS schedule was constructed using the goods market in the Keynesian cross model and how the LM curve was derived using the market for liquidity in terms of money. The two schedules combine to provide us with a 'general equilibrium' in the economy where the goods and money markets are simultaneously equilibrated with one level of output and one interest rate.

In what follows, we will show how we can use the IS/LM/BP model to predict the reactions of the economy to both monetary and fiscal policy under two different exchange rate systems – under a regime of free floating exchange rates and under a regime of fixed exchange rates. The chapter begins by laying out the open economy IS/LM/BP model using simple extensions to the standard closed economy versions of the IS and LM schedules, before a discussion of the reasoning behind the balance of payments schedule in the model – the schedule that provides us with our most visual departure from the closed economy version of the model.

To help us do this, we will make use of the explicit functional forms of the components of aggregate expenditure – consumption, investment and government expenditure and net exports – introduced in Chapter 7 and the mathematical representation for the balance of trade, that we discovered in Chapter 3.

Learning Outcomes

By the end of this chapter you should be able to:

- Identify and build the different components of the IS/LM/BP model, both diagrammatically and algebraically.
- Understand the key assumptions of the small open economy.
- Describe the key transmission mechanism in the IS/LM/BP model, between policy, capital flows and exchange rate movements.
- Assess the effects and economic consequences of economic policy using the IS/LM/BP schedules, under floating exchange rates.
- Assess the effects and economic consequences of economic policy using the IS/LM/BP schedules, under fixed exchange rates.
- Explain major international economic events and crises using the IS/LM/BP.

12.2 Building the IS/LM/BP model diagrammatically

This small open economy IS/LM/BP model is made up of three schedules: the investment savings IS schedule, the liquidity money preference LM schedule and the balance of payments BP schedule. We often use a star above the letters IS, to remind us that this is the open economy version of the investment savings schedule (IS*). *R*emember that the assumption of fixed prices carries over from the closed economy version described in Chapter 11, but now with further assumptions of a fixed interest rate (fixed at the world interest rate, r^*) and perfect capital mobility. Allowing the free movement of capital will mean that capital flows can facilitate discrepancies in the balance of payments position or, in other words, enable international trade. A flow of goods across borders must be matched by an equal flow of capital in the opposite direction (goods received must be paid for).

EXAMPLE 12.1

Real world example: Small open economy – Singapore

Singapore is a good example of an economy that operates under the assumptions of the Mundell–Fleming small open economy model of given world interest rate and unrestricted capital movement.

World interest rate

Singapore has a very open financial system which has no influence on world interest rates; as a result they are taken as given for this economy. The Monetary Authority of Singapore (MAS) targets the exchange rate, rather than the domestic interest rate.

Capital movement

In Singapore there are no restrictions on the movement of capital in and out of the country; investors can respond quickly to movements in the world interest rate. When US interest rates rise, this induces capital outflow, causing downward pressure on the Singapore dollar, as investors seek higher returns abroad.

The open economy IS* and LM schedules

This small open economy model provides us with an opportunity to introduce the important trade balance component of expenditure, missing from our closed economy version in the previous chapter. National income is now the sum of domestic expenditure and net expenditure from abroad, *NX*. As we learnt in Chapter 3, the trade balance can be modelled simply by adding a fourth term to our closed economy version of the income identity, net exports.

$$Y = C + I(r^*) + G + NX$$

where *NX* is equal to the difference between export and import expenditure, both of which depend on the exchange rate:

$$NX = X - M = NX(\varepsilon)$$

National income is now categorized by consumption expenditure *C*, investment expenditure *I*, government expenditure *G* and net exports *NX*. Notice that just as with the closed economy, the investment function is endogenous on the interest rate, but that this is now set at the world interest rate, r^* to reflect the power of foreign interest rates and the inability of a small open economy to make any impact on those by itself. The economy is therefore an interest rate 'taker'; we can imagine an economy that has no financial power in the context of international financial markets. Remember also, as discussed earlier in Chapter 3 and Chapter 8, that the net export function is dependent on the exchange rate ε. Net exports and the exchange rate are negatively correlated (an increase in the exchange rate is consistent with a fall in net exports).

We can now write our open economy IS curve as:

$$Y = C + I\,(r^*) + G + NX\,(\varepsilon)$$

Notice that our adjusting mechanism has changed, from the interest rate (which is now fixed) to that of the exchange rate. It is the exchange rate that will adjust to ensure equilibrium in the economy. We can build the curve, just as we did before, but with the open economy version of the Keynesian cross. The IS* curve is shown in Figure 12.1; notice that the interest rate is fixed at r^*, the world interest rate.

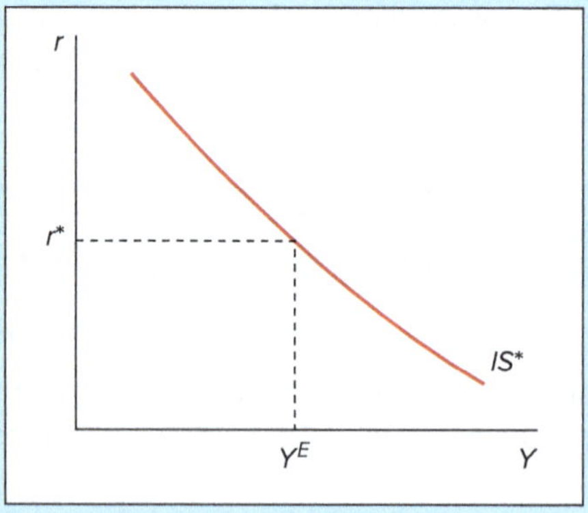

Figure 12.1 The IS* schedule in interest rate/output space

To represent the monetary side of the economy, we also need an open economy version of the LM schedule. Changes in the exchange rate in the economy will affect investment decisions, leading to changes in output and thus money demand. Although this channel between the exchange rate and money demand exists, we have no need to model money demand as endogenous on the exchange rate. Essentially, our LM function for the open economy is the same as for the case of the closed economy with one exception: that the interest rate is now set at the world interest rate r^*. We can now write our LM for the open economy as:

$$L(r^*,Y) = \_M \ \_P$$

The money market is in equilibrium when the demand for money, which now depends on a fixed world interest rate along with the prevailing level of output, is met by the real money supply. We draw the LM schedule in interest rate output space in Figure 12.2.

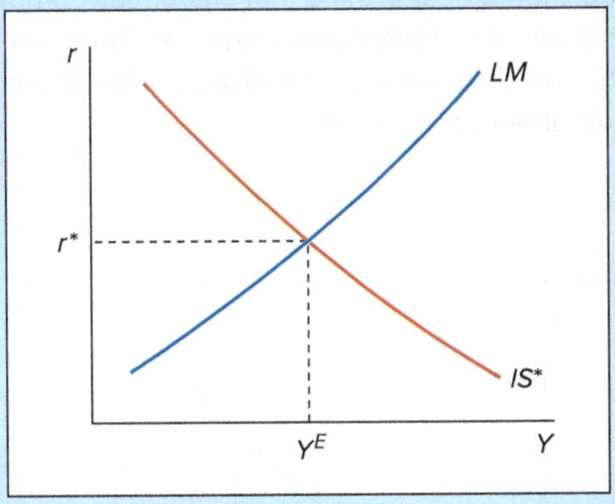

Figure 12.2 Adding the open economy LM schedule in interest rate/output space

At the fixed world interest rate, r^*, equilibrium income is determined by the intersection of the open economy IS* and LM schedules, as shown in Figure 12.2. Essentially, the interest rate is now set, exogenously (or outside of the model) by external financial factors with the exchange rate adjusting in the background to ensure general equilibrium.

EXERCISE 12.1

1 How does the Mundell–Fleming open economy IS*/LM model differ from the closed economy IS/LM model?
2 How will the investment savings IS* schedule react to an increase in the exchange rate?

The balance of payments (BP) schedule

Finally, we need to close the model with a condition on the **balance of payments** to connect the real and monetary sides of the economy and to allow the **exchange rate** to act as the adjusting mechanism. International trade is financed in a viable way when real flows (through net exports) are equal and opposite to financial flows (through net capital outflow):

$$BP = TB - NCO$$

The balance of payments, *BP*, is equal to the difference between the trade balance, *TB*, and net capital outflow, *NCO*. Changes in the trade balance need to be met by equal and opposite changes in the flows of finance (capital). In this particular description of the model we will assume that the **capital flows** can instantly adjust to satisfy the requirements presented by any trade balance disturbances – in other words that *BP* is normally equal to zero. Furthermore, we assume that net capital outflow is 'super' sensitive to changes in the domestic interest rate – upward pressure on the domestic interest rate will attract very fast capital inflow to accommodate any current account surplus, and vice versa.

Balance of Payments: An accounting term used by the National Statistics Office. A balance sheet that equates the current account (measuring net exports) and the financial account (measuring net capital outflow). The value of goods and services sold to abroad must be equal to the flow of money used to buy those goods and services.
Exchange Rate: The exchange rate at which one currency is traded for another. If there is a surplus or deficit in the balance of payments, then the exchange rate will adjust to rebalance the difference between the current and financial accounts.

Capital Flows: International movements of financial capital in exchange for domestic currency for the purpose of investment. To invest in another country, you will first have to exchange your funds into the local currency, in the foreign exchange market.

We can add the BP schedule to our previous diagram to show the Mundell–Fleming small open economy equilibrium, in Figure 12.3.

Anywhere along the BP schedule, the balance of payments is equal to zero at the world interest rate, any BP disturbance will cause upward or downward pressure on the domestic interest rate, even though it is fixed at the world rate.

You should bear in mind that authorities do not have perfect control over the balance of payments – changes in the exchange rate will affect net exports, and changes in the relative position of domestic to world interest rates will affect capital flows.

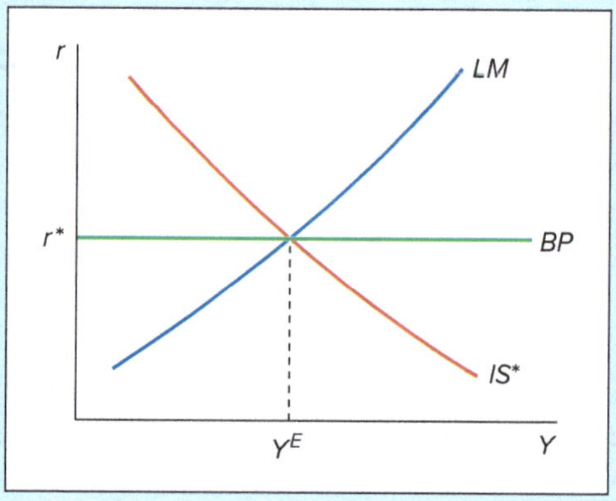

Figure 12.3 The Mundell–Fleming open economy model in general equilibrium

Notice that for the case of the open economy the IS* and LM schedules have the usual slopes. The IS* curve slopes downward, reflecting that higher interest rates decrease investment and thus output in the usual way, but now a change in the exchange rate will cause a shift in the IS* curve due to the change in net exports. The LM curve slopes upward, reflecting that higher output leads to higher money demand and higher interest rates in the financial sector, though bear in mind that monetary policy can now create movements in the exchange rates via the international sector.

The BP line is horizontal, reflecting perfect capital mobility. In other words, any change in economic activity that causes a balance of payments disturbance will attract any necessary capital inflow/outflow to finance the trade activity without friction. As an example of this, imagine an increase in national income, leading to an increase in imports and a trade deficit – the deficit must be financed by capital inflow and it is assumed that this balancing act is immediate (i.e., no capital restriction).

In reality, we could draw the BP schedule slightly upward sloping to reflect the disturbances caused by increases in income, but for simplicity we will focus on the case of perfect capital mobility. Finally, notice that in general equilibrium the BP line is drawn with intercept at the world interest rate. This is one of the key assumptions of the IS/LM/BP model, that the economy is small and with no influence over international capital markets. Without this assumption, changes in the domestic rate would cause massive capital flows of their own; an increase/decrease in the interest rate would attract/repel capital from international investors looking for returns on investment capital.

EXERCISE 12.2

1 How would you expect the money demand function to react to a decrease in output in the money market?

2 Does this change provide us with 'a movement along' or 'a shift' in the open economy LM schedule?

12.3 Economic policy analysis under floating exchange rates

We now look at economic policy using the Mundell–Fleming open economy model in an economy where the exchange rate is determined freely in the foreign exchange market. In doing so, we can describe the channels through which policy feeds through to the real economy. From here onwards we drop the star over the IS schedule, given that we now understand the difference between the closed economy and open economy IS/LM model, but acknowledge that the IS schedule is that referred to above, as the IS*.

Fiscal policy in the IS/LM/BP model

From our long-run equilibrium position shown in Figure 12.3, we can now use the IS/LM/BP model to predict the effects of monetary and fiscal policy in an open economy context. This allows us to consider the exchange rate transmission mechanism, where departures from the BP line result in exchange rate movements leading to real effects (movements in output) through the changes in exports and imports that make up the trade balance. Having a channel within the model for exchange rate movements, also allows us to consider exchange rate policy. With this in mind, we can categorize our policy analysis under two exchange rate regimes – free **floating exchange rates** and **fixed exchange rates** – starting with fiscal policy under a floating exchange rate.

Floating Exchange Rates: An exchange rate policy whereby the exchange rate is determined freely in the international foreign exchange markets.
Fixed Exchange Rates: A deliberate policy of exchange rate government intervention in the foreign exchange markets, designed to influence the domestic exchange rate, often with the ultimate aim of manipulating a country's share of international trade.

Starting from the long-run equilibrium in Figure 12.4 where the red IS and blue LM schedules cross, an increase in government expenditure shifts the IS schedule to the right (green arrow); output increases and there is upward pressure on the domestic interest rate in the money market. With equilibrium now above the BP schedule there is a balance of payments surplus; we can see this from the balance of payment schedule presented earlier – an increase in government spending will reduce national saving, meaning that net capital outflow ($S - I(r^*)$) is reduced. With lower net capital outflow, and the position of the economy away from the BP schedule, there is a positive balance of payment disturbance. Massive capital inflow will ensue due to the upward pressure on the domestic interest rate.

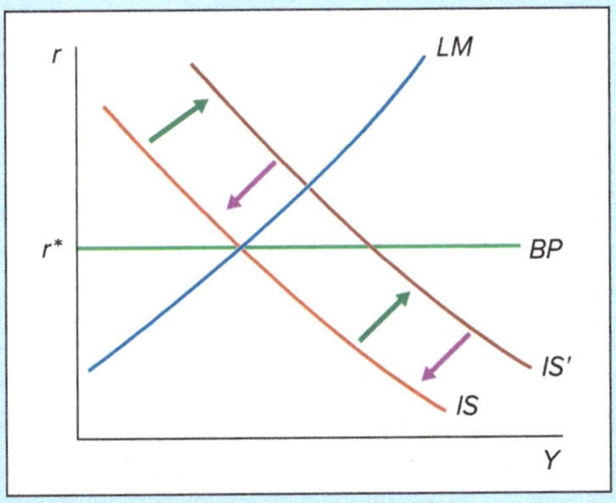

Figure 12.4 Fiscal policy under floating exchange rates

The upwards pressure on the domestic interest rate will give rise to an appreciation in the exchange rate, driven by the additional demand for domestic currency from foreign investors seeking higher returns. In turn, the exchange rate appreciation will have the effect of making exports more expensive to foreigners and imports less expensive to domestic consumers; net exports will therefore reduce. The reduction in net exports will cause the *IS* schedule to shift back left to its original position (purple arrows). The IS/LM/BP model predicts that expansionary fiscal policy under a regime of floating exchange rates is ineffective, as output has not increased. The exact cancellation of the fiscal expansion in real life is actually dependent on two counteracting effects: the strength of the multiplier from the increase in government expenditure and the crowding out of net exports from the increase in the exchange rate. One way to test this prediction for any particular economy is to embark on an empirical investigation, a process that we describe in detail in Chapter 18.

Monetary policy in the IS/LM/BP model

In Figure 12.5, we consider the case of expansionary monetary policy under floating exchange rates. Starting from an initial long-run equilibrium position (where the red IS and blue LM schedules cross), an increase in the money supply will shift the LM schedule right to LM′ (green arrows); this is reflecting the higher real money balances at every interest rate in the money market. The increase in aggregate demand will increase output and the economy moves to a new general equilibrium (green dot); notice that the new equilibrium is below the BP schedule, consistent with a balance of payments deficit.

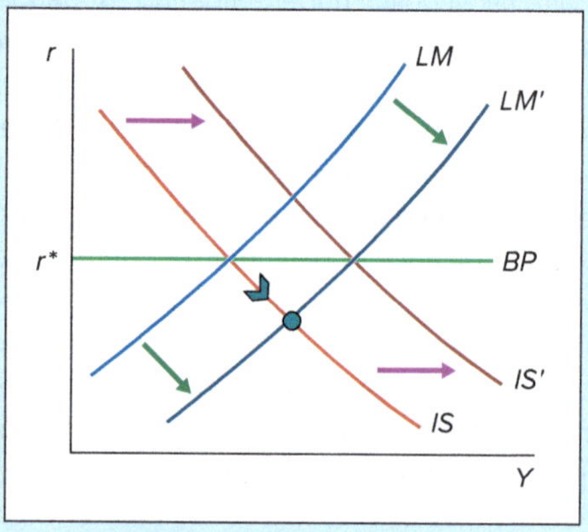

Figure 12.5 Monetary policy under floating exchange rates

The negative balance of payments disturbance will induce a massive capital outflow as investors withdraw their capital. This will put downward pressure on the exchange rate and cause an excess supply of domestic currency. With the lower exchange rate, there will be an impact upon the goods market; an increase in net exports from the currency depreciation and this will shift the IS schedule to the right (purple arrows). The process continues until the balance of payments is once again zero, where the flows in trade match the new position in the capital markets. With the IS eventually at IS* we can see that the IS/LM/BP model predicts that monetary policy is highly effective under a floating exchange rate regime.

EXERCISE 12.3

Fill in the blanks in the following:

In a small open economy, under floating exchange rates, a decrease in the money supply will lead to a balance of payments ___________ and a/an ___________ in the exchange rate. This can be shown by a ___________ shift in the *LM* curve followed by a ___________ shift in the IS curve in the IS/LM/BP model.

12.4 Economic policy analysis under fixed exchange rates

Now that we have covered economic policy under floating exchange rates we can now consider the case for a fixed exchange rate regime. A fixed exchange rate regime is one where a government will 'intervene' in currency markets, with a view to keeping the domestic exchange rate higher or lower than the rate that would normally prevail under free market conditions. In other words, the exchange rate is kept fixed at some predetermined level by the central bank.

The reasons for intervention are quite intuitive since we know that the net exports component of expenditure is directly affected by exchange rate movements. A lower exchange rate will favour domestic firms who are required to export goods to bring employment to the domestic economy, so the incentive to intervene one way or another is strong. One question you might ask is: how do we know when a government is manipulating its exchange rate? This can often be seen in the time series data for the domestic exchange rate; you might see prolonged periods where the series is flat at one particular rate (meaning that intervention is most likely taking place in an attempt to fix the exchange rate).

Once again, under the alternative exchange rate regime, we see counteracting effects from the use of economic policy, and we must bear in mind that the prediction of total ineffectiveness is one that can only be verified by thorough empirical investigation for a particular economy. In Chapter 18, we discuss the strategies for testing these predictions.

Fiscal policy in the IS/LM/BP model

We now consider economic policy using the IS/LM/BP model under fixed exchange rates, where the policymaker is expected to intervene in the foreign exchange market (buying and selling domestic currency) whenever the exchange rate is away from its announced or privately agreed fixed rate. In Figure 12.6 we examine the case of fiscal policy under fixed exchange rates.

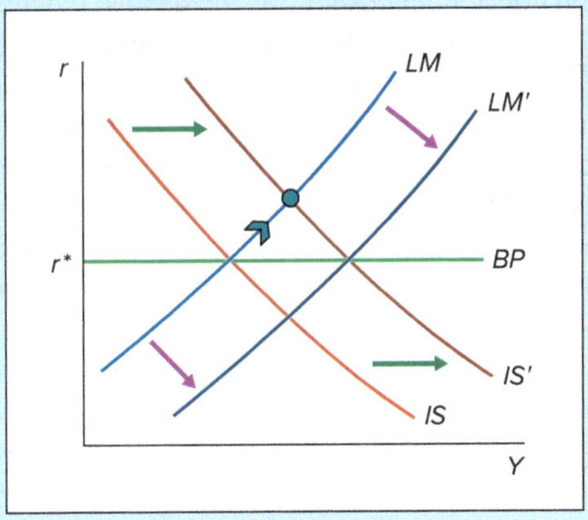

Figure 12.6 Fiscal policy under a fixed exchange rate regime

Starting from long-run equilibrium and following Figure 12.6, an increase in government expenditure under a fixed exchange rate regime, shifts the IS schedule to the right (green arrow); output increases and the economy moves upwards (blue dot), reflecting a positive balance of payments disturbance. Due to the position of the economy there is now massive capital inflow, giving rise to an appreciation in the exchange rate. However, the exchange rate appreciation will cause a problem for the monetary authority who is committed to the fixed exchange rate.

The central bank is forced to sell domestic currency in the foreign exchange market to undo the appreciation. Selling the domestic currency has the effect of increasing the money supply, shifting the LM curve right to LM′ (purple) until the balance of payments is once again at zero.

Finally, the predetermined exchange rate is restored and output is increased, though this time it has been increased by fiscal 'and' monetary policy, leaving us with the conclusion that fiscal policy under a fixed exchange rate regime is highly effective.

Monetary policy in the IS/LM/BP model

A fixed exchange rate regime poses problems for the monetary authority – if the central bank is busy in international foreign exchange markets, it is going to be very difficult to simultaneously intervene to enact monetary policy due to the needs of the business cycle. Increasing the money supply will always be consistent with a falling exchange rate, so if the business cycle requires monetary expansion, but the exchange rate must be kept constant, this raises a dilemma for the bank. In Figure 12.7, we consider the case of expansionary monetary policy under fixed exchange rates.

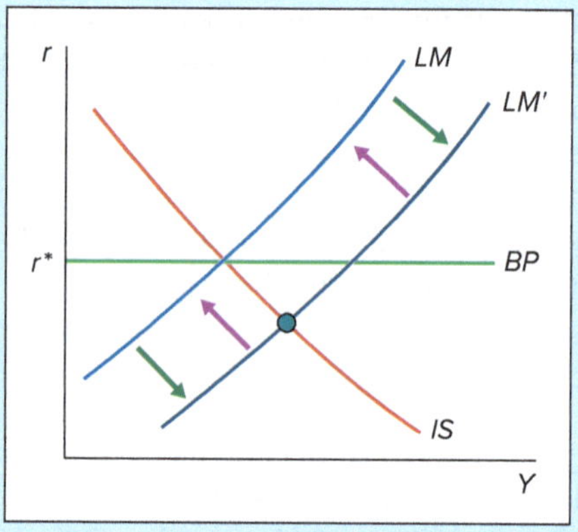

Figure 12.7 Monetary policy under a fixed exchange rate regime

Starting from a long-run equilibrium position, an increase in the money supply will shift the LM schedule right to LM′ (green arrows), reflecting the higher real money balances at every interest rate in the money market. The increase in aggregate demand from higher money balances will increase output and the economy will move to a new general equilibrium (blue dot); notice that the new equilibrium is below the BP schedule, consistent with a balance of payments deficit. The deficit will induce massive capital outflow, as investors take flight, putting downward pressure on the exchange rate caused by an excess supply of domestic currency.

With the lower exchange rate, there will again be a requirement for the central bank to intervene to restore the fixed exchange rate. It will do this by buying domestic currency in the foreign exchange market, causing excess demand for the domestic currency, increasing the exchange rate and decreasing the money supply. The LM curve will shift back leftwards until the balance of payments once again returns to zero. Finally, the predetermined exchange rate is restored but output has not increased, leaving us with the conclusion that monetary policy under fixed exchange rates is totally ineffective. The message from the Mundell–Fleming model is clear: the cost of maintaining a fixed exchange rate is the loss of monetary policy altogether.

ASSESSMENT ADVICE

It would be good to discuss the reasons that lie behind the assumption in the Mundell–Fleming model of a fixed interest rate. From our discussion on macroeconomic modelling in Chapter 4, remember that in a diagrammatical model we can only capture the relationship between 'two' variables; it is a two-dimensional diagram. So, while this assumption of a fixed interest rate is convenient for easier analysis (as it allows us to use the exchange rate as the adjusting mechanism instead of the interest rate), is it justifiable?

EXERCISE 12.4

Fill in the blanks in the following:

In a small open economy under a floating exchange rate regime, any balance of payments disturbance will cause an adjustment in the ___________ ___________. This adjustment will be reflected by a shift in the ___________ schedule.

Using the model to explain a sovereign debt crisis in a monetary union

The IS/LM/BP model allows us to dig deeper into the exchange rate transmission mechanism, as we can explain more exactly how the exchange rate moves in reaction to shifts in the open economy versions of the IS and LM schedules. This is particularly useful when we want to explain the forces acting upon the exchange rate during a period of deep economic uncertainty – for instance, after a period of emergency remedial fiscal measures by policymakers during an economic crisis.

As a more specific example, we can take the case of the aftermath from the global financial crisis of 2008 – governments had taken extraordinary measures to protect the banking sector from a potentially dangerous financial collapse. Governments across the globe spent large sums recapitalizing commercial banks, after wide-scale subprime loan default and heightened uncertainty. Over time, the governments themselves began to look vulnerable in terms of the ability to repay the accrued resulting public debt; a realization of the situation by credit rating agencies led to governments spending unsustainable amounts on interest from reservicing public debt, with some countries having to offer much higher yields as bonds reach maturity.

Thinking of the additional amount of interest paid by governments on **sovereign debt** in times of uncertainty as the **risk premium**, we adapt the IS/LM/BP model:

$$r = (r^* + \theta)$$

The interest rate r now incorporates the additional amount that governments must pay to service sovereign debt in times of uncertainty or due to poor macroeconomic performance. Our IS and LM curves can now be written:

$$Y = C + I\,(r^* + \theta) + G + NX\,(\varepsilon)$$

and

$$L(r^* + \theta, Y) = \frac{\overline{M}}{P}$$

It is worth noting here that, unlike a majority of the other variables in the IS and LM schedules, changes in θ affect both the IS and LM simultaneously; a change in the risk premium will have a goods market and money market effect.

Sovereign Debt: When the government borrows money to carry out its expenditure it gets the funds from the central bank. In return the government provides the central bank with IOUs called government bonds; also referred to as 'sovereign debt'.
Risk Premium: An addition to the normal rate of interest that prevails across the economy. This extra amount of interest is dependent on the perceived credit worthiness of an individual government. The safer the country is to lend to, the lower the interest rate it will pay.

With this adapted structure in mind, we can now use the IS/LM/BP to analyse the specific case of a country participating in a currency union and facing a sovereign debt crisis; to think of an example from recent history we can take the experience of Greece in 2010. In the aftermath of the financial crisis of 2008, several European countries have been identified by ratings agencies as over indebted and vulnerable to default on sovereign debt. Subsequently, a selection of countries with the notable case of Greece find themselves in the unfortunate position of having sovereign credit ratings downgraded in a time of need.

With the Greek government facing high debts alongside an untimely need to re-service its existing borrowing, rating agencies indirectly imposed a risk premium upon Greece of between 20 per cent and 30 per cent. This effective interest rate for public borrowing is what we might normally associate with consumer credit cards. Of course, Greece was unable to sustain such an interest rate without the prospect of default and now we use the IS/LM/BP model to explain events from this moment onwards. We start with the imposition of a risk premium for Greece resulting in a shift upwards in the BP line in Figure 12.8.

As the BP schedule shifts upwards, this creates a negative balance of payments disturbance; there is massive capital outflow ensuing. Normally we would see this disturbance as resulting in

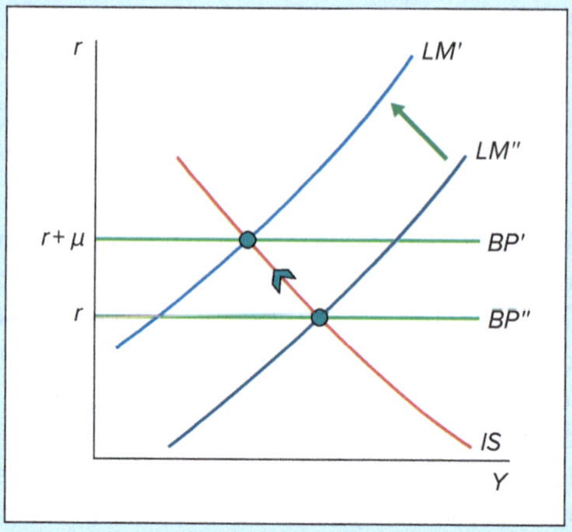

Figure 12.8 Debt crisis adds a risk premium, shifting the *BP* upwards

downward pressure on the exchange rate. However, Greece is part of a monetary union and the usual adjustment of the exchange rate is impinged upon.

From this point forward and with the natural adjustment of the exchange rate, we would expect the IS schedule to shift to the right as net exports increase but instead, with the exchange rate unable to adjust, the only reaction is an increase in prices and real money balances fall back across the economy. The LM schedule shifts back to LM′ *to* reflect this and output is now reduced to below its normal rate.

Naturally, this event leaves Greece in a very difficult position. Money is needed to revive the economy, although with the rate at which it can re-service debt being unrealistically high, this is not a possibility. In 2010 the Greek government benefited from an EU bailout package that effectively gave a guarantee for the sovereign debt; this event removes the risk premium. In our model we see the BP line shift back down towards BP′′. The price for such a remedy from the EU is a condition that Greece must impose austerity measures to ensure future fiscal discipline. The imposition of fiscal discipline sees government spending fall back and we see this reflected in Figure 12.9 as a leftward shift in the IS schedule; output falls further back.

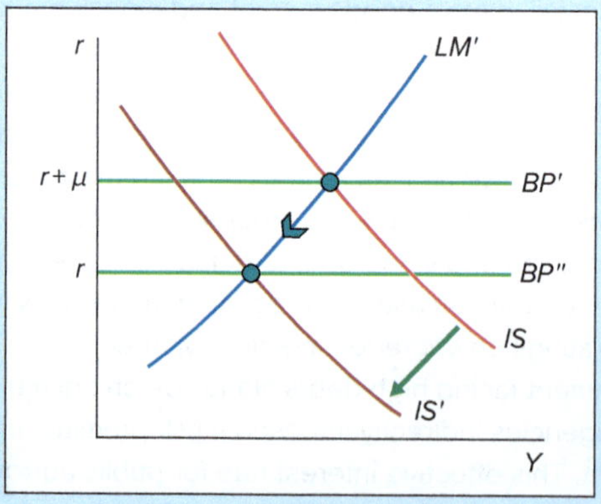

Figure 12.9 EU reduces the risk premia, pushing the *BP* line back down

We can use the model's usual prediction for the return to the long-run equilibrium for Greece as a very long-run and ongoing recovery towards normality. As you can see, the situation has been made worse by the fact that Greece is part of a monetary and yet no fiscal union; this halfway house towards full political union itself has its own unique characteristics and challenges. In a crisis this has left Greece in the unenviable position of having to face its problem with sovereign debt without the safety net or option of devaluing its own currency.

For the future, Greece has to wait for its own inflation rate to subside so that real money balances recover. Remember that the real exchange rate is affected by the relative difference between the domestic (Greek) and foreign (EU) inflation rates. We see the long path back to normal output represented in our model in Figure 12.10; the LM schedule eventually shifts right so that output returns to its normal rate.

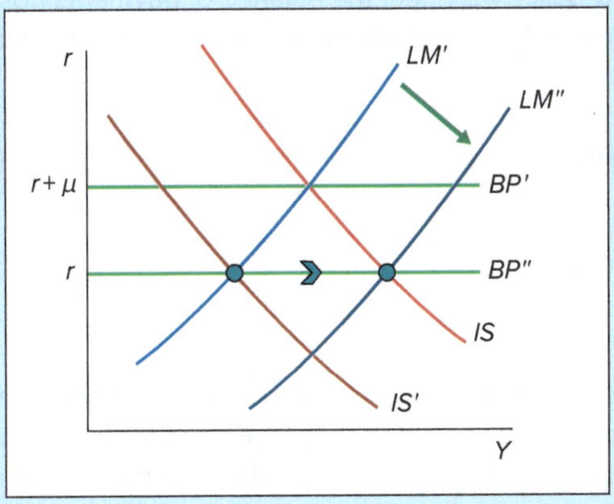

Figure 12.10 The return to long-run equilibrium with lower real money balances

12.5 Chapter summary: Putting it all together

In this chapter, we have learnt about the open economy version of the IS/LM model which uses the concept of a general equilibrium between the goods market and the money market in one two-dimensional diagram, for the small open economy. The model helps us to understand how the real economy is affected by economic policy through the channels of international capital flows and movements in the exchange rate, rather than the usual closed economy explanation of the interest rate channel.

We could say that the model is more realistic, given its ability to account for exchange rate movements and flows of international capital. We must bear in mind, though, that the model assumes that the interest rate is fixed at the world interest rate and there is perfect capital mobility, so can only be applied to a small open economy. How realistic is this? Well, one way to think about this is that, compared to the world economy, any economy can be thought of as small by comparison, so that the assumption of small is not so unrealistic.

It is also indeed the case that some countries still engage in capital restrictions (imperfect capital mobility); especially when an economy is underperforming, there is always a temptation to impede capital flight. A country that has been forced to borrow in terms of foreign currency will have to make higher repayments as the exchange rate falls or deplete foreign exchange reserves. In the modern globalized world, capital controls are becoming increasingly difficult to enforce, especially with the advent of the internet and digital currencies, making it easier for large-scale investors to move capital around to seek out higher returns elsewhere. It is better for policymakers to engage in macroprudential policies that aim to attract foreign investment, and negate the need for capital controls in the first place.

We finish the chapter with a specific case of a country that struggles to raise finance for government spending during a crisis; a case further complicated by the constraints imposed by membership of a currency union. Whenever a crisis hits an economy, there are policy options that can be applied to mitigate the harm passed on to society. Sometimes, a membership of a union, or agreement to harmonize currencies can impinge on efforts to lessen the negative impacts of such an event, and we should bear in mind these limits when forming political agreements.

Assessment question

Using the IS/LM/BP model, explain the reaction of an open economy to remedial monetary policy following a financial crisis in an economy with floating exchange rates. A central bank may need to react to falling asset prices by lowering the cost of borrowing and stimulating demand for assets. Highlight the details of the linkages across the macroeconomic variables, and explain how policy will affect the balance of payments position of the economy. What pressures will this place on the domestic interest rate and what effect will this have on international capital flows?

Cases

The IS/LM/BP model in Singapore (post-COVID economic policy response)

Background

Singapore is a small, open economy that is highly dependent on trade and foreign investment. Its government and central bank (the Monetary Authority of Singapore – MAS) are renowned for the responsive and disciplined macroeconomic policies historically. Singapore maintains a managed float exchange rate regime and has near perfect capital mobility due to open capital markets and a globally integrated financial system.

In the aftermath of the COVID-19 pandemic (2020–2022), like many countries, Singapore faced a severe economic contraction. Policymakers responded with aggressive fiscal and monetary policies to support households and firms.

IS/LM/BP framework context

The IS/LM/BP model can be used to analyse the interaction between:

- IS curve: Goods market equilibrium (investment = saving)
- LM curve: Money market equilibrium (money supply = money demand)
- BP curve: Balance of payments equilibrium (external sector)

This model is especially insightful when applied to small open economies, particularly under perfect capital mobility.

Assumptions in the case of Singapore

- Perfect capital mobility: Investors can move capital in and out of Singapore freely. This implies that the domestic interest rate must match the world interest rate in the long run.
- Small open economy: Singapore's policies do not affect world interest rates or global demand.
- Flexible exchange rate (managed float): MAS uses the exchange rate (through a trade-weighted basket) as the main policy tool rather than setting interest rates directly.

Policy response and effectiveness

1. Fiscal policy (IS shift):
    - The Singapore government implemented large fiscal stimulus packages ($100 billion SGD) during 2020–2021.
    - This shifted the IS curve rightward, increasing output.

- Under perfect capital mobility and a flexible exchange rate, the fiscal expansion appreciated the Singapore dollar, which partially offset the demand boost through reduced net exports.
- Nonetheless, due to strong consumer and business confidence and the targeted nature of government spending (e.g., wage subsidies, business grants), fiscal policy proved somewhat effective.

2. Monetary policy (LM curve):
   - MAS does not use interest rates but adjusts the exchange rate policy band instead.
   - During the COVID crisis, MAS flattened the slope of the policy band, effectively allowing a depreciation to support exports and growth.
   - This shifted the LM curve for Singapore rightward (increasing money supply due to more relaxed financial conditions).
   - However, under perfect capital mobility, interest rates remain fixed at the global rate, meaning an expansionary monetary policy is likely to cause capital outflows, putting downward pressure on the currency.
   - MAS balanced this with its managed float mechanism, showing that monetary policy can still be effective if the exchange rate is not strictly fixed.
3. Balance of payments (BP curve):
   - Capital mobility ensured that any deviation from the global interest rate would lead to capital flows restoring equilibrium.
   - This put pressure on the exchange rate, which MAS managed via forex interventions.

Outcome

Singapore recovered relatively quickly post-COVID, with GDP growth rebounding to 7.6 per cent in 2021. The coordinated fiscal and monetary responses, alongside credible policy institutions and a flexible exchange rate regime, made the IS/LM/BP framework relevant and visible in the country's macroeconomic management.

Questions

1. Explain how the assumption of perfect capital mobility affects the shape and position of the BP curve in the IS/LM/BP model. Use Singapore as an example.
2. Evaluate the effectiveness of Singapore's fiscal policy in 2020–2021 using the IS/LM/BP model. Consider the exchange rate regime and capital mobility in your answer.
3. Discuss why monetary policy is generally considered ineffective under perfect capital mobility and a floating exchange rate regime. Then explain how Singapore's managed float might allow some effectiveness.
4. Using the IS/LM/BP framework, explain what might happen to output, interest rates, and the exchange rate in Singapore if the government increased spending while MAS tightened the exchange rate band to prevent depreciation.

Problems

EASY

1. In the IS/LM/BP framework, which of the following statements about the BP curve is correct?
   a) It is vertical in interest rate output space when capital is perfectly mobile
   b) It shows combinations of interest rates and output associated with goods market equilibrium
   c) It is horizontal in interest rate output space under perfect capital mobility
   d) It shifts left when the domestic interest rate rises
   e) It represents monetary policy effectiveness for a closed economy

MEDIUM

2. In the IS/LM/BP model with fixed exchange rates and perfect capital mobility, if the government increases spending, what is the most likely short-run effect on output?
   a) The central bank will tighten monetary policy to reduce inflation
   b) The increase in demand will be offset by a currency appreciation
   c) Output will rise as monetary policy accommodates the fiscal expansion to maintain the peg
   d) Output will remain unchanged because fiscal policy is ineffective under fixed exchange rates
   e) Investment will fall due to higher interest rates, crowding out investment
3. Under floating exchange rates and perfect capital mobility, a monetary expansion in a small open economy will:
   a) have no effect on output but cause an increase in the price level
   b) lead to massive capital inflow and an appreciation of the currency
   c) result in a lower exchange rate, higher net exports and rising national income
   d) force the central bank to defend the exchange rate by selling foreign reserves
   e) be completely offset by a fall in private investment
4. When a country with floating exchange rates implements expansionary fiscal policy, what is the likely result, according to the Mundell–Fleming model?
   a) Increased output and a depreciation of the domestic currency
   b) Increased output and an appreciation of the domestic currency
   c) No change in output due to the assumption of perfect capital mobility
   d) A fall in interest rate and a net capital outflow
   e) A rightward shift in the LM curve due to the fiscal stimulus of the economy
5. Consider a small open economy with the following components of aggregate demand:
   - Consumption: $C = 100 + 0.6Y$
   - Investment: $I = 150 - 10r$
   - Government spending: $G = 200$
   - Net exports: $NX = 50 - 0.1Y$
   - World interest rate: $r = 5\%$
   - The exchange rate is floating and capital mobility is perfect. Prices are fixed.

   a) Derive the investment savings curve for the economy.
   b) Calculate the equilibrium level of output (Y) using the given interest rate.

HARD

6. Which of the following is an implication of perfect capital mobility in the Mundell–Fleming IS/LM/BP model?
   a) The domestic interest rate can diverge from the world interest rate without capital flows
   b) Any attempt to change the money supply under a fixed exchange rate is futile
   c) Fiscal policy becomes completely ineffective under floating exchange rates
   d) The *IS* curve becomes vertical in interest rate output space
   e) Exchange rates cannot influence output under perfect capital mobility
7. Which policy is the most effective for stimulating output in a small open economy with floating exchange rates?
8. Explain how the effectiveness of monetary policy differs under fixed versus floating exchange rate regimes in the Mundell–Fleming model. Why does this difference arise?
9. Discuss the implications of perfect capital mobility for the autonomy of domestic monetary policy in a small open economy. How does the exchange rate regime influence this?

CHAPTER 13

The AS/AD Model

Chapter contents

At a Glance The AS/AD model

The issue

The most commonly taught model in macroeconomics is the AS/AD model – the economy is split between those demanding goods and services and those supplying goods and services. How useful is this model in comparison to the general equilibrium IS/LM model from Chapter 11?

The understanding

Being a macroeconomic model, it uses the controversial assumption of representative agents, the average consumer making up demand and the average firm used to model supply in the economy; effectively, all consumers and suppliers are assumed to be identical. The AD curve follows the law of demand, that output demanded is negative in prices, and the AS curve follows the theory of the firm, where supply increases with increases in price.

The usefulness

The AS/AD model is useful in that it can capture inflationary effects through movements in the price level. This is somewhat of a limitation for the IS/LM model that assumes prices are fixed. Here, we can also use the AS/AD model to capture the concept of output gaps in the macroeconomy.

13.1 Introduction

A popular macroeconomic model used to represent the market for goods and services is the aggregate supply and aggregate demand (AS/AD) model. This is a two-dimensional model where two agents, the firm and the consumer, interact to determine the level of output in the economy. The model helps to explain how the demand and supply side come together to explain changes in output brought about by economic shocks and the use of economic policy. As an explanation of short-run deviations in output from its trend, the model can be seen as a benchmark, not least due to its simplicity and ease of use but also because of the intuitive structure. However, the model is not without its critics and so we begin with a brief discussion on the scope and usefulness of the model for explaining movements in economic activity.

In the most basic version of the circular flow model, first introduced in Chapter 4, the economy is assumed to have two economic actors: the representative consumer and the representative firm. Using an average representation in this way might seem 'far-fetched' but in the context of the 'macro' economy may be quite reasonable too. Why reasonable? For one thing, we know that government institutions such as the central bank will react to variables such as inflation and output – remember that inflation is an economy-wide change in the 'average' price in the economy. The central bank has to set the one interest rate based on the change in this 'average' price level. There is one interest rate and one inflation rate, so perhaps it is not so unreasonable to have one 'average' consumer and one 'average' firm. In any case, if the economic question being asked of a model requires a level of heterogeneity (or to control for different characteristics among differing groups of agents), then a model can be adapted to account for it with theoretical innovations.

EXAMPLE 13.1

Real world example: The representative agent assumption

A real example of where the use of representative agents could be justified exactly is that of the German labour market during the early 2000s. German households were characterized by moderate income equality, a highly skilled and fairly homogeneous workforce and an efficient social welfare system.

Simplification over accuracy

These factors contributed to a relatively uniform behaviour by households in terms of labour supply decisions, and saving and consumption choices. Under such circumstances the use of representative households offers a simplification that does not sacrifice accuracy.

Macroeconomic models

Many macroeconomic models use representative households to avoid the complications of controlling for different household types, each displaying different behaviours. In Germany's case this allowed economists to evaluate labour market reforms and monetary policy within the euro area.

Another criticism of the AS/AD model is that it makes use of the concept of general equilibrium, which some might see as an abstract or even mythological concept – a special place in the market where variables gravitate, pushed by the market forces of disequilibrium, towards a place where everything is equal and nothing happens. While it is not so difficult to justify the concept of equilibrium at the microeconomic level, at the macroeconomic level this is more difficult. One way to think of the movements away from equilibrium in real life is the cyclical ups and downs of a variable above and below its average rate.

Table 13.1 summarizes some of the commonly cited strengths and weaknesses of the AS/AD model.

Table 13.1 Strengths and weaknesses of the AS/AD model

Strengths	Weaknesses
Simple 2D model	Unable to capture inflationary effects
Highly intuitive	Uses concept of general equilibrium
Easy to use for policy exercises	Time invariant

Now that we have discussed the shortcomings and advantages of the model we can introduce the AS/AD model in more detail. The model assumes that there are two agents – the representative firm and the representative consumer – modelled by the aggregate supply curve and the aggregate demand curve, respectively. The two agents interact (the curves cross) to determine an equilibrium economy-wide level of output and price level; this is the reason that they are drawn in output/price space (*P* and *Y* are on the axis). The individual curves show the level of output demanded and the level of output supplied at every price level in the economy.

In this chapter, we begin by introducing the two agents (consumers and firms) individually and in detail, building the model diagrammatically. When we introduce the supply side we allow for both the short-run and long-run reaction of firms to changes in the price level. Remember that we first discussed the issue of the short run versus the long run in Chapter 4, when we used the slope of the aggregate supply curve to differentiate between two time frames and two schools of economic thought. After closing the model with the concept of general equilibrium, we then show how we can use the AS/AD model to analyse the effects of economic shocks and economic policy. Finally, we complete our description by taking a mathematical perspective of the model before concluding with some more critique and discussion of the model's limitations.

Learning Outcomes

By the end of this chapter you should be able to:

- Explain the aggregate supply aggregate demand (AS/AD) model in diagrams.
- Understand how to use the AS/AD model to explain how national income is determined in the economy.
- Use the AS/AD as a tool to explain the effects of economic shocks and economic policy.
- Understand the basic mathematics of the AS/AD model.
- Evaluate the limitations of a static and agent-based model.

13.2 The aggregate supply and aggregate demand model

For a model to achieve the status of 'benchmark' or be considered 'mainstream' it must be universally accepted by economists and non-economists alike. The language has to be simple and the predictions accurate. A politician will want to know how an increase in taxes will affect the economy without referring to a highly complex modern macroeconomic DSGE model. Simple models are successful because they are easy to transmit an economic prediction with. So, despite the limitations of the AS/AD model it will continue to be universally taught and used by professional economists as a framework to communicate better-known policy implications. Let us start by adding some detail to the structure of the AS/AD model.

Aggregate Demand: The sum of all demand in the economy. We can think of demand as 'planned expenditure'; when we are planning to spend, we are in a position of demand.
Aggregate Supply: The aggregated sum of the revenues of all firms in the economy.

The AS/AD model is a static agent-based model displayed in two dimensions with two schedules (or curves) representing the supply and demand sides of the economy – the supply side being the representative (or average) firm and the demand side being the representative consumer. We can use both diagrams and mathematics to describe the model: as a diagram in the form of a graph with price and output on the vertical and horizontal axis respectively, or as a set of two equations in two variables (prices and income). It is also quite possible to describe the model in a few paragraphs of words, though I leave this to you as a worthy exercise having read this chapter. Below we introduce the **aggregate demand** and **aggregate supply** schedules.

The aggregate demand curve

The aggregate demand curve represents the economy-wide reaction of demand to changes in the price level. The schedule is downward sloping in prices/output space reflecting that at higher prices we see lower demand for goods and services and at lower prices this demand increases. At a micro level, the assumption of utility maximization, is consistent with the proposition that consumers will tend to substitute away from goods that are increasing in price. The aggregate demand curve simply reflects the downward sloping nature of all the individual market demand curves. Figure 13.1 plots the aggregate demand curve.

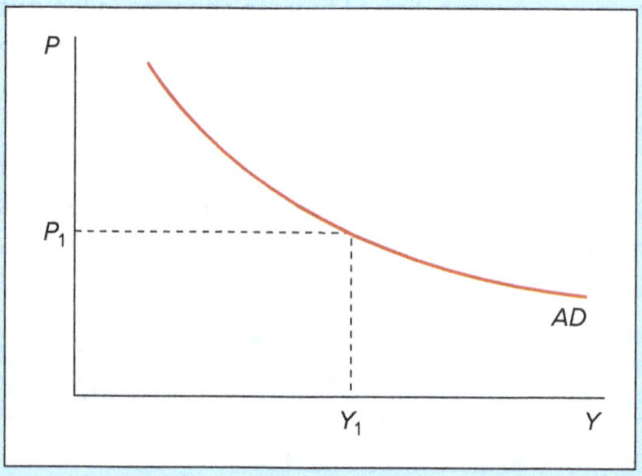

Figure 13.1 The aggregate demand curve drawn in price-output space

The result that higher prices reduce goods and services demanded is highly intuitive. A change in the price level will move us along the aggregate demand curve and a change in anything else that effects demand will shift the curve. In our model, shifts can occur via economic shocks and economic policy. Shocks and policies that increase economic activity shifts the curve rightwards (or out) and those that reduce activity leftwards (or in). As a couple of examples, we can imagine a negative economic shock such as the recent credit crunch reducing economic activity and so shifting the AD curve left, and an increase in the money supply by the central bank increasing economic activity and so shifting the AD curve right.

In Figure 13.2 we map the specific case of fiscal policy aimed at increasing economic activity (expansionary); by increasing spending, the government increases demand for goods and services at every price level and so the AD curve will shift rightwards to reflect this change.

We can split policy into two categories: expansionary and contractionary. Expansionary policy is designed to increase output or expand the economy, and contractionary is the opposite.

Expansionary fiscal policy is an increase in government spending or a reduction in taxation and expansionary monetary policy is an increase in the money supply. Notice from the diagram that after the increase in demand we have higher output demanded at any particular level of

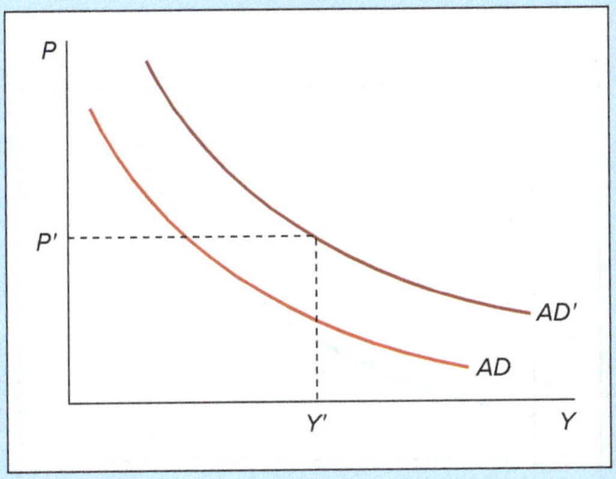

Figure 13.2 The aggregate demand curve showing a rightward shift caused by expansionary economic policy

prices. Needless to say, if we had taken the case of contractionary policy (a policy designed to reduce output/ or cool the economy) we would have shown this as a leftwards shift in the aggregate demand curve. In the AS/AD model the use of monetary and fiscal policy is only reflected in the demand curve, and for this reason these types of policy are often referred to as 'demand management'. As a useful guide, Table 13.2 outlines the reaction of the demand curve to different types of economic policy and shocks.

Table 13.2 Reaction of demand curve

Policy or shock	Shift of aggregate demand curve	
Increase in government spending		Right
Decrease in government spending	Left	
Increase in taxes	Left	
Decrease in taxes		Right
Increase in money supply		Right
Decrease in money supply	Left	
Stock market boom		Right
Stock market crash	Left	
Credit crunch	Left	
Increase in confidence		Right

The short-run and long-run aggregate supply curve

The aggregate supply curve represents the set of firms in the economy, modelled as the representative (or average) firm. We can think of the aggregate supply curve over two time frames: the short run where prices are assumed fixed or sticky; and the long run where prices are assumed flexible. In the short run firms will react to an increase in the price level by increasing output above its natural rate, but in the long run firms will be exposed to higher costs and output will fall back to its natural rate.

So the short-run aggregate supply curve (SRAS) gives us the 'supply' side reaction to changes in the price level in the economy. The schedule is upward sloping in prices/output space, reflecting that at higher prices we see a higher willingness to supply goods and services from firms in the economy. Figure 13.3 plots the short-run aggregate supply curve in price/output space.

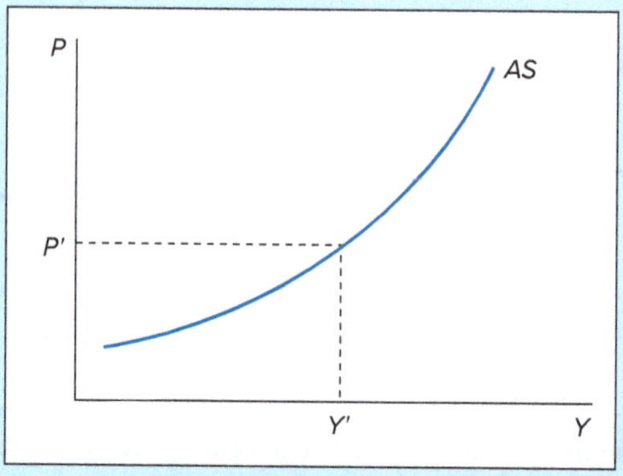

Figure 13.3 The short-run aggregate supply curve (SRAS)

At the microeconomic level, the proposition that higher prices are likely to attract more suppliers into the individual market is quite intuitive. The upward sloping SRAS simply aggregates this proposition so that higher prices in the economy increase aggregate supply. As with any two-dimensional model, notice that if the values of the variables on the axis change then there is a movement along the curve but if anything else connected with supply changes then the curve will shift. Such changes to consider are factors affecting suppliers, economic shocks and supply-side policy.

As an example, imagine that the government enact a policy that will lower the costs of firms in the economy. Intuitively, we know that firms will enjoy lower costs and our intuition is correct – the short-run aggregate supply curve shifts right (or outwards) and production of goods and services increase at every price level.

EXERCISE 13.1

In 2008 there was a sudden hike in the global oil price (to $147 on 11 July) which many economists saw as a major economic shock.

Use the AS/AD model to show the predicted effect of the shock on the economy. Start by working out which schedule (AS or AD) is affected and how.

Even though the AS/AD model is a static explanation (something we might call a snapshot) one useful addition to the AS/AD model is a schedule that helps us to capture the difference between the short run and the long run. As the model is set in price/output space it makes sense to use the supply side for this purpose; so we can include a 'long-run' aggregate supply curve also. The long-run aggregate supply (LRAS) curve shows us where we expect output to be in the long run, and also has important implications for economic policy. Long-run output is held fixed in the short run determined by the fixed level of labour and capital in the economy. You might think of long-run output as the natural rate or the average rate. It is drawn as a vertical line upwards from the horizontal axis (output) at the value of the natural rate of output.

In Figure 13.4 we see how to draw the LRAS curve in the AS/AD model. Aggregate supply will be at its natural rate in the absence of price shocks. In other words, production will be at its natural rate when prices are as expected. This is why the short-run aggregate supply and long-run aggregate supply curves cross at the expected price level in the economy P^e. If the price is away from its expected level, we have a price surprise and output will deviate away from the natural rate. This deviation will only last for a short period, as the economy will return to its natural state when expectations have adjusted so that the new price is no longer a surprise.

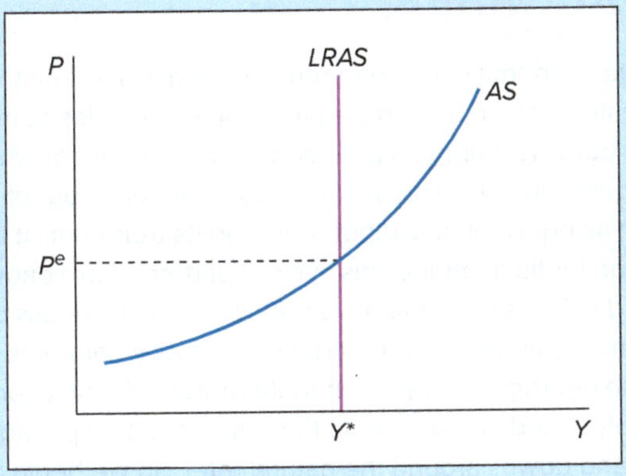

Figure 13.4 The short-run and long-run aggregate supply curves together

Long-run and short-run equilibrium in the AS/AD model

Now that we have fully described both the demand and supply side in our model for the macro economy, we can put everything together to discuss general equilibrium. In Figure 13.5 we bring the individual components, aggregate demand (AD), short-run aggregate supply (SRAS) and long-run aggregate supply (LRAS), together in one diagram. Where the aggregate demand and supply curves cross is the economy-wide equilibrium level of prices and output. Notice that if we consider the long run by including the LRAS, then this equilibrium level of output coincides with the natural rate of output Y^* in the absence of economic shocks or changes in economic policy.

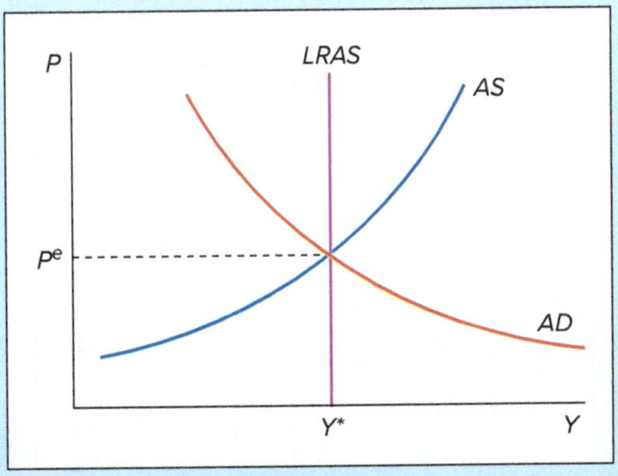

Figure 13.5 General equilibrium in the AS/AD model

Short-Run Equilibrium: The intersection of the short-run aggregate supply and demand curves. Output will not be at its natural rate and so prices will adjust to return the economy to its long-run equilibrium in the absence of intervention by policymakers.
Long-Run Equilibrium: The intersection of the short-run aggregate supply, aggregate demand and long-run aggregate supply together. Prices will not need to adjust because they are at their expected level and output is at its natural (long-run) rate.

It is worth noting that the short-run intersection of the AS and AD curves does not necessarily have to exist at the natural rate of output. The **short-run equilibrium** can exist either to the left or to the right of Y^*. For the **long-run** position, the combination of prices and output that clear the market for goods and services is the expected price level P^e and natural rate of output Y^*. In the next section, we consider the short-run equilibrium that comes after an economic shock or economic policy.

13.3 Economic policy analysis using the AS/AD model

We have seen that in the long run we can assume that the equilibrium between aggregate demand and aggregate supply coincides at the natural rate of output, but what happens after an economic event or when policy disturbs the status quo? One way to explain the cyclical behaviour of output is as a variable that fluctuates away from its equilibrium. Output is around its trend until it becomes disturbed and we witness a deviation (or fluctuation). This cyclical pattern of prolonged expansion followed by periods of prolonged decline is something we refer to as the business cycle, with output increasing as the economy expands and output decreasing as it contracts. In the context of the AS/AD model the long-run aggregate supply schedule represents the economic trend and the short-run aggregate supply schedule represents the deviations that provide our explanation of the fluctuations (the ups and downs around the natural rate). So we begin our static comparisons by using policy as a shock that moves us away from equilibrium in the short run.

Measuring the impact of supply-side policy

We start with a policy example designed to encourage inward investment with the ultimate aim of reducing domestic unemployment. To make the economy attractive to foreign firms the government might lower its corporation tax rate. In 2010 the incoming UK coalition government announced such a policy and consequently we have since seen the corporation tax rate drop from 28 per cent in 2010 to 20 per cent in 2016. How can we analyse this policy using the AS/AD model?

First, we can identify which part of the economy is immediately affected by the change in economic policy. You may have already realized that this policy will affect the short-run aggregate supply curve. The lower tax rate encourages firms to produce more and we see an increase in supply at every price level (a rightward shift in the SRAS). Figure 13.6 shows the economy in the long run before the SRAS shifts outwards from AS to AS′.

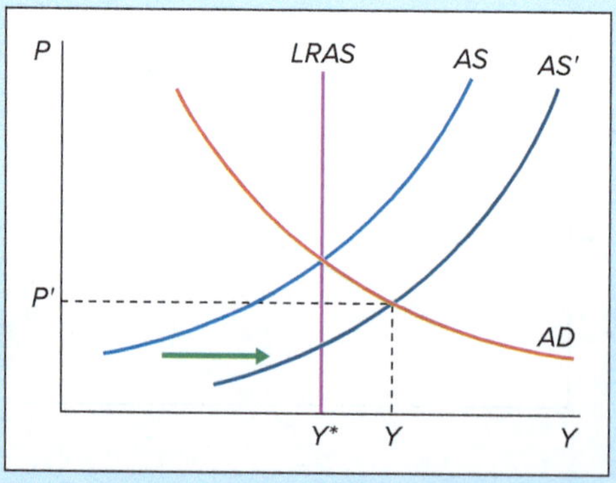

Figure 13.6 Using the AS/AD model to analyse supply-side policy

As we can see, the reaction to the supply-side policy of reducing corporation tax is favourable in terms of higher output and lower prices. Firms, seeing lower costs, are keen to raise production – given the potential for higher profits – and at the same time the lower taxes may attract firms from abroad, increasing output supplied and lowering prices through competition. However, this is not the end of the story: output is now above its long-run rate (the new short-run position) and over time the increased activity will begin to push up prices. When these higher prices feed into the suppliers cost base aggregate supply will begin to fall back again. The economy will return to equilibrium as the SRAS shifts leftwards; we see prices rising and output returning to its long-run value.

Our example above shows the reaction of the economy to a positive supply side shock. If we were studying the case of a negative shock, then output would have fallen below the natural rate and prices would have fallen to restore long-run equilibrium. Now that we have seen some analysis of supply-side policy we turn our attention to demand-side economic policy (something we also refer to as **demand management**).

Demand Management: Actively managing the level of economic activity in the economy using fiscal or/and monetary policy. Using demand-side policy is generally thought of as short run.
Adjusting Mechanism: The variable that changes to restore equilibrium in our model. This is normally the variable on the vertical axis. In the AS/AD the adjusting mechanism is the price level. If output is above its natural rate, prices will rise, if output is below the natural rate, prices will fall. If the economy is in equilibrium, no adjustment is necessary.

Demand management in the AS/AD model

In our supply-side example above, the economy returned naturally to its long-run equilibrium through the **adjusting mechanism** of prices. At the new short-run equilibrium, output was above its natural rate causing prices to rise, leading supply to fall back again. In fact, after any shock or economic policy change the AS/AD model will be out of equilibrium; output will be away from its natural rate and prices will adjust to bring the economy back.

Instead of this natural adjustment to the long run, authorities can use demand-management policies (monetary or fiscal policy) to force the economy back to equilibrium rather than waiting. We can also think that the options open to the policymaker involve a choice between 'intervention' and 'non-intervention' – intervening in terms of using demand management policy or non-intervention in terms of allowing the economy to return to its long-run position naturally. In the following example, we can use the recent and global financial crisis of 2008 as a real-life case for the AS/AD model to demonstrate government intervention during a recession.

We begin our explanation of the financial crisis as a liquidity shock to the financial markets. After the shock to liquidity, banks reduced the availability of loanable funds in the financial markets, meaning that consumers were unable to raise funds for purchases. Consequently, we can represent this in our AS/AD model as a negative demand shock that shifts the aggregate demand curve leftwards. From this short-run position, we can explain an intervention from the government or central bank aimed at restoring the economy back to long-run equilibrium. Figure 13.7 shows the economy 'after' a negative credit shock and work forwards from a short-run position.

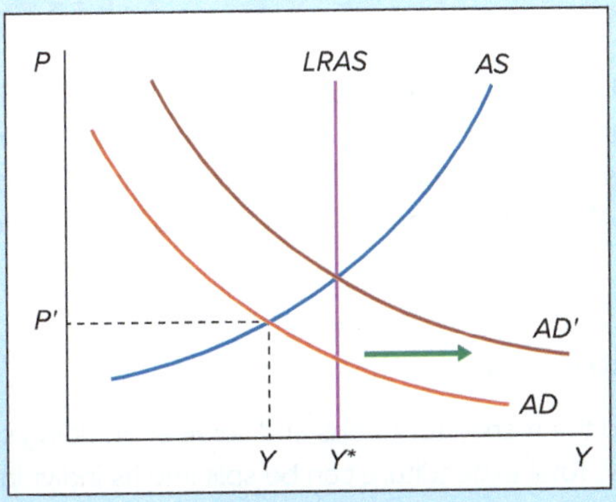

Figure 13.7 Demand management in the AS/AD model

The economy is in short-run equilibrium with output below its natural rate – the credit shock has caused a recession. The policymaker may want to increase economic activity to reduce job losses and avoid reduction of capacity rather than wait for the long-run natural adjustment to take place. The tool required for this objective is expansionary economic policy (increasing the money supply or increasing government spending). So we begin with the economy with the equilibrium to the left of the LRAS, where the AS and AD curves intersect. The policymaker increases aggregate demand by either increasing the money supply (through lowering interest rates) or by increasing government spending. Consequently, the AD curve shifts to the right (upwards) and the short-run equilibrium moves up along the AS curve to its new position, which coincides with the *LRAS* at the natural rate of output.

So, what would have happened if the economy would have been allowed to adjust naturally? Are these outcomes the same, and if so, why would the policymaker ever wait? To answer this question, we can go back to the original short-run position where the economy was in recession. In a recession, output is below its natural rate, prices will fall, suppliers will start to benefit from lower costs and supply will increase. As supply increases, output returns to its natural rate, but this time with lower prices than the case of intervention where the policymaker forced the economy back to the long-run position. The exercise provided below will reinforce your understanding.

EXERCISE 13.2

1 Use the AS/AD model and starting from the short-run equilibrium of a recession, draw out the options open to a policymaker (i.e., intervention or non-intervention). You will need two graphs to display the two different scenarios.

2 Compare your case of non-intervention with the case of intervention (given above). Given the differences in terms of prices and output, what lesson does the AS/AD provide us in terms of the arguments for and against intervention?

It is worth remembering that throughout our examples above we have referred to economic policy rather than individually, in terms of monetary and fiscal policy. In the AS/AD model the outcomes for both types of policy are the same – an increase in the money supply and an increase in government spending both shift the aggregate demand schedule right and decreases shift the demand schedule left. Why is this? For monetary policy, remember that in Chapter 5 we introduced the market for money where an increase in the money supply is consistent with a reduction in the interest rate. This reduction in rates feeds higher investment which increases demand. For the case of fiscal policy, an increase in government expenditure feeds higher demand for goods and services. So, both monetary policy and fiscal policy affect aggregated demand in the same way – policy that increases activity (expansionary) shifts the AD schedule right and policy that decreases activity (contractionary) shifts the schedule left.

13.4 The mathematics of the AS/AD model

So far, we have only used words and diagrams to explain the AS/AD model and for a working knowledge of the model this is sufficient. However, a mathematical framework is also very useful as it gives us another perspective on the mechanics of the model's predictions. Additionally, it helps us to relate the AS/AD to other types of model and further develop complexities for more specific policy analysis.

The AD and AS functions

In Chapter 6 we introduced the market for goods and services; in doing so we also made use of the aggregate demand identity. Total expenditure can be split into its individual components to provide us with an identity. The sum of the components 'must' be equal to the original variable's components.

$$Y \equiv C + I + G$$

To help us develop the economic concept of aggregate demand we can assert that all expenditure has to be 'planned' at some point, and at this stage it represents 'demand'. So, we can write a version of the income identity to provide a relation for aggregate demand:

$$AD = C + I + G$$

Aggregate demand is equal to the sum of all planned expenditure, that is, consumption, investment and government expenditure. This identity is useful in that it allows us to see quickly how monetary and fiscal policy drive aggregate demand.

Fiscal policy:	Change in government expenditure affects aggregate demand via the AD identity.
	Change in taxation affects aggregate demand via consumption then via the AD identity.
Monetary policy:	Change in the money supply affects interest rate via the money market, then investment via the investment function, finally via the AD identity.

Now that we have seen the channels through which economic policy affects aggregate demand we can write a functional form for the AS/AD model in output/price space:

$$Y = \left(\frac{M}{P}\right)^d$$

Aggregate demand can be written simply as a function of real money balances demanded. In the case of monetary policy, an increase in the money supply M increases real money balances (via the money market), in turn increasing aggregate demand. In fact, we can also think of fiscal policy driving real money balances via the increase in the money supply from government spending (assuming constant taxation). So both demand management policies are captured by this simple relation. Notice that an increase in the price level will reduce real money balances and in turn aggregate demand so that the function is consistent with our downward sloping aggregate demand curve. Lastly, we rewrite our aggregate demand function in log form, where y is the log deviation from its natural rate:

$$y = m - p$$

Movements in output are driven in the same direction as exogenous monetary policy but in the opposite direction in terms of price. Notice that variables multiplied together are separated when taking logs (+ for variables on the nominator and – for variables on the denominator).

In Chapter 9, we derived an aggregate supply relation from the expectations-augmented Phillips curve and we can also write a version of this in log form:

$$y = \delta(p - p^e)$$

This aggregate supply equation is also known as a 'Lucas' type supply equation after an economist Robert Lucas (1973) who developed an explanation for aggregate supply in response to Milton Friedman's natural rate hypothesis (NRH). The surprise supply equation predicts that output will be around its natural rate ($y = 0$) in the absence of any price shock. If prices turn out to be higher than expected, then there is a price surprise and suppliers move to increase production. As we would expect from our earlier discussions, the aggregate supply function predicts an upward-sloping relationship between prices and output, consistent with our drawn *AS* curve.

Solving the model under rational expectations

If we can be more specific about the formation of expectations in our model, we can solve for equilibrium output and prices. Here we will assume that expectations are formed rationally and keep in mind that our result for equilibrium is sensitive to this choice. In its most simple form we can write out the economy as a system of two equations and allow for an aggregate demand shock ε – for example, an unanticipated change in the money supply.

We consider the following economic system:

(Equation 13.1) $$y = m - p + \varepsilon$$

(Equation 13.2) $$y = \delta(p - p^e)$$

where y is output, p is the price level, p^e is the rational expectation of the price level, m is the money stock set exogenously by the central bank and ε a normally distributed demand shock with mean zero to capture departures from equilibrium. All variables are in logs.

To solve for equilibrium, we can start by eliminating the dependent variable y and then solving for the independent variable p. Equate the two right-hand sides of Equation (13.1) and Equation (13.2):

(Equation 13.3) $$m - p + \varepsilon = \delta(p - p^e)$$

Taking expectations of Equation (13.3), bearing in mind that the expectation of the exogenously set money supply is just itself, $E(m) = m$, and that the expectation of the shock is its mean, $E(\varepsilon) = 0$, and also that $E(p) = p^e$:

(Equation 13.4) $$m - p^e = \delta(p^e - p^e)$$

then simplify and solve for the expected price:

$$p^e = m$$

Now substituting our solution for the expected price into Equation (13.3):

$$m - p + \varepsilon = \delta(p - m)$$

solving for p:

$$(1 + \delta)p = (1 + \delta)m + \varepsilon$$

gives our solution for equilibrium price:

$$p = m + \frac{\varepsilon}{(1 + \delta)}$$

This solution tells us that the equilibrium price is determined by changes in the money supply and some proportion of the economic shock. It is intuitive that increases in the money supply drive up prices, although we will see that the solution for output is less intuitive. We can find the solution for output by substituting the solution for equilibrium price into the aggregate supply curve (Equation 13.2) just as we would for simultaneous equations in mathematics. Once we have the solution for one variable we can use either of the original equations to extract the remaining solution.

Substituting our solution for price and the expected price into Equation (13.2):

$$y = \delta\left(\left(m + \frac{\varepsilon}{(1 + \delta)}\right) - m\right)$$

and simplifying gives our solution for output:

$$y = \left(\frac{\delta}{1 + \delta}\right)\varepsilon$$

Output is simply a function of the demand shock – an unanticipated upward movement in the money supply will cause output to increase, but only for as long as the shock remains a shock. Unlike the solution for price, the solution for equilibrium output does not have the exogenous money supply as a driving force (on the right-hand side) and this provides us with the most notable implication. Only unanticipated monetary policy can affect output through the shock. An anticipated increase in the money supply m will have no effect on equilibrium output, meaning that policy is ineffective and that the central bank can only raise output briefly. Further, the cost of raising output, even for a short while, is permanently higher prices (notice m is on the left-hand side for the solution in price).

13.5 Criticism and limitations of the AS/AD model

The AS/AD model presented in this section gives us the implication that policy is ineffective, at least in the long run. After a monetary expansion, the increase in output is temporary and carries the undesirable cost of permanently higher prices. Depending on the speed of transition to the long run we could say that this implication supports the view held by classical economists that all interventions by policymakers will only feed through to nominal changes with no real effects on the economy.

In reality, output spends prolonged periods away from its natural rate; output is increasing and decreasing in durations of years rather than months. This cyclical pattern to the path of output is something we call the **business cycle**. The explanation of this cycle is a contentious issue for economists, centred on the thorny issue of the driving force of the fluctuations and its consequence for the role of economic policy. A 'classical non-interventionist' would explain the deviations as real movements driven by productivity shocks but a 'Keynesian interventionist' would prefer to use nominal shocks such as money, underpinning the role of monetary policy in the evolution of output.

To account for real effects from policy a macroeconomic model needs a mechanism to slow the adjustment of prices in the model and thus slow down the return of output to its natural rate. Keynesian economists such as Guillermo Calvo (1983) and John Taylor (1980) developed models specifically for this purpose; an explanation of sticky prices that could be applied to macro models that otherwise would have supported the classical outcome. These innovations have been termed **nominal rigidities** and used widely to explain longer price durations, though in reality a good proportion of the inertia (smoothness) in the data is actually caused by the process of aggregation rather price rigidity. Nevertheless, the AS/AD model remains a simple and useful tool for practising economists to explain the most basic movements of the economy.

Business Cycle: The cyclical path that the growth in output follows historically – prolonged periods of expansion followed by prolonged periods of contraction. The source of these fluctuations is a source of popular debate.
Nominal Rigidities: Also termed 'sticky prices'. A theoretical explanation of the sluggish behaviour of prices. Modelling prices as sticky helps to explain the smoothness we see in inflation data (the time series is nearly flat) and allows models to predict a usefulness for demand management.

13.6 Chapter summary: Putting it all together

In this chapter, we have introduced a model that can represent the economy as a whole in output/prices space that makes use of the concept of general equilibrium, with two agents representing the demand and supply sides of the economy. The demand side of the economy is assumed downward sloping in prices and the supply side sloping upwards. The adjusting mechanism that restores equilibrium after a shock in the model is the price level. While the model is very simple it is also intuitive and useful to explain the basic movement of the economy after a shock or economic policy.

Monetary and fiscal policy are explained as shifts in the aggregate demand schedule and observations in aggregate supply contain both an element of long-run aggregate supply and the short-run deviation from the long run. We have also learnt how to use the model to describe supply- and demand-side policy and through this, the macroeconomic difference between non-intervention and intervention after an economic shock. Finally, we have produced the mathematical functions for aggregate demand and aggregate supply and made use of the simplifying assumption to solve the model for equilibrium. Under an assumption of rational expectations, the AS/AD model predicts that monetary policy is ineffective.

Assessment question

Use the model of aggregate supply and demand to explain the real effects of monetary policy in the short run and in the long run. What does this prediction tell us about the use of quantitative easing by the Bank of England during the financial crisis of 2008?

Cases

The United Kingdom's energy price shock (2021–2023)

Context

In 2021–2023, the UK economy experienced a significant energy price shock, caused by two major geopolitical events. First, the COVID-19 crisis had led to the interruption of global supply chains in the energy sector; and secondly, the invasion of Ukraine by Russia in 2022 led to a significant loss of gas supply across Europe. These events led to soaring gas and electricity prices, which had profound short-run and long-run macroeconomic effects on the UK economy.

Short-run effects (SRAS and AD impact)

1. Cost-push inflation (the SRAS shifts left): Higher energy prices raised production costs for firms, especially in energy-intensive sectors such as manufacturing and transport. This caused a leftward shift in the short-run aggregate supply (SRAS) curve, increasing the price level and reducing real GDP (a situation often termed stagflation).
2. Reduced real incomes and consumption (the AD shifts left): With real incomes eroded by higher energy bills, household consumption fell, contributing to a leftward shift in the aggregate demand (AD) curve. This compounded the decline in output and added pressure to the labour market.
3. Monetary policy response: The Bank of England raised interest rates to combat the cost-push inflation, further dampening aggregate demand by discouraging borrowing and spending, and reinforcing the downward pressure on growth.

Long-run effects (economic capacity and the LRAS)

1. Investment in renewable energy and efficiency (*LRAS* to shift right): In response to volatile fossil fuel prices, the UK government and private sector increased investment in renewable energy and energy efficiency. Over time, these investments can improve productivity and shift the long-run aggregate supply (LRAS) to the right, increasing economic capacity.
2. Labour market adjustments: In the long run, the labour market may adjust through wage negotiations and structural shifts into more resilient sectors (e.g., green tech), supporting a return to fuller employment.
3. Improved energy security: Policy measures to reduce reliance on imported fossil fuels may reduce future vulnerability to external energy price shocks, enhancing macroeconomic stability.

Evaluation

- Time lags: Long-run supply-side improvements, such as energy infrastructure, take years to materialize. Short-run pain may persist in the meantime.
- Policy dilemmas: The Bank of England faced a policy trade-off – raising the interest rate to tackle inflation at the risk of deepening an economic slowdown.
- Distributional effects: Lower-income households were disproportionately affected by energy inflation, highlighting the regressive nature of such negative energy price shocks.
- Global interdependence: The UK's inflation was heavily influenced by global commodity markets, limiting the domestic ability to intervene against external shocks.

Questions

1. What happened to the SRAS during the energy price shock in the UK?
2. How did the UK's aggregate demand respond and why?
3. Describe the long-run consequences of the energy shock on the UK economy.
4. What policy actions did the UK government and Bank of England take?
5. Evaluate whether the UK can fully recover from this shock in the long run.

Problems

EASY

1. In the short run, an increase in government spending is most likely to:
   a) shift the long-run aggregate supply curve to the right
   b) shift the aggregate demand curve to the right
   c) increase both short-run and long-run output permanently
   d) shift the short-run aggregate supply curve to the right
   e) reduce inflationary pressure in the economy
2. If the economy is operating above its normal output level, and in the absence of policy intervention, what is the most likely macroeconomic outcome?
   a) Aggregate demand will continue to increase without limit
   b) Prices will fall and output will remain elevated
   c) Nominal wages will rise, shifting the SRAS curve leftward
   d) The SRAS curve will shift rightward as technology improves
   e) Government spending must increase to stabilize output

MEDIUM

3. What are the short-run implications of the central bank raising interest rates?
   a) Aggregate demand will shift right and the price level will rise
   b) Aggregate demand will shift left and output will fall
   c) Aggregate supply will shift left due to higher borrowing costs
   d) Long-run aggregate supply will increase
   e) Prices will fall and real output will rise
4. In the AS/AD model, a supply-side shock such as a sudden increase in the oil price will typically:
   a) shift the SRAS curve to the right
   b) cause a rightward movement along the AD curve
   c) shift both AD and SRAS to the right
   d) shift the SRAS to the left, increasing prices and lowering output
   e) Have no meaningful effect in the long run
5. When the economy is below full employment, the most appropriate short-run policy response would be:
   a) a contractionary fiscal policy to lower inflation expectations
   b) raising the interest rate to increase the level of savings
   c) increasing taxes to reduce the budget deficit
   d) expansionary fiscal or monetary policy to boost AD
   e) a reduction in the money supply to shift the SRAS to the right
6. Discuss how a central bank might use monetary policy to return an economy to long-run equilibrium after a demand-driven recession. Use an AD/AS diagram to support your explanation.

HARD

7. Which of the following is true about the distinction between the short run and the long run in the AS/AD model?
   a) In the short run, prices and wages are fully flexible
   b) In the long run, output depends entirely on demand

c) In the long run, the economy always returns to its natural level of output

d) In the short run, the LRAS curve is drawn vertical

e) In the long run, fiscal policy is always more effective than monetary policy

8. An economy has a full-employment level of output (Y^* = £500 billion), but is currently producing only £470 billion in real GDP. The marginal propensity to consume (MPC) is 0.75, and the government is considering a fiscal stimulus package. However, due to expected partial crowding out, only 80 per cent of the total increase in aggregate demand will translate into increased output in the short run.

   a) Calculate the size of the output gap.

   b) Calculate the value of the government purchases Keynesian multiplier.

   c) Calculate the amount of government spending needed to close the output gap, taking into account the partial crowding out effect.

   (Assume a one-time increase in government spending and no change in taxes.)

9. Evaluate the effectiveness of fiscal policy in the short run versus the long run in stabilizing output. Consider potential trade-offs and limitations.

CHAPTER 14

The Flexible Price Model

Chapter contents

At a Glance The flexible price model

The issue

The exact behaviour of the price level in the economy is pivotal for the debate surrounding the effectiveness of economic policy. How does the assumption of total price flexibility affect economic policy advice? What comparison can we make against models with sticky or fixed prices, such as the IS/LM introduced in Chapter 11?

The understanding

On the face of it, the notion of flexible prices might seem a little fanciful. The assumption suggests that all markets clear instantly and the economy is always in a state of equilibrium. In this chapter we introduce the neoclassical flexible price model which takes the form of a slightly more elaborate aggregate supply and aggregate demand (AS/AD) model that was laid out in Chapter 13.

The usefulness

Understanding the implications for economic policy under flexible prices is equally important as that under fixed prices. The flexible price outcome provides us with a prediction that focuses on the long-run effects upon the economy from shocks and policy.

14.1 Introduction

The classical flexible price model uses the concept of market clearing and in both the labour markets and capital markets, quantity demanded is always equal to quantity supplied. To facilitate this state, prices such as the real rental rate and the real wage need to be fully flexible. If prices and wages did not adjust we would be operating outside of equilibrium and output would be away from its potential, even in the long run. The name of the model reminds us of this important assumption. Output in the economy is determined by the factors of production associated with those market clearing factors that suggests that economic activity is always at its optimum level where resources are fully employed. Consequently, the model implies that output is always at its full potential, a level we associate with long-run aggregate supply.

Macroeconomic Disequilibrium: A state where the economy is away from equilibrium. In a market clearing model the prices adjust quickly to restore economic equilibrium after a shock or economic policy.

With output at long-run supply the model has the implication that economic policy can be an inappropriate tool to attempt to affect or manage **macroeconomic disequilibriums**. Money is ignored in the model, as is the price level, so there is no way to account for monetary policy, but this is not the same for fiscal policy. One of the most basic implications of the model is that expansionary fiscal policy will only lead to higher interest and therefore policy will be crowded out through lower investment. The implication of policy neutrality facilitated by immediate price adjustment might seem a little far-fetched and I expect that a good student might wonder what use a model can be with such a prediction. Well, the key here is to see the usefulness in the context of what the model represents.

With both factors of production assumed fixed at their flexible price levels, the model becomes a long-run perspective; where prices adjust without any impediment. Output, which depends on the efficient levels of capital and labour, consequently appears fixed also, perhaps justified by the tendency of developed economies to gravitate around their natural rates of output at low price levels under certain economic conditions. On this basis the model becomes a very useful reminder of the long-run impact from economic shocks and economic policy – a reminder to policymakers of the dangers of overusing demand management and risking destabilization in the economy, or after a large economic shock, as we have seen recently during the 2019 COVID crisis when large interventions by policymakers contributed towards the causes of a prolonged period of higher inflation and interest rates.

EXAMPLE 14.1

Real world example: The United States

A market clearing economy relies on free markets to provide the efficient allocation of resources. The forces of supply and demand determine prices where the amount of goods and services demanded will be matched by supply so that there are no demand shortages or supply gluts. The idea that free markets can provide efficient allocations of resources comes from theories born in the classical schools of economics.

The stock market in the United States

In the United States an example of a free market exists in the form of the stock exchange, where shares in firms are traded freely and without intervention from any authority. The New York Stock Exchange facilitates the constant trade in shares and other financial assets, with buyers and sellers participating in continuous auctions. When demand for shares is high, prices will tend to rise quickly in reaction to the increase in demand and higher trading volume; the upward adjustment of the price serves to dampen the excess in demand automatically, restoring equilibrium. While this example is close to the assumption of market clearing, all markets have some kind of real life imperfection, such as the time taken for trades to clear.

In terms of structure, the heritage borrows from the aggregate supply and aggregate demand model. We include:

- The standard production function to represent aggregate supply
- The components of expenditure to represent aggregate demand
- A decision-making process for the firm in terms of how much capital and labour are utilized, based on the level of the marginal products.

This is a two-dimensional **agent-based model** where the two agents, the firm for the supply side and the consumer for the demand side, interact to determine the level of output in the economy. The model helps to explain how the demand and supply side come together to explain changes brought about by economic shocks and the use of certain economic policies over the long run.

Agent-Based Model: Most macroeconomic models have components that represent the behaviour of the relevant actors in the economy. These are often the representative agents.

We can sum up with some commonly cited strengths and weaknesses of the flexible price model in Table 14.1.

Table 14.1 Strengths and weaknesses of the flexible price model

Strengths	Weaknesses
Simple two-dimensional model	Unable to capture unemployment
An intuitive process for the firm's behaviour	No account for financial variables
Easy to use for policy exercises	Time invariant
Helpful long-run predictions for monetary and fiscal policy	Short-run deviations not explained
Long-run impacts for economic shocks	Money is ignored

Now that we have discussed this shortcoming and advantages of the model we can introduce the flexible price model in more detail.

The model enjoys a very simple structure which is easy to interpret. The demand side is modelled through the usual components of expenditure in the form of consumption, investment and government spending; and the supply side is modelled with the long-run representation of aggregate supply using a production function. In this chapter we keep things parsimonious by using a closed economy version, though the open economy extension is simple. The restoration to equilibrium after an economic disturbance can only come through changes in the interest rate and in turn investment. The model is a challenge to present diagrammatically since we might expect, as we have done in the preceding chapters, to draw aggregate demand and aggregate supply in the same diagram. To get around this we can make use of the concept of national savings, where we can include national income as a proxy for aggregate supply.

In this chapter, we begin by introducing two structures: first, aggregate demand by defining consumption, investment and the government budget; and second, aggregate supply through the production function. Firms make the decision on how much to supply by using the relation between the marginal factor products and the real given prices for labour and capital. After some basic policy analysis we discuss the implications for economic policy and the usefulness of the flexible price model more generally.

Learning Outcomes

By the end of this chapter you should be able to:

- Interpret the flexible price model laid out in diagrammatic form.
- Understand how to connect the structures of aggregate demand and aggregate supply through the concept of national savings.
- Use the flexible price model to explain the long-run effects of economic shocks and economic policy.
- Demonstrate a basic understanding of the mathematics behind the flexible price model.
- Evaluate the limitations of a static, agent-based model where prices are flexible and the economy is at potential output.

Long Run: An economic time frame that can span years, rather than the months associated with the short run.
Economic Shocks: Disturbances caused by factors that we consider to be exogenous, or outside our usual analysis. We can think of expansionary fiscal policy as such an exogenous change.

14.2 Building the flexible price model

In the **long run**, the economy behaves differently; prices have time to adjust fully and firms can make long-run decisions about production. This closed economy model allows us to capture the long-run effects of economic policy and **economic shocks**, through the normal channel of aggregate demand when resources are fully employed and both labour and capital markets clear. The processes that make up the structure of this model are kept simple, though extensions are not too difficult; as an example, we might account for the open economy by adding net exports to the demand side.

Flexible prices, assumptions and implications

It is generally understood among economists that prices take time to adjust after an economic disturbance. A sudden increase in aggregate demand will take time to filter through to the real economy, mainly due to the time that prices take to fully react. In the short run we can think of prices as fixed, or at least sticky, but over the longer time frame this stickiness dissipates, and the price adjustment will be complete.

As the name given to this model implies, the most important assumption of the flexible price model is that there is no price stickiness, so that prices are totally flexible. Consequently, we consider that this model lies within the category of long-run explanations of the economy. Another important assumption of this model is that the factors of production will be set at a level whereby actual output is equal to potential output; prices and wages adjust so that markets clear and the economy works at full employment. The implications of flexible prices are stark in terms of policy – both fiscal and monetary policy are totally ineffective, so that interventions by the government and the central bank are futile. Expansionary policy will only lead to a rise in the price level with no real effect on the economy.

The demand side and the adjusting mechanism

The demand side for our flexible price model shares the same set-up as the AS/AD model. Aggregate demand is modelled by the components of GDP: consumption, investment and government expenditure. Being a closed economy, we can neglect the open economy component of the trade balance, net exports.

We can set out the basic structure as follows.

Aggregate demand:

$$AD = C + I + G$$

Consumption expenditure, C, is linear in disposable income so that:

$$C = a + b(Y - T)$$

where a is autonomous consumption, b is the marginal propensity to consume, Y is income and T is the level of taxation. This linear consumption function is drawn in expenditure-output space, upward sloping in income, as we see in Figure 14.1. Notice that the slope of the linear consumption function is the marginal propensity to consume and that autonomous consumption is the value of the intercept.

Investment expenditure, $I(r)$ is negative in the interest rate and follows:

$$I = c - d(r)$$

where c is autonomous investment and d is the sensitivity of investment to changes in the interest rate. The investment function depicted in Figure 14.2, shows that the investment function is downward sloping in the interest rate, reflecting that when borrowing costs are high, firms and households are less likely to borrow to invest. The interest rate is the variable that adjusts to ensure equilibrium after an economic disturbance in the flexible price model.

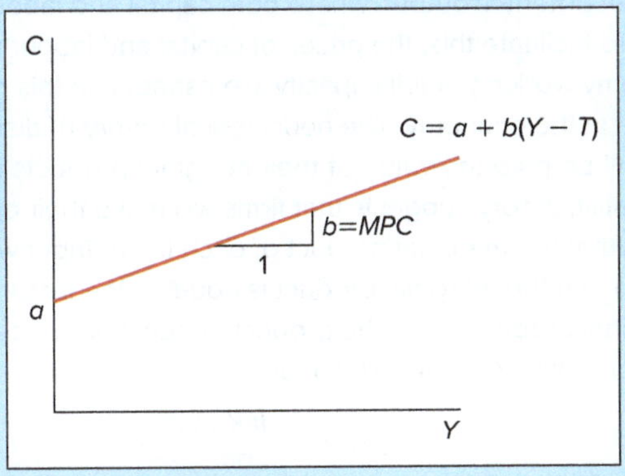

Figure 14.1 The consumption function drawn upward sloping in income

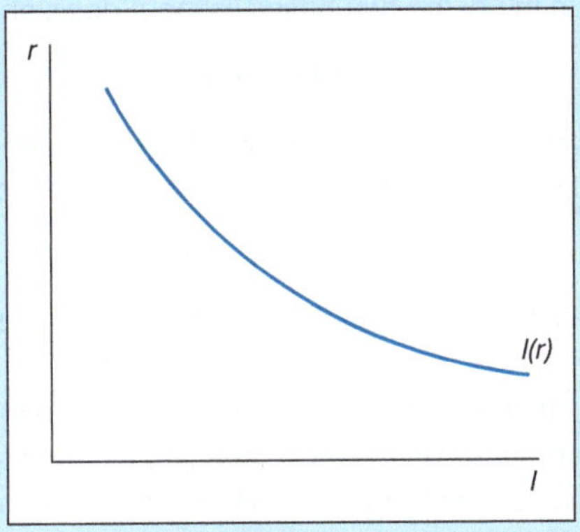

Figure 14.2 The investment function is drawn negative in the interest rate

Lastly, we specify our public policy variables for fiscal policy as:

$$G = \overline{G} \text{ and } T = \overline{T}$$

In words, both government expenditure and the level of taxation are set by the fiscal authority as part of fiscal policy – the difference between the two being the government financial budget also known as public saving. Monetary policy is not accounted for in this model explicitly and because of this is omitted from our economic policy analysis.

As we will see when we discuss general equilibrium later in this chapter, it is worth highlighting here that the adjusting mechanism in this model is the interest rate. For this reason the interest rate will feature as our vertical axis when we map together the supply and demand sides of the economy in one diagram. The role of the adjusting mechanism in a two-dimensional model was discussed in Chapter 1. To connect the demand and supply side in a meaningful way we can make use of the loanable funds model discussed in Chapter 8.

Aggregate supply curve and the marginal products

In the flexible price model; aggregate supply is modelled using the production function:

$$Y = f(K, L)$$

This equation tells us that aggregate output supplied is a function of the variable capital, K and labour, L. Remember our discussion from earlier that a key assumption of the model is that both capital and labour are the result of total market efficiency in the labour and goods market. To reflect this we can also present the production function:

$$Y = f(\overline{K}, \overline{L})$$

Output supplied is at potential output, where both capital and labour are assumed set at market clearing levels. To facilitate this, the prices of capital and labour must be fully flexible. As a result of the economy working at full capacity, we cannot use this model to explain the reality of unemployment in the economy. The neoclassical theory of distribution states that all factors of production will be paid the value of their marginal products in equilibrium. Neoclassical, or marginalist, theory suggests that firms will make their optimum choices for each input using the concept that the marginal product of each factor input will be equal to its value, or the respective prices, so that the marginal product is equal to the factor price.

To derive the marginal products from the production function we can simply differentiate with respect to the factor inputs, capital and labour:

$$MPK = \frac{df(K,L)}{dK}$$

and

$$MPL = \frac{df(K,L)}{dL}$$

With the marginal products in mind, the firm bases its input decision on the following conditions:

$$MPK = R/P$$

Real Rate of Return: This is the real rate of the return on capital in the market for capital. In practice this will be closely related to the interest rate in the economy.
Real Wage: The price of labour in the labour market is the real wage, which is the nominal wage divided by the price level.

The firm will employ capital K exactly at the point where the marginal product of capital will be equal to the **real rate of return** on capital, R/P and:

$$MPL = W/P$$

The firm will employ labour, L, exactly at the point where the marginal product of labour will be equal to the **real wage**, W/P.

The intuition behind these decisions need little more than common sense to understand. As an example, imagine a coffee shop where the manager has to decide whether or not to hire another member of staff. The product that will come from the additional unit of labour is the marginal product (additional revenue) that will result from the hire. Of course, if the wage required for the worker is more than the additional revenue from the hire the firm will not make the addition. Whereas, if the firm considers that the additional revenue will be greater than the wage, then the hire will go ahead. With the marginal products set to the factor prices, the firm is assumed to be maximizing profits.

The resulting level of capital and labour employed by firms provides us with aggregate supply:

$$Y = f(\bar{K}, \bar{L})$$

As we have mentioned earlier, it is important to understand that aggregate supply is not fixed by the fixed factors of production but by the assumptions of the model. The efficient levels of capital and labour, $\bar{K}$ and $\bar{L}$ mean that the economy will produce at potential output always. We can now begin the connection between the supply and demand sides in the economy by making use of the concept of national savings.

National savings and general equilibrium

The concept of national savings, first introduced in Chapter 8, helps us connect aggregate demand and aggregate supply together. National saving is the sum of all public saving and all private saving, which we can define as all income in the economy minus that which is spent by all households and government. We can write this as follows:

$$\bar{S} = \bar{Y} - \bar{C} - \bar{G}$$

Notice that national savings depend on fixed output $\bar{Y}$ and fixed government expenditure $\bar{G}$. Consumption itself relies on fixed income $\bar{Y}$ and fixed taxation $\bar{T}$, thus it is also fixed.

In equilibrium, national savings are equal to investment, and so we can write the economic structure as:

$$\bar{S} = \bar{Y} - \bar{C} - \bar{G}$$

and

$$I = I(r)$$

In equilibrium, savings are equal to investment so we can now write:

$$Y - C - G = I(r)$$

Notice also that this equilibrium condition can be arranged so that it is presented as goods market equilibrium, which I leave to you as an exercise. We now plot equilibrium in Figure 14.3.

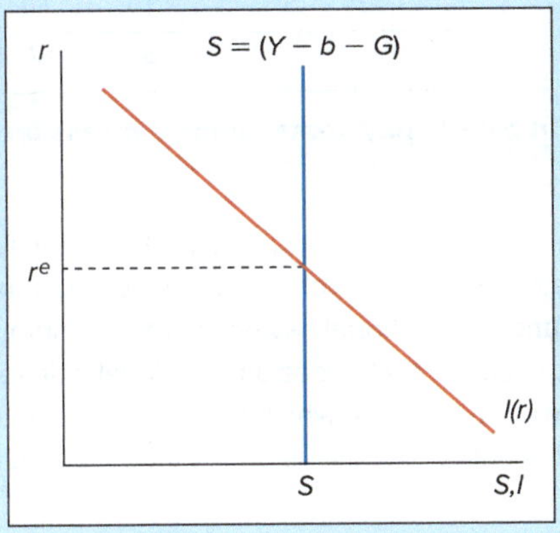

Figure 14.3 Equilibrium in the flexible price model using the market for loanable funds

The flexible prices model is shown using the market for loanable funds, where the supply of loanable funds is made up of public and private savings and the demand for loanable funds being represented by the investment function. Aggregate supply, Y, is represented in the supply of loanable funds schedule and components of aggregate demand, C, I and G, split between both. We can see that at the point of intersection between the investment function and the schedule for national savings, there exists an economy-wide rate of interest, r^e.

14.3 Economic policy analysis using the flexible price model

The ability of the flexible price model as a tool for economic policy analysis is limited but there is an absence of any process to account for the movement of money in the economy. Nevertheless, with the inclusion of government spending and taxation, we are afforded the analysis of fiscal policy. Aside from demand management, we also have the ability to discuss other policy types such as legislation aimed at the level of investment.

Investigating the impact of economic policy

In terms of demand side policy, we can begin with a simple example of government spending to avert the full effects of an economic slowdown. With the onset of a slump in economic activity, the government introduces emergency measures to reduce the impact of the recession on the level of unemployment, perhaps by increasing social security benefits to maintain consumption. The increase in government spending, G, will reduce national saving:

$$S\downarrow = Y - C - G\uparrow$$

We can see how the model reacts to this policy change using Figure 14.4 (overleaf).

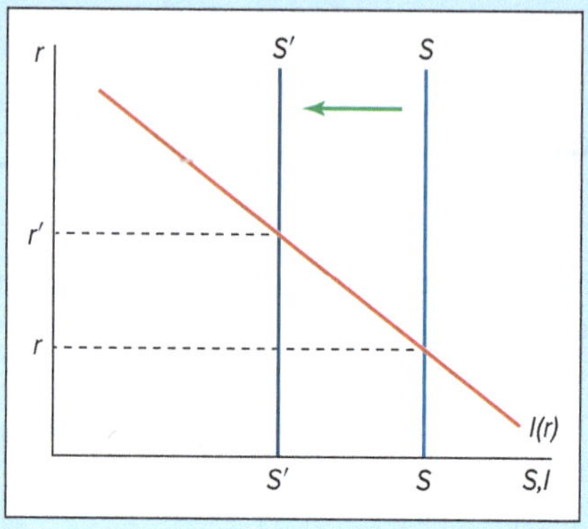

Figure 14.4 An increase in benefit payments during a recession

We begin in equilibrium where the original savings schedule meets the investment function at equilibrium interest rate, *r*, and level of savings at *S*. The increase in expense for the government reduces public and thus national savings in the economy. To reflect this, the national savings schedule shifts left, the interest rate rises and the level of investment falls. Output is still at its potential level but with lower investment, which has crowded out the increase in government spending. The lesson from this policy exercise is that in the long run, fiscal policy will not expand the economy.

EXERCISE 14.1

Imagine an autonomous reduction in consumption – perhaps caused by a credit crunch – a lack of availability of credit for consumers due to a lack of confidence in financial markets. An environment of economic instability might cause commercial banks to make it more difficult to get consumer credit.

Use the loanable funds model to predict how the reduction in consumption affects investment and the interest rate.

Fiscal policy is not the only type of economic policy we can analyse with the flexible price model; we can also predict the effects of legislative policy. As an example of legislative policy, imagine the government wants to increase the level of investment in the economy by offering a tax break to investors.

Recall our investment function from earlier in the chapter:

$$I = c - d(r)$$

The variable that represents autonomous investment (the part of investment that does not rely on changes in the interest rate) is c. To achieve a change in autonomous investment the government can utilize schemes such as grants, tax incentives or even legislation to achieve higher investment across the economy more generally. Under flexible prices the tax break shifts the investment schedule outwards left and this increases investment at every interest rate in the economy (see Figure 14.5). The higher investment will eventually increase pressure in financial markets and the interest rate increases as a result. Unfortunately, the increase in investment in the economy is short-lived as the level of savings in the economy are unable to accommodate the expansion. The lesson here for the government is that expansion through legislation is ineffective if channelled through investment.

Comparison of flexible price and fixed price outcomes

Focusing on expansionary fiscal policy, you might think that the difference in the model predictions for the IS/LM and the flexible price model are much the same – an increase in

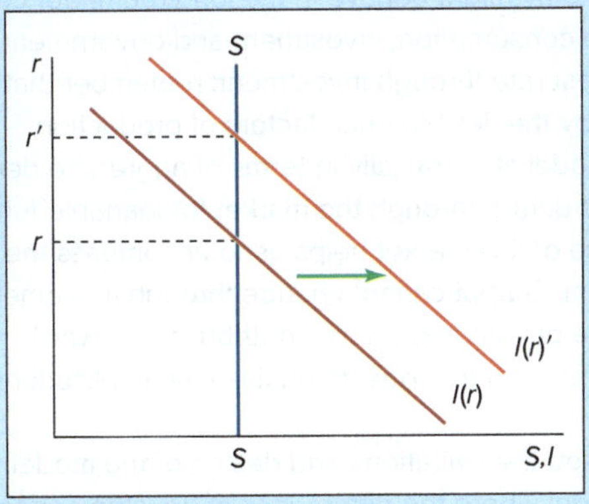

Figure 14.5 Impact of legislation affecting investment

government spending leads to higher interest rates and the crowding out of investment, albeit to varying degrees. Whereas with the flexible price outcome there is total crowding out, for the IS/LM this phenomena is only partial.

However, if we look at how an exogenous decrease in consumption might affect the economy, the models are further apart. Imagine a forthcoming recession and a desire by consumers to save money. We might think that saving more would be a virtuous action to take, but in fact according to the IS/LM it can harm the economy. A reduction in consumption might lead to a further fall in output, leading to a further drop in consumption and so on. This phenomena is known as the 'Paradox of Thrift'. The IS/LM model predicts this paradox, but the flexible price model does not. The flexible price outcome in this case increases national saving, which leads to lower interest rates and higher investment.

14.4 Criticism and limitations of the flexible price model

The flexible price model has some serious limitations, especially in the inability to capture short-run fluctuations in the economy; it also has no account for financial variables such as money or the price level. Further to this is the market clearing assumption, which is really an extreme of a well-functioning free market economy, whereas some factor markets will inevitably suffer from market imperfections. Also, a labour market that clears is inconsistent with the reality of 'always on' unemployment.

However, this does not mean that the flexible price model is without good purpose – its prediction for an exogenous increase in saving is more sensible than the Keynesian prediction and if we consider its suitability for providing longer-run insights. The model also helps us to see how the economy would behave in the absence of market imperfections or how it might return to long-run equilibrium after an economic shock. Lastly, you might look at how the model has performed in light of the recent COVID-19 crisis – even though both the IS/LM and the flexible price model predicted higher interest rates after the huge fiscal interventions during the crisis, perhaps the flexible price model did better at predicting the outcome for economic activity.

> **Market Clearing:** The markets for capital and labour clear instantly, there are no market imperfections. This is due to the assumptions of total price flexibility in factor markets; the real wage in the labour market and the real rate of return in the market for capital are fully flexible.
> **Market Imperfections:** These are the frictions that can prevent prices from adjusting quickly. For example, a labour market friction can prevent wages from adjusting in the labour market.

14.5 Chapter summary: Putting it all together

In this chapter, we have introduced the flexible prices model that can provide a long-run view of economic impacts from supply and demand side fiscal policy. Even though the assumptions of the model stretch the role of the adjusting mechanisms to the limit, the model gives us a benchmark of how the economy might behave in the long run under certain economic conditions. In the model, any change to consumption, investment and government spending is counteracted by a reaction from the interest rate through investment; remember that aggregate supply is determined independently by the flexible price factors of production.

We have laid out the model algebraically in terms of aggregate demand and aggregate supply and presented the structure through the market for loanable funds where savings are equal to investment. The use of this market helps us to encompass the supply and demand sides in a two-dimensional diagram. Output cannot change through movements in aggregate demand but the balance between the private and public contributions towards national income can. This balancing act helps us to use the model to analyse the implications of both demand side and supply side fiscal policy.

Finally we have discussed the limitations and design of the model, making a comparison with the short-run IS/LM model where the differences of how the economy reacts to reductions in consumption are more notable. As a predictor of economic policy impacts under strong assumptions, the model stands up fairly well to the fact of the histories of large-scale fiscal intervention in the long run.

Assessment Question

Describe government interventions during COVID-19 and explore which channels the Flexible Price Model covers and which ones it doesn't. How well does the model explain and predict the state post-COVID economies?

Cases

Extending the flexible price model to an open economy

Introduction

The neoclassical flexible price model is a fundamental framework used in macroeconomics to explain how economies reach equilibrium. In this model, prices adjust quickly to clear market disturbances, meaning there is no persistent unemployment or excess demand in the long run. This model is often presented in a closed economy setting, where all goods and services produced are consumed domestically and no international trade takes place.

However, in the real world, economies are interconnected through international trade, capital flows and exchange rates. With this in mind, we can extend the closed economy flexible price model to account for a more real-life open economy, where international interactions play a key role. The extended model incorporates factors like exports, imports and exchange rates, which influence the equilibrium of the domestic economy also.

The neoclassical flexible price model in a closed economy

In a closed economy, the focus is on the interaction between aggregate demand (AD) and aggregate supply (AS). The economy reaches equilibrium when:

$$AD = C(Y) + I(r) + G$$

where:

- $C(Y)$ is consumption as a function of income Y
- $I(r)$ is investment as a function of the interest rate r
- G is independently set government spending.

The aggregate supply (AS) is vertical, reflecting the assumption that prices and wages are fully flexible and adjust to clear the market, as we might expect in the long run. This implies that output is determined solely by factors such as capital, labour and technology, rather than by demand-side factors.

Extending the model to an open economy

To extend the neoclassical model to an open economy, we can incorporate exports (*X*), imports (*M*), and net exports (*NX*) into the aggregate demand equation. Accordingly, aggregate demand becomes:

$$AD = C(Y) + I(r) + G + X(Y,E) - M(Y,E)$$

where:

- $X(Y,E)$ is exports, which depend on foreign income *Y* and the exchange rate *E*
- $M(Y,E)$ is imports, which depend on domestic income *Y* and the exchange rate *E*.

Exchange rates: The exchange rate *E* plays a crucial role in determining the price competitiveness of a country's goods in international markets and this is why it is often referred to as a country's 'terms of trade'. A depreciation of the domestic currency makes exports cheaper and imports more expensive, stimulating exports and reducing imports, while an appreciation in the exchange rate has the opposite effect.

The role of exchange rates in open economy equilibrium

The equilibrium in an open economy involves not just the domestic factors of production but also international trade. When the domestic price level is flexible, an increase in domestic demand (due to higher government spending, for example) can cause inflationary pressure. In an open economy, this might lead to an increase in imports (due to higher domestic income) and a reduction in net exports (due to a possible appreciation of the domestic currency). Thus, the adjustment mechanism is influenced by both domestic and international factors.

Case study example: A country increasing government spending

Suppose a small, open economy is experiencing a recession, and the government decides to increase spending to mute the effects of an economic slump. In the closed economy model, this increase in government spending directly boosts aggregate demand, leading to higher output and income.

In the open economy version, however, the increase in government spending also affects net exports. As income rises, demand for imports increases. If the exchange rate remains constant, the economy may not experience as large an increase in output, as some of the increased demand is satisfied by imports rather than domestic production. If the central bank allows the currency to depreciate (or if the currency naturally depreciates), this could help increase exports, offsetting the import effect and boosting domestic production.

Conclusion

The flexible price model provides a useful starting point for understanding how an economy reaches equilibrium. Extending this model to an open economy allows for a more comprehensive view of the interactions between domestic and international economic factors, such as trade and exchange rates. In the open economy, these factors play a significant role in determining output and price levels, making the model more reflective of real-world dynamics.

Questions

1. What is the key assumption of the flexible price model in a closed economy?
2. How does the inclusion of international trade (exports and imports) alter the aggregate demand curve in an open economy?
3. What role does the exchange rate play in the extended open economy version of the model?
4. In the open economy version of the flexible price model, what happens when the government increases spending? How does international trade influence this outcome?
5. How does the flexible price model in a closed economy differ from the open economy version in terms of output determination?

Problems

EASY

1. In the flexible price model, what happens to output in the short run when there is an increase in government spending?
   a) Output decreases due to higher interest rates.
   b) Output increases as prices adjust to the increase in demand.
   c) Output remains unchanged because the economy operates at full employment.
   d) Output decreases because demand for labour decreases.
   e) Output increases due to a decrease in wages.
2. Which of the following best describes the adjustment mechanism in the flexible price model?
   a) Prices and wages are sticky, and adjustment occurs through output changes.
   b) Prices and wages adjust instantaneously, and output remains constant.
   c) Prices adjust only in the long run, but wages adjust in the short run.
   d) Output adjusts quickly, but prices are rigid in the short run.
   e) Both prices and wages are rigid in the short run, and only output adjusts.

MEDIUM

3. In the context of the flexible price model, what is the primary reason the economy returns to full employment after a demand shock?
4. Which of the following is true about the relationship between price levels and output in the flexible price model?
   a) There is an inverse relationship between price levels and output in the short run.
   b) The price level is constant, regardless of changes in output.
   c) A higher price level leads to higher output due to higher demand for goods.
   d) The economy's output is fixed at the natural level of output, irrespective of the price level.
   e) A higher price level causes a decrease in output due to higher interest rates.
5. In the flexible price model, if there is an unexpected increase in aggregate demand, what is the likely outcome in the short run?
6. In the flexible price model, what happens if autonomous consumption (a) rises?
7. Consider a simple economy described by the following variables:
   - C = Consumption, which is a function of disposable income ($Y - T$), where the marginal propensity to consume (MPC) is 0.75.
   - I = Investment, which is given as a constant of 100.
   - G = Government spending, which is 150.
   - T = Taxes, which are 100.
   - Y = National income.

   Using the Keynesian cross model, calculate the equilibrium level of national income (Y) in the economy. Assume that the economy is closed, and there is no foreign trade (exports or imports).

HARD

8. Explain the key assumptions of the neoclassical flexible price model. How does the model explain the adjustment of prices and output in the long run? Discuss its implications for economic policy, particularly in relation to inflation and unemployment.
9. Critically evaluate the role of flexible prices in the neoclassical model. How does the model address the concept of market clearing, and what are its limitations when applied to real-world economies? Provide examples to illustrate your points.

CHAPTER 15

Modelling Economic Growth

Chapter contents

At a Glance — Modelling economic growth

The issue

In the previous chapters throughout this textbook we have modelled aggregate supply as an upward sloping schedule in prices/output space, where the amount of output supplied increases with increases in the price level. However, this does not tell us much about the economic capacity of the economy. How do we represent aggregate supply in terms of its potential? And how do policymakers grow the economy as a whole over time?

The understanding

To model the long run capacity of the economy we use the long-run factors of production in a structural form called the production function. While we can include all manner of aggregate inputs, such as labour, capital, enterprise and land, we tend to focus on just two – both labour and capital as right-hand side variables driving long-run output.

The usefulness

Policymakers understand that to grow the economy in the long run we need to increase capacity and efficiency. Increasing the labour force and the amount of capital in the economy will achieve that, but so will how we utilize those factors; this is captured by technology in the production function.

15.1 Introduction

So far, we have discussed how economic activity fluctuates around its 'normal' level in a cyclical pattern, something we call the business cycle. This helps us to explain the changes in real output from quarter to quarter, but it does not explain how the economy grows over the longer time horizon. Growth in real output is an economic variable that is measured and reported quarterly as the percentage change in the level of output. If the change in growth is more positive than it is negative over the longer term horizon, then the 'normal' level of economic activity is increasing. In reality, we observe that most economies tend to grow consistently in their natural levels, not just on a quarter to quarter basis, and to model this behaviour we need a theory of growth.

Growth is a fact that we observe but it is also a policy outcome. An increase in output, equivalent to an increase in production, is most likely to lead to a decrease in unemployment. Growth provides a boost to incomes, an increase in living standards and even increases in the ability of governments to repay sovereign debt through increases in tax receipts. It is no surprise, then, that growth is highly desirable to the authorities that govern us.

The question for the authorities will undoubtedly be how to achieve sustained growth, or for a more modern society, how to achieve 'sustainable' growth. The desire to achieve growth provides us with a motivation in the science of macroeconomics, to build models that can guide politicians with this aim, but to do so we need to identify the driving forces behind economic expansion. We can categorize the forces behind growth into the quantity of labour, quantity of capital and also the state of technology (Table 15.1).

Table 15.1 The driving forces behind growth

Driving growth	How?
Labour	A greater supply of labour will increase employment and in turn production.
Capital	Machines and tools allow workers to produce more, increasing production.
Technology	Improvements in the way we use labour and capital increases production.

The benefits of growth are rather obvious, but what about the drawbacks? A most obvious constraint is that resources on our planet are 'finite'. The inputs required to achieve growth are not unlimited; economics is often cited as 'the study of the allocation of scarce, rather than unlimited resources'. The contribution from growth theorists on the important issue of sustainability is not yet reflected in mainstream economics. Should every government have ever-increasing growth as a prime strategic ambition?

In this chapter, we begin by introducing the key functional form used for growth theory, known as the production function. We use the production function to explain the concepts of diminishing returns for the factors of production in a marginal analysis for capital and labour and discuss a particular function introduced by economists Charles Cobb and Paul Douglas (1928).

Armed with our explanation for the movement of output we introduce two explanations of growth theory – a simple classical explanation shown in a diagrammatic fashion before presenting a more formal explanation introduced by Robert Solow and Trevor Swan (1956) with exogenous (or fixed) technology where the role of policy is limited to the short run. Finally, we discuss the implications of relaxing the assumption of exogenous technology before discussing more recent developments in growth theory, including an entirely alternative and simple framework centred on the pressures provided by limited global resources.

Learning Outcomes

By the end of this chapter you should be able to:

- Understand the concept of economic growth.
- Develop key results for growth theory using the production function.
- Understand the two alternative classical approaches to modelling economic growth.
- Use the Solow–Swan model to investigate the role of economic policy aimed at economic growth.
- Critique key approaches in growth theory, highlighting the different assumptions used and resulting performance against the real world.

15.2 The production function

So how do we model growth? Intuitively, for the economy to grow we need our firms to grow and so an obvious candidate for a theory of economic growth is a model of aggregate supply that can capture the longer-run movements in national income.

The factors of production and the production function

Economy-wide production requires the coming together of inputs, something we call the factors of production. We can identify those factors subjectively by listing them – factors such as **labour**, **capital**, **technology**, human capital, financial capital and so on. In the simplest case we could identify the factors of production as capital and labour, that is, the number of machines and the number of labour hours used to create output. The production function relates the factors of production, capital and labour, with the economy-wide production and is good for this purpose. In implicit form, we can write the production function as:

$$Y = f(K, L)$$

Using this implicit form, we can clearly imagine that an increase in economy-wide capital or labour increases output. The exact functional form of the production function reflects the technology of the economy it is trying to describe. For instance, for an economy that is more competitive than another, we would expect to see the functional form predict a higher level of output from changes to capital and labour than the production function representing the less competitive economy.

> **Labour:** The total number all working hours utilized in the economy by the sum of all producers.
> **Capital:** The total number of machines utilized in the economy by the sum of all producers.
> **Technology:** The functional form of the production function representing the efficiency of aggregate production.

The explicit functional form dictates the 'return' on changes to the exogenous inputs and we can categorize these returns between decreasing to increasing returns to scale. For instance, on any particular explicit form we can measure the returns from changes to the inputs as we have in Example 15.1. We can see that multiplying capital and labour by a factor m produces an increase of m^2 times output, and so we have increasing returns to scale. An increase in exactly m times output would indicate constant returns to scale and an increase of less than m would indicate decreasing returns to scale. We can also apply different functional forms to individual countries to reflect their respective levels of technology. Example 15.1 provides a worked example of how we can measure the returns to scale from a production function.

EXAMPLE 15.1

Worked example: Production function

$$Y = f(k, L) = \frac{1}{2}(KL)$$

Multiply the inputs by a common factor, say *m*, then measure the effect on output:

$$Y = \frac{1}{2}(mK)(mL)$$

Now rearrange to get:

$$Y = m^2\frac{1}{2}(K)(L) \quad \text{which is the same as} \quad Y = m^2 f(K, L)$$

So increasing the inputs by a factor of *m* produced $m^2 \times$ output. This function exhibits increasing returns to scale.

The marginal products of capital and labour

An important concept in economics is the measurement taken at the margin, something we call marginal analysis. If we take one more step forward how will that change the landscape? If we add one more worker to our production line, how will that affect output? It is a useful question to ask in everyday life, not just in economics. Knowing the marginal effect can inform us on when to stop or when to add further to the mix.

The marginal analysis in the context of the production function is a measurement of the effect of adding one more unit of labour or adding one more unit of capital. These marginal effects are known as the marginal product of labour (MPL) and the **marginal product of capital** (MPK). To measure the marginal product of labour and capital we can either differentiate the production function with respect to labour or capital, or we can write it using an implicit functional form. To keep things simple, we will present the latter, though you will also find an example of the differentiation later in the following section. We begin with the marginal product of labour and show how the representative firm uses this information to maximize its profits.

Marginal Product of Capital/Labour: The additional output achieved by the firm from the act of employing one more unit of capital/labour.

The marginal product of labour can be defined as the additional output received from adding one more unit of labour, so we can write this mathematically:

$$MPL = f(K, L + 1) - f(K, L)$$

The marginal product of labour is the difference between the output from the production function with one more unit of labour added, minus the production without the additional unit of labour.

A real life feature we see commonly applied to the functional form of the production function is one of diminishing marginal returns. As we add more labour to the same number of machines (capital) the gain in terms of output tends to diminish; the same applies when workers are added to production, the gain in output gets smaller each time. We can imagine a scenario where there is one machine in a factory. When we apply the first worker, that worker is very productive, but as we add more and more workers the machine becomes overcrowded until the addition of workers has no effect. We can see this more clearly with the help of a diagram (Figure 15.1).

Assuming the firm is aware of the marginal product, the firm will continue to add more labour to its workforce so long as the cost of hiring the labour is less than the additional production that comes from it (the MPL). As labour increases, the increase in output becomes smaller and smaller.

We can also write this decision out explicitly; the firm will hire more labour until:

$$MPL = \frac{W}{P}$$

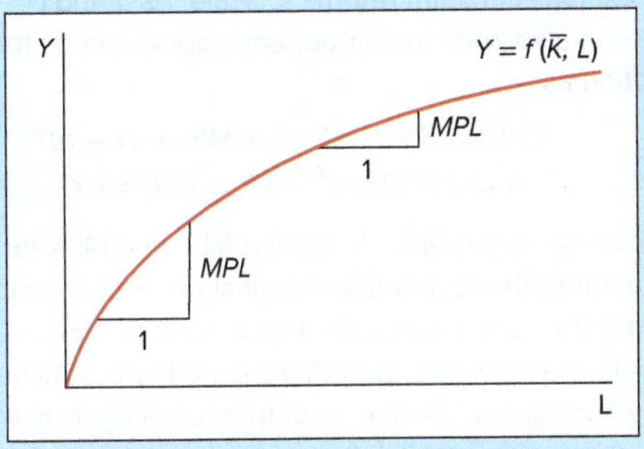

Figure 15.1 A production function displaying diminishing marginal returns

where $\frac{W}{P}$ is the real wage and also the additional real cost of hiring the additional labour. This is the firm's decision on how much labour to hire. Because the firm uses this condition to form its labour hiring decision we can also think of the MPL as the labour demand schedule from Chapter 5.

EXERCISE 15.1

Now that you have seen how the firm makes its hiring decision in terms of labour, derive and write down the decision for how much capital to rent, bearing in mind that the cost of renting one unit of capital is the real rental price *R/P*.

The decision of the firm on how much labour to hire or capital to rent can also help us to calculate the share of income that comes from labour and capital respectively. For the **labour share**, recall that the firm will place hires up and until the marginal product of labour is equal to the real wage, where profit turns from positive to zero. So in equilibrium we can say that labour is paid its marginal product; labour income must be equal to the quantity of labour L times the price of labour, the real wage $\frac{W}{P}$. Given that the real wage is equal to the marginal product of labour in equilibrium, we can write this mathematically:

Capital/Labour Share: The proportion of national income that can be attributed solely to the employment of capital/labour.

$$Labour\ Share = L \times \frac{W}{P} = L \times MPL$$

and in the same way for capital:

$$Capital\ Share = K \times \frac{R}{P} = K \times MPK$$

The Cobb–Douglas production function

An important qualification for any model in macroeconomics is the ability to bear some relation to reality, perhaps through an empirical investigation (testing the model with actual data). In 1923, an economist called Paul Douglas noticed that the contributions towards national income from labour and capital remained roughly constant over time, something we now refer to as 'constant factor shares'. With the help of a mathematician, Charles Cobb, a convenient functional form was born that was both analytically convenient and managed to replicate the fact of constant shares.

The Cobb–Douglas production function is written:

$$Y = f(K, L) = AK^{\alpha}L^{(1-\alpha)}$$

National income Y is determined by the inputs of capital K and labour L with constant technology A and α, a constant parameter representing the share of capital. Notice that the shares of labour and capital must sum to the value of one by design, and because of this the

Cobb–Douglas function exhibits constant returns to scale. As α and $(1 - \alpha)$ are given as shares of national income Y, we can also write the labour and capital shares for the case of the Cobb–Douglas production function as:

$$Labour\ Share^{CD} = L \times MPL = (1 - \alpha)Y$$
$$Capital\ Share^{CD} = K \times MPK = \alpha Y$$

In order to calculate these shares, first derive the MPL and MPK for the Cobb–Douglas and then multiply each factor to the respective marginal product. Example 15.2 shows the mathematical derivation for the labour share for the case of the Cobb–Douglas production function. Notice that to calculate the MPL, we differentiate the production function with respect to labour; we are effectively finding the 'change' in output resulting from the 'change' in labour. The mathematics for the share of capital is left as a very useful exercise.

EXAMPLE 15.2

Worked example: Cobb–Douglas labour share

$$Y = AK^{\alpha}L^{(1-\alpha)}$$

Differentiate Y with respect to L:

$$MPL = \frac{dY}{dL}\ (1 - \alpha)\ K^{\alpha}L^{(-\alpha)}$$

$$\begin{aligned} Labour\ Share &= L \times MPL \\ &= L(1-\alpha)\,K^{\alpha}L^{(-\alpha)} \\ &= (1-\alpha)\,K^{\alpha}L^{(-\alpha)}.L \\ &= (1-\alpha)\,K^{\alpha}L^{(1-\alpha)} \\ &= (1-\alpha)\,Y \end{aligned}$$

EXERCISE 15.2

Begin with the Cobb–Douglas production function and show, in a similar fashion to the example given, that the capital share of income is equal to αY.

15.3 Classical growth models

We can now begin to see how growth actually occurs by making use of the production function and the marginal product of labour. The production function shows us how the factors of production are combined to create output, and the marginal product provides us with both the incentive and the limiting factor for firms to grow. We begin by using the production function, again plotted against the associated labour costs of production.

A simple model of economic growth

A simple model of growth can be drawn from the work of classical economists such as David Ricardo and Adam Smith where changes in production are part of a cycle of changes and effects. Initially, we can imagine that firms produce output according to a production function in capital, labour and land, where only land is fixed. Workers are paid a minimum sustainable wage W_{min}, below which they are not prepared to supply labour effort.

In Figure 15.2 we have drawn the production function with a wage schedule which increases proportionately with the amount of labour hired. Beginning at L', we can see that the firm sees positive profits (wages are less than turnover) and decides to increase production, hiring more labour. The increase in demand for labour pushes up wages and this leads to an increase in the working population as the labour supply also increases. The increase in the labour supply

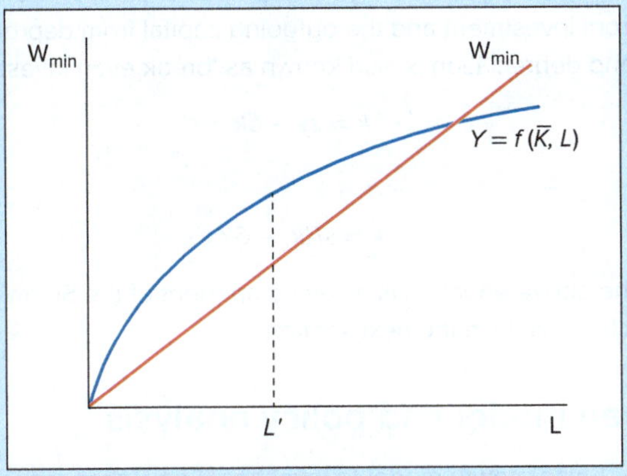

Figure 15.2 The classical model of growth theory

causes wages to fall back again to the subsistence wage W_{min}. This process continues but with decreasing incentive; remember that as the firm hires more labour the difference between output and the wage is decreasing because of diminishing marginal returns. Eventually, growth will stall altogether where the wage schedule and the production function intersect.

The outcome of this model is a little stark and we might consider this classical model unrealistic. Surely increases in technology play a role, bringing new opportunities for profit as the marginal products decline? Think about the proposition that growth will stall as countries develop – though it could be argued that we are already seeing evidence of this in the developed world.

Turning to the path of capital

So far, we have deliberately focused the explanation of growth on the role of labour, and for labour-intensive industries this may seem reasonable. However, we cannot discuss the role of technology in growth without recourse to the evolution of the stock of capital and so we begin here.

If we divide the production function through by the quantity of labour we can represent the production function in **per capita** terms, that is:

$$Y/L = f(K/L, L/L)$$

or

$$y = f(k)$$

Per Capita: The term we use to describe variables that have been divided by the variable that represents labour. Effectively 'per capita' variables are measurements 'per head'.

where lowercase letters in growth theory represent the 'per capita' equivalents – uppercase Y is output but lowercase y is output per capita where the variable has simply been divided by L. This is also analytically convenient as we can now focus on capital and technology from this point onwards. The two key drivers towards the change of our capital stock are investment, that adds to capital, and depreciation that dissolves it. Investment feeds into the capital stock and depreciation feeds out.

Just as in the circular flow model of Chapter 4, we can imagine two sectors in our economy so that all income is either spent (consumed) or saved and then invested via the financial market. So we can write investment very simply as a fraction s of output, where s is the saving rate:

$$Investment = sy$$

As we have discussed, investment is the flow into the capital stock and so to complete the path we need an explanation for the flow out; we can do this using the concept of depreciation. In a similar way we can say that the capital stock depreciates at a constant rate given by the fraction δ and write:

$$Depreciation = \delta K$$

The path of capital $\dot{k}$ is simply the change in capital over time, or the difference between the incoming capital from investment and the outgoing capital from depreciation. This difference between investment and depreciation is also known as 'break even investment'.

$$\dot{k} = sy - \delta k$$

or

$$\dot{k} = sf(k) - \delta k$$

We will see that the above equation is a key component of the Solow–Swan model for economic growth which we build in the next section.

The Solow–Swan model and policy analysis

We can use the Solow–Swan growth model to investigate how changes in the depreciation rate, savings rate and population growth rate affect the steady state level of output per capita (per worker) in the economy. We think of the steady state level of output per capita as the rate at which the economy stops growing until there is a change in one of the key parameters. We begin by using the per capita version of the production function with the investment and depreciation schedules. Notice that the production function and saving schedule are non-linear and increasing in capital at a decreasing rate, yet the depreciation schedule is linear and increasing in the level of capital per worker.

In Figure 15.3 we see the per capita production function $y = f(k)$, investment function $sf(k)$, and depreciation (or break-even investment) schedule δk. At k^* notice that investment is equal to depreciation and so the path of capital $\dot{k}$ is equal to zero; we are at the steady state of capital per worker and the economy will not shrink or grow.

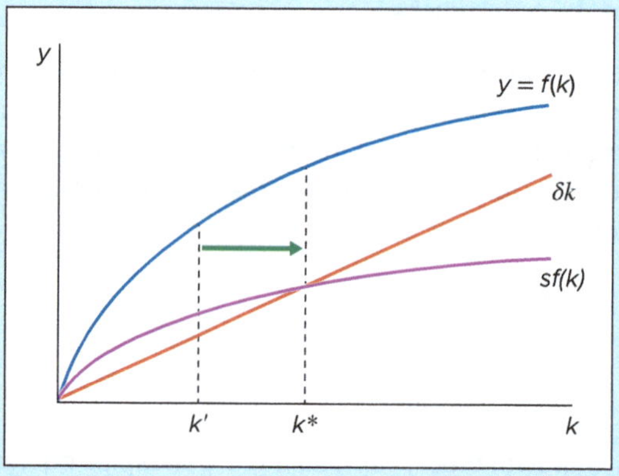

Figure 15.3 The Solow–Swan model showing the steady state

Imagine that the economy begins at k' where capital is below its steady state; notice that investment is higher than depreciation at this point and so the capital stock will grow towards k^*. The production function predicts that as capital per worker increases so does output per worker and so we see the economy expanding. This continues until capital reaches its steady state value, where investment is equal to depreciation. As growth in the capital stock ceases so does the increase in output per worker; economic growth can continue, but only at the rate of population growth. Essentially, the Solow–Swan model predicts that for an economy with its capital stock per worker away from the steady state, there are driving forces bringing the economy upwards or downwards towards its long-run equilibrium.

We can also extend this by adding some account for the growth in the working population. New workers require capital to maintain the capital to labour ratio and so an influx of workers will require a level of investment equal to the growth rate in the population. If the population grows at a rate of n, then the capital stock will also need additional investment of amount ($n \times k$). To capture this, our equation for the path of capital becomes:

$$\dot{k} = sy - (n + \delta)k$$

Figure 15.4 shows how the break-even investment schedule changes when we account for growth in the working population in the Solow–Swan model. Break-even investment now requires that investment accumulates capital at a rate equal to the depreciation of existing stock and also the capital required to equip incoming workers, $n \times k$.

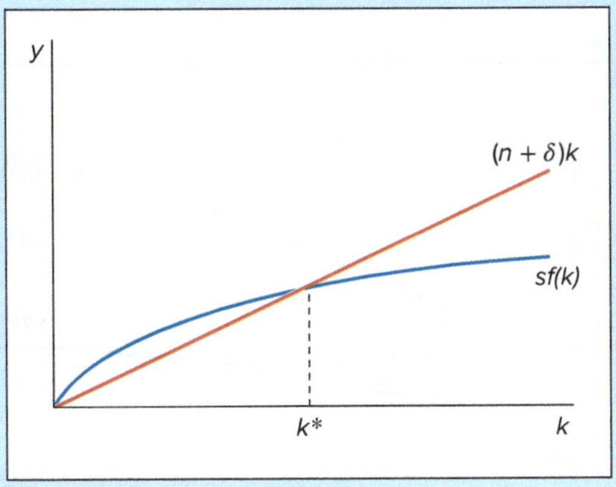

Figure 15.4 Steady state capital with population growth

With the additional term on the depreciation line, the steady state now accounts for population growth. We can see that an increase in the rate at which the population grows (n) reduces steady state capital per worker and output per capita. This result might sound counterintuitive if we normally associate immigration with a boost to national income, but we should bear in mind that the model is measuring the effect on output per head.

We now turn to economic policy in the context of the Solow–Swan model of economic growth. How can a policymaker use this tool to manage the economy with positive effect? An obvious way to achieve growth using this model is to increase the saving rate. A government can encourage and achieve higher saving through the careful and targeted use of fiscal policy, the higher saving rate will mean higher investment and, with unchanged depreciation, a higher stock of capital.

In Figure 15.5 we see that with a higher saving rate the investment schedule shifts upwards from *sf(k)* to *sf(k)′*. The prediction of higher output from higher savings rates in the Solow–Swan model is consistent with our observations from the real world. Many economies that begin development with high saving rates grow at a faster pace than economies with lower savings rates.

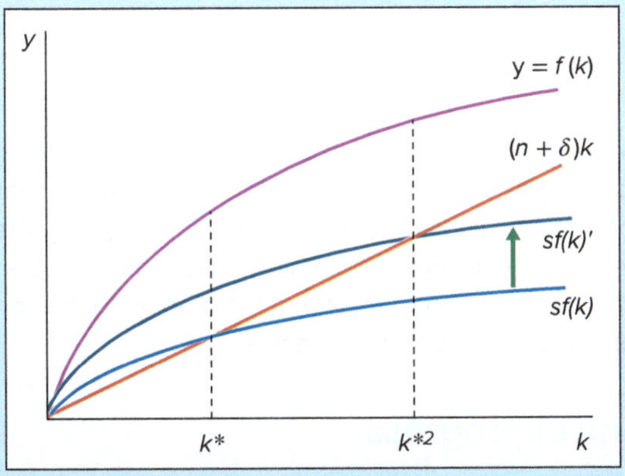

Figure 15.5 An increase in the saving rate in the Solow–Swan model

The Solow–Swan model predicts a relationship between the savings rate and growth, raising a question of what savings rate a policymaker should aim for. The maximum possible? Remember that earlier we have made the assumption that the whole of national income is either saved or consumed. So if the savings rate is very high then consumption will be too low. An economy needs some balance between consumption and investment.

The policymaker should target a rate of saving that provides the investment/consumption balance, and that target rate should be where consumption is maximized. As we can see from Figure 15.6, this point occurs where the distance between income and the depreciation line is maximized.

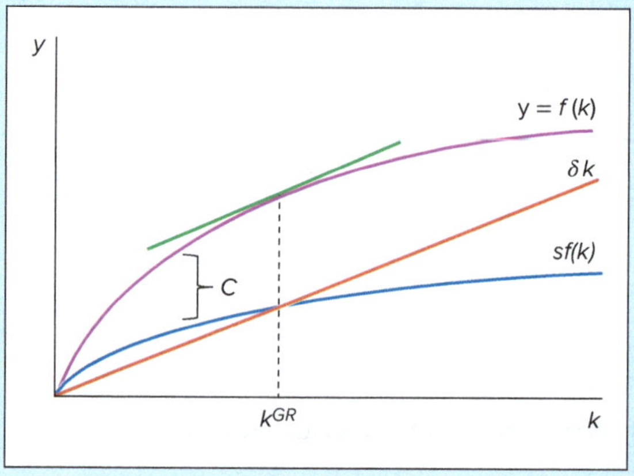

Figure 15.6 The Solow–Swan economy at the golden rule level of capital

Golden Rule Level of Capital: A level of steady state capital that achieves maximum consumption in the steady state. We find this level by equating the marginal product of capital (*MPK*) and the slope of the depreciation line (δ).

The **golden rule level of capital** per worker is achieved when the policymaker can deliver a savings rate so that the steady state coincides with the point of maximum distance between the depreciation line and the production function (maximum consumption c). We can express this mathematically where the slope of the depreciation line δ is the same as the slope of the production function (MPK); here the economy is at the golden rule level of capital:

$$MPK = \delta$$

In summary, the Solow–Swan model predicts that population growth can inhibit growth without an accompanying increase in capital, that a policymaker can use the saving rate to achieve higher income per capita and that the optimal level of capital per worker exists where the slope of the production function is equal to that of the depreciation schedule.

15.4 Developments in growth theory

Beyond the basic Solow–Swan model we can account for a reality, so far ignored, such as the influence of technological progress on growth. We understand that the working population requires capital in the form of machines to produce, but what happens when those machines become more productive, or new machines become available that bring entirely new productivities? We can think of the internet as one of the biggest technology shocks to bring new efficiencies to production; surely we cannot ignore this.

Exogenous technical progress

Up and until now we have kept the description of the Solow–Swan model simple by making use of the implicit function form, but to introduce technology and maintain the intuitive approach, we will make use of an explicit example with a result instantly recognizable from our implicit results above. We introduce an economy where output in goods and services follows the Cobb–Douglas production function given by:

$$Y = AK^{\alpha}L^{1-\alpha}$$

Output comes from the factors of production capital K and labour L where the weights of the factor contributions are determined by the key parameter α, which lies between the value of zero and one. The parameter A represents technology, which we can think of as the efficiency in the way the economy makes use of capital and labour, more simply the productivity of the economy. We can write the Cobb–Douglas production function in 'per capita' form by dividing by labour and writing the per capita variables in lowercase.

$$y = Ak^{\alpha}$$

It is worth restating here that the value of α is less than one and this is consistent with our requirement up and until now that the functional form exhibits decreasing marginal returns. Without decreasing returns, we would not achieve a steady state in the model, with the gap between investment and depreciation actually widening as capital increases. Just as with our implicit example above we can write out the path of capital for this economy, which will be of a familiar form:

$$\dot{k} = sAk^{\alpha} - (n + \delta)k$$

From our equation for the path of capital, we can see the effects of policy when we control for productivity in the Solow–Swan model. An increase in the savings rate or in productivity will increase investment and in turn steady state capital, which will feed higher output per worker. As before, an increase in population growth or in the depreciation rate will have a negative effect on steady state capital per worker.

A model with endogenous growth

In the previous section we introduced a role for technology, adding a more realistic extension to the Solow–Swan model. We showed how we can account for the effect of increases in technology on economic growth and obtained the intuitive result of higher growth from higher technology. However, up and until now we have not discussed the causes of technology or examined the possibility that this variable might be affected by economic policy. We also failed to model the persistent growth rates we see for developed economies across the world.

It is not unreasonable to assume the existence of technology and simply 'bolt it on' to existing models, but how do we know if we have modelled it correctly? If a macroeconomic model is mis-specified, then the predictions that it makes can be biased and misleading. If we have assumed a functional form for technology, then it is also worth considering a cause for technology to give us a better idea of its correct specification. If we model technology as the end event of a process, we are proposing that the variable is endogenous in that process. Up to now we have made use of the assumption of diminishing marginal returns for capital; the reducing return is key to the existence of a steady state level of capital.

The AK model of Rebelo (1991) answers both the endogeneity and persistence issues by making use of a mathematical convenience, the proposition that the income share of capital is equal to one. The AK model suggests that technology is an accidental result of investments made in the stock of knowledge such as education, innovation and research. We can write the stock of knowledge B as:

$$B = Ak^{(1-\alpha)}$$

with the production function:

$$y = Bk^{\alpha}$$

Combining these two functions we have:

$$y = Ak^{(1-\alpha)}k^{\alpha}$$

which conveniently simplifies to:

$$y = Ak$$

After working through the mathematics, it becomes apparent why this model is called the 'AK' model. The capital share is equal to one (k is to the power of unity) and the production function is no longer increasing at a decreasing rate. It is just increasing in a linear fashion and as a result, the savings schedule will not dip to cross the depreciation schedule. The steady state has been removed and continuous growth explained.

From Figure 15.7 we can see that the production function is now restricted so that it is linear in capital; in this case, the savings schedule and depreciation line will never cross. The AK model shows that we can explain persistent growth and also endogenize technology. The model carries an important implication that policy may play an important role in economic growth. However, there is little evidence to suggest that growth and higher tax rates are related.

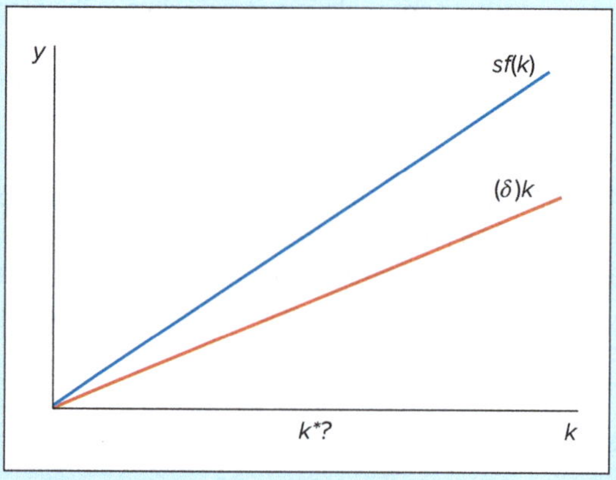

Figure 15.7 The AK model can explain persistent growth

EXERCISE 15.3

Check that the production function in the endogenous technology AK model has constant returns to scale.

An alternative heterodox approach

The endogenous growth model in the previous section allowed us to explain the persistent growth we see in more developed countries rather than the stagnation predicted by models with exogenous technology. Capital accumulation is the driving force for production, which can increase forever without any negative consequence or limit. In reality, we know that economic development is not a costless exercise; in many cases, growth uses up natural and finite resources. It remains to be seen whether or not growth can be achieved through increases in technology alone and some might argue that the proposition of sustainable growth is still a utopian dream.

One model that does address the issue of cost in economic growth is the Doughnut model of Kate Raworth (2018) represented in Figure 15.8. The model uses indicators from recent advances in Earth-system science to propose that some critical **planetary boundaries** are being violated. This key feature introduces the concept of an environmental limiting constraint – so far missing from traditional models – that can help us understand key issues surrounding economic growth.

Planetary Boundaries: The safe limit of pressure that humanity can put on critical Earth systems without pushing Earth out of its benevolent and resilient Holocene state.

The planetary boundaries are a set of nine critical Earth-system processes that help to sustain the benevolent conditions of Earth's Holocene epoch of the past 11,000 years, such as a stable climate, a protective ozone layer and healthy oceans.

Planetary boundaries:

1. Ozone depletion
2. **Climate change (violated)**
3. Ocean acidification
4. **Biodiversity loss (violated)**
5. Freshwater use
6. Chemical pollution
7. **Land use change (violated)**
8. **Nitrogen and phosphorous cycles (violated)**
9. Atmospheric aerosol loading (unclear)

Recent Earth-system science finds that four of the boundaries – climate change, biodiversity loss, nitrogen and phosphorous cycles, and land use change – have been transgressed (Steffen et al. 2015).

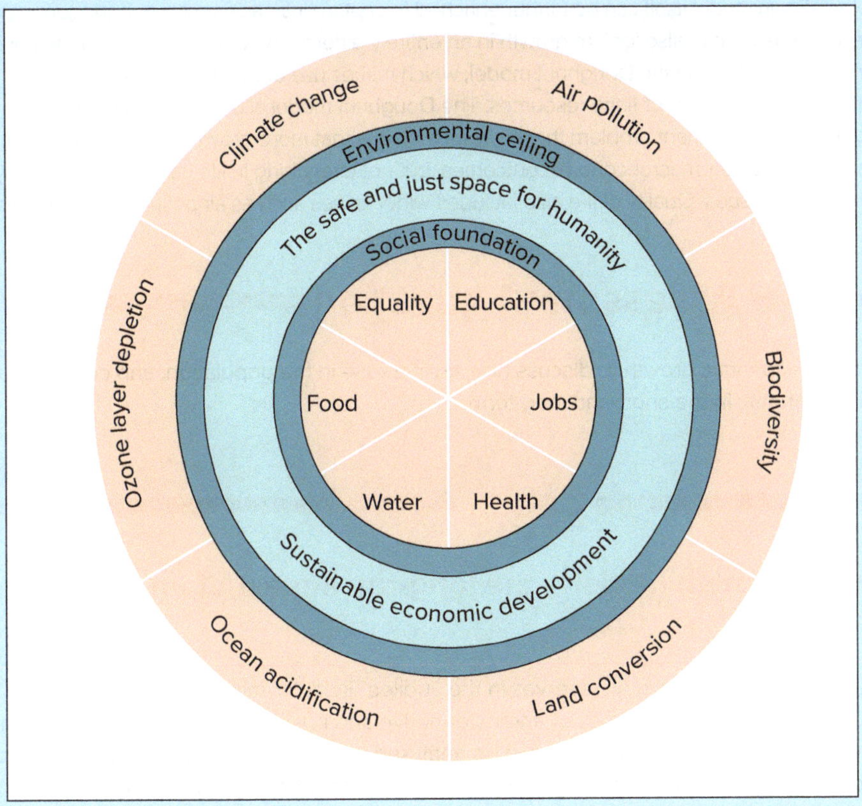

Figure 15.8 The Doughnut model showing the safe and just space for humanity

Obviously, we cannot eradicate humanity's pressure on Earth's systems altogether, so the Doughnut proposes a balance between meeting the rights and needs of all people (bringing everyone above the 'social foundation') while safeguarding the planetary boundaries on which the planet's health and resilience depend (staying within the 'environmental ceiling').

In between the social foundation and the environmental ceiling is the '**safe and just space** for humanity' shown as the doughnut itself. The doughnut now represents a space for inclusive and sustainable economic development, and in doing so it asks whether (or what kind of) economic growth is compatible with achieving that? Inside the safe space the concept of optimal growth can hold after accounting for the binding

Safe and Just Space: The concept of a space for humanity that lies between a minimum social floor and maximum environmental ceiling.

constraints of the planetary boundaries, as identified by the Doughnut model. The model is visually appealing and projects its implications to policymakers in an immediate and intuitive fashion at the same time as making evident the shortcomings of the earlier efforts to model growth while ignoring the environmental implications.

15.5 Chapter summary: Putting it all together

In this chapter, we have discussed the subject of economic growth, why our policymakers desire a growing economy and identified the economic forces that contribute to longer-run increases in economic activity. These driving forces are the combination of the factors of production together with technology, which measures the efficiency in our use of the 'factors'.

For each economy, we can measure technology through the functional form of a production function, which we can specify to reflect the realities of the economy that we observe. For instance, we can use decreasing returns to scale in capital to reflect diminishing returns and the slowing growth of more developed economies. We can make use of simple models such as the classical theory or make use of the path of capital to further understand slowing growth in Solow–Swan type models.
The Solow–Swan model itself can be further enriched to capture intricacies such as endogenous growth.

Beyond this we can also look at growth in an entirely different way, bearing in mind the constraints of our natural world, using the Doughnut model, which makes use of the undeniable limitations presented to us by the fact of finite resources. The Doughnut model allows us to immediately appreciate the predominant problem that lies with the view that more growth is always better. Higher growth provides better macroeconomic outcomes, but not everything in life can be measured by the macroeconomic issues. Quality of life also includes wider issues such as air pollution and biodiversity.

Assessment question

Use the Solow–Swan model of economic growth to discuss how an increase in the population, and consequently the labour force, will impact the economy in the short and long term.

Cases

Ghana and the Solow growth model – the long-run impact of an oil discovery

Introduction

In 2007, Ghana discovered substantial offshore oil reserves in the Jubilee Field, 37 miles from the coast and production began in 2010. This event sparked hopes of a transformative and positive impact on the Ghanaian economy. From a macroeconomic perspective, this case can be analysed using the Solow growth model, which explains how savings, population growth and technological progress affect economic growth in the long run.

Application of the Solow growth model

1. The Event – Oil discovery and initial economic impact

   The discovery and production of oil presented a positive economic shock to capital accumulation in Ghana. In the Solow model framework, this can be interpreted as a temporary increase in investment, leading to faster capital accumulation and higher GDP per capita in the short run.

   - Capital deepening: The inflow of foreign direct investment (FDI) into the oil sector boosted the Ghanaian capital stock.
   - The discovery improved incomes and, initially, GDP per capita rose significantly due to oil exports.
   - In terms of infrastructure spending the government invested some of the oil revenues on infrastructure, aiming to build economic capacity.

2. Medium to long-run trends

   According to the Solow model, in the absence of any sustained technological progress or increased savings, the growth effects of a one-time capital increase will diminish over time. The economy will return to a steady state growth path determined by population growth and technological change.
   In Ghana's case:

   - GDP growth moderated after the initial oil boom. By the mid-2010s, growth had slowed due to falling oil prices, inefficiencies in revenue management and over-reliance on oil.
   - Fluctuation in saving and investment rates worsened, and volatility in oil prices contributed towards economic instability.
   - Technological progress and diversification in production lagged, limiting productivity gains in other sectors like agriculture and manufacturing.

3. Evaluation and structural challenges

   - Dutch disease risk: The oil boom appreciated Ghana's currency, hurting other export sectors like cocoa and manufacturing, a situation also referred to as a resource curse.
   - Revenue volatility: Heavier dependence on oil made public finances more vulnerable to global price shocks.
   - Policy responses: The government created a Stabilization Fund and Heritage Fund to manage oil revenues better, but issues of fiscal discipline and accountability persist.

   The Solow model highlights the importance of considering long-term factors, especially technological progress and effective use of resources, towards achieving more sustainable growth. Ghana's experience illustrates how a temporary capital shock can boost growth, but without structural reforms the effects fade over time and prove detrimental to long-term stability.

Questions

1. According to the Solow model, what is the main driver of long-run growth in per capita income?
2. In the context of the Solow model, Ghana's oil discovery represents:
   a) A permanent shift in the steady-state growth rate
   b) A temporary increase in capital accumulation
   c) An increase in labour productivity due to better education
   d) A decrease in the savings rate
3. Why did Ghana's initial growth spurt after oil discovery not lead to sustained high growth rates? Use the Solow model in your explanation.
4. Evaluate the effectiveness of Ghana's policies in managing oil wealth to achieve long-run growth.

Problems

EASY

1. Which of the following best describes the marginal product of capital (MPK)?
   a) The additional output produced when all inputs are increased by one percentage point
   b) The total output produced from all units of employed capital and labour
   c) The additional output produced by employing one more unit of capital, holding the amount of labour constant
   d) The cost of producing one more unit of output, holding the amount of labour employed constant
   e) The decrease in output when capital is reduced by one unit, holding the amount of labour constant
2. In a Cobb–Douglas production function $Y = AK^{\alpha}L^{1-\alpha}$, what does the parameter α represent?
   a) The rate of capital depreciation
   b) The marginal product of labour

c) The share of output earned by capital

d) The elasticity of the labour supply

e) The level of technology or productivity

MEDIUM

3. Which of the following conditions implies constant returns to scale in the Cobb–Douglas production function?

    a) $\alpha + (1 - \alpha) = 0$

    b) $\alpha + \beta > 1$

    c) $\alpha = 1$

    d) $\alpha + (1 - \alpha) = 1$

    e) $\alpha = \beta = 0.5$

4. In the Solow growth model (without technological progress), what happens in the steady state?

    a) Output per worker continues to grow indefinitely

    b) Capital per worker and output per worker remain constant

    c) Capital grows faster than output

    d) Labour productivity will decline over time

    e) The savings rate will eventually fall to zero

5. Which of the following is *not* an assumption of the Solow growth model?

    a) Returns to capital are diminishing

    b) The savings rate is constant

    c) Technological progress is endogenous

    d) Population growth is exogenous

    e) Markets are competitive

6. Explain the economic intuition behind the concept of diminishing marginal returns to capital. How does this principle affect long-term economic growth in the Solow model?

HARD

7. If the savings rate increases in the Solow model, what is the long-term effect on output per worker?

8. Consider a Cobb–Douglas production function of the form $Y = AK^{0.3}L^{0.7}$. Suppose that total factor productivity $A = 2$, capital $K = 100$, and labour $L = 64$. Calculate:

    a) Total output Y

    b) The marginal product of capital (MPK)

9. Discuss the role of total factor productivity (TFP) in explaining the difference in income levels across countries. How does the Solow model account for TFP, and what are its limitations in this respect?

CHAPTER 16

Economic Growth – Policy and Frameworks

Chapter contents

At a Glance Economic growth – Policy and frameworks

The issue

The subject of macroeconomics allows us to predict and plan for the future. An important part of those plans will involve how we can grow the economy in a sustainable way. The human characteristic of altruism will encourage us to pass on a better world to future generations; so how exactly do we go about planning for a responsible macroeconomic route to the future?

The understanding

This chapter follows from Chapter 15, where we discussed frameworks for modelling economic growth, the content we would normally expect to see in a textbook on macroeconomics. This chapter introduces some relatively new areas not normally included in traditional macroeconomics textbooks, namely the circular economy, environment and governance, and the framework of equality, diversity and inclusivity. So far discussions in this area have been limited to the arena of macroeconomic research.

The usefulness

The frameworks covered here are covered in all kinds of disciplines and widely discussed by agencies in the private sector. What you are less likely to find is the connection between these concepts and macroeconomics. We can think of the macroeconomist perspective on these issues surrounding socially responsible strategies employed by firms and policies employed by government.

16.1 Introduction

In Chapter 15 on growth theory, we built an understanding of how the economy grows using some of the more established frameworks and some new ones – from the classical growth models, through to the more sophisticated endogenous growth model, finishing with the more heterodox explanation of Kate Raworth's doughnut model. All of these models are useful as tools to help us describe the path and determinants of economic growth.

Good questions remain, however: How do we promote and maintain economic growth? What steps should we take, to ensure the economy grows in an efficient, yet sustainable manner? How can we help our producers to flourish while minimizing the impacts on our environment? Recently, policymakers have been more concerned about these questions and are more motivated to design policies that can enable the type of growth that society expects and prefers. These concerns are relatively new in the field of economics, just as they are a more recent concern for our media. Of course, the government and the central bank have the more traditional policy tools to play with, in the forms of fiscal, monetary and international trade policy; and let us not forget that firms will tend to grow naturally over time as they expand their portfolios and increase their shares of the markets in which they operate. Over and above the use of these more traditional types of policy, the government can utilize legislation and other less obvious means to help the economy to grow in a way that is consistent with the values of its citizens.

Here we learn more about recent thinking in terms of 'how' we should grow. Just as Kate Raworth has highlighted, using her doughnut model introduced in Chapter 15 on economic growth, the challenges posed by unlimited growth are significant. Here we take a detailed look at three main areas that have been associated with growing an economy in a more sustainable manner: the **circular economy**; the environment, social and governance (**ESG**) considerations; and equality, inclusivity and diversity (EDI). Of course, it is not universally agreed upon that these frameworks or categories of ideas are the best ways to frame how new growth in the economy might be achieved, but it is a good starting point to lay them out and understand them in the context of macroeconomics.

> **Circular Economy:** An economy where the production processes of firms are designed to consider the 'whole' life cycle of a good – from sourcing raw materials to end of life, to reuse.
> **ESG:** A framework that promotes the inclusion of the environment and the welfare of society into the objectives and practices of institutions.

EXAMPLE 16.1

Real world example: Unlimited growth in China, 1980–2010

China has experienced what might be considered exponential growth after the economic reforms of 1979, led by rapid industrial expansion from the 1980s.

Side effects

While it has lifted millions of citizens out of poverty and boosted GDP, there has also been negative environmental effects such as depletion of resources and increases in pollution.

Sustainability

Unlimited growth can undermine long-term sustainability and bring doubt to the use of GDP as a measure of economic success. More recently China has implemented policies to limit the environmental impact of economic growth and promoted green technologies.

Another question that presents itself in the context of the field of macroeconomics is: Are these issues relevant to our science – what place does this content have in a textbook for core macroeconomics? This is a valid question and one that deserves to remain at the forefront of our minds as we work our way through this chapter. One of the most widely cited definitions of macroeconomics is that the subject is 'the study of the economy as a whole'. A chapter that focuses on the subject of growth theory definitely fits well, and so another chapter that discusses 'how' we grow should be equally fitting.

Throughout this chapter, I will focus on how these three concepts and their associated components are related to the science of macroeconomics. Remember that these topics will feature in many other disciplines of discussion; and so we can do our bit by discussing these topics through the lens of a macroeconomist.

In this chapter, we begin by laying out how we go about defining some of the sustainability concepts in the context of the field of macroeconomics (see Table 16.1), before discussing them in detail individually. The circular economy is a framework to help us think of how we can design production processes and consider our environment at the same time – where the initial product design, product consumption and end of life recycling are all connected, following a cyclical pattern rather than a linear path from creation to destruction. We will take the opportunity that this topic lends us to learn a modern modelling technique referred to as 'input/output' (I/O) modelling. This technique will also feature as a learning outcome of this chapter, providing us with a more formal framework in which to analyse the concept of the circular economy.

Table 16.1 Sustainable growth frameworks

Concept	Description
The circular economy	A framework that helps us to design and produce goods to be consumed and reused in a way that is sustainable for the environment.
Environment, social and governance	How firms can produce in a way that internalizes the externalities that they create during production through the act of production and trading.
Equality, diversity and inclusivity	Ideals driven by the values of modern societies. These ideals might be associated with more progressive thinking and considered virtuous attitudes by those that champion them.

The way that firms behave while carrying out their core activities has drawn more attention in recent times. There is a growing expectation that they will act in a way that is consistent with not only maximizing their profits, but also taking steps to minimize their impact on wider society. We are indeed seeing firms go beyond the more basic considerations and thinking more about these impacts, drawing in the factors normally considered external to them. Some economists believe that this behaviour is only rational in any case, and the firm will benefit indirectly and in the long run from its non-core initiatives aimed at the well-being of society. The actual concept of firms behaving in a way that considers their wider impact on the economy is called ESG, which stands for environmental, social and governance.

Finally, we look at the emerging field of equality, diversity and inclusivity through the lens of the macroeconomist. Few would disagree with these goals or desirable attributes, but how do we square these aims with the behaviour we normally expect from a firm in carrying out its core duties? Is government intervention required to achieve growth consistent with better policy? Should we revisit the exact framing of the virtues of sustainability and equality as theories in this area develop?

Learning Outcomes

By the end of this chapter you should be able to:

- Understand the concept of the circular economy and how it fits into our current understanding of growth theory.
- Apply the input/output model to interpret the circular economy.
- Outline key environmental, sustainability and governance initiatives in the relation to macroeconomics.
- Critically analyse the concepts that have been developed through popular debate aimed at progressing the behaviour of society, particularly in the context of equality, diversity and inclusivity.
- Discuss the role macroeconomics can play in equality, diversity and inclusivity.

16.2 The circular economy

The name circular economy is one that gives us an immediate sense and intuitive feel for this growing field in macroeconomics – designing our production processes so that the construction, act of using and recycling of a product are seamlessly connected in a circular way makes obvious sense if you believe in the premise that waste is not a want in society, merely an unwanted by-product of our consumption. To ensure completion of the cyclical process, firms must consider objectives that go beyond the normal profit maximization and market share concerns. Producers may require incentivization to produce goods whose **life cycle** follows through from purchase, to use, to end of life, and around back to recycle for new purchase. Designing goods and services in this manner makes obvious sense, but does require a lot of planning and perhaps a good deal of investment.

Defining the circular economy

The main objective that lies behind the concept of the circular economy is that of minimal waste. It is commonly understood that reducing waste is a good idea if we want to protect the environment in which we now live and especially in the future. A producer can design and build a car that can be dismantled after use in such a way that the resulting pieces can be reused to build the next new car. Designing a product that can be dismantled and recycled in its entirety is a very sustainable way for society to consume and still pass on a quality environment to future generations.

Of course, it might not be economically viable to produce all goods in this way, and so it is up to policymakers to set rules and regulations to ensure that firms have to internalize the costs of this circular production. If it costs more to produce a car that can be 100 per cent recycled, then consumers will have to accept the additional cost to enjoy the benefits of this cleaner economy.

In summary, the circular economy is one where economic activity takes place in a manner which minimizes waste, contributes towards **sustainable economic** growth, and respects the wider environment – an economy that is characterized by verbs such as share, reuse, recycle, lease, repair, refurbish and recapture. Currently there are limited ways to classify and trade

> **Life Cycle:** The span of time between conception, design, production, sale, use, maintenance and disposal. In the past, a product might be designed specifically for the earlier parts of the life cycle, with no consideration for maintenance and disposal.
> **Sustainable Economy:** An economy where activity can continue in a way that minimizes its impact on the environment.

end-of-use goods or waste products, partly due to environmental and health grounds and other concerns about the impact on CO_2 levels. A mixture of technology and good economic policy may address this in the future.

An input–output model for the circular economy

To help us understand the concept of the circular economy we can use a modelling structure called input–output modelling (or more commonly termed the IO model). The benefits of using such a model type are twofold: first, the structure is relatively simple in its most basic form; and secondly, for graduates, the usefulness in terms of employability. These types of models are commonly used by practising economists for a wide range of issues, especially where the traditional theories are difficult to fit with the data of real life.

Social accounting matrices (SAMs) and computational general equilibrium models are pivotal tools for understanding fundamental macroeconomic questions, such as the economic impacts of tariffs, wars, pandemics, environmental disasters, and so on, on trade, employment and sectoral output, to name only a few. Practitioners, such as governments and international institutions, also use such tools to answer policy-relevant economic questions, such as the impact of Brexit on the Scottish economy. **Input–output models** are also fundamental building blocks for the national accounting framework. Lastly, designated models are developed to highlight and quantify specific aspects of macroeconomic questions, such as the costs of global value chain dependence and resilience and the heterogeneous impacts of policies on poorer households, and so on.

Input–output Model: A model that can interconnect the different sectors of the economy, taking account of the interdependencies between the two industries.

Let us begin with the simplest case. In our two-sector economy there are producers of normal goods and producers of recycled goods; the production of both producers can be split into the demand required for each respective sector. Imagine that we have estimated that the total final consumer demand for normal goods is 12 (million) units and for recycled goods is 4 (million) units. We can write this out mathematically so that it is easier to visualize.

Let the output of producers who focus on non-recycled (or normal) goods be represented by the variable X and the output of the producers primarily concerned with recycled goods be represented by variable Y. We can write out the production of each producer:

$$X = 0.1X + 0.5Y + 12$$

$$Y = 0.25X + 0.03Y + 4$$

The first equation tells us that the production of normal goods (X) can be split into the production that it requires for its own use (which we can think of as intermediary goods), how much goods are required by the recycling sector and how many goods are required by consumers, which we can think of as final demand. In a similar fashion, the second equation tells us that of the goods produced by the recycling sector (Y), 25 per cent will be of use to the normal goods sector as inputs, 3 per cent will be required as inputs within its own sector and a total of 4 units will be required by consumers, also in the form of final demand. In our example we can write this in matrix form:

$$\begin{pmatrix} X \\ Y \end{pmatrix} = \begin{pmatrix} 0.1 & 0.5 \\ 0.25 & 0.03 \end{pmatrix} \begin{pmatrix} X \\ Y \end{pmatrix} + \begin{pmatrix} 12 \\ 4 \end{pmatrix}$$

Solve these two for X and Y to get the optimal production mixture. If the observed mixture is above or below the optimal level, then the government might take action to intervene in the market for either normal or recycled goods.

For the general case we can write the problem out as:

$$\begin{pmatrix} X \\ Y \end{pmatrix} = \begin{pmatrix} a & b \\ d & e \end{pmatrix} \begin{pmatrix} X \\ Y \end{pmatrix} + \begin{pmatrix} c \\ f \end{pmatrix}$$

where a, b, d and e represent the input shares of both goods X and Y that contribute towards the final production of both goods individually. The parameters c and f are the value of the final demand for X and Y respectively. To do this implicitly requires a good share of detail in matrix algebra, but with values for the parameter set this reduces down to a simple simultaneous equation problem.

EXERCISE 16.1

1. Now that you have seen how input–output models are written out, why not take some time to solve for the circular economy above. What is the right mixture of new and recycled goods, and what policies might the government adopt to change this?
2. Imagine the government wants to move closer to a circular economy by raising the level of recycled goods in production from 25 per cent to 50 per cent. How does this affect the production of normal goods?

Research in the area of the circular economy

Input–output models can be used for research purposes, where there is a requirement to further understanding of the interconnectedness of different economic sectors across the economy. The framework is useful for analysing the impact of economic shocks and policy on the economy as a whole but with a breakdown of the impact on individual sectors. These models can also bring social factors into play in any analysis, such as the environmental impacts, normally external to other traditional models used for the same purpose. Being able to delineate across sectors allows a deeper understanding of the heterogeneous effects, such as breaking down an economic question into a regional contribution analysis.

The field of circular economy research in macroeconomics will look at questions in sustainability and the protection of the environment. Examples of research questions are:

- **How do we reduce waste?**
- **How do we make manufacturing more efficient?**
- **How do we foster sustainable supply chains?**
- **How do we make the most of innovation and technology?**
- **How do we involve stakeholders in the design process?**

Five principles that can help us to define the scope of circular economy research are shown in Table 16.2.

Table 16.2 The principles that define the scope of the circular economy

Principle	Explanation
Design	Durability and longevity in the design process
Reuse	Ensure maintenance and the ability to refurbish
Recycle	Life-cycle design to allow repurposing of goods
Reduce	Minimizing inputs and lowering production waste
Regenerate	Ability to regenerate natural systems

The five principles set out the objectives of typical research in the area of the circular economy. Manufacturing processes may need to be entirely reimagined, especially for older and more established industries. For larger industries the scale of investment required may be so high that government intervention is required to facilitate a transition and maintain a level playing field for the stakeholders in these industries. These interventions may also have significant second-round effects to areas of the economy such as international trade and the domestic labour market.

Aside from the difficulties of transition, the benefits of adopting such frameworks are easier to imagine. A circular economy is going to come with the benefits of a cleaner and less polluted economy, the scope to mute climate change and reduced biodiversity loss. On the subject of 'how we grow' is certainly a good starting point.

EXERCISE 16.2

Imagine a two industry economy characterized by the following interconnectivities between the two industries. The production of Good A is made up of 15 per cent of itself and 20 per cent of Good B; Good A is also consumed by the public to the tune of 20 units. Good B, however, is made up of only 1 per cent of itself, 35 per cent of Good A, with 45 units consumed. What is the optimal production of Good B?

16.3 Environmental, social and governance (ESG)

In the context of macroeconomics, the firm is assumed to behave in a manner that will maximize its profits, by considering its total revenue and its total cost. The external impacts caused by the firm's activities are irrelevant for that consideration; of course, in reality these impacts are not irrelevant. ESG helps us to frame the debate around firm accountability and transparency in the economy and how the government might internalize the negative **externalities** caused by production without resorting to distortionary taxation.

Externalities: The indirect costs or benefits of economic production. These costs are outside of the firm's objective function and can be internalized by the government through taxation and legislation.

We can encourage firms to consider their wider impact on society through the way that consumers make choices and through soft legislative policy. ESG is a framework that considers these external effects through a corporate sustainability strategy and is made up of three fundamental pillars. These pillars are environmental, social and governance. It is believed that building the economy around these pillars can result in an economy that is more sustainable and has less impact on the environment for its civilians.

Producers may require incentivization to internalize the negative externalities that they contribute towards; for example, firms can deliberately focus on hiring and buying more locally if the impact on profit margins is minimal, with this initiative promoted by the government. From the firm's perspective, ensuring that practices are completed in a socially responsible manner is important, especially when you consider the more recent preference sets of investors and consumers, looking to invest in clean technologies and with firms that maintain good reputations in these areas.

ESG and macroeconomics

Macroeconomics concerns itself with the higher-level workings of the economy, so you might wonder why this area appears within the content of this textbook? ESG is certainly a microeconomic consideration, but even in the field of microeconomics this new area is allocated to the field of externalities. The firm will only consider the problem of profit maximization; other objectives such as the impacts of production on society are left for the government to deal with via its own expenditure or by internalizing the problems for the firm through legislation or taxation. This should be the end of the story, but something is happening more recently.

Recent pressures from environmental campaigners have brought the problem of the environment into focus at a national level – governments are now more likely to consider macroeconomic policy that addresses the issue of the limited objective for the firm. Firms are now rethinking their own mission statements to include ESG among their goals of existence. Pressure from campaigners and more generally from consumers is driving firms to re-evaluate their over-simplified objective and include environment, sustainability and better governance. Will this fundamental shift in attitude and objectives survive the harsh realities of the business cycle over the long term? This remains to be seen when the new approaches are tested by the next prolonged and significant downturn in economic activity.

The three pillars of ESG

The ESG framework, which has evolved since the early part of the new millennium, captures the essence of a movement in strategic thinking in organization behaviour split into the three areas of environmental, social and governance. We summarize these in Table 16.3 overleaf.

Table 16.3 ESG pillars and aims

The Three Pillars	An Organization Should:
Environmental	seek to minimize its impact of its activities and processes on the immediate and wider environment
Social	seek methods to ensure that its activities have a positive effect on stakeholders including impacted communities
Governance	administrate its activities in an integral and transparent manner – an organization should be accountable and report honestly

The three pillars are a useful framework to measure a firm's performance in the area of social responsibility. Of course, it would be hard to make comparisons across firms if the framework itself is not consistent or follows some accountability standard. For this requirement specifically, we really need coordination and consistency at a higher level than individual boardrooms. In this regard there is an obvious role for the government to legislate more specific requirements for firms to follow and to ensure a level playing field for firms that will be competing in markets across the economy.

To give an idea of the kinds of practices we can include in an ESG strategy, we begin with the 'environmental' pillar. Environmental considerations include such practices as a lower dependence on fossil fuels, the careful use of natural resources, manufacturing at a minimum scale in terms of pollution, a minimal impact on the climate, reduction in the use of hazardous chemicals and a switch to renewable energy. Secondly, we consider the practices we can include in the area of strategies in the 'social' arena: equality and diversity in terms of workforce, producing safer products and accepting liability, the health and safety of employees, adequate provision of training and staff development, lower reliance on animal testing, accounting for the mental health of employees, and supply chain transparency. Finally, we consider 'governance': employing good practices in the areas of employee remuneration, governing board diversity, ethical accounting and tax strategies, identifying corruption and facilitating whistle blowing, values in ethics, and maintaining the rights of shareholders.

Recent criticisms of ESG

The decision of whether or not to implement an ESG strategy will most probably come down to a cost–benefit analysis of the impact on the financial performance of a firm. The first drawback will be the lack of direct contribution to the return that shareholders will receive – the firm is unlikely to profit from any of the initiatives listed under the pillars. Another consideration is the time frame – the benefits that a firm might expect to enjoy will probably all appear outside the typical accounting window or might not even be captured directly due to accounting standards. Lastly, it is also possible that firms can use these frameworks as marketing tools, rather than as seriously intended strategy – this kind of shortcoming can lead to a loss in confidence or reputation of the whole idea of ESG.

Research in this area draws attention to the lack of return from such activities – recent research has failed to find a link between sustainable exchange-traded funds and investors' returns. Other studies have failed to find a link between firms receiving responsible investment funds and above average financial market performance. Nevertheless the reality is that the opinion of investors and the wider public do matter; investment decisions are gravitating towards more ESG-oriented vehicles. If you couple this with the lack of evidence for drag on value of investment, then you might come to the conclusion that ESG is positive for financial performance for companies over the longer-term time horizon.

16.4 Equality, diversity and inclusivity

Another relatively recent concept surrounding the issue of social responsibility and sustainability is that of equality, diversity and inclusivity (EDI). Although it is difficult to link such initiatives directly to positive macro outcomes, research in this area is gaining momentum; often through extensions to the production function as an example. In a world of equal opportunity and in the absence of human bias, you might question the need to adopt such a concept or include EDI as part of a production strategy or mission statement for an organization.

Unfortunately, in the real world, biases and inequalities exist naturally as we tend to behave selfishly and repel anything new or 'foreign' in our everyday lives; people prefer the known to the unknown, for example. Historical events also produce biases in the way that different societies think about each other. Being biased is human, but it can have very negative effects for those that make up minority groups. Whenever individuals are judged based on their characteristics or alleged/assumed group identity, this undermines the agency of the individual and should, therefore, be rejected. Here we take a look at each component of EDI using the lens of a macroeconomist, though we can keep in mind that there are many perspectives on the topic of EDI, of which this is only one. There are three pillars that capture the essence of this framework: equality, diversity and inclusivity.

Equality and macroeconomic equilibrium

We can revisit the topic of macroeconomic equilibrium here; typically the economy is in a state of rest and there is an absence of economic shocks that might change that. To use the example of the aggregate demand and aggregate supply model, supply in the economy meets demand at a specific level of prices and level of output. With the economy in equilibrium, the driving factors of excess supply or demand are absent and consequently there is no motivation for firms or consumers to take any action. In the context of macroeconomics, equilibrium is a state devoid of new activity, until the status quo is disturbed by an economic shock.

From a macroeconomic perspective, the concept of equality might be a familiar one – everyone should be treated equally. Equity, on the other hand, can be interpreted as the idea of everyone having access to the same opportunities. While they can be defined distinctly the two concepts are in fact related. A society that strives for equality will need to ensure that resources are allocated fairly through the efficiency brought about by a state of equilibrium. Long-run equilibrium requires markets to clear and that all resources are fully utilized – there is balance across the economy and social stability. Equilibrium is a state that we are always moving towards but one that we rarely arrive at. In the same way that the movement towards equality is attractive, is it achievable in absolute terms? And would this be a state where we could happily remain? Absolute equality would need some drastic intervention from a totalitarian social planner.

Absolute equality requires the equal division of resources to be applied to the economy – imagine a state where everybody is paid the same, treated the same and defining characteristics are overlooked, extra effort is unrewarded and careful frugality pointless. I can not think of any student who would be happy to complete a degree only to receive the same salary as everybody else. You can see this conflict even more clearly by searching for the definition of equality – it is very difficult to pin down. An advocate will explain: 'what is meant by equality is . . .'; 'It is not about equality exactly, but something else more detailed', such as 'equal opportunity' or 'equal treatment under some specific circumstances'. The trouble about the notion of equality is that it is an absolute concept in the first place; it cannot be defined by attaching caveats. I imagine that this is one of the reasons that even though it is understood that equality might be seen as a noble aim, in reality the actual outcome might be seen as a lot less attractive – somewhere where we might want to move towards but not to arrive at.

Despite the challenges thrown up by the reality of the definition of equality, huge inequalities remain in the world. A capitalist system that rewards human endeavour has to allow for the accumulation of wealth, but what do we do when all of the world's resources end up in the hands of a very small number or people? Attempts to address the problem of wealth distribution have had little success, and the problem is one of the biggest global challenges.

One way to address the problem posed by the definition and reality of equality is to take a rethink on this controversial pillar of EDI. More recently we have seen calls for the replacement of the concept of equality with the concept of equity. Whereas the concept of equality faces a challenge in interpretation, the concept of equity does better. Equality could be interpreted and is most clearly defined as treating everybody the same; whereas the aim of equity is to provide everyone with the opportunity to achieve success in terms of a meaningful role in the economy.

Diversity and the distribution of wealth

Diversity in the context of the framework of EDI can be explained quite simply as 'the presence of the widest spectrum of characteristics, backgrounds and perspectives within a social group or institution'. As the concept itself is both relative and evolving it is not an easy task to define exactly. Broadly speaking we can think of diversity as the practice of involving people from a range of social and ethnic backgrounds. How do we account for diversity in the field of macroeconomics?

Macroeconomics itself has faced a good deal of criticism for its over-reliance upon simplistic assumptions and models that ignore the complexities of real life; something we have already touched upon in Chapter 4. The economist Thomas Piketty is renowned for discussing these shortcomings in his book *Capital in the Twenty-first Century*[1]. The mainstream macroeconomic models fall short in dealing with the sort of useful detail provided by the distribution of wealth. As an example, the AS/AD model of Chapter 13 describes the economy with just two agents: the representative firm and the representative consumer. Every consumer is assumed to have identical wealth, but the distribution of wealth is important for economic policy; taxation should take account of the fact that wealthy people spend a much smaller proportion of their income on food, for instance. Treating everyone the same can lead to a disproportionate impact of economic policies.

For the science of macroeconomics, there is a need to make better account for diversity of wealth at the very least. As Piketty points out, this debate is ongoing and much work needs to be done in this area. One way we can address this shortcoming is to introduce more layers to our macroeconomic models; we can make space for the heterogeneity displayed in the real life distributions, by introducing more sectors, or types, of consumers in our models.

Inclusivity and internalization

The Firm's Objective: The problem that the firm solves in deciding how much to produce, or which price to set for its output. Normally, we assume that the sole objective for the firm is the maximization of profits.

In the context of EDI we can think of inclusivity as the practice of creating environments where all social groups feel valued, respected and empowered to participate regardless of ability, background or identity. As we have discussed earlier in this chapter, we assume that **the firm's objective** relies solely on the maximization of profits; externalities such as pollution output or any other social disturbance do not matter for the decision of how much to produce.

Government intervention can address the societal problem of externalities by internalizing the problem; in other words, bringing the firm's wider impact into play in the firm's objective function, through taxation or legislation. For macroeconomics there is little to discuss beyond this policy fix, until we think about the issue of inclusivity. How do we make sure that policies and the reactions of firms to the problem of externalities are implemented in an inclusive manner?

EXAMPLE 16.2

Hypothetical example: Inclusivity and internalization

As an example imagine that a social media platform is fast growing and very popular – fast growth can lead to growing pains; problems that appear in processes are sidelined by expansion efforts. One of these problems manifests itself in the form of mental problems for younger users of the platform and this leads to significant negative health outcomes for these users. Under pressure from relatives of the afflicted, the government exerts pressure on the platform to improve practices and the firm duly responds with a new process that puts a lower limit on the age of users in a bid to mitigate the problem. How could the concept of inclusivity have helped here?

If the government had been more specific in its communication to the platform firm, it might have also insisted that measures were taken to ensure that the response and resulting fix had considered the issue of inclusivity. An inclusive solution might have involved the victims and relatives of those impacted in the decision-making process, who ultimately decided on the proposed fix to the problem.

By encompassing the goal of inclusivity in the framework of EDI, we can ensure that the process of internalizing externalities is itself designed to encompass fairness to those impacted. It is important that the burdens of economic activity are not disproportionately felt by vulnerable sections of society.

16.5 Chapter summary: Putting it all together

In this chapter, we have discussed the subject of modern frameworks for sustainable growth. A capitalist system that rewards human endeavour has to allow for the accumulation of wealth, but what do we do when all of the world's resources end up in the hands of a very small number of people? Attempts to address the problem of wealth distribution have had little success to date, and the problem is one of the biggest challenges for the capitalist economic systems. Another challenge for our economic system is how we design policies that can foster a responsible economy – how do we ensure equal opportunity, with the richness of diversity, where every member of society can enjoy a meaningful role?

We have also looked at three core areas of public policy that can help us to achieve sustainable growth – policies that can foster a circular economy, practices surrounding environmental sustainability and governance and finally, by encouraging the use of the three pillars of EDI, equality, diversity and inclusivity. Where a government should focus such efforts is yet to be determined in the evolving field; frameworks and policies take time to evolve and need careful consideration to avoid conflicts that new initiatives might bring. In this evolution it is important to take into account the perspectives of all social sciences, and that includes that of the macroeconomist.

Assessment Question

Imagine that an institution is thinking of writing down a policy to be circulated across an entire organization. The policy is aimed at encouraging a more diverse workforce in terms of ability and background. Discuss the long-run benefits and costs that might be enjoyed or endured by the institution as a result of this policy. You should write this short essay as a report to the governing board responsible for key decision making.

Cases

Sweden and the integration of ESG principles into macroeconomic policy

Overview

Sweden is renowned for the use and integration of environmental, social and governance (ESG) principles into national economic policy. Rather than treating ESG as a separate or secondary concern, Sweden has incorporated these principles directly into its macroeconomic frameworks, particularly through fiscal policy, labour market strategy and industrial policy.

Environmental (E): A green fiscal policy approach

Sweden was one of the first countries to introduce a carbon tax in the 1990s. This tax has been applied to fossil fuels used in transport and the provision of energy.

Where we might expect slower growth as a result of ESG type initiatives due to higher costs of production, Sweden has experienced sustained positive economic growth at the same time. This coincidence can be referred to as 'decoupling' economic growth from carbon emissions.

Revenues from the taxes raised are used to fund further investments in clean energy, green infrastructure and environmental innovation, stimulating new sectors of the economy and creating jobs. This approach demonstrates how environmental goals can align with macroeconomic objectives such as employment growth, increased productivity and long-term sustainability.

Social (S): Inclusive labour market policies

Socially, Sweden places higher emphasis on equal opportunity and inclusive participation throughout the economy. High investment in education and vocational training ensure that the workforce is adaptable to changes in demand, particularly as the economy transitions toward more sustainable industries.

Policies such as paid parental leave, subsidized childcare and gender equality legislation help to enable higher labour force participation, particularly among women. These policies contribute positively toward long-run economic growth, reducing structural unemployment and increasing the capacity of the economy.

Governance (G): Transparency and accountability

The existence of strong institutions and a high level of government transparency reinforces the success of ESG-type policy integration. Public trust and low corruption levels ensure that environmental taxes and social spending are more widely accepted and efficiently implemented.

Sweden's independent fiscal policy council's remit is to ensure responsible management of the public finances, providing oversight and long-term planning guidance. This in turn reinforces macroeconomic stability and investor confidence, both of which are vital for sustainable growth.

Positive macroeconomic outcomes

- Stable GDP growth alongside reduced carbon emissions (decoupling)
- Lower unemployment and higher labour force participation
- More resilient public finances and higher credit ratings
- Growth in green industries and levels of exports, including clean technology and sustainable forestry

Sweden's case illustrates how integrating ESG principles into macroeconomic policy can support long-term economic stability, social cohesion and environmental sustainability.

Questions

1. What makes Sweden's approach a good example of ESG in macroeconomics?
2. What macroeconomic outcomes has Sweden achieved through ESG integration?
3. How can this example be linked to macroeconomic models?

Problems

EASY

1. Which of the following best captures the primary objective of the circular economy?
   a) To maximize profits for producers by reducing operating costs
   b) To increase consumption through mass production
   c) To minimize waste and encourage the sustainable use of resources
   d) To extend the role of government in the production process
   e) To increase international trade in recyclable goods
2. Why might firms be reluctant to adopt circular economy principles without government intervention?
   a) The cost of redesigning and repurposing products can be economically impractical without incentives
   b) Consumers are typically unwilling to buy products made from recycled components

c) Circular production might lead to a decrease in consumer demand

d) Most firms lack the technical capacity to implement circular models of production

e) Firms are only encouraged to produce recyclable goods with government approval

3. Which of the following best explains why ESG considerations are becoming relevant in macroeconomic discussions, despite traditionally being seen as microeconomic concerns?

a) ESG principles can directly improve GDP figures and inflation targets

b) Consumer pressure is influencing firms and governments to integrate ESG objectives into broader economic policy

c) ESG policies are promoted across the economy by international central banks

d) Most ESG benefits are immediately measurable in national income accounts

e) ESG only affects multinational organizations, hence its macroeconomic relevance

4. Which of the following is a major challenge faced by firms when implementing ESG strategies?

a) ESG strategies normally require government approval before implementation

b) Investors tend to reject ESG principles due to ideological concerns

c) ESG investments often yield benefits outside the conventional financial reporting periods

d) ESG frameworks are generally standardized but costly to adhere to

e) Environmental strategies always lead to higher short-term profits but lower long-term profits

MEDIUM

5. In macroeconomic terms, why might absolute equality be seen as an unattractive or impractical societal goal?

a) It leads to a decrease in government intervention

b) It eliminates the need for taxation

c) It might disincentivize personal effort and achievement

d) It is inconsistent with long-run economic growth

e) It improves the accuracy of macroeconomic modelling

6. Why is accounting for diversity important when designing macroeconomic models?

a) It makes inflation forecasting more accurate

b) It simplifies aggregate supply and demand interactions

c) It allows policymakers to ignore wealth inequality

d) It enables models to reflect the heterogeneity that exist in real-world economies

e) It ensures all consumers behave identically in fiscal policy design

HARD

7. Discuss how input–output (IO) modelling can help policymakers and economists understand and promote the idea of the circular economy. In your answer, refer to the strengths of the IO model framework and explain how it can reflect the relationship between sectors in an economy.

8. Evaluate the role of government policy in the promotion of ESG practices. In your answer, consider both the limitations firms face when acting independently and the macroeconomic rationale for state intervention.

9. Explain how the three pillars of EDI – equality (or equity), diversity and inclusivity – can influence macroeconomic policy design and implementation. Discuss the challenges each presents and how macroeconomists might respond to them in theory and in practice.

Endnote

1. Thomas Piketty, Capital in the Twenty-first Century. Harvard University Press, 2014.

CHAPTER 17

Introduction to Intertemporal Macroeconomics

Chapter contents

At a Glance — Introduction to intertemporal macroeconomics

The issue

In real life the linkages that connect the macroeconomic variables are rather complex and seldom follow the basic structures suggested by macroeconomic theory. To connect the actual facts observed to the economic models requires some control for the time lags and multi-directional interdependencies. How do we adapt models to allow for these more intricate connections?

The understanding

In this chapter we introduce a formal algebraic method for dealing with macroeconomic flows between time. Accounting for the changing pattern in macroeconomic variables over time starts with the study of intertemporal macroeconomics.

The usefulness

Intertemporal macroeconomics allows us to consider agents' choices over time, connecting the concepts of an intertemporal budget constraint with the notion of consumer choice through a utility function. We consider the optimal choice of the private sector faced with a limited lifetime budget and close by encompassing the public sector to review the theory of Ricardian equivalence for policy analysis.

17.1 Introduction

Up until now, this book has focused on macroeconomic models that are static in nature. There is an assumption that changes over time do not matter for the model's predictions. The issue of changes over time are less important for the outcome of the major policy implications, but this is not necessarily a good reason to ignore them. As an example, consider the aggregate supply aggregate demand (AS/AD) model – equilibrium output depends on the levels of demand and supply in the economy, and changes over time are irrelevant for this outcome. If the level of demand changes over time, we would account for this with a shift in the demand schedule; what we have actually done is use the 'shift' to depict a new model with a new equilibrium. Accounting for changes over time using static models would mean using a series of models where equilibriums 'jump' from one period to another. The study of dynamics in macroeconomic modelling allows us to explain these jumps.

A natural question arises as to why these dynamics are interesting or even important. They are important because, in reality, macroeconomic variables are significantly time dependent; one period's consumption is closely connected to the next period; restricting our models to account for this connection makes them more life-like, better able to explain the data and avoids the important problem of model mis-specification.

Table 17.1 The dynamics of macroeconomic modelling

Macroeconomic Variable	Real life – dynamic behaviour
Consumption	Every period's consumption is strongly related to the next period; the consumer is habitual in spending.
Investment	Investment is volatile, so is less related to time. Investment is considered a leading indicator for forthcoming changes in the business cycle.
Government spending	Another habitual variable connected to the spending and tax decisions which determine government debt.

Consumption is a good example; remember in our Keynesian cross from Chapter 7, that we model consumption as an upward sloping line in consumption/output space. Consumption increases in income at a rate equivalent to the marginal propensity to consume, *mpc*.

$$C = a + mpc\left(Y^d\right)$$

This expression might be a sufficient explanation for the behaviour of consumption over time, though it is limited in its ability to match certain facts about consumption observed in real life from the dynamics displayed in the data – for example, the real life behaviour of habitual spending. What we consume day to day has elements that are unlikely to change as much as the change in income exactly.

What we see in the time series for aggregate consumption is a smoothness from period to period; we can adapt our model to replicate this 'inertia'. We can model consumption as a function of itself in the previous period:

$$C_t = hC_{t-1} + \varepsilon_t$$

The parameter which describes the smoothness of the path of consumption is captured by the constant *h*, which we can also think of as the structural parameter that captures the 'habits' of consumers in the model. If *h* is close to unity, then we can surmise that consumption is close to constant, or doesn't change over time.

Consumption is not the only variable that has a significant relationship with time, or linkages with other variables. Investment tends to act as a leading indicator for economic activity and we could specify this in a model with output being dependent on investment, but only in a previous 'lagged' period. Government spending can also be specified as dependent on the spending and borrowing decisions made by the government in each period. In this chapter, and to keep things simple, we will focus on the paths of consumption and government spending. We will do so in a two-period model that represents the early and later years across a lifetime. Consumers choose what to spend and save in the first period and spend those savings in the later period; governments borrow in period one but have to repay that debt in period two.

In this chapter we look more carefully at the dynamic interdependencies of the macroeconomic variables and explain the importance of the flows which belie the transmission of shocks and economic policy into the real economy. Understanding these time-dependent relationships completes our intermediate understanding of the science of macroeconomics. We will draw comparison between the static IS/LM model and our first understanding of dynamics in consumption and the government budget.

We introduce the two-period model, the simplest way to introduce dynamics, so that we can build behavioural equations for the household and the government. We refer to these behavioural building-blocks as the private and public budget constraints, which we can consolidate for the economy as a whole. Finally, we derive the decisions for the consumer by optimizing utility, given a budget constraint. and show that the government choices across periods are inconsequential for the economy over the lifetime span.

Learning Outcomes

By the end of this chapter you should be able to:

- Understand the importance of time as a determining factor of key macroeconomic variables.
- Model macroeconomic flows into mathematical expressions.
- Compare and contrast two alternative approaches to modelling the macroeconomic economy.
- Build and use a two-period macroeconomic model to understand consumer behaviour in the light of fiscal policy choices.

17.2 A dynamic approach to the goods market

Up until now, the only way we have been able to account for changes over time is through additional equilibriums that can jump around from one period to the next. We depict these jumps as 'shifts' in our schedules or curves in two-dimensional diagrams. Each period is represented by a separate model, which we can think of as a series of photographs of the economy or economic sector taken over time. These shifts have allowed us to explain the effects from economic shocks and economic policy. Intertemporal macroeconomics allows us to gain a more exact understanding of these equilibrium jumps, using a mathematical structure that maps out the dynamics more precisely.

Why dynamics matter for macroeconomic modelling

Throughout this text we have taken time to consider different approaches towards modelling the macroeconomic markets – for example, our treatment of the labour market in Chapter 10 Section 2, where we compare both a static approach and a dynamic perspective. The way that macroeconomic variables flow across time and into one another gives a deeper insight into the condition of the markets which they help to represent and can inform more targeted and more efficient economic policy. Sticking with the labour market, remember that the variable unemployment can be viewed in a static way, as a stock measured at one period in time, or as a rate of change which describes how the variable is moving and in which direction. Both perspectives provide us with different information; that is, 'unemployment is currently standing at 10,000 workers' or 'unemployment has risen by 5% in just one month'. From this example, we can see that the dynamics are just as important as the current picture or state of the level.

EXAMPLE 17.1

Real world example: Intertemporal effects in the UK 2008

The economy of the United Kingdom is hit disproportionately by a significant negative liquidity shock emanating from the global financial crisis of 2008. We discuss the initial shock, dynamic response and intertemporal effects below:

Initial shock

A sizeable negative liquidity shock brings financial institutions close to collapse leading to a sharp contraction in commercial bank lending. Lower business investment and consumer confidence contribute towards the deepest recession in the UK since World War II.

Dynamic response

Falling output causes a reduction in consumption, further reducing aggregate demand, which itself leads to lower output and higher unemployment; a classic negative demand-side feedback loop. Despite a monetary expansion from the Bank of England, consumption remained subdued.

Intertemporal effects

A key reason behind the slow recovery for consumption was the forward-looking nature of consumers. Fearing a prolonged economic slump, many consumers chose to save recovered incomes and delay expenditure. This highlights how consumption depends on a number of factors, including time itself. **Dynamic models** need to incorporate intertemporal choice decisions to make more accurate economic predictions.

Dynamic Model: An economic model that accounts for changes in variables over time. We can spot these mathematically, by the use of number or 't' subscripts attached to the variables in the structural equations.

There is another reason why dynamics are so important – macroeconomic variables are interdependent upon one another. A movement in one variable will most likely cause movements in other variables, sometimes simultaneously and sometimes in a lagged or delayed way. As an example, we would expect firms to offload workers during an economic slump, but it is important to notice how this happens exactly. First of all demand will shrink, a firm's production will fall, and then after a while when the demand does not recover, the firm will realize that it has to reduce the number of employees. From this example, we can imagine why unemployment tends to fall a few periods 'after' a fall in output. By understanding this behaviour a macroeconomist can make the prediction that unemployment will react in a lagged way to a change in economic activity. Understanding the intricate dynamics of a macroeconomy provides us with very useful predictions and facilitates better advice to policymakers.

Comparing the IS/LM and intertemporal frameworks

Up to now we have considered the AS/AD and IS/LM family of macroeconomic models. Both models are static by nature – they represent a picture of the economy with time held still. This assumption could be considered reasonable if the question that we are asking the model is not dependent on the underlying dynamics of the macroeconomic linkages in an economy. However, if we are looking for more detail and consider that dynamics are important for our economic question, then time should not be overlooked. Here we focus on the main differences between the IS/LM class of models and the intertemporal frameworks. In Table 17.2 we compare the structures of the different approaches using the goods market.

Table 17.2 Static vs intertemporal approaches

Approach	Basic structure
Static	$Y = C + I(r) + G$ $C = a + b(Y - T)$ $I(r) = c - dr$ $G = \overline{G} \quad T = \overline{T}$
Intertemporal	$C_1 = Y_1 - S_1$ $C_2 = Y_2 + (1 + r)S_1$ $G_1 = T_1 + B_1$ $G_2 = T_2 - (1 + r)B_1$

For the **static model** set up we can see that time does not feature in the relationship between state variables; the relationship between Y, C and G is governed by the structural parameters a, b, c and d. On the other hand, the intertemporal setup allows for interdependence of variables across time where saving, S, and government borrowing, B, can affect the values of variables such as C and G in the future. What happens in one period matters for the next. This is the reason that the intertemporal models are better suited to applications that use time series data, though notice the lack of structural parameters in the second case; here we have simplified the sensitivities to unity, but we could specify them as otherwise as we did for the habit parameter earlier.

Static Model: An economic model where time is assumed constant and where we are concerned with how one variable reacts to a change in another.

The intertemporal model differs to the standard static setups in three key ways. First, the model allows for a timeframe; here we consider the simplest case of just two periods. Second, the agents in the model can make decisions based on their preferences and the constraints that they face. They aim to maximize their lifetime consumption and utility – bundles that achieve higher consumption levels are generally considered better. Finally, decisions made today are set up to constrain the choices available to agents in the future, in the same way that constraints affect our choices in real life.

17.3 Intertemporal choices in a two-period model

Here, we introduce the option choices available to the consumer (which makes up our private sector) and to the government (which makes up our public sector). The model is set in two periods; the first period is the early period, for instance while the consumer is young, and the second period is the later period, for instance while the consumer is old. This assumption is rather limiting as we can imagine many periods in our lifetimes, but having two periods is sufficient to demonstrate our important results.

The private sector budget constraint

We make the further assumptions that the agents in our model are rational, that is, that more is good, and that all income is spent exactly over the complete lifetime of the agents. An agent can spend more or less than their income in each period by borrowing or saving. For a net borrower any borrowing in Period 1 has to be repaid with interest in Period 2. Likewise, for a net saver, any saving made in Period 1 has to be spent in Period 2. Let us begin by describing the choices open to the consumer in terms of income, saving and consumption across the two periods. The consumer's choice options can be written algebraically across the two periods as follows.

The consumer has income Y_1 in Period 1 which can either be consumed in whole, or in part, the remainder being saving:

$$Y_1 = C_1 + S_1$$

writing in terms of saving:

$$S_1 = Y_1 - C_1$$

Further, we can write out the choice for Period 2, that consumption is made up of income in Period 2 plus any saving (minus any borrowing) made in Period 1.

$$C_2 = Y_2 + (1 + r)S_1$$

Notice that both periods are connected by the variable S_1, as such we can combine them using substitution of S_1, to find a lifetime budget constraint:

$$C_1 + \frac{C_2}{(1+r)} = Y_1 + \frac{Y_2}{(1+r)}$$

This relation tells us that the present discounted value of lifetime consumption must be equal to the present discounted value of income. All income (wealth) must be spent over the lifetime. The right-hand side of the equation also gives us the maximum wealth available to spend, which we can think of as potential wealth, depicted by the intercept at *v* in the following figure:

In Figure 17.1 we can see the problem posed by the constraint laid out in a diagram. Here we are comparing the consumption choices available to the consumer over the lifetime of both periods, when young and when old. The consumer has the following choices: to consume all of Y_1 and the discounted equivalent of Y_2 in the first period (W), or all income from both periods in the second period (potential wealth, V), or anything in between. We can also see the special case of the decision to consume at A, where the consumer spends exactly the income received in each period.

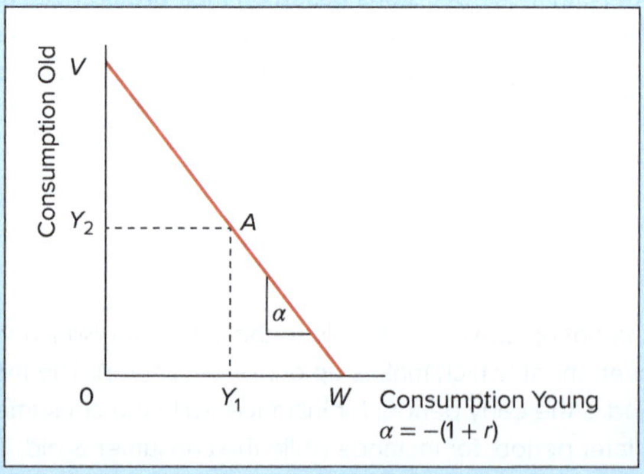

Figure 17.1 The budget constraint for the consumer

The choice of consumption between the two periods will depend on the consumer's preference set. Some consumers are less cautious and are prepared to borrow, and some are more comfortable when saving. We can imagine a sensible strategy – to borrow when current income is much lower than future income – though it is important to stress that the decision is made by the consumer based on individual preferences.

EXERCISE 17.1

Imagine the case of a football player in the premier league who has managed to agree a contract with one of the best ranked teams in the league year on year. Use the knowledge you have acquired up until now to map the player's typical preferences on the budget constraint in Figure 17.1.

This is a convenient point at which to delve a little deeper into the mathematics surrounding the choices available to the consumer. We can derive an expression to capture the path of consumption in our model. To do this, we solve the private sector lifetime budget constrain for C_2 and then differentiate with respect to C_1 to obtain the slope of the constraint, which is also a measurement of how consumption is changing across periods. Solving the lifetime budget for C_2, we get:

$$C_2 = (1 + r)Y_1 + Y_2 - (1 + r)C_1$$

Then differentiating to find the slope of the budget constraint:

$$\delta C_2 / \delta C_1 = -(1 + r) = \alpha$$

You may not be surprised to learn that the slope of the budget constraint is just the relative difference between initial wealth W and potential wealth V which comes from the mark-up due to the interest rate. We can see clearly that the path of consumption depends on the interest rate.

The public and consolidated budget constraints

The government finances government spending via two channels: receipts from taxation T and borrowing through the issuance of government bonds B^G. This reality presents us with an algebraic relationship:

$$G_1 = T_1 + B_1^G$$

Government spending in Period 1 will be equal to financing of that spending, that is, the taxation received in the same period plus finances raised through government bonds. Should the government run a surplus, then $B^G < 0$.

For Period 2, we have a similar relation that accounts for **discounting** across time:

Discounting: Allowing for the opportunity cost that comes from time. This is often most easily identified as the interest rate paid, or through a discount factor that measures an agent's preference to receive something earlier or later.

$$G_2 = T_2 - (1 + r) B_1^G$$

Government spending in Period 2 will be equal to the taxation receipts for the same period minus the borrowing from the previous period plus any interest that has accrued. At this stage it is worth highlighting the important assumption that the private sector and public sector borrowing rates of interest are the same.

We can combine the two previous relationships for government spending to derive a lifetime public sector budget constraint:

$$G_1 + \frac{G_2}{(1 + r)} = T_1 + \frac{T_2}{(1 + r)}$$

Government spending across time will always be equal to taxation in the long run. This is an important result, because it encourages us to re-evaluate fiscal policy. We discuss this further in our section on Ricardian equivalence later.

Going further, we can write the public sector budget constraint in terms of the government budget surplus ($T - G$) and deficit ($G - T$).

$$G_1 - T_1 = \frac{T_2 - G_2}{(1 + r)}$$

In words: the current value of the budget deficit will be equal to the future present discounted value of the budgets surplus.

Now that we have covered the topic of public sector budgets we can extend our schedules for the private sector so that they account for taxation. This is done easily by replacing income Y, with disposable income ($Y - T$) in the private sector lifetime budget constraint:

$$C_1 + \frac{C_2}{(1 + r)} = Y_1 - T_1 + \frac{Y_2 - T_2}{(1 + r)}$$

The present value of lifetime consumption must be equal to the present value of lifetime income – an intuitive proposition that reinforces that all income is consumed over the household's lifetime.

Finally, we can combine the private sector and public sector lifetime budget constraints to arrive at the consolidated national lifetime budget constraint:

$$C_1 + \frac{C_2}{(1 + r)} + G_1 + \frac{G_2}{(1 + r)} = Y_1 - T_1 + \frac{Y_2 - T_2}{(1 + r)} + T_1 + \frac{T_2}{(1 + r)}$$

which simplifies neatly to:

$$C_1 + \frac{C_2}{(1 + r)} + G_1 + \frac{G_2}{(1 + r)} = Y_1 + \frac{Y_2}{(1 + r)}$$

The present value of consumption and government expenditure will be equal to the present value of national wealth.

EXERCISE 17.2

Practise the algebraic steps to derive the expression for the lifetime public sector budget constraint, by combining the two relations for government spending in Periods 1 and 2.

Hint: Start by dividing the relation for government spending in Period 2 through by (1 + r); combine this with the expression for spending in Period 1.

17.4 Optimality and fiscal policy implications

Forward from here we discuss some important results from the **intertemporal** framework for macroeconomics, namely that we can now specify exactly how the consumer makes the rational consumption choice, with implications for personal taxation. We finish with a discussion on how we can use the framework to open the debate into fiscal policy effectiveness.

Intertemporal: In the context of dynamics, concerning the changes that are evident over time. Intertemporal models provide us with explanations of the dynamic relationship between structural variables. They are easily identified by the presence of numbered or '*t*' subscripts in the structural equations.

Constrained utility optimization

Like all consumers in real life, we make purchase decisions based on our ability to pay and our ability to pay is determined by our income. Of course, our ability to pay is not the only consideration; we have to want to make the purchase in the first place, it has to provide value. Our preference set helps us to make the choice decision over other competing priorities or wants. These priorities and considerations of value are modelled using the concept of utility. In a two-dimensional analysis we can map out consumption bundles made up of a mixture of two goods. In this context the two goods are consumption now and consumption later.

The preferences for these different bundles are mapped using indifference curves, such that each individual curve becomes a locus of points for which we are indifferent between consumption bundles. In an effort to satiate, a consumer will try to consume along the highest possible indifference curve while making a choice on how much to consume today (when young) and how much to consume tomorrow (when old).

In Figure 17.2 we can see these indifference curves diagrammatically, where the consumer would prefer to obtain consumption on the utility curve furthest away from the origin; in this case, I_3. Anywhere along the indifference curve, the consumer is indifferent between different combinations of consumption between when young (C_1) and when old (C_2). The indifference curve, then, measures a consumer's utility, which we can write implicitly in functional form in consumption across the two periods:

$$\text{Utility } U = U(C_1, C_2)$$

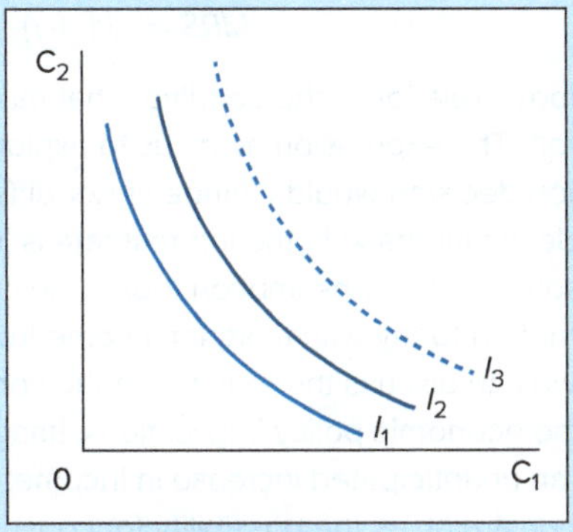

Figure 17.2 Indifference curves, mapping utility for intertemporal consumption

A key feature of the indifference curve is its slope, which also represents the consumer's marginal rate of intertemporal substitution (MRS). We can think of the MRS as the amount of future consumption we are happy to give up for more consumption today, and vice versa. To find the MRS, we can divide the change in utility after changes in C_1, by the change in utility after changes in C_2:

$$MRS = \frac{dU / dC_1}{dU / dC_2}$$

Optimal consumption is achieved at the point where the consumer maximizes utility bearing in mind the limits presented by the budget constraint. To maximize utility the consumer will choose the indifference curve the furthest away from the origin, a point where the two schedules are tangent to one another or where their slopes are equal. In Figure 17.3, we see this consumption decision precisely, as point *A*.

Optimal: The characteristic of a choice made to maximize utility within the boundaries of a limiting constraint.

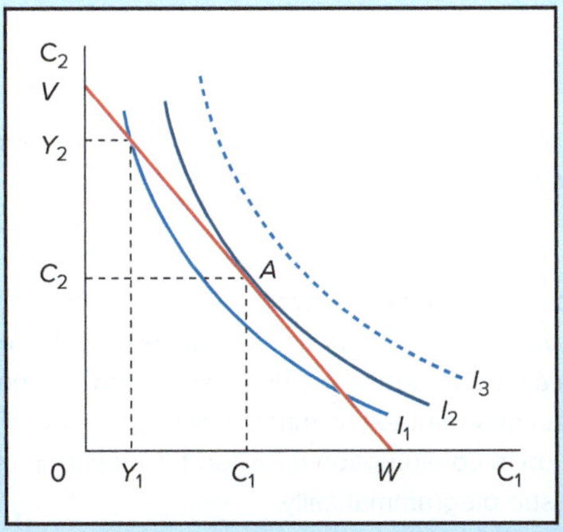

Figure 17.3 Combining the budget constraint and indifference curves

With the indifference curve I_1, we can see that the two consumption choices that use all available budget are given by the two points where the constraint and I_1 intersect. However, from I_1, the consumer can achieve higher utility without violating the budget, as point *A* on utility curve I_2. You can also see that I_3, although preferred by the consumer, is not achievable due to the limits placed by the constraint.

We can also express this algebraically. We know that at the point of optimal consumption the two schedules (the utility curve I_2 and the budget constraint *VW*) have the same slope (they are tangent to one another); so that $-(1 + r)$ must be equal to the slope of the indifference curve – the **marginal rate of substitution** (MRS).

Marginal Rate of Substitution: The amount we are prepared to give up to obtain one more unit of a substitute that is equally satisfying. We can think of this as our willingness to substitute one good for another.

$$MRS = -(1 + r)$$

The above relation is the condition that must be met for optimal consumption. The expression helps us to explore how the optimal consumption decision would change under different circumstances. For example, an increase in the interest rate is likely to lead the consumer to switch some of the consumption today into consumption tomorrow; it is more attractive to delay consumption today with a higher income from money saved.

Lastly and in this context, we can discuss the reaction of the consumer to a change in income, and from this draw some economic policy implications. Imagine from Figure 17.3 that we provide our consumer with an unanticipated increase in income; consequently there will be a right shift out for the budget constraint, as the possibility for consumption in both periods will increase also. Will the consumer consume more now, more later or increase both? Obviously this depends on the preferences of the consumer, but there is more that we can deduce than to identify these basic choices alone.

We can discuss two cases: a permanent rise in income and a temporary rise in income. For the case of a permanent increase in income, it is intuitive that the consumer will simply choose to consume more in both periods, knowing that the new income will be received in every period in the future. For the temporary increase, the consumer faces the disutility of a drop in income in the future. With this cost in mind, there is an incentive for the consumer to save some of the unanticipated windfall and minimize a fall in income in the future. There is a definite incentive to save in the first period for the case of a temporary increase; thus, not all of the income will be consumed, some will be saved.

What can we deduce from this analysis? That in order to encourage an increase in saving across society a government could use this result in policy formulation; by targeting net borrowers or savers or keeping the changes in income from taxation and changes to benefits unanticipated. We can go further than this and think about the way that government introduces policy – should the government announce policy in advance, or give forward guidance to reduce uncertainty? As an example, consider the case of an announcement of a decrease in future taxes. Armed with this knowledge the consumer may be induced to borrow, meaning that the policy will be less effective at changing wealth over immediate consumption.

The Ricardian equivalence result

In order to fully understand the effects of fiscal policy we can revisit our expression for the present value of national wealth:

$$C_1 + \frac{C_2}{(1 + r)} + G_1 + \frac{G_2}{(1 + r)} = Y_1 + \frac{Y_2}{(1 + r)}$$

National wealth available is consumed in two ways: by the private sector in the form of consumption and by the public sector in the form of government spending. Changes in government spending drive a wedge between private spending and national income. The consolidated lifetime budget constraint tell us that a fiscal expansion would be met by a reduction in consumption. The reduction in consumption is visited through an increase in taxation. Figure 17.4 highlights the issue diagrammatically.

With no government spending the private sector is on the budget line *VW*, and as government spending is introduced the budget line shifts inwards by exactly the same amount

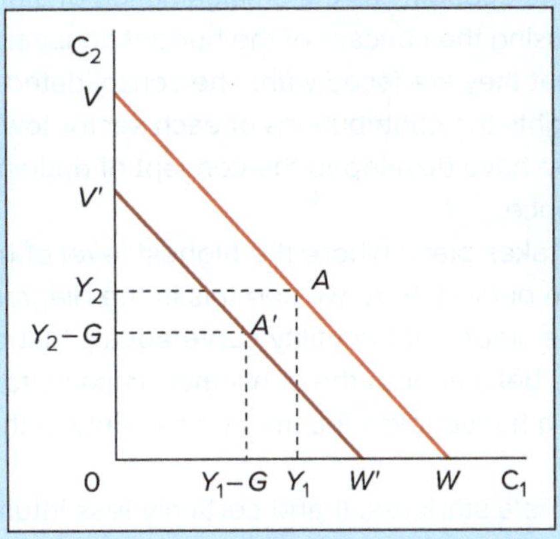

Figure 17.4 The budget constraint with government expenditure G

to V′ W′. Government spending is internalized by the private sector, meaning that it simply shifts wealth from the private sector (through taxation) to the public sector; it cannot affect the real economy.

An important result here is that the 'pattern' of government spending does not matter for national wealth either. If the government changes the timing of the expenditure – that is, higher spending with a higher deficit in Period 1, or lower spending with a lower deficit/surplus in Period 2 – the budget has to be settled over the lifetime in any case, and any disturbance caused by a change of pattern is simply internalized by the private sector.

As an example, imagine that the government attempts an economic expansion by increasing government spending – the private sector will know that taxes have to increase in the future and reduce spending accordingly; tax payers anticipate tax rises in the future and save to pay for them later. This result is called the Ricardian equivalence result. Fiscal policy is said to be ineffective upon the real economy and thus attempts to manipulate demand are futile.

What can we take away from this discussion on fiscal policy effectiveness? First, that the Ricardian equivalence result derives from a model whereby the sum of private and public wealth must be equal to nation wealth – the model is built upon a constraint. From this we can deduct that fiscal policy has no impact on the real economy, neither does the pattern of that impact over time – the private sector can see through the veil of government promises about public debt and expenditures.

EXERCISE 17.3

Think about the implications of Ricardian equivalence for the debate surrounding fiscal discipline or the government policy known as austerity, specifically as a method to restore economic growth.

17.5 Chapter summary: Putting it all together

In this chapter, we have discussed the subject of dynamics in macroeconomic modelling, why it is an important consideration, and drawn richer lessons from the extended macroeconomic analysis to encompass important features, displayed by key macroeconomic variables. Initially we have made a comparison between the static IS/LM framework and the two-period intertemporal explanation of the goods market. In the IS/LM framework, the impacts of policy are represented by shifts in equilibriums, whereas these movements are captured more precisely in the intertemporal model, which accounts for time.

We have also framed the economy as the amalgamation of a private and public sector, describing each sector by using the concept of the budget constraint, where the sectors are modelled by the choices that they are faced with. The consolidated budget constraint for the economy as a whole highlights the contributions of each sector towards national wealth. From these budget constraints we have developed the concept of optimality in consumption and the result of Ricardian equivalence.

Optimal consumption takes place where the highest level of utility is achieved against the constraint posed by the budget; here we see this in the diagrams without difficulty – optimality occurs where the slopes of the utility curve equals that of the consumer's budget constraint. Considering the behaviour of the consumer helps us to analyse economic policy, which involves changes in a household's income. Uncertainty in the path of income can induce private saving.

Ricardian equivalence is a stark result and certainly less intuitive than optimal consumption. Is it possible that consumers automatically internalize government spending so that it has no impact on economic activity across the lifetime? Looking a little deeper, the result becomes less surprising, especially when we are considering the lifetime effect. The Keynesians will use this result as evidence that governments can borrow money without impeding economic performance; higher interest rates paid by the government are simply received by the private sector that hold the bonds that finances the public debt in the first place. Looking even deeper, you might consider the financial market effects of a switch from equity into bonds. What are the consequences for the accumulation of capital against investment for the case of a fiscal expansion? This last consideration I will leave for your own economic research.

Assessment question

During the lockdown at the beginning of the global pandemic of 2020, the UK government announced a temporary increase in benefits for citizens claiming Universal Credit of £20 per week. With hindsight, use your knowledge to evaluate the policy decision on whether or not the government should have made the increase temporary or permanent.

Cases

The United Kingdom and the cost-of-living crisis (2022–2024)

Background

In the wake of the COVID-19 pandemic and during the Ukrainian war, the UK experienced a significant rise in inflation between 2022 and 2023. Prices for essentials like food and energy soared significantly. The Bank of England responded by raising interest rates aggressively to tackle inflation, increasing the policy rate from near-zero levels to over 5 per cent.

At the same time, the UK government altered its fiscal policy multiple times. In 2022, a new administration announced large-scale tax cuts (especially for higher earners), but these were quickly reversed due to market backlash. The expectation of rising debt levels raised bond yields for government debt, adding further to the prospect for government debt. By 2023 and 2024, the government had reversed its fiscal expansion by increasing taxes and reducing support payments. These measures were especially targeted at the working-age population.

These changes impacted households' intertemporal consumption decisions on how they chose to consume or save at the time (Period 1) versus the future (Period 2).

Applying the two-period intertemporal model

In this model, individuals decide how much to consume today versus tomorrow, based on:

- Current and expected future income.
- Interest rates (the cost/return of saving or borrowing).
- Current and future taxes.

Interest rate effects

As interest rates rose, borrowing became more expensive and saving became more rewarding. Households with mortgages saw their monthly repayments increase sharply. For UK households:

- Present consumption decreased, as more income was spent on debt repayment.
- Future consumption expectations were also adjusted, depending on their belief about how long the higher rates would last.

Meanwhile, savers (often older households) benefited from higher interest income and in some cases increased their present consumption slightly.

Tax changes

The reversal of 2022's tax cuts and later tax increases led to:

- A decline in disposable income, especially for middle-income workers.
- A negative wealth effect, as people anticipated higher future taxes or lower government transfers.

This discouraged both current consumption and future spending, as households became more cautious and saved more.

Consumption behaviour observed

- Lower-income households were especially squeezed: high inflation, rising mortgage or rent costs, and lower real wages led to decreased current consumption. Many relied on credit or savings available to them.
- Middle-income households reined in spending, delaying major purchases (like cars or holidays), and increased precautionary savings.
- Higher-income and older households, who may have benefited from higher interest rates on savings, were more stable in their consumption but still became more cautious due to economic uncertainty.

Summary of key insights

- Interest rate hikes reduced present consumption for borrowers, while increasing returns for savers.
- Tax increases reduced both present and expected future disposable income, causing households to save more and consume less.
- The two-period model helps us to explain how these macroeconomic policies (monetary and fiscal policy) impacted households differently based on their income, assets and age.

Questions

1. Why did rising interest rates lead to reduced consumption for some UK households but increased income for others?
2. How would an expected future tax increase affect a household's current consumption decisions in the two-period model?
3. How might a student loan borrower and a retired saver respond differently to interest rate increases?
4. What role does uncertainty (e.g., about future inflation or taxes) play in the intertemporal consumption decisions?

Problems

EASY

1. What is the main assumption underlying the Ricardian equivalence proposition?
   a) Taxes are distortionary
   b) Consumers are liquidity constrained
   c) Government spending is productive in the long run
   d) Consumers are forward-looking and internalize government budget constraints
   e) The Interest rate is constant over time

MEDIUM

2. In a standard two-period consumption model, individuals maximize utility by choosing a level of consumption for each period subject to an intertemporal budget constraint. Which of the following would cause the individual to consume more in the first period, holding everything else constant?
   a) An increase in the real interest rate
   b) A decrease in first-period income
   c) A temporary decrease in the interest rate
   d) A decrease in second-period income
   e) A preference for future consumption increases
3. In a two-period intertemporal model with perfect capital markets (common interest rate) and no uncertainty, if a consumer is initially a borrower and the interest rate increases, their optimal consumption plan will typically:
   a) Stay the same
   b) Shift towards more first-period consumption
   c) Shift towards more second-period consumption
   d) Become infeasible
   e) Lead to a government intervention
4. Suppose the government cuts taxes today but does not cut spending. According to Ricardian equivalence, how should rational consumers respond?
   a) Increase consumption today and forgo consumption tomorrow
   b) Save the tax cut to pay for future tax increases
   c) Reduce their labour supply accordingly
   d) Lobby for more government borrowing
   e) Spend the full amount of the tax cut today
5. Which of the following violates the assumptions needed for Ricardian equivalence to hold?
   a) Lump-sum taxation
   b) Consumers live forever or care about their heirs
   c) No credit market imperfections
   d) Consumers who cannot borrow
   e) Full information about fiscal policy

6. A representative consumer lives for two periods. Their income in the first period is £50,000 and in the second period is £60,000. The private and public sector share a common real interest rate of 10 per cent in each period. There are no taxes and they can borrow or lend at the interest rate.
   a) Write down the consumer's intertemporal budget constraint.
   b) Suppose they want to smooth their consumption perfectly across both periods. How much do they consume in each period?
7. Explain how a consumer decides on the optimal level of consumption in a two-period model. Discuss the role of the intertemporal budget constraint and how the interest rate influences the consumer's choices.

HARD

8. According to the concept of Ricardian equivalence, a temporary increase in government spending financed by borrowing, will:
   a) Increase private consumption permanently
   b) Leave lifetime private consumption unchanged
   c) Increase national income in both periods
   d) Reduce total savings in the economy
   e) Cause a budget surplus in the future
9. Discuss the Ricardian equivalence proposition. What are the key assumptions, and why might they not hold in practice? Give at least two examples of conditions that would cause deviations from Ricardian equivalence.

CHAPTER 18

Macroeconometrics

Chapter contents

At a Glance Macroeconometrics

The issue

All of the models we have covered in this textbook can provide us with policy implications – the policy analysis can be focused on specific policy types, such as fiscal policy, while others include monetary policy, trade policy, legislation, or even a mixture of these. This focus can help us to decide which model to use but how do we measure how well a particular model performs against the economic reality, or against its peers more generally?

The understanding

The answer lies in the data, or the reality of actual economic activity. Using observations of macroeconomic variables over time we can measure model performance using empirical analysis. By writing a model in terms of its dynamics we can match the model with the facts that are collected over time.

The usefulness

Matching a model with the data allows us to tailor the model to reflect the characteristics of a particular economy or event. Empirical analysis allows us to tailor fit a model for a specific purpose and provide the best predictions and thus advice available to the policymaker.

18.1 Introduction

Throughout this text we have introduced and explained numerous ways to represent the economy with macroeconomic models. These models are theoretical, meaning that they are borne from logic and ideas. This chapter introduces students to the idea of taking the model to the data. Models can be tested using macroeconomic time series data to see how they perform under real life conditions. Does the outcome, predicted by the macroeconomic model, stack up to the facts? How accurate is the theory? Using data to test a model is the best way to see how the model's predictions can be measured for accuracy over the passage of time.

The study of macroeconometrics uses a form of statistical analysis known as econometrics to test models in the area of macroeconomics specifically. Because our models are built to measure economy-wide issues, the data we use in macroeconometrics is also of the aggregate variety. As an example, if we were to test the framework known as the aggregate production function, we would be interested in testing it against the macroeconomic time series data for output Y, capital K and labour L. Using data for this purpose allows us to assign parameter values to the model and these parameter values can represent the characteristics of an economy.

Once we have taken the time to measure the parameters of a model for a specific economy, we are then in a position to provide much more information to policymakers. We can supply historical averages or trends, we can provide more accurate information about the relationships between the macroeconomic variables and with all this done we can also make predictions about the future, or provide scenario type analysis. For example, we are able to determine characteristics such as the natural rate of unemployment, identify linkages between variables such as government debt and economic growth and provide 'what if' scenarios to policymakers.

A note of caution here: economies are notoriously complex to model exactly with multiple one- and two-way flows between variables that make up their complex interdependencies. Attempting to model and capture these intricate complexities is no small task – a bit like trying to map out the exact workings of a human brain! Some compromise is inevitable and that is why the economist will fall back on the convenient tool of simplification through limiting assumptions. Econometrics as a science itself relies on the fundamental assumption that all dependent variables are driven by variables that are independently determined. What does this mean exactly? It means that an independent variable (that sits on the right-hand side of any equation) has evolved exogenously to the dependent variable (on the left-hand side of an equation). This is called the assumption of exogeneity and is crucial for the accurate and unbiased estimation of the model's parameters, that we have discussed above. The act of matching data with the algebraic structural form of a model is termed a 'regression'. The regression is the procedure of estimating a model using data with the aim of identifying the strengths and directions of the relationships between the variables for a specific set of data.

Using the algebraic structure of a model we can estimate the parameters that can be applied to a specific economy in a number of ways, by simply estimating the equations simultaneously or in a more sophisticated way which allows for dynamic linkages over time and between the variables under investigation. One way in which we can attempt to account for the more dynamic linkages between macroeconomic variables is through the analysis of causality. As an example, we might be interested to know how consumption and income are related between periods. To account for time in this way we can use the analysis of causality, a way of testing data for dependencies on values of itself and other variables over the course of time; estimating these causal relationships can provide us with better information on the time that policy will take to receive due impact and how long these impacts are likely to last.

In this chapter we focus on time series analysis due to the nature of the macroeconomic variables that we make use of – macroeconomic variables are measured over time and so this makes perfect sense. We will begin by looking at how we can use time series data to make some preliminary data analysis, plotting the data and making some factual observations; this is probably the most useful part of any macroeconometric analysis. Once this is complete, we will learn how to construct a basic simple linear regression from a theoretical structure, estimate a model's coefficients, test the model itself and then draw inference from the results that we obtain. Lastly we will discuss the issue of causality using a model made up of multiple structures in an attempt to deal with the problem posed by the assumption of exogeneity.

Learning Outcomes

By the end of this chapter you should be able to:

- Understand the importance and purpose of testing a macroeconomic model using time series data.
- Articulate the challenges presented by the problem of exogeneity for the accurate estimation of a macroeconomic model.
- Build a simple linear regression model to estimate the parameters that reflect the characteristics of an economic structure.
- Compare and contrast the approaches that can be applied to overcome endogeneity issues in successful estimation.
- Design a regression that can test for one- or two-way causality between two specific macroeconomic variables.

18.2 Macroeconomic time series data

Macroeconomic time series are made up of the observations of real life macroeconomic variables recorded over time. Examples include national income, economic growth, unemployment, inflation and the exchange rate. The time series provide us with an indication of the condition of the economy through the three markets: the market for goods and services, the labour market and the market for money. The ordering of these observations over time allows us to construct profiles for the variables, which we can then plot, either separately or together with other profiles of selected variables that we may choose to analyse. The profile of these time series can help us to understand the behaviour of the economy and its reaction to economic events and policy. We can observe the cyclical patterns that are driving economic activity and draw some predictions about how these variables are connected; in other words, we can look for dynamic interdependencies or **correlations** between variables.

The data from macroeconomic times series also allows us to measure the appropriateness of structures in macroeconomic models. Something we can think of as 'taking the model to the data' for theoretical validation. We can estimate the sensitivities of the components in a model so that it reflects the characteristics of an economy we are trying to represent. With this task completed we can even use the model to make predictions about the consequences for the after-effects of policy and economic shocks. The techniques that we can employ may range from a simple ordinary least squares (OLS) estimation to a more sophisticated structural vector **autoregression** (SVAR) approach, depending on how deeply we want to analyse the data. Whichever empirical techniques we employ, it is important to bear in mind the assumptions that we will have to accept to make the analysis meaningful. More advanced techniques may require the relaxation of certain assumptions and the adoption of others.

Correlation: A measure of how closely two variables are related in linear terms. If the relationship is linear then it is constant over time.

Autoregression: An algebraic representation where a variable is expressed as a sequence over time. We use autoregressive relations in our dynamic models, where variables carry a t (time) subscript.

Aside from the challenges mentioned in the introduction, the use of time series data to estimate the parameters for a macroeconomic model normally requires some preparation, careful assessment and possible transformation. Macroeconomic data may already contain attributes that should need to be treated so that they are suitable for accurate estimation. These include pre-existing trends, seasonal impacts (from recurring calendar events) and other impacts such as an increase in prices. We can ensure that the data is stationary to remove time trends, adjust data for seasonal effects and use real variables to control for inflation. Lastly, it is also possible that data may suffer from measurement errors, the need for harmonization across countries or from highly unusual observations. These kinds of issues can be picked up in a preliminary data analysis, or through careful visual observation of time series plots.

Preliminary data analysis

Any macroeconomic investigation should also involve a thorough initial examination of the data. This might be carried out using time series plots or through basic correlations between the variables of interest. Time series plots can reveal obvious flaws in the data, such as seasonal effects or the presence of trends. Seasonal effects will give the profile of a time series a jagged look, whereas an upward trend will appear as a steady increase over time – a problem referred to as serial correlation, or the presence of a **unit root**. In the case of a unit root, the data will also need to be made stationary to remove the trend to prepare the variable for successful estimation.

Unit Root: A characteristic of a time series where the data is mean reverting, meaning that it evolves around a stochastic trend or can be modelled as a random walk with drift.

EXAMPLE 18.1

Real world example: Tossing a coin and unit roots in time series

Imagine we are tossing a coin and recording the results as a way of constructing a time series of observations. Experience will tell us that the series can go in any direction for any length of time. We may have a series of heads, followed by an instance of tails, followed by another series of heads.

Problems with unit roots

The profile generated will have no particular direction and will display the properties of a classic random walk. The mean and variance will change over time, meaning that basic assumptions surrounding empirical techniques are violated and the series is non-stationary or displays evidence of a unit root.

Real world example

In the real world we see the traded prices of assets, such as stocks and commodities, appear heavily reliant on their past values, in these cases they are difficult to predict and any inference we draw from a statistical analysis is risky.

The preliminary data analysis acts as an important bridge between the collection of data and successful estimation of the model. The process should involve some checks for completeness of data (i.e., no missing observations), possible data errors, inconsistencies or extraordinary observations caused by one-off exogenous events. The impacts of exogenous events, for example COVID-19, may be very short lived or might take time to dissipate. Such events might even cause structural changes to the economy over time. These kinds of data issues can significantly distort the results from a model estimation, which can lead to misinference. Another consideration is that of the frequency of the data collected; consistency is necessary especially if the data is required for the estimation of a model. If the variable being estimated is quarterly, then it makes sense that all the predetermined variables are collected or converted to the same frequency. It is worth bearing in mind that converting data to a lower frequency will involve the loss of information – data will appear smoother in a time series plot as a result, and intra-annual dynamics will be lost in the process.

A preliminary data analysis should include the visual inspection of time series plots, histograms or scattergrams. These plots will provide early indications of any problems that may be present or any treatments required to deal with trends, cycles, seasonality, volatility clusters or structural break points in the data. Once identified, an analysis will require more detailed scientific checks, before fixes can be applied. As an example, the visual identification of a trend will require an official test such as an Augmented Dickey–Fuller Test for a stochastic trend, something known as a unit root in the data. The trend needs to be removed so that the data is stationary so that the mean and variance are constant over time. An official test can confirm the existence of a unit root and determine whether the data requires treatment before it can be used for the purpose of an estimation. Common treatments for this problem include the differencing of data or transformation into growth rates through the use of natural logs.

Descriptive data statistics and analysis

Another way to quickly identify any problems that we might encounter when estimating a macroeconomic model is by collecting a report on the data descriptive statistics. The statistics will quickly summarize any underlying characteristics of any time series data. The values of the statistics can provide: a central tendency, such as the mean; the dispersion of observations, such as the variance; and general distributions of the sample as a whole. A successful process will provide a preliminary understanding that can be attained before a more complex econometric estimation. Key measures that should be utilized are: the mean, median and mode for central tendency; variance and standard deviation for dispersion; and skewness and kurtosis for the shape of the distribution of the data as a whole. As an example, we might use the mean across subsamples to identify episodes of price instability; and the variance of output to identify periods of economic turbulence.

In the context of macroeconometrics, descriptive statistics might also help us to investigate relationships between macroeconomic variables. Correlation matrices can help to identify the direction and strength of linear relationships between macroeconomic variables that we find specified in macroeconomic theory – for example, the unemployment rate and the rate of inflation specified in the Phillips curve. Where this fails we can take the analysis further by controlling for more dynamic linkages, perhaps by adding time lags to a regression or other variables that might be part of the interdependencies between parts of a real life economy. Identifying correlations can also help with correct variable selection during the regression design process.

Further to the use of correlograms, we can also plot independent and dependent time series together to make a visual inspection for both lagged and synchronous co-movements and richer dynamic interdependencies. A visual inspection can reveal possible relationships that will not show up in basic linear regressions, which we can later test for in a more scientific way through the use of vector autoregressive models or theoretical structures like dynamic general stochastic equilibrium models (DSGEs). A visual inspection may also reveal anomalies in our collected data, such as outliers of one-off economic events that may need to be controlled for so that structural changes can be identified and be included in the investigation.

Overall, a thorough descriptive analysis will minimize the possibility of a faulty interpretation of the results obtained from an empirical regression, something we sometimes refer to as statistical misinference. This exercise serves as a critical foundation in empirical macroeconomic research, guiding the transition from raw data to normative policy implications and advice.

18.3 Simple linear regressions

A simple linear regression is a statistical procedure to examine the relationship between dependent and independent economic variables. That relationship between variables has both direction and strength and a linear simple regression can provide early indications of the nature of that relationship, the foundations of which will lie in the data that we use. The simple linear regression marks a first step before the use of more complex methods that can account for richer dynamic or non-linear relationships.

The simple linear model

The simple model is a first order straight line relationship between two or more variables. In the most simple case we can specify the model algebraically:

$$Y = \beta_0 + \beta_1 X + \varepsilon$$

Here, Y represents the dependent (response) variable, X is the independent (predictor) variable, β_0 is the intercept (where the fitted line will intersect the vertical axis), β_1 is the estimated parameter representing the strength the effect of X upon Y and ε is the allowance for the difference between the estimated line and the actual observation from the data – this difference is called the error term. Remember that not all data observations will sit on the estimated line – the line can only ever be a best fit, not an exact fit – so inevitably there will nearly always be a gap between the fitted line and the actual observations. We can also think of the error terms as accounting for variation not explained by the model.

The model has assumptions – first, that the relationship is linear (straight line); secondly, that the error terms are distributed normally around a zero mean and that the variance in those errors is constant (homoscedasticity), or evenly spread over the sample; lastly, that the error terms are independent of one another.

In Figure 18.1 we can see this graphically; the line, estimated using our simple linear regression, is plotted against the actual observations of coincidences between the variables, the crosses. The line estimated is the 'best fit', but as we can see, there is rarely a case of the observations being on the line itself. These gaps are called the errors (residuals) from the estimation. The fitted regression line is 'best fit' because it minimizes the difference between the observation values and the predicted values from the model (the errors).

As an example, imagine that Variable 1 is in fact the time in between observations of Variable 2, in this case Figure 18.1 reverts to a time series plot. The fitted line helps us to visualize and perhaps investigate for an upward trend in Variable 2 over time. The process of

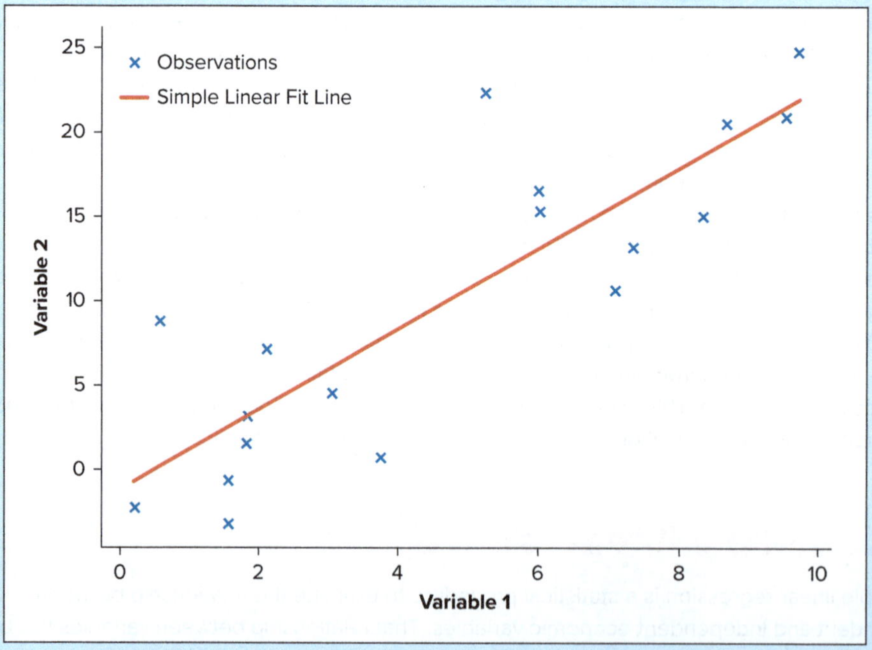

Figure 18.1 A fitted line from a simple regression model plotted with actual observations

carrying out a formal test for this upward trend in the data can begin with the method of ordinary least squares, which we will now go on to discuss. Despite the simplicity of this technique the simple linear procedure is useful as part of any estimation strategy because it provides us with our first scientific measurements beyond the preliminary data analysis as part of an overall empirical investigation.

EXERCISE 18.1

Assumptions for ordinary least squares

Imagine that in Figure 18.1 you can see uneven clustering of the observations that lie above and below the fitted red line. Which assumption of the simple linear regressions model might this violate?

Estimating the model coefficients

To estimate our simple linear model we can employ the method of ordinary least squares (OLS); under the assumptions of the model, we can estimate the value of the **coefficients** β_0 (the intercept of our fitted line) and β_1 (the slope of our simple linear fit line). The ordinary least squares method minimizes the sum of the squared errors (the residual distance between the observations and the fitted line). The reason that the errors are squared is that we can compare the distance evenly regardless if the error is above (positive) or below (negative) the fitted line; positives and negatives are treated equally as distances. It makes sense that this method provides the best fit with the errors minimized in this way.

Coefficients: An estimated constant that can be applied to the beginning of an independent variable to reflect the strength of its impact on the dependent variable.

From our algebraic form of the simple model we can write the estimated slope of our line as:

$$\widehat{\beta}_1 = \frac{\sum_{i=1}^{n}[(x_i - \overline{x})(y_i - \overline{y})]}{\sum_{i=1}^{n}[(x_i - \overline{x})^2]}$$

and our intercept as:

$$\widehat{\beta}_0 = \overline{y} - \widehat{\beta}_1 \overline{x}$$

both $\overline{y}$ and $\overline{x}$ represent the means of the dependent and independent variables respectively. The slope $\widehat{\beta}_1$ tells us how much Y is expected to change after a one unit increase in the variable X, and the intercept $\widehat{\beta}_0$ tells us how much the variable Y will be when the value of X is zero. Together the two values fully identify the model that we originally estimated, allowing us to make predictions outside the sample of the observations taken.

Once the coefficients $\widehat{\beta}_0$ and $\widehat{\beta}_1$ are estimated, we can move on to assess how well the model fits the data using especially designed tests. The most common way to test the goodness of fit is by using the R^2 measure, also known as the coefficient of estimation, and also by plotting the residuals. The goodness of fit R^2 test statistic indicates the proportion of the variance on the dependent variable explained by the independent variable in a model. A higher value of R^2 indicates a better fit, though the power of the test is relatively weak because it cannot measure the level of causation.

Interpreting the results and basic hypothesis testing

The collection of coefficients obtained from an empirical estimation are often referred to as 'the results'. Once we have the results we can make some scientific interpretation of the values by conducting a **hypothesis test**. The hypothesis test will determine the level of statistical significance of the model.

Hypothesis Test: A statistical process used to evaluate a proposal (hypothesis) about a parameter of a model that has been estimated empirically.

The most commonly used test involves testing the slope coefficient $\widehat{\beta}_1$. To do this we need two hypotheses; the null hypothesis and the alternative hypothesis. The null hypothesis (H_0) is the proposal that the estimated slope coefficient $\widehat{\beta}_1 = 0$; In other words; that there is no relationship between the variables estimated (*x* and *y*). The alternative hypothesis (H_A) asserts all else, that is, that $\widehat{\beta}_1 \neq 0$, indicating a significant linear relationship between *x* and *y*.

To test these hypotheses we can use a *t* test of the form:

$$t = \frac{(\widehat{\beta}_1 - 0)}{\text{s.e.}(\widehat{\beta}_1)}$$

where s.e.($\widehat{\beta}_1$) is the standard error of the estimated slope coefficient. Notice that the hat version of the coefficients is the value obtained from the estimation. The resulting value for the *t* test is then compared to a critical value from the *t*-distribution or more often assigned a probability value for significance. For example, if the chosen significance level is, say 5 per cent, then we would reject the null hypothesis of no statistically significant relationship.

Another way to interpret the results obtained from an estimation is through an interpretation of the value of the slope itself. For each one unit increase in *X*, the dependent variable *Y* changes by $\widehat{\beta}_1$ units, assuming *ceteris paribus*. The intercept might be less useful, but helps us to analyse exogenous changes which can result in upward shifts of the fitted line, or through structural breaks in the data.

To add a level of robustness to our analysis and to appreciate the uncertainty of parameter estimates, we might also consider making use of confidence intervals for the estimated parameter, often presented through a range of values within which the slope of the fitted line most likely lies.

Finally, the use of residual plots and test for normality can help to check that the assumptions of the model have not been violated. If the plots of the residuals show patterns or skewness, then this may indicate that the model is misspecified or that some transformation is required.

18.4 Multiple linear regressions

Not all theoretical relations can be expressed as simple relations between two variables, for example, the income identity $Y = C + I + G$ has a total of four – *Y* the dependent and *C*, *I* and *G* the independent variables. These kinds of structures require estimation in multiple dimensions, and can help us to gain insight from more complex relationships in macroeconomic data. Beyond the simplification of linear relationships we can employ more advanced techniques such as **Structural Vector Autoregressions** (SVARs) and **Granger causality** testing.

Vector Autoregression Model: A statistical model built to capture the dynamic relationships of multiple variables over time. Past, present and future values of variables can be included in a simultaneous estimation.
Granger causality: A statistical concept that can be used to test if one macroeconometric time series can be predicted using the time series properties of another variable.

More than one independent variable

We can use multiple linear regression (MLR) models to show how one continuous variable changes in response to multiple independent variables, which we can think of as the collection of driving forces that lay behind changes in the variable under investigation (dependent variable). For a dependent variable *Y* and several independent factors ($X_1, X_2, X_3, \ldots, X_n$) we can write the MLR model as follows:

$$Y = \beta_0 + \beta_1 X_1 + \beta_2 X_2 + \ldots + \beta_n X_n + \varepsilon$$

Here, the intercept β_0 is the usual intersection of the vertical axis; remember this model is in multiple dimensions so the value is determined where 'all' other variables are set to zero. The slope variables β_1 to β_n are the coefficients which determine the impact on *Y* from a one-unit change in the respective variables ($X_1, X_2, X_3, \ldots, X_n$). Remember that error term ε captures the residuals from the model estimation, or the distance between the fitted line and the actual observations. With a multiple linear estimation equation such as this we can investigate how macroeconomic variables are impacted by multiple factors.

Key assumptions of the MLR model:

- **Linearity: The true relationship between variables is linear**
- **Independent errors: There is no relation between errors**
- **Homoscedasticity: Constant variance (equal spread) of error terms**
- **No multicollinearity: Independent variables are not closely related**

EXAMPLE 18.2

Real world example: Government spending and UK output 2015–23

During the COVID-19 pandemic the UK government increased spending significantly to mitigate the effects of the forced lockdowns on UK GDP.

Economic question

The data collected over the preceding period can be used to investigate how powerful the effect of the new spending was on economic activity. We can use time series data to analyse this impact empirically.

Approach

After some preliminary investigation involving time series plots and tests for stationarity we can carry out a simple linear regression between the two variables. A positive and statistically significant slope would suggest that increased government spending boosts GDP.

To make the analysis more robust and to capture dynamic effects, an economist might then construct an SVAR, involving more variables (e.g., inflation). Such analysis allows policymakers to understand the timing, magnitude and longevity of the impacts from policy. This ensures that policy implications from the analysis are grounded from evidence and not just theory.

EXERCISE 18.2

Assumptions of multiple linear regression

You plot two independent variable in a correlogram and you notice a close one-to-one relationship (observations are concentrated around the 45 degree line). What characteristic might be indicated here, and what, if any, model assumption might be violated?

Granger causality testing

The SVAR approach relies on some prior beliefs about the underlying linkages acting out in the economy. Those linkages have a direction and so it is a worthwhile exercise to test that direction as accurately as possible. The simple Keynesian model specifies income as a function of consumption in the income identity, but also that the consumption itself is dependent on income. Setting up the causal chain correctly is often important if we want to map out the macroeconomic linkages accurately, and obtain a successful model.

Granger causality testing can help us to determine the most likely directions of how one variable affects another, and which direction that the effect takes. It cannot determine true causality in the philosophical sense, but it can provide a predicted causality based on the data we have made use of.

A variable, X, Granger causes a variable Y if the past values of X contain information that helps to predict the future values of Y over and above the information that is already present in the past values of Y. More formally we set up the following two models:

The restricted model (without X)

$$Y_t = a_0 + a_1 Y_{t-1} + a_2 Y_{t-2} + \ldots + a_n Y_{t-n} + \varepsilon_t$$

The unrestricted model (with X)

$$Y_t = a_0 + a_1 Y_{t-1} + \ldots + a_n Y_{t-n} + \beta_1 X_{t-1} + \ldots + \beta_n X_{t-n} + \varepsilon_t$$

The null hypothesis for this test is that X does *not* Granger cause Y, and if we can show that the unrestricted model is a better fit, then we can reject the null hypothesis and show that by including past values of X in our explanation of Y improves the prediction of the variable Y. To test for goodness of fit we can use an F test to compare the variances from the dataset, especially in the case where we have the models nested as versions of each other. A restricted version of the model is a special (nested) case of an unrestricted, wider, model. Officially, an F test is a statistical test used to determine how well an observed frequency distribution matches an expected frequency distribution. Goodness of fit is then measured by comparing the variability explained by the model to the unexplained variability from the errors.

In summary, Granger causality testing is a very useful way to check the direction of flows between macroeconomic variables – the dynamic linkages that we can discover help us to correctly identify the structures for macroeconomic models with better powers of prediction for successful policy analysis. Several important conditions must be met: the data used must be stationary, the lag length needs to be appropriate and care taken not to omit other important variables that may contain useful information about the linkages we are searching for. It is also important to appreciate that the presence of Granger causality does not necessarily prove or confirm a direct cause and effect relationship, but it does suggest that one variable contains predictive information about another variable.

18.5 Chapter summary: Putting it all together

Macroeconometrics is the subject surrounding empirical macroeconomic modelling – how we can measure the success or otherwise of our macroeconomic models and how we can use time series data to test our economic theory and find a strategy for a successful empirical investigation. We now understand the importance of time-ordered macroeconomic variables in our search for information about the economy – tracking economic trends, interpreting policy impact and for model validation. Recognizing patterns in our data helps us to design models that better reflect the real economy.

An important part of this process is the preliminary data analysis where we can visually inspect and examine time series plots of macroeconomic variables. We carry out basic checks for stationarity, interpret descriptive statistics and view distributions and central tendencies. Plots of our data can reveal important characteristics such as outliers, seasonal effects and structural breaks. This process avoids fundamental errors in our strategy that might not get picked up later during the more technical stages of our investigation.

Building on the preliminary analysis, we have examined the basic scientific tools that we can apply in our quest to take a macroeconomic model to the data. These tools range from the simple linear to the multiple linear regression approaches. Ordinary least squares can help us to quantify a relationship between two or more variables; we can extract that relationship and make further analysis through the intercept coefficient and slope of the fitted model. From the estimates we can take the analyses further by interpreting the slope coefficient of the fitted model, performing t-tests to check for significance and construct confidence intervals for our estimates.

Beyond the basic linear methods we take a more sophisticated approach, one that better matches the real life characteristics of time series data. The Structural Vector Autoregressive model allows us to encompass models with more complex structures, with theoretical equations that need to be estimated together as part of an economic system. The SVAR also allows us to make a detailed analysis of the effects that propagate from economic shocks. The Granger causality test complements our dynamic approach by helping us to identify the correct specifications for our more complex economic structures – how we specify the direction of relationships and the nature of the time lags in real life is important for model performance. A more accurate specification will lead to a model with more explanatory power and ultimately provide us more meaningful economic policy implications.

Assessment question

Using the Keynesian cross model for a closed economy, discuss how you would approach an empirical investigation for a particular economy of your choice. You could discuss how you would collect data for your empirical analysis and which type of regression you might use to capture the more intricate connections between variables as part of your investigation.

Cases

Understanding macroeconomic interactions in India using time series analysis

Context

India, as one of the world's largest emerging economies has experienced significant macroeconomic fluctuations in recent years, driven by global shocks, domestic reforms and pandemic recovery policies. Understanding how inflation, interest rates, exchange rates and output growth interact is crucial for policymakers and analysts.

Objective

To investigate the interrelationships among key Indian macroeconomic variables – inflation, real GDP growth, interest rate (repo rate), and the INR/USD exchange rate –using empirical time series methods.

Step 1: Preliminary data analysis

Data sources (2020–2024)

- **Inflation (CPI):** Reserve Bank of India (RBI), Ministry of Statistics
- **Real GDP growth rate:** National Statistics Office (NSO)
- **Interest rate (Repo rate):** RBI
- **Exchange rate (INR/USD):** RBI

Descriptive analysis

- **Inflation** has been volatile post-COVID, peaking in 2022 due to food and energy prices.
- **GDP growth** sharply rebounded in 2021–22 but moderated in 2023–24.
- The **repo rate** was increased multiple times between 2022–2023 to combat inflation.
- The **INR/USD exchange rate** depreciated during global tightening cycles.

Stationarity check

Augmented Dickey–Fuller (ADF) tests suggest the variables are non-stationary in levels but are stationary after applying first differences, indicating that the use of a VAR/SVAR in terms of first differences may be appropriate.

Step 2: Basic linear regression model

Research question

Does the interest rate in India significantly affect inflation in the short run?

Simple OLS model

- Dependent variable: Monthly CPI inflation
- Independent variable: Lagged repo rate

Findings

- A weak or insignificant relationship is detected in the basic OLS setup.
- Residuals show autocorrelation, suggesting omitted variable bias.
- The model cannot account for the feedback loop between interest rates and inflation.

Conclusion

A linear regression is insufficient to capture the complex interactions among macro variables, especially with endogeneity concerns.

Step 3: Structural Vector Autoregression (SVAR)

Motivation

SVAR allows us to model contemporaneous and lagged relationships while imposing theoretically motivated restrictions (e.g., interest rate responds to inflation with a lag, not contemporaneously).

SVAR setup

- **Variables:** Inflation, GDP growth, repo rate, exchange rate
- **Identification restrictions**
  - Inflation is affected contemporaneously by interest rates and exchange rate shocks.
  - GDP growth responds with a lag to inflation and interest rates.
  - Interest rate is set responding to inflation and growth, but not contemporaneously to exchange rate.

Key insights

- Inflation shocks have a delayed and persistent negative effect on GDP growth.
- Interest rate hikes gradually reduce inflation but also dampen growth – confirming a policy trade-off.
- Exchange rate shocks (such as dollar strengthening) increase inflation temporarily reflecting imported inflation effects.

Value addition

- SVAR allows us to see dynamic responses through impulse response functions.
- It reveals bidirectional causality, notably between interest rates and inflation.
- The model allows for policy simulation: for example, estimating the inflation response to a hypothetical 100 bps rate hike.

Conclusion

This case study illustrates how we start with a basic empirical question, test it using simple regression, and then improve our investigation using SVAR to uncover deeper dynamics. In the context of India's recent macroeconomic environment, SVAR modelling reveals crucial insights into how policy tools like the interest rate affect inflation and growth, particularly amid global uncertainty.

Questions

1. Why is preliminary data analysis important in macroeconomic time series research?
2. What were the limitations of using a simple linear regression model in this case?
3. How did SVAR improve the empirical investigation?
4. What does the reaction of inflation to interest rate changes tell us in India's case?
5. What real-world policy relevance does this analysis offer?

Problems

EASY

1. What is the primary purpose of using time series data in macroeconometrics?
   a) To study the interactions between individual consumer preferences
   b) To analyse cross-sectional variation between producers
   c) To validate macroeconomic theories using real-world historical data
   d) To test for the impact of political decisions on individual income levels
   e) To compare market shares of publicly quoted institutions

MEDIUM

2. In a simple linear regression of the form $Y = \beta_0 + \beta_1 X + \varepsilon$, the coefficient β_1 represents:
   a) The random fluctuation in the model's explanation of Y
   b) The average value of Y when the value of $X = 0$
   c) The change in X caused by a one-unit increase in Y
   d) The change in Y due to a one-unit increase in X
   e) The total variation in X explained by the model
3. Which of the following best describes the assumption of exogeneity?
   a) The dependent variable causes changes in the independent variable
   b) The independent variable evolves independently of the dependent variable
   c) All variables are correlated with each other across observations
   d) The model can allow for multicollinearity between a dependent and independent variable
   e) There exists some relation between individual errors in the model
4. What issue is most likely present if a time series displays evidence of a 'unit root'?
   a) The model is overfitted and needs re-specification
   b) There is multicollinearity with other variables in the model
   c) The variable being used for the estimation is not stationary
   d) The residuals from the estimation are homoscedastic
   e) The value of the estimated intercept is reliably constant

5. The following time series data from two macroeconomic variables is listed below:

X (independent variable)	*Y* (dependent variable)
1	3
2	5
3	7
4	9
5	11

Estimate the parameters β_0 and β_1 for a linear model $Y = \beta_0 + \beta_1 X$ using the ordinary least squares formulas provided in the text.

6. Discuss the importance of performing a preliminary data analysis before estimating a macroeconomic model. List some of the issues that can be detected and how they might affect the accuracy of the estimation.

HARD

7. Which of the following is not an assumption of the multiple linear regression model?
   a) Linearity of relationships
   b) Multicollinearity among independent variables
   c) Homoscedasticity of residuals
   d) Independence of errors
   e) Normality of error distribution
8. Granger causality implies that:
   a) A variable causes another in the philosophical sense.
   b) A variable's past values are irrelevant to another's prediction.
   c) Predictive content from one variable's lag values, helps forecast another.
   d) Correlation always implies causation, if the assumptions are not violated.
   e) Stationarity is not required to estimate causal relationships reliably.
9. Discuss the differences between a simple linear regression and a Structural Vector Autoregression (SVAR) model. In what types of macroeconomic research would each method be appropriate?

Glossary

A

Adjusting Mechanism The variable that changes to restore equilibrium in our model. This is normally the variable on the vertical axis. In the AS/AD the adjusting mechanism is the price level. If output is above its natural rate, prices will rise, if output is below the natural rate, prices will fall. If the economy is in equilibrium, no adjustment is necessary.

Agent-Based Model Most macroeconomic models have components that represent the behaviour of the relevant actors in the economy. These are often the representative agents.

Aggregate Demand A force that drives economic activity, not to be confused with economic activity (or output) itself. Aggregate demand drives changes in production and becomes output at the point of transaction.

Aggregate Supply The sum of all production; The schedule of aggregated supply decisions of the firm based on the level of prices in the economy.

Autoregression An algebraic representation where a variable is expressed as a sequence over time. We use autoregressive relations in our dynamic models, where variables carry a t(time) subscript.

B

Balance of Payments An accounting term used by the National Statistics Office. A balance sheet that equates the current account (measuring net exports) and the financial account (measuring net capital outflow). The value of goods and services sold to abroad must be equal to the flow of money used to buy those goods and services.

Bond Maturity The term for which the bond is issued and this can vary considerably. The term of the bond also dictates which interest rate the bond yield would align to; for instance, a GILT bond would be related to the long-term interest rate.

Bond Yield The distance between the face value and market price of a bond as a proportion of the market price. Normally quoted as a percentage so that it can be compared to the interest rate.

Business Cycle The oscillating pattern that we see in economic activity over the longer time horizon. Recessions and booms are a feature of this cycle, one that policymakers hope to influence through economic policy. The business cycle is characterized by prolonged periods of expansion followed by prolonged periods of contraction.

C

Capital The total number of machines utilized in the economy by the sum of all producers.

Capital Flows International movements of financial capital in exchange for domestic currency for the purpose of investment. To invest in another country, you will first have to exchange your funds into the local currency, in the foreign exchange market.

Capital/Labour Share The proportion of national income that can be attributed solely to the employment of capital/labour.

Causality The issue of what is causing what, or the order in which macroeconomic variables determine or 'lead' each other.

Ceteris Paribus A key assumption required for a typical 2 dimensional analysis. Everything that might affect the economic agents outside our space is assumed to remain constant; direct meaning 'all other things equal'.

Circular Economy An economy where the production processes of firms are designed to consider the 'whole' life cycle of a good – from sourcing raw materials to end of life, to reuse.

Coefficients An estimated constant that can be applied to the beginning of an independent variable to reflect the strength of its impact on the dependent variable.

Consumption Function The behavioural equation that describes consumption as linearly dependent on disposable income ($Y - T$).

Correlation A measure of how closely two variables are related in linear terms. If the relationship is linear then it is constant over time

CPI Inflation A measure of inflation that accounts for the change in the cost of living faced by the economy's consumers using an estimated and average fixed basket of goods.

D

Demand Management Actively managing the level of economic activity in the economy using fiscal or/and monetary policy. Using demand-side policy is generally thought of as short run.

Discounting Allowing for the opportunity cost that comes from time. This is often most easily identified as the interest rate paid, or through a discount factor that measures an agent's preference to receive something earlier or later.

Dynamic Model An economic model that accounts for changes in variables over time. We can spot these mathematically, by the use of number or '*t*' subscripts attached to the variables in the structural equations.

E

Economic Shocks Disturbances caused by factors that we consider to be exogenous, or outside our usual analysis. We can think of expansionary fiscal policy as such an exogenous change.

Economic Slack The difference between actual activity and the 'normal' rate of economic activity. In terms of the labour market we can think of labour market slack as the difference between the normal rate of unemployment and the actual rate of unemployment.

Endogenous Variable A macroeconomic variable that 'depends' on another variable in some way. Nearly all variables are dependent to some degree.

Equilibrium An economic state where the economy is assumed to be 'settled' and no further change will take place without some movement in economic policy or shock. If we are not in equilibrium, then there is always a driving force back towards it, through the powers of excess supply and excess demand.

Equilibrium Unemployment Similar in definition to the normal rate of unemployment, more exactly: the labour market clearing level of unemployment. Unwanted changes to equilibrium unemployment requires 'long-run' economic policy.

ESG A framework that promotes the inclusion of the environment and the welfare of society into the objectives and practices of institutions.

Exchange Rate The exchange rate at which one currency is traded for another. If there is a surplus or deficit in the balance of payments, then the exchange rate will adjust to rebalance the difference between the current and financial accounts.

Exogenous Shock A sudden or unanticipated change to a variable, *not* caused by a change in a variable on the axis of our two-dimensional model. An exogenous shock comes from outside the model.

Exogenous Variable A macroeconomic variable that is considered totally independent from other variables; we often call these variables 'fixed' or predetermined.

Expectations The expected value of an economic variable in the future. If inflation turns out as expected, then unemployment and output would be at their natural rates.

Externalities The indirect costs or benefits of economic production. These costs are outside of the firm's objective function and can be internalized by the government through taxation and legislation.

F

Fiat Money A monetary base that has no tangible backing. The notes issued by the central bank are underwritten by the credibility of the issuing authority.

Final Goods A finished product aimed at an end user, also one that is made up of components bought from intermediate goods producers. An example of a final good is a car sold in a showroom.

Firm's Objective The problem that the firm solves in deciding how much to produce, or which price to set for its output. Normally, we assume that the sole objective for the firm is the maximization of profits.

Fiscal Policy The use of taxation and government spending to make short-run impact on economic activity. An increase in government spending *G* will increase output, through changes in aggregate demand.

Fixed Exchange Rates A deliberate policy of exchange rate government intervention in the foreign exchange markets, designed to influence the domestic exchange rate, often with the ultimate aim of manipulating a country's share of international trade.

Floating Exchange Rates An exchange rate policy whereby the exchange rate is determined freely in the international foreign exchange markets.

G

GDP Deflator Inflation A measure of inflation that measures the change in the aggregate price level using the relative change between nominal and real GDP.

Golden Rule Level of Capital A level of steady state capital that achieves maximum consumption in the steady state. We find this level by equating the marginal product of capital (*MPK*) and the slope of the depreciation line (δ).

Goods Market The real side of the economy where goods and services are exchanged for domestic expenditure. We can think in terms of suppliers producing goods and consumers providing revenue to the firms in return.

Government Expenditure The amount that the government spends on goods and services excluding transfer payments. We use changes in this exogenous variable to measure the effects of policy in our model.

Granger causality A statistical concept that can be used to test if one macroeconometric time series can be predicted using the time series properties of another variable.

Gross Domestic Production (GDP) A measure of national income calculated by the summing up of domestic production (on home soil). There are three main methods to calculate GDP: the production method, expenditure method and income method.

H

Hypothesis Test A statistical process used to evaluate a proposal (hypothesis) about a parameter of a model that has been estimated empirically.

I

Inflation The measured change in the price level, also defined as 'the continuous rise in the price of goods and services sold in the economy'.

Input–Output Model A model that can interconnect the different sectors of the economy, taking account of the interdependencies between the two industries.

Intermediate Goods A good that is manufactured and intended for use as a component in an end-user good. An example of an intermediate good is a micro-chip inside of a laptop computer.

Intertemporal In the context of dynamics, concerning the changes that are evident over time. Intertemporal models provide us with explanations of the dynamic relationship between structural variables. They are easily identified by the presence of numbered or '*t*' subscripts in the structural equations.

Investment Function The behavioural equation that describes non-residential and residential investment as dependent positively on output and negatively on the interest rate.

IS Curve The schedule (locus) of different combinations of *r* and *Y* that represent equilibrium in the goods market. The IS curve is built via the Keynesian cross.

IS/LM Long-Run Equilibrium The equilibrium in the IS/LM model where the economy returns to after a short-run change in the model from economic policy or a shock. The return to equilibrium is explained by the adjustment of prices. The level of output in long-run equilibrium is shown by the LRAS curve at Y^{LR}.

L

Labour The total number all working hours utilized in the economy by the sum of all producers.

Labour Demand The total number of working hours demanded by firms at the current wage rate.

Labour Supply The total number of all working hours willing to be supplied by households at the current wage rate.

Life Cycle The span of time between conception, design, production, sale, use, maintenance and disposal. In the past, a product might be designed specifically for the earlier parts of the life cycle, with no consideration for maintenance and disposal.

Liquidity The speed at which a financial asset can be converted into its most liquid form: money in the form of cash.

LM Curve The schedule (locus) of different combinations of r and Y that represent equilibrium in the money market, given by the intersection of the money supply and money demand schedules.

Long Run An economic time frame that can span years, rather than the months associated with the short run.

Long-Run Equilibrium The intersection of the short-run aggregate supply, aggregate demand and long-run aggregate supply together. Prices will not need to adjust because they are at their expected level and output is at its natural (long-run) rate.

M

Macroeconomic Disequilibrium A state where the economy is away from equilibrium. In a market clearing model the prices adjust quickly to restore economic equilibrium after a shock or economic policy.

Marginal Product of Capital/Labour The additional output achieved by the firm from the act of employing one more unit of capital/labour.

Marginal Rate of Substitution The amount we are prepared to give up to obtain one more unit of a substitute that is equally satisfying. We can think of this as our willingness to substitute one good for another.

Market Clearing The markets for capital and labour clear instantly, there are no market imperfections. This is due to the assumptions of total price flexibility in factor markets; the real wage in the labour market and the real rate of return in the market for capital are fully flexible.

Market Equilibrium A unique outcome where the natural driving forces of the market come to an end. After a disturbance in the market, changes in the market price will drive the economy back towards equilibrium. In equilibrium, the price clears the market, ending the process of adjustment.

Market Imperfections These are the frictions that can prevent prices from adjusting quickly. For example, a labour market friction can prevent wages from adjusting in the labour market.

Monetary Assets An asset that could be used as money or as a form of security that ranges in liquidity from the most narrow to the most broad.

Monetary Policy Changes in the money supply aimed at managing economic activity in the short run. An increase in the money supply M will increase output.

Money A financial asset that can be used to facilitate the purchase of any good or service or to pay wages. An asset needs to meet three conditions to be considered as money:

1) It should be universally accepted for the purpose of transactions
2) It should help us to measure value of goods and services
3) It should keep its value stable over time.

Money Demand The demand for central bank money, or base money, dependent on the interest rate (negative) and income (positive).

Money Market The monetary side of the economy where the money supply is set by the central bank and money is demanded to facilitate the transactions taking place in the goods market.

Money Supply The supply of money set by the central bank; this is independent of the interest rate and drawn vertically in the money market.

Multiplier the factor by which an increase in government expenditure will increase output. This factor depends on the marginal propensity to consume.

N

Natural Rate of Unemployment The level of unemployment that would prevail when the labour market is in equilibrium.

Nominal GDP The market value, measured at current prices, of all goods and services produced by domestic producers in any one year. We can think of this measure as the 'value of transactions' (prices multiplied by the quantities)

Nominal Rigidities Also termed 'sticky prices'. A theoretical explanation of the sluggish behaviour of prices. Modelling prices as sticky helps to explain the smoothness we see in inflation data (the time series is nearly flat) and allows models to predict a usefulness for demand management.

Nominal Variable A variable presented at face value, and measured in current prices. These variables are not adjusted for inflation, so that changes in nominal variables can reflect both movements in prices and quantities.

Normal Rate of Unemployment The rate of unemployment that would exist in normal times or in the absence of economic shocks. The normal rate is sometimes referred to as the 'long-run' or 'natural' rate of unemployment.

O

Optimal The characteristic of a choice made to maximize utility within the boundaries of a limiting constraint.

Output Gap The difference between the actual and potential output. This difference can be in the levels or measured as a proportional deviation. If the output gap is positive, it is thought to be inflationary.

P

Participation Rate The percentage of the working-age population that are currently participating in the labour market.

Per Capita The term we use to describe variables that have been divided by the variable that represents labour. Effectively 'per capita' variables are measurements 'per head'.

Planetary Boundaries The safe limit of pressure that humanity can put on critical Earth systems without pushing Earth out of its benevolent and resilient Holocene state.

Planned Expenditure Expenditure that is anticipated or planned and assumed to be realized in the near future, also the forcing variable to drive changes in economic activity. We can think of planned expenditure as aggregate demand (AD).

Preliminary Data Analysis An analysis, or visual inspection, that comes from the observation of a basic presentation of economic data. This may be in the form of summary statistics, or from the profiles and directions of the time series data itself.

Price Level A number estimated by the office of statistics, often in index form, that reflects movements in the average price in the economy.

Production Production is the sum of the value-added revenues of firms in the economy, also known as 'output' or 'aggregate supply'.

R

Real GDP The value of all goods and services measured using a fixed base year set of prices. This measure washes out the inflation element of the market value 'nominal' measure.

Real Rate of Return This is the real rate of the return on capital in the market for capital. In practice this will be closely related to the interest rate in the economy.

Real Variable A variable that measures a physical quantity and is constructed with prices held fixed. Changes in real variables will only reflect changes in quantities as they are adjusted for inflation.

Real Wage The price of labour in the labour market is the real wage, which is the nominal wage divided by the price level.

Risk Premium An addition to the normal rate of interest that prevails across the economy. This extra amount of interest is dependent on the perceived credit worthiness of an individual government. The safer the country is to lend to, the lower the interest rate it will pay.

S

Safe and Just Space The concept of a space for humanity that lies between a minimum social floor and maximum environmental ceiling.

Schedule A line or a curve in an economic model. The schedule reflects the behaviour of an agent inside the model; for example, the representative consumer or representative firm.

Security A financial instrument that can be traded between two financial entities, for example bonds, stocks, exchange traded funds (ETFs), options, futures, derivatives and other financial innovations. A security represents 'ownership'.

Seigniorage The profit made by the government when increasing the amount of money in circulation, also known as 'printing money'. Adding to the money stock can devalue that money already in circulation by causing prices to rise.

Separation Rate The rate at which employed workers lose their jobs, flowing from employment into unemployment. All fires are separations, but not all separations are fires.

Short-Run Equilibrium The intersection of the short-run aggregate supply and demand curves. Output will not be at its natural rate and so prices will adjust to return the economy to its long-run equilibrium in the absence of intervention by policymakers.

Sovereign Debt When the government borrows money to carry out its expenditure it gets the funds from the central bank. In return the government provides the central bank with IOUs called government bonds; also referred to as 'sovereign debt'.

Static Model An economic model where time is assumed constant and where we are concerned with how one variable reacts to a change in another.

Stylized Facts The facts that we see reflected by the macroeconomic data. For example, the business cycle and the negative relationship between output and unemployment.

Sustainable Economy An economy where activity can continue in a way that minimizes its impact on the environment.

T

Technology The functional form of the production function representing the efficiency of aggregate production.

Time Series Data A series of observations from a macroeconomic variable, constructed or collected by the Office of National Statistics. Data may be in the form of a level, an index or a percentage.

Trade Deficit Net exports are negative because imports are greater than exports.

Trade Surplus Net exports are positive because exports are greater than imports.

U

Unemployment Gap The difference between the actual rate of unemployment and the natural rate of unemployment. We can think of this gap as the short-run deviation from the long run.

Unemployment Rate The percentage of the workforce that are without work but willing and able to work at the current wage rate.

Unit Root A characteristic of a time series where the data is mean reverting, meaning that it evolves around a stochastic trend or can be modelled as a random walk with drift.

V

Vacancy Filling Rate The rate at which job vacancies are filled by workers looking for jobs. A higher vacancy filling rate is associated with a more flexible labour market.

Value Added The value created by each contributing producer in the chain of production towards completion of a final good. If the production of a final good involves more than one company, the total value added of the final good is split between producers by contribution.

Value of Transactions The total sum value of the sale prices multiplied by the sale quantities of all goods and services sold in any year. This variable is equivalent to the nominal value of gross domestic product.

Vector Autoregression Model A statistical model built to capture the dynamic relationships of multiple variables over time. Past, present and future values of variables can be included in a simultaneous estimation.

Velocity of Money The speed at which money flows around the economy. The higher the speed the less demand there will be for real money balances.

W

Workforce Also known as the labour force; the subset of the working age population willing and able to work at the current wage. Workers who retire or give up looking for work are no longer in the workforce.

Working Age Population The set of individuals between the legal age for starting work and the age of retirement. For the UK, this is currently age 16 to 65.

Index